Tool-Being

Tool-Being

Heidegger and the Metaphysics of Objects

GRAHAM HARMAN

OPEN COURT
Chicago and La Salle, Illinois

This book has been reproduced in a print-on-demand format from the 2002
Open Court printing.

To order books from Open Court, call toll-free 1-800-815-2280.

Open Court Publishing Company is a division of Carus Publishing Company.

© 2002 by Carus Publishing Company

First printing 2002

Printed and bound in the United States of America.

Library of Congress Cataloging-in-Publication Data

Harman, Graham, 1968–
    Tool-being : Heidegger and the metaphysics of objects / Graham Harman.
        p.   cm.
    Includes bibliographical references (p.) and index.
    ISBN 0-8126-9444-9 (trade paper : alk. paper)
    1. Heidegger, Martin, 1889–1976—Contributions in concept of object.
    2. Object (Philosophy) I. Title.

B3279.H49 H275 2002
193—dc21   2002075265

Contents

Note to the Reader

It has become customary to begin any academic work with a page of acknowledgements to friends and acquaintances who have contributed to its development. This habit is rooted in the most generous impulses of human nature—few among us have not profited greatly from the timely suggestions of a colleague. Furthermore, this new type of standard preface shows how far we have come from the days when philosophers were forced to preface their works with obsequious bows to princes and bishops.

But whatever the merits of publicly recognizing those who have assisted us, this now-standard practice can also have an unintended and harmful effect. Standing at the entry to a book like some Praetorian guard, a long list of names often serves to intimidate readers, to make them feel outclassed by a competent network of college professors, research institutes, and fellowship foundations. Whether consciously or not, a subtle message is transmitted: "To disagree with me, you must contend with all of these others as well. Do you dare?" There is a similar effect when the author dates his preface from an especially prestigious location, whether it be Athens, Jerusalem, the remote archive of a famous writer, or simply a respected university campus. In this way, the possible objections of a talented but uncredentialed reader are silenced in advance—less by the actual skill of the author than by the mass of his external qualifications and friendships.

Wishing to avoid any trace of this effect, I have chosen to thank those who helped me in a more private way; wherever possible, I have done so with material gifts. The book *Tool-Being* should be regarded as addressed to each reader *directly*, rather than through the medium of any institutional machinery. In principle, any disagreements between us might easily be hammered out in person (among other possibilities, e-mail can be sent to toolbeing@yahoo.com). I make no appeal to any authority beyond the merits or flaws of the book itself. In return, I ask only that the reader extend the same courtesy to me.

Introduction

This book begins with a somewhat unorthodox commentary on the thought of Martin Heidegger and ends with an outline of what will be called an "object-oriented philosophy." To define this phrase, and to show how it emerges inevitably from Heidegger's basic insights, is a task best left to the body of the book. But a brief preview may be of interest to the reader.

The key to my argument lies in a fresh reading of the famed tool-analysis of *Being and Time*. Although hundreds of scholars have already commented on this masterful analysis, I am not aware of any who have drawn sufficiently radical conclusions from it. Of the few interpreters who have been willing to give center stage to the drama of tool-being, all have followed Heidegger too closely in regarding human Dasein as the biggest star in the theater. The tool-analysis is read as the triumph either of practical activity over theoretical abstraction, or of the network of linguistic signs over the ever unpopular "things in themselves." Such readings of Heidegger prevail among both analytic and continental philosophers. Against these standard readings, I claim that the tool-analysis is neither a theory of language and human praxis, nor a phenomenology of a small number of useful devices called "tools." Instead, Heidegger's account of equipment gives birth to an ontology of *objects themselves*.[1] Contrary to the usual view, tool-being does not describe objects insofar as they are handy implements employed for human purposes. Quite the contrary: readiness-to-hand (*Zuhandenheit*) refers to objects insofar as they withdraw from human view into a dark subterranean reality that never becomes present to practical action any more than it does to theoretical awareness. This already runs counter to the usual readings of Heidegger, since it denies from the start that the tool-analysis tells us anything about the difference between theory and praxis. What is first at stake is an absolute gulf between the things and *any* interaction we might have with them, no matter whether that interaction be intellectual or merely manipulative.

1

But my argument goes another step further. When the things withdraw from presence into their dark subterranean reality, they distance themselves not only from human beings, but *from each other* as well. If the human perception of a house or tree is forever haunted by some hidden surplus in the things that never becomes present, the same is true of the sheer causal interaction between rocks or raindrops. Even inanimate things only unlock each other's realities to a minimal extent, reducing one another to caricatures. It will be shown that, even if rocks are not sentient creatures, they never encounter one another in their deepest being, but only *as present-at-hand*; it is only Heidegger's confusion of two distinct senses of the as-structure that prevents this strange result from being accepted.

But this means that, contrary to the dominant assumption of philosophy since Kant, the true chasm in ontology lies not between humans and the world, but between *objects and relations*. Moreover, this duality holds equally true for all entities in the cosmos, whether natural, artificial, organic, or fully human. If we read Heidegger's tool-analysis in the right way, the lingering priority of Dasein in his philosophy is vaporized, and we encounter a strange new world filled with shocking possibilities for twenty-first-century philosophy. Certainly, Heidegger deals yet another mortal wound to metaphysics of the old-fashioned kind, the kind that is slapped and pummeled still further by Derrida, Wittgenstein, and others. But by the same stroke, he unknowingly suggests a possible campaign of *guerilla metaphysics*. Tool-beings turn out to be a strange variant of traditional *substances*, though they are as irreducible to physical particles as they are to the traces they leave in human perception. They are substances that exceed every relation into which they might enter, without being ultimate pieces of tiny matter. But this leaves only one possibility: for the first time in a long while, Heidegger pushes philosophy to the point where it has no choice but to offer a renewed theory of *substantial forms*. The reasons for this unusual claim will become clearer to the reader as the book progresses.

The result of all this is that, despite his glaring statements to the contrary, Heidegger accidentally incites a new age of metaphysics. Accordingly, we are finally in a position to oppose the long dictatorship of human beings in philosophy. What emerges in its place is a ghostly cosmos in which humans, dogs, oak trees, and tobacco are on precisely the same footing as glass bottles, pitchforks, windmills, comets, ice cubes, magnets, and atoms. Instead of exiling objects to the natural sciences (with the usual mixed emotions of condescension and fear), philosophy must reawaken its lost talent for unleashing the enfolded forces trapped in the things themselves. It is my belief that this will have to be the central concern of twenty-first-century philosophy. The purpose of this book is to sketch an object-oriented theory that can help address this concern.

washed up dead on the shore, no longer immersed in their withdrawn reality. It is impossible to define tool-being as a linguistic network or culturally coded system of "social practices," as many commentators do. Tool-being is that which *withdraws* from all such networks, as this book will argue. Hence, what Heidegger opposes to theory is not *human praxis*, but a mysterious capital "X," a brutal subterranean realm which we can glimpse only at second hand.

More controversially, I hold that the same structure of withdrawal occurs even on the *inanimate* level: just as we never grasp the being of two pieces of rock, neither do they fully unlock the being of *each other* when they slam together in distant space. Contra Heidegger, withdrawal is not a specific feature of human temporality, but belongs to *any relation whatsoever*. That tool-beings retreat into a silent background means not only that they are invisible to humans, but that they they exceed any of their interactions with other tool-beings. In this sense, tool-beings are unearthly, otherworldly. Then far from *abolishing* the transcendent world of things in themselves, Heidegger inadvertently *rejuvenates* this notion in a form that no dialectic can overcome. In this respect, he is a full step beyond most of his successors, who continue to wage war against a naive brand of Billiard Ball Realism that is no longer a threat to anyone.

3. The theory of tool-being revives metaphysics as a reflection on the fundamental nature of reality *without* relapsing into metaphysics as ontotheology. It achieves this by undermining from the outset any possible *presence* of tool-beings. Against what is often assumed, the paradox of metaphysics does *not* arise from claiming that there is a real world distinct from appearances, but only from assuming that this real world can be especially incarnated in certain privileged entities at the expense of others. Although the very mention of the word "metaphysics" will raise suspicions in some quarters, there is little reason to worry—the style and content of the book will quickly prove that conservatism is not my motive.

4. I regard as irrelevant the question of whether Heidegger *meant* to grant the prominence to tool-being that it receives in this book. As is often observed, Heidegger himself frequently tells us that any interpreter must bring to the fore those topics that the original author passes over in silence. But even this observation misses the point, since it implies that we need Heidegger's permission to think for ourselves—what could be more oppressive than this? A philosophy is not a private introspective diary to which the philosopher has unique access. Better to think of it as a thought experiment, a process of smashing fragments of reality together to see what emerges. Just as the legendary Michelson-Morley experiment was retroactively transformed by the interpretations of Planck and Einstein, you and I have the right to pursue the implications of tool-being in ways that Heidegger might not have suspected, and even in ways that he might have

condemned. In short, the goal of this book is not to understand Heidegger better than he understood himself, but to understand *tool-being* better than he understood it. These are two very different ambitions.

5. Heidegger studies has often been sidetracked by a serious misunderstanding of the term *ontic*. While many readers behave as though it meant "pertaining to objects," it actually means "pertaining to presence-at-hand." Due to this misinterpretation, readers of Heidegger tend to think they are on the right track whenever they move as far away from specific objects as possible. The belief seems to be that *entities* are the source of our philosophical problems, and that the solution is to retreat ever deeper into the *conditions* underlying these entities, into the very conditions of these conditions, and even back into the "clearing-opening play" in which these conditions of conditions emerge. Since it is widely believed that Heidegger's path of thinking consists in precisely this retreating movement, it should be no surprise that his successors are always trying to further his work by offering an even deeper, even more "forgotten" condition that Heidegger himself never saw fit to uncover.

To give two examples, it seems to me that Luce Irigaray's *L'oubli de l'air* is guilty of trying to outgun Heidegger in this unfruitful way, and that Reiner Schürmann's highly regarded *From Principles to Anarchy* is marred by its employment of a similar method. The approach I have adopted is the opposite of these—a military campaign driving back toward the *surface* of reality. What interests me is not the forgotten site of the ground of the condition of all that appears—but rather snowflakes, whales, flames, stars, and rubies. To repeat, the problem for Heidegger's philosophy is not objects: the problem is *Vorhandenheit*. His own discussions of bridges, jugs, and temples are more than enough to show that objects *per se* are not contraband in his thought. And even if they were, why should we care?

6. Although I will argue that Heidegger's philosophy is *compatible* with a discussion of numerous concrete themes, I also claim that none of these themes can actually be found in his writings. Heidegger is a thinker not only of profundity, but of profound monotony. Scratch the surface of his *Stimmung*, *Zeitlichkeit*, *Spielraum*, or *Zwitterwesen*, and you will find that they are only nicknames or aliases for a single obsessive reversal between the poles of "concealed" and "revealed," ready-to-hand and present-at-hand. Heidegger is an unparalleled master at showing how any specific ontic term is always grounded in something deeper. He is not as skilled in showing how this monotonous depth is related in different ways to different zones of reality; the movement is always one of *implosion*. Heidegger could have escaped this perpetual collapse into a repetitive dualism only by developing his sketchily proposed "metontology," a theory of the *metabole*: the *Umschlag* or turnabout between an object's infrastructural depth and its sparkling exterior contours. In the absence of such a theory,

most of his specific terminology gives us nothing more than a distracting variety of literary figures for a recurrent duel of light and shadow. This last claim is the topic of my opening chapter.

7. We should oppose all developmentalist readings of Heidegger, which are satisfied only when they have identified every least turn and micro-shift in every semester of the philosopher's career. This procedure may be useful for writing Heidegger's intellectual biography, but not for advancing his insights (and so far, it has not even been useful for the purposes of biography). With Theodore Kisiel,[2] I hold that Heidegger's lifelong subject matter is already perfectly visible as early as 1919, in the masterful lectures assembled in *Gesamtausgabe* Volume 56/57, *Zur Bestimmung der Philosophie*. The fully ripe tool-analysis offered by the 29-year-old Heidegger already signals the high-water mark of twentieth-century philosophy, an inexhaustible thought experiment to which the remainder of his career serves as a series of footnotes. If this sounds wildly implausible, it is only because tool-being continues to be misread as a provisional first step along Heidegger's path, one that has to be progressively deepened, layer by layer, over a period of decades. My own view is that Heidegger never goes any "deeper" than tool-being, precisely because it is almost impossible to do so. The full-significance of the tool-analysis is still anything but clear even in the year 2001; indeed, it still contains enough puzzles to fuel a revolution. When commentators rush past the analysis of equipment toward all points further south, this only shows that tool-being has been distorted into a practical concept of knives and forks. And the proper way to overcome the philosophy of knives and forks is not to abandon objects, but to abandon the view that human *praxis* was ever the theme of the tool-analysis.

8. I do not share the near-universal admiration for Heidegger as a *historian* of philosophy, an admiration often granted even by his bitterest enemies. Just as Heidegger's discussions of time, space, theory, and animal life soon implode into a dualistic mantra of exteriority and depth, so too do his thousands of pages of historical writings begin to assume an almost numbing uniformity. As a rabid Heideggerian since my late teens, and as someone who has carefully reviewed every extant volume of the *Gesamtausgabe*, I do not make this claim flippantly. Certainly, there are moments of pleasure awaiting those who follow Heidegger through his readings of Aristotle or Kant or Nietzsche. Professor Heidegger was not only a man of impressive erudition, but one for whom historicity was a decisive theme. But whatever the textual details of his various historical analyses, his conclusion is inevitably the same: here, the question of being has not been posed, and therefore some form of presence-at-hand is still secretly privileged, whether as *idea, energeia, existentia,* representedness, or will to power. While this is certainly a powerful way for Heidegger to establish the

novelty of his own standpoint, it leads him to offer interpretations that are less sympathetic and less *informative* than those of less ingenious historians. After all, it is never true that any of the great historical thinkers can be *fully* reduced to puppets of *Vorhandenheit*. The vigorous and crafty historical works of Gilles Deleuze, even the honest and thorough summaries of Frederick Copleston, remind us by way of contrast that Heidegger's history of being is interesting mostly for what it tells us *about Heidegger*. This is why enthusiasts of Greek philosophy are often less excited by the commentaries of Heidegger than by those of Ross or Zeller or Jaeger or Leo Strauss, none of whom can equal his originality as a philosopher. Heidegger shows great brilliance in compressing thousands of years of philosophy into a single foundational problem, but often lacks the versatility of a true *aficionado*, the willingness to free up a *plurality* of basic concepts in an author's works.

9. Heidegger abuses his notion of the "as-structure" in a way often repeated by his admirers. On the one hand, the "as" is supposed to be a global structure found everywhere and at all times: all experience is experience of something "as" something, no matter how marginal or hazy it may be. But at the same time, he also tends to use the "as" as a kind of measuring-stick that singles out privileged *cases* of reality. This happens, for example, when theoretical comportment is praised as an *especially clear* version of the as-structure.

On the one hand, the "as" is so universal that even a glazed and empty staring at a mountain faintly recognizes this mountain *as* a mountain, rather than as some other sort of landmark. Even an animal would have to encounter it, however vaguely, *as* a familiar mountain rather than as a dangerous fire.

But on the other hand, Heidegger also wants to invoke an exemplary, turbocharged version of the "as," such that some forms of the as-structure would give us the "as" *par excellence*. This can be seen in the hasty distinctions he draws between humans and animals, who are denied full access to the as-structure despite the fact that they must live amidst *some* version of the "as" if they are to be more than sheer automata. Worse yet, these supposed gradations continue even within the *human* realm. We are told that mere gazing does not reveal the world "as" world to as significant a degree as other experiences do. Supposedly, the geologist should be able to see the mountain "as" mountain *more* than a drunken loiterer would; in turn, an ontologist would be able to liberate the thing in its being *even better* than the geologist, who is stranded on the level of positive science.

This illicit appeal to the souped-up "as" recurs throughout the works of Heidegger and his interpreters, above all in reflections on the artwork, which is continually said to exhibit earth in a way that simple equipment does not. But this claim is based on assumptions that cannot withstand close scrutiny. In short, Heidegger's duplicitous use of the as-structure is the epitome of metaphysics in the *bad* sense. And although I by no means fight under the banner of Derrida, this duplicity cannot survive the first five pages of *Speech and Phenomena*. The as-structure is a powerful concept, but it is ill-suited to the task of establishing gradations and differences among entities.

10. I have already suggested that fundamental ontology begins by reducing *everything* to the eternal duel of shadow and light, tool and broken tool. Nonetheless, a *second* axis is faintly visible in Heidegger's thought. The two becomes a four; reality is made up of *quadrants*. It is from this crossing of two axes, already fully visible in 1919, that there emerges the obscure notion of the "fourfold." This concept has been increasingly neglected in recent years—largely through Heidegger's own fault, since it is he who offers such painfully obscure and even precious overviews of this theme that it has become an international laughing-stock even among his admirers. But although I understand why most readers throw up their hands in frustration at the merest mention of *Geviert*, I do not feel obliged to follow them. Sufficient clues are available for piecing together the meaning of the fourfold, at least in a preliminary way.

11. The dominant theme in recent books on Heidegger has been that of "the political": or in franker terms, Nazism. In the present book, I prefer to make only passing reference to this problem, which is both grim enough and timely enough that it tends to overshadow anything else that might be said about Heidegger. Since I am concerned with a colder and more elusive theme, it seems better to keep explicit political questions in the background. Nonetheless, my views on Heidegger's ontology are not unconnected to my views on his politics, which are discussed briefly in chapter 1.

12. There is a bumper crop of excellent peripheral reasons to focus our attention on the concept of tool-being: (a) As already suggested, Heidegger's tool-analysis holds good for *all* entities—human beings not excluded. Hence, the tool-analysis is far more encompassing than the famed analytic of Dasein. (b) Every idea in Heidegger's works makes sense only when understood as part of an ongoing critique of presence-at-hand, a critique played out most clearly in the analysis of tools. (c) As further circumstantial evidence, note that the tool-analysis is in some respects the first passage of *Being and Time*. If we ignore the introduction to the work (which was written last anyway) and the preliminary reflections on the phenomenological method, the hammer and broken hammer are the first personae to appear on Heidegger's philosophical stage. Although this is hardly enough evidence to close the case, it sheds intriguing additional light on the central role of tool-being. (d) As already mentioned, tool-being provides the subject matter for Heidegger's earliest surviving lecture

course, the 1919 Freiburg Emergency War Semester. (e) The tool-analysis marks Heidegger's definitive break with Husserl, and hence the fateful point of rupture between two of the giants of contemporary philosophy. (f) The tool-analysis offers the best opportunity for bridge-building between continental and analytic readers of Heidegger, since the latter group tends to favor this passage above all others. (g) Finally, the description of the tool and its breakdown is the most *popular* theme in all of Heidegger, the one most often remembered by intelligent readers of *Being and Time* outside the ranks of university professors. For this reason, it offers the best opportunity to export Heidegger's insights beyond the skirmishes of academia into the emerging community of freelance and renegade philosophers: whether they be novelists, sculptors, translators, web designers, physicists, or imaginative slackers.

*   *   *

It seems best to conclude this introduction with a sketch of the three chapters of the book. Chapter 1 develops the most general features of tool-being, a concept which applies not just to wrenches and anvils and linguistic signs, but to everything under and over the sun. A general theory of equipment must have a boundless field of application. And just as the tool-structure applies to all beings, so too does the memorable description of the "broken tool." Every entity is already caught up in the turning movement of equipment, torn between presence-at-hand and readiness-to-hand. The opening chapter sketches the leading traits of this conflict in the heart of objects, one of such universal breadth that every specific theme mentioned by Heidegger quickly collapses into a single recurring opposition. However minutely he tries to describe space, theory, time, animal life, and dozens of other themes, they soon implode into the same ontological niche occupied by the failed hammer. In this sense, *the theory of the tool and its reversal makes up the full content of Heidegger's philosophy*. But the appearance of a second axis in reality soon indicates that Heidegger is confronted with a vague *fourfold* rather than a simple duality.

Chapter 2 contains my views on some of the most prominent secondary literature on Heidegger. Obviously, I have had to limit not only my selection of commentaries, but also my choice of Heideggerian concepts. Bearing this in mind, my strategy has been to focus on a narrow syndicate of concepts of such undeniable prestige for Heidegger studies that the burden of proof will shift onto my potential opponents. The concepts I have selected are: Dasein, being, time, truth, Ereignis, language, and technology.

In chapter 3, I make use of the results of the first chapter to sketch the outlines of an object-oriented philosophy. I borrow the term "prehension" from the marvelous philosophy of Whitehead, who far exceeds Heidegger in his appreciation for the inanimate realm, despite Heidegger's tacit superiority in refusing to reduce objects to the sum of their relations. I cite Emmanuel Levinas for his dramatic sense of the strife between the visible and withdrawn faces of the things themselves, and praise Xavier Zubiri for insisting that the essence of any object must be incommensurable with all of its relations. I also criticize Aristotle and Leibniz for enforcing an absolute distinction between substances and composites.

On this basis, I begin to develop an alternative theory of substances, with the following features: (1) A substance is not one kind of entity among others, but a way of being belonging to *all* entities, even those that seem at first to be mere composites. Contra Leibniz, the Dutch East India Company is no less substantial than the diamond of the Grand Duke. And since every relation can also be regarded as an entity, the world is jampacked with entities; there is no room for "nothingness" in ontology. (2) Since tool-beings are always more than what they present to humans and to other entities, they must lie somewhere outside of Heidegger's "world," in some *metaphysical vacuum* whose features are yet to be determined. (3) Since objects remain partially concealed from one another even during physical causation, they never touch one another directly. But if direct causality is impossible, then it is necessary to revive some form of *occasional cause*. I hold that this can be done on a "local" level without strange and arbitrary invocations of a hidden God. These three problems are formulated solely on the basis of what was learned from Heidegger in chapter 1—there are no extraneous last-minute appeals to Platonism or to theological concepts. In closing, I make nothing less than a call to arms: the problems raised in this book are not be solved by the traditional metaphysics that Heidegger attacks, but only by the guerrilla metaphysics that he *provokes*. In the final paragraphs of the book, I invite the reader to participate in the liberation of objects from the philosophical ghetto where they have been confined for far too long.

It is only at the conclusion of chapter 3 that my reading of Heidegger should be judged, since the primary standard of judgment should be whether the book has succeeded in securing a new and compelling subject matter. Lacking this, even the most irrefutable arguments vanish from our lives without a trace, often in a matter of hours.

Chapter One

The Tool and
Its Reversal

*Commentaries in the history of philosophy should
represent a kind of slow motion. . . .*

—GILLES DELEUZE,
from the opening to *Difference and Repetition*

§1. The Invisible Realm

Martin Heidegger's famous analysis of equipment has never been denied its due share of attention. Few passages from *Being and Time* have been cited as frequently or with such persistent enthusiasm. The most casual readers of this work are often able to provide expert accounts of the hammer and its breakdown; surely, no published commentary has passed over the topic in silence. Even so, this celebrated description of the tool has been consistently displaced from the thematic center of Heidegger studies. The analysis of equipment is treated *historically*, explained as a reworking of issues arising from Aristotle's discussion of praxis. It is praised *biographically*, as a fine piece of phenomenology accomplished by a rising student who has now surpassed even the inventor of his method. Or it is viewed *developmentally*, as the first hint of a later full-blown critique of technology. In chapter 2, I will discuss some of these approaches by name. While all of them treat equipment with a reasonable degree of well-earned respect, it soon becomes clear that the commentator is just passing through, en route to more prestigious topics. The real action is assumed to lie elsewhere—whether in the depths of a relation to history, or in one of the more remote and complicated problems found in Heidegger's abundant writings.

Against these tendencies, the present book advocates a more extreme position: that the theory of equipment contains *the whole of the Heideggerian philosophy*, fully encompassing all of its key insights as well as the most promising of the paths that lead beyond them. In negative terms, I will argue that Heidegger's tool-analysis has nothing to do with any kind of "pragmatism," or indeed with any theory of human action at all.[1] Instead, the philosophy of Heidegger forces us to develop a ruthless inquiry into the structure of *objects themselves*, and to a greater extent than he himself would have endorsed.

Numerous misunderstandings can be averted if I begin with a word about the method of interpretation employed in this book. My goal is *not* to reconstruct Heidegger's own understanding of the tool-analysis. Nor is it my claim that previous interpreters have mistaken his authorial intentions, as if I were in a position to reveal his esoteric doctrine, hidden from the vulgar until now. Indeed, I am convinced that he would revile much of what I have to say. This book is an attempt at an improved understanding, not of *Heidegger*, but of the concept of *tool-being*, which he was the first to identify with such precision. The term "tool-being" is not to be found in Heidegger's own writings. It was coined by a close friend of mine almost a decade ago, in joking reference to the dominant status of the theme of *Zuhandenheit* in my reading of Heidegger.[2] The joke was more appropriate than he suspected, for my claim is that the analysis of equipment does give us the preliminary answer to the question of the meaning of being. *The meaning of being is tool-being,* and the near future of philosophy may hinge in large part on the further exploration of this Heideggerian insight.

The identification of being with tool-being will come as a shock to most readers, insofar as Heidegger's tool-analysis seems to deal with a specific class of utensils, while being itself is supposed to be withdrawn from any contact with specific entities, and is held to be accessible at all only through an analysis of human being. But my argument on behalf of tool-being is quite simple and, in my opinion, decisive. Heidegger poses the question of being by launching a ferocious assault on all forms of presence-at-hand (*Vorhandenheit*). He does this phenomenologically through the tool-analysis; he does it rhetorically through his repetitive use of the word "mere" to dismiss all ontic arguments; he does it historically through his assertion that presence-at-hand has dominated the history of metaphysics. The goal of Martin Heidegger's career was to identify and to attack the notion of reality as something present-at-hand. And although his proposed alternative to *Vorhandenheit* remains underdeveloped in his writings, it is in no way vague—that which first resists any reduction to presence is tool-being, performing its dynamic effect amidst the cosmos, always partly withdrawn from anything that might be said about it.

But every great insight in the history of philosophy is shadowed by a great error. Heidegger's error lies in the assumption, typical of the post-Kantian era, that a reflection on *human being* is the key to passing from an unphilosophical perspective to a philosophical one. Heidegger seems to think that human *use* of objects is what gives them ontological depth, frees them from their servitude as mere slabs of present-at-hand physical matter. And this is the point at which contemporary philosophy needs to part company with Heidegger in the most radical way: *objects themselves* are already more than present-at-hand. The interplay of dust and cinder blocks and shafts of sunlight is haunted by the drama of presence and withdrawal no less than are language or lurid human moods. As a result, philosophy must break loose from the textual and linguistic ghetto that it has been constructing for itself, and return to the drama of the things themselves. Contrary to Heidegger's own belief, his criticism of *Vorhandenheit* does not end metaphysics, but revives it. But since even physical matter can no longer be regarded as sheer present-at-hand mass, it will have to be a metaphysics of a very different kind from that which Heidegger criticized.

To remain true to the contours of tool-being quite often requires that we jettison Heidegger's own stated opinions about it. Any citations of his works are not meant as an appeal to authority; therefore, I ask that they not be opposed by such appeals. I footnote particular texts only for the same reason that mapmakers label rivers and monuments: to prevent the traveler from losing track of the landscape. We are no more obliged to follow Heidegger's own understanding of tool-being than we are to follow the itinerary of Lewis and Clark when driving from St. Louis to Portland, or to limit our uses of electrical power to those devices patented by Thomas Edison himself. The historical greatness of explorers or inventors or philosophers does not guarantee that they have exhausted their own subject matter.

I have sometimes found it necessary to repeat my arguments more than is usually the case in philosophical books. This is consistent with the old pedagogical maxim that a subject is learned best when it is presented six different times in six different ways. It is also my attempt to address a disturbing fact about the nature of reading that is usually overlooked by authors in highly technical fields such as Heidegger studies. If I now asked you to list your five favorite articles of all those published in your field of speciality, you could probably do so without much difficulty. But if I then asked you to repeat the precise argument of each of these articles, without looking at them again, you would probably have a much more difficult time. Even the best scholarly writing presents a series of arguments that many readers either do not long remember, or which consists of so many distinct steps that readers take what they like, and ignore or misuse the rest.

By way of contrast, consider how much better we all know the major landmarks in the neighborhood where we live. Here, we are absolute masters, and can summarize accurate details to anyone who asks, often to the point of annoying those around us. All of us find it hard to forget the sequence of restaurants and bars visited during the course of an especially memorable weekend, or the order in which songs occur on our favorite compact discs. We will always know the physical geography of our lives far better than we know the works of any particular philosopher. This is not because philosophy is more difficult than everyday life—for some people, quite the contrary. The real reason is that arguments and citations are only *secondary* forms of proof and therefore are easily forgotten.

The best model for communicating with a reader is not the dry expertise of the university overlord, but rather the native tact with which we guide a newly arrived visitor through the streets of Iowa City or Leipzig. A tour of this kind is usually only successful if it is repeated the following morning, and perhaps even once or twice more. When merely stating an argument, it may be enough to list your claims in a withering and exhaustive sequence. But when trying to teach your guests how to operate independently in an unfamiliar city, it is often necessary to visit the same cafés or streetcar stops on multiple occasions before expecting them to remember. "Right over there is where we were last night"; "no, this *is* the same techno club, it just looks different in the sunlight"; "when you're ready to head back to my apartment, just go past where all those bookstores were and follow the diagonal road." Only a rude and pompous host would give directions a single time and then snap at his guest for forgetting them the next day (sadly, we all know such people). The same is true, *mutatis mutandis*, for technical subjects.

The method of this chapter, then, is phenomenological rather than historical or expository. Its pace is designed to explore a single concept repeatedly and thoroughly, rather than to run wild with dozens of assorted claims drawn at random from the primary and secondary literature. The concept we will explore, of course, is *tool-being*. If by the end of the book any open-minded reader does not have a clear sense of the importance of this concept, the fault will be my own.

*   *   *

Heidegger's account of "readiness-to-hand" (*Zuhandenheit*) is so widely familiar that any paraphrase quickly becomes tedious. But we can begin by recalling his insight that human beings do not usually encounter entities as discrete visible objects, as substances present-at-hand (*vorhanden*). Heidegger demonstrates that our primary interaction with beings comes through "using" them, through simply *counting on them* in an unthematic way. For the most part, objects are implements taken for granted, a vast environmental backdrop supporting the thin and volatile layer of our explicit activities. All human action finds itself lodged amidst countless items of supporting equipment: the most nuanced debates in a laboratory stand at the mercy of a silent bedrock of floorboards, bolts, ventilators, gravity, and atmospheric oxygen. Only rarely, most often in cases of malfunction, do we come to notice any of these subterranean elements of our lives. Our attention is focused instead on that luminous plane where our overt hopes and struggles unfold.

In this way, Heidegger shows that we normally do not deal with entities as aggregates of natural physical mass, but rather as a range of *functions* or *effects* that we rely upon. Instead of encountering "pane of glass," we tend to make use of this item indirectly, in the form of "well-lit room." We do not usually contend with sections of cement, but only with their outcome: an easily walkable surface area. As a rule, tools are not present-at-hand, but *ready-to-hand*. For the most part, they work their magic upon reality without entering our awareness. Equipment is forever *in action*, constructing in each moment the sustaining habitat where our explicit awareness is on the move.

I immediately place special emphasis on the work or effect executed by tools themselves in order to counter a nearly universal error regarding the concept of readiness-to-hand. This typical mistake presumes that the theory of equipment is concerned primarily with *human beings*, that it leads us in the direction of a "practical philosophy."[3] It is clear enough that the liberating power of Heidegger's theory of equipment lies in its subversion of the traditional dominance of *Vorhandenheit*. The problem lies in the additional assumption, often encouraged by Heidegger himself, that *human existence* is the hero that frees entities from the present-at-hand realm. This approach wrongly casts Dasein in philosophy's starring role, while preserving the unfortunate belief that the world itself is made up of sheer physical objects: neutral slabs of material accidentally shuffled around or colored by human viewpoints, stable substances volatilized only by an external force. But it is precisely this thesis of natural present-at-hand entities that is permanently crushed from the first step of Heidegger's analysis, whether he fully recognizes this or not. For presence-at-hand is simply not an adequate description of the being of *any* entity—person, hammer, chandelier, insect, or otherwise.

Contrary to one widespread reading of equipment, the tool-analysis *does not* serve to criticize the notion of independent objects, as if to champion instead a subjective human realm of gadgets or linguistic signs. The concept of Dasein is not introduced in order to rough up the notion of a world-in-itself. The revolution cannot begin with an equipmental or linguistic subjectivism, since it is not the human *use* of tools that threatens the dominance of *Vorhandenheit*. Quite the contrary: only when equipment somehow *enters* the province of human awareness does its veiled performance or execution become concealed behind some present-at-hand configuration. I will show that objects themselves, far from the insipid physical bulks that one imagines, are already aflame with ambiguity, torn by vibrations and insurgencies equaling those found in the most tortured human moods. It is mistaken to follow a literal reading of *Being and Time* and assume that only human being is filled with riddles, as if only Dasein were irreducible to traditional categories. Heidegger's philosophical achievement goes far beyond this. To repeat: inanimate objects are not just manipulable clods of matter, not philosophical dead weight best left to "positive science." Instead, they are more like undiscovered planets, stony or gaseous worlds which ontology is now obliged to colonize with a full array of probes and seismic instruments—most of them not yet invented.

Heidegger's voluminous history of being has been taken as justification for the ongoing explosion of historical studies by his followers. Meanwhile, the philosopher's promising insights into the structure of *things* have barely been developed at all. Against the ever-increasing calls for "historical awareness" in Heidegger studies, I would suggest that it is time to try the opposite approach. Rather than endless summer symposia about "Heidegger and the Greeks," we should ask to hear more about jugs and artworks, as well as about oceans and diamonds and earthquakes. Instead of aloof reflections on the enframing mechanisms of technology, it ought to be possible to discuss subways and radio telescopes. And enough with clever references to the "dice-throw" as an avant-garde literary image: dice and slot machines and playing cards *themselves* should now be our theme— as should fireworks, grasshoppers, moonbeams, and wood.

If the trail stretching toward these possibilities seems to be a long one, we should not forget that serious work on it began long ago, with Husserl's famed return to the things themselves. Although I regard Heidegger's criticisms of his teacher as definitive,[4] they hardly oblige us to abandon the things of the world for a consuming focus on either language or the history of philosophy. In fact, Heidegger does *anything but* abandon objects; his discovery of tool-being even restores the things to the very center of philosophy, transforming them from *phenomena* into equipmental *events*. As will be seen below, this theory of equipment is not jettisoned by the later Heidegger at all, but is gradually reshaped into the forgotten theme of the "fourfold." By patiently developing his account of tools into a theory of the quadrants of reality, Heidegger provides us with the initial elements of an object-oriented philosophy. The present book is an attempt to summarize and extend his raw initial catalog of these elements.

In any event, the key result of Heidegger's analysis of tools is not that "equipment becomes invisible when serving remote human purposes," an uninspired and trivial claim. It should already be evident that the crucial insight has nothing to do with the human *handling* of tools; instead, the transformation takes place on the side of *the tools*. Equipment is not effective "because people use it"; on the contrary, it can only be used because it is *capable of an effect*, of inflicting some kind of blow on reality. In short, the tool isn't "used"—it *is*. In each instant, entities form a determinate landscape that offers a specific range of possibilities and obstacles. *Beings in themselves* are ready-to-hand, not in the derivative sense of "manipulable," but in the primary sense of "in action." The tool is a real function or effect, an invisible sun radiating its energies into the world before ever coming to view. In this way, the world is an infrastructure of equipment already at work, of tool-beings unleashing their forces upon us just as savagely or flirtatiously as they duel with one another. Insofar as the vast majority of these tools remain unknown to us, and were certainly not *invented* by us (for example, our brains and our blood cells), it can hardly be said that we "use" them in the strict sense of the term. A more accurate statement would be that we silently *rely* upon them, taking them for granted as that naive landscape on which even our most jaded and cynical schemes unfold. Heidegger's analysis by no means leads to a "practical philosophy." At most, we might speak of a *pragmatic* philosophy: not a pragmatism, but a theory concerning the *pragmata*, the tools themselves.[5]

The entire theme of this book is nothing but these tools themselves. Heidegger teaches that equipment is not to be understood as a solid mate-

rial bulk, as an atom lying before us in obvious presence. In order to examine the alternative, we can abandon the stale example of the hammer and
consider a basic piece of infrastructure: a bridge. The reality of the bridge
is not to be found in its amalgam of asphalt and cable, but in the geographic fact of "traversable gorge." The bridge is a bridge-effect; the tool
is a force that generates a world, one in which the canyon is no longer an
obstacle. It is crucial to note that this is not restricted to tools of human
origin: there are also dependable earth-formations that provide useful car-
avan routes or hold back the sea. At each moment, the world is a geography of objects, whether these objects are made of the latest plastics or were
born at the dawn of time.

This is the true scenario of Heidegger's tool-being: equipment as an
agent thoroughly deployed in reality, as an *impact* irreducible to any list
of properties that might be tabulated by an observer. Advancing rapidly
into this subject matter, we can isolate several distinct features of equipment. Heidegger has shown that its first notable trait is *invisibility*. As a
rule, the more efficiently the tool performs its function, the more it tends
to recede from view: "The peculiarity of what is proximally ready-to-hand
is that, in its readiness-to-hand, it must, as it were, withdraw
[*zurückziehen*] in order to be ready-to-hand quite authentically."[6] But
this familiar point is rarely grasped in a sufficiently rigorous way. It is not
just that equipment is generally invisible as long as it is working properly.
Such a notion can never surpass the level of empirical anecdote, and only
invites free-wheeling attempts at contradiction ("but then we noticed that
it worked a lot better if you stared *right at* the damn thing"). The truth
is far more radical than this. In the first instance, there is an eternal chasm
between equipment and its tool-being. The wrench as reality and the visible or tactile wrench are incommensurable kingdoms, solitary planes
without hope of intersection. The function or action of the tool, its tool-
being, is *absolutely* invisible—even if the hammer never leaves my sight.
Neither gazing at an object nor theorizing about it is enough to lure its
being from concealment.

Someone might object that the tool is always invisible "only in a certain respect" rather than absolutely. And sure enough, a table obviously
does not vanish into the ether once it begins to function as a support for
plates or apples. But this complaint once again presupposes the idea of the
table as a natural object, portions of its reality momentarily visible and others unseen. On the contrary, it is not the chance fluctuations of human
attention that determine whether the ready-to-hand is invisible or not. To
say that the tool is unseen "for the most part" is ultimately superfluous,
even incorrect. Whatever is visible of the table in any given instant can
never be its tool-being, *never* its readiness-to-hand. However deeply we
meditate on the table's act of supporting solid weights, however tena-

ciously we monitor its presence, any insight that is yielded will always be something quite distinct from *this act itself.*[7]

A tool exists in the manner of enacting itself; only derivatively can it be discussed or otherwise mulled over. Try as hard as we might to capture the hidden execution of equipment, we will always lag behind. There is no gaze capable of seizing it, despite Heidegger's claims to the contrary.[8] Insofar as any aspect of the table is represented to us, it is *already present-at-hand,* loitering in the very dimension of surface-apparitions that the analysis of tools was born to undermine. Thus, we find that there are two separate facets to equipment: (1) its irreducibly veiled activity, and (2) its sensible and explorable profile. In more familiar Heideggerian terms, there is the tool viewed "ontologically" and the same tool viewed "ontically." For the moment, we have no way of bringing these worlds into communion, other than to say that one is primary and the other *not* primary. Soon, I will examine the way in which Heidegger attempts to relate these two dimensions by means of the as-structure. For now, it remains preferable to develop the two moments in isolation from one another.

The next major feature of equipment is its *totality.* The tool is never found in isolation, but belongs to a system: "Taken strictly, there 'is' no such thing as *an* equipment. To the being of any equipment there always belongs a totality of equipment, in which it can be this equipment that it is."[9] Here again, there is the danger of rushing into facile agreement with Heidegger. The crux of the matter does not lie in the observation that equipment is always found in conjunction with related items, a superficial claim easily snuffed by any master of counterexample. What is essential is that at the level of readiness-to-hand, the idea of a single tool reposing in its solitary effect is shown to be untenable. Instead, individual equipment is already dissolved into a global tool-empire.

Bolts and wires taken alone enjoy a rather minimal reality. In combination with thousands of other minutely engineered pieces, they blend into the composite visible equipment known as a bridge. But these tiny devices would bring about an utterly different state of affairs if reassigned elsewhere, whether as scrap metal or as segments of a bomb. The reality of the tool-pieces is different in each of these cases. Although we know *ontically* that most equipment has enduring substantial parts that can be separated and removed, we do not yet have a legitimate way of importing this fact into Heidegger's ontology. On the level we have currently reached, there *are* no individual tool-pieces with discrete personalities, but only totalitarian machines that have already enslaved their pieces in the name of a more encompassing reality. Bolt and wire are the specific equipment that they are only within the system they currently happen to occupy: suspension-system, explosive-system. In the case now under discussion, the being of the individual pieces is swallowed into the larger framework of the bridge.

In turn, the bridge as a whole is not a self-evident, atomic finality; rather, it functions in numerous different equipmental ways, swept up into countless larger systems. Usually, it enacts an official plan of efficiency, shaving ten minutes from the drive around a bay. But in certain regions of the world, separating hostile factions, it is monitored by snipers. The bridge can be the unforgettable site of a fateful conversation (nostalgia-equipment), the location of a distant relative's suicide (memorial-equipment), or perhaps it is simply stalked in a troubling insomnia. It is an object of study for architectural critics or material for sabotage by vandals. In the lives of seagulls and insects, it takes on altogether different aspects.

The key is not to argue that there are independent objects that mean different things "depending on the context," which would be to slip once more into the naturalistic error we have encountered twice already. The crucial point is that at any given moment, every tool is plugged into certain limited systems of machinery while excluded from others: for Heidegger, equipment *is* its context. And furthermore, even this context is manifold, since bird and sniper encounter the bridge as different realities in precisely the same moment. Every implement exerts a determinate and limited range of effects in each instant, and is equally determined by the equipment that surrounds it. The tool gives birth to one particular world of unleashed forces, and no other—even if that world is mirrored in an indefinite number of perspectives. I might point out that even the most insignificant shard of metal is not without importance, since it at least enacts the effect of "harmlessness." Placed elsewhere, it might take on a disastrous role: causing illness if ingested, ruining an engine when inserted at decisive temperatures.

The totality of equipment means that each tool occupies a thoroughly specific position in the system of forces that makes up the world. Or to be more precise, the totality of equipment *is* the world; not as a sum of ontic gears and levers, nor as an empty horizon in which tool-pieces are situated, but as that unitary execution in which the entire ontic realm is already *dissolved*. The action of individual tools has already receded from view, as it exerts its force against all other equipment, even if only by remaining at a safe enough distance so as not to impede or damage it. We cannot presuppose the notion of the tool as an impenetrable, self-sufficient unity that shifts between contexts, for this is already to view it from the standpoint that Heidegger has worked to discredit. This would be to offer an implicit theory of substance existing independently from the relations in which it is involved. Nothing could be more foreign to Heidegger's philosophy, or indeed to any of the leading thinkers of the twentieth century, who as a rule earned their living with a thoroughly *relational* theory of reality. One of the unconventional claims of this book is that this relational theory has already performed its historical mission, and is now burdening us with its own excesses. A theory of substance is inevitably reborn from the ashes of Heidegger's criticism, as I will argue in chapter 3. But first things first: it is impossible to understand Heidegger without seeing that he believes he is annihilating all possibility of independent objects existing in a vacuum outside the world of relations, functions, significations. For him, the tool in the reality of its labor belongs to a world-system, one that has swallowed up all individual components into a single world-effect. It is only from out of this system that specific beings can ever emerge. *The world of tools is an invisible realm from which the visible structure of the universe emerges.*[10]

In the remainder of this chapter, I will argue that this reversal between concealed tool and visible tool (that is, the "broken" tool) is the sole subject matter developed throughout the entirety of Heidegger's works. But his discovery of the reversal within tool-being requires a shift away from the various linguistic and textual philosophies still dominant today. What is demanded is a fresh and concrete research into the secret contours of objects.

§2. Reference

For Heidegger, tool-being is notable both for its invisibility and for its totality. Always in action, the tool assumes a determinate stance in the midst of reality: compressing other entities into submission, while also giving way beneath the forces they return. As such, the work of the tool forever recedes behind its radiant surface profile. The tool-being of the ready-to-hand is not simply withdrawn from view "for the most part," since by definition it is irreducible to anything that could ever be seen. From here on out, I will use the phrases "equipment," "the ready-to-hand," and "tool-being" to refer *exclusively* to the level of their subterranean reality which never comes openly to view. Insofar as the hammer is present to me in any way, it is *not* equipment in the sense that emerges from Heidegger's analysis. Wherever we might look, tool-being always lies elsewhere. Hence, it is necessary to purge Heidegger's term *Zuhandenheit* of every connotation of mallets and screwdrivers, a false overtone that leads so many commentators astray from the outset.

Forever withdrawing from view into a distant background, *equipment is invisible.* And for Heidegger, tools also cannot be regarded as discrete natural substances that enter into systems only accidentally, as if they were independent solids that retained their integrity even when entering into the wildest combinations. Equipment seems to be a unitary effect, its various tool-pieces absorbed into the *Imperium* of function that it inaugurates, each of them separable from it only by way of abstraction or outright physical removal. Hence, *equipment is total.* I gladly repeat these results of the previous section, hoping that a variety of reformulations will eventually bring every reader to a clear grasp of my theme. In §1, several positive features of this subject matter were introduced. The present section takes a more critical tack, showing that numerous pieces of supposedly diverse Heideggerian terminology quickly collapse into the simple situation that has already been described.

In the interest of clarity, both major features of equipment can be combined in a single term: *referentiality*. The tool is referential, in a twofold sense that should now be briefly recounted. It has already been seen that equipment functions by pushing us beyond itself, by vanishing in favor of the visible reality that it brings about. By disappearing from view in this way, it allows the ultimate reference to swallow all of its component forces into an invisible system or network lying silently beneath it. In this *first* sense, the "reference" of the tool is the encountered finality or terminus to which it anonymously contributes: the miniature bolts "refer" to the bridge, while the carpenter's tools tend to vanish in favor of the house as a whole.

But in each case, a lost race of tool-beings is smothered beneath these end-points, vanishing into the machinery whose dominance finally halts in some impenetrable surface. In a *second* sense, then, reference is the act of an entity's *withdrawal* into its unseen efficacy, hidden away in its function or execution or performance: "The structure of the being of what is ready-to-hand as equipment is determined by references or assignments [*Verweisungen*]... The assignments themselves are not observed; they are rather 'there' when we concernfully submit ourselves to them."[11] The function or reference of the tool is effective not as an explicit sign or symbol, but as something that vanishes into the work to which it is assigned.

To all of this we can add the famous terms "significance" and "world": "The relational totality of this signifying we call '*significance*' [*Bedeutung*]. This is what makes up the structure of the world—the structure of that wherein Dasein as such already is."[12] The dual referentiality described by all of these concepts (function, action, reference, significance, world) is the subject matter of the current section. It is important to point out that all such terms are strictly *synonymous* in Heidegger's thought. All arise in connection with the theme under discussion: the unified totality of equipment and the manifold distinct entities that erupt from it. Otherwise, we are too easily led astray by an illusory abundance of Heideggerian concepts, a misleading plenitude which only masks the beautiful austerity of a single ontological paradox.

As we have seen, the being of equipment is *Vollzug*, execution or performance, a shifting of the issue beyond itself: a "reference" toward the end it accomplishes. Then the tool is reference; for the tool, to be is to *mean*. To solidify this observation, we can briefly repeat the content of the preceding paragraphs, substituting the term "meaning" [*Sinn*] for "reference" [*Bedeutung*].[13] Note the following: (1) The tool's "meaning" is nothing other than the visible termination of its underground action. Just as the meaning of a signal-arrow is the region to which it alerts us by pointing, just as a word evokes its meaning by deflecting attention away from itself, so too do cable and pillars "mean" the bridge-system by vanishing into it. Here, the meaning of equipment is the final explicit reality that it serves to bring onto the stage. (2) In another respect, meaning is quite the opposite. For instance, we know that the phenomenological method aspires never to be stupefied by the simple presence of any phenomenon; rather, this method earns its living by gradually drawing out the countless hidden layers of categorial structures implicit in the merest appearance. In this way, it pursues the *meaning* of the phenomenon. This second, *concealed* kind of "meaning" is analogous to what I have called the tool-being of the entity, an act of primal effectiveness that eludes every possible view.

Thus, equipment is "meaning" or "reference" in *two* distinct senses. It is the performance of a withering subterranean force, but a force that also acts to summon up some explicitly encountered reality. This ambiguity of meaning is nothing but the ambivalence of the tool itself: a *reality* that is also somehow an *appearance*, or a *verb* that is also a *noun*. It is as if Heidegger had set out to compose a vast philosophical thesaurus, in which "equipment," "reference," "meaning, "world," and other terms became versatile synonyms for a single reversal between the withdrawn tool-being of the world and its present-at-hand fragments.

Perhaps most surprisingly of all, we can easily add the word "being" to this list of synonyms. Commentators have often pointed to the close relation in Heidegger between *Sinn* and *Sein*. However we decide to approach these terms, there are numerous reasons to sidestep any attempt to deal with them by means of word-play.[14] But I avoid it here mostly because there is no swirling chiasm between the two words, no remarkable oscillating relation between "unreadable" poles. Things are much simpler than this: in fact, the being of the tool and its meaning are *one and the same*. After all, the *being* of the tool is what that tool actually is, the impact it attains, its anonymous labor behind all that is present-at-hand. Yet in spite of this labor, it somehow also emerges as a specific visible tool—as the tangible outline of a screwdriver or nail, or as the house that these utensils are helping to build. But this same dual status is what has just been shown to be characteristic of the tool's *meaning*. Thus, Heidegger's analysis of equipment is the cradle of this pivotal concept in his work, the *Sein* that is a *Sinn*. Then the "question of the meaning of being" is a reversible tautology, one whose answer can be found only in that living tautology—*equipment*. I postpone until chapter 2 a further review of this claim.[15]

This is a good time to address one of the most likely objections to any supremacy of tool-being among Heidegger's concepts. It will be said that the analysis of equipment is only a starting point. From here, after all, the reader is treated to a progressively deeper account, one that takes the form of a *grounding* analysis. Thus, it is not enough to focus on the use of implements, for these can be encountered only insofar as Dasein has the structure of "concern." Additionally, concern is possible only on the basis of being-in-the-world, which is only possible on the basis of "care," which in turn is based in the structure of temporality. Countless intermediate steps can be added at the commentator's pleasure. But this manner of presenting the case is essentially a distraction. However popular it may be, it resembles too closely the method of an old children's slumber party chant, still in circulation during the 1970s: "Near a dark, dark star, there's a dark, dark planet. On the dark, dark planet, there's a dark, dark nation. . . ." The song moves on fearfully in this way through the whole run of ever smaller dark geographies—state, city, neighborhood, street, house, room, door, closet, coat, pocket—until we reach the final surprise: "in the dark, dark pocket is a pink jelly bean!"[16] Aside from the inverse order, a good deal of Heidegger commentary differs from this hypnotic progression only through the insistence that *its* jelly bean is unapproachable, cloaked in some sort of "irreducible negativity."

Accordingly, I would recommend that this form of grounding exposition be scrapped, despite Heidegger's own use of it. On a related note, it is also not very helpful to insist on minute distinctions between every piece of Heideggerian terminology that is even remotely related to the tool (for instance, "involvement," "unobtrusiveness," "discoveredness") as if these were anything more than additional figures of speech for a very simple insight that must be grasped as clearly as possible if it is ever to be overcome.

The initial aim of *Being and Time* is to exhibit beings in their predominant mode of being, a process beginning with the famous tool-analysis that is the focus of this chapter. Along this path, the single error to be guarded against lies in the ingrained habit of regarding beings as present-at-hand, as representable in terms of delineable properties rather than acknowledged in the *actus* of being what they are.[17] But this first step is not abandoned once Heidegger's more ethereal terminology replaces his various hammer and turn-signal examples. "World," for instance, is not an independent void or projective screen standing at a distance from beings; it is the referential contexture in which these beings themselves are stationed, and *which they alone enact*. Equally, "time" is not some remote structure blissfully uncontaminated by contact with objects; rather, it is a temporality acting *in the heart of entities themselves*, undercutting their claim to mere presence. All talk of a retreat into successive horizons is valuable only as a method to prevent our being duped by the possible naturalistic connotations of any given term in the series. Strictly speaking, *there is no such thing as a horizon*. There are only being and beings. The "horizon" is a creature of the intellect, an artificial index finger rather than a real structure.

In short, the point is not to abandon specific entities in favor of ever deeper foundations, but *to overthrow the regime of presence-at-hand*. And tool-being already does this! Provided that the tool is conceived with sufficient rigor from the outset, and not just lazily identified with bargain-bin hammers, it already brings the key insights into view—and with a sorely needed immediacy of intuition that Heidegger's later developments tend to muffle. As long as a jigsaw is not misread as a physical tool-thing, there is no need to retreat into supposedly deeper strata, since the theme of the jigsaw and its being will already be in play from the start.

It is fruitless to debate the possibility or impossibility of "thinking being apart from beings"; as is often the case when it comes to Heidegger, ample textual ammunition is available to both sides.[18] The crucial point is that the fear of conceiving being in terms of entities is valid only when it reflects the danger of approaching being along the path of *present-at-hand* entities. *This* procedure, and not the focus on individual objects, is what Heidegger condemns as the repeated lapse of the Western tradition.[19] As already noted, his own later writings are populated with numerous individual entities—jugs, bridges, temples—none of them leading to any sort of retro-onto-theology (as was usual *prior* to Heidegger), and none to a purely metaphorical or figural discourse (as has been usual *since* Heidegger). Whether he succeeds or fails, the main difference between Heidegger and most contemporary continental philosophers is that he at least *tries* to talk about real jugs and bridges. Thus, there is no great danger if the present book now demands a renewed theory of specific objects. Beings taken as naively present-at-hand are already dead—and tool-being is the murderer. By nervously avoiding all mention of specific entities, one continues to lose sleep over an enemy that has not existed for seventy years.

My aim so far has been to focus undivided attention on the scenario of equipment, which I believe to contain the entirety of Heidegger's philosophical advance. To this end, it has been vital that we keep equipment itself firmly in view, and reject the notion that it is the human *use* of tools that is at stake. One potentially major distraction along this path stems from Heidegger's attempt to distinguish between the "in-order-to" (*Um-zu*) of the tool and the human "for-the-sake-of" (*Um-willen*), the final vantage point that is said to ultimately provide meaning to any referential contexture. I have already cited the in-order-to as the *reference* by which every tool vanishes into something beyond itself: "Equipment is essentially something 'in-order-to...', such as serviceability, conduciveness, usability, manipulability."[20] Forever withdrawn, equipment disappears in favor of the landscape it brings into view, the tangible reality that it allows to enter the spotlight. But at this point, Heidegger makes the additional claim that the system of tools ultimately gains its meaning from Dasein's "potentiality for being": "The primary 'towards-which' (*Wozu*) is a 'for-the-sake-of-which' (*Worumwillen*)."[21]

At first glance, this seems irrefutable. We know that the covered railway platform is not a simple fusion of wooden beams. Its usefulness as a piece of sheltering equipment is due to the existence of a rain-system, which is significant only insofar as Dasein, unlike amphibians, needs to stay dry. Furthermore, even these higher references would obviously make sense only in light of the structure of *care*: that is to say, none of these implements would have meaning if they were not somehow "at issue" for Dasein, if human beings were not concerned with their own being at all.

Given this priority of human care for the referential system of equipment, all arguments for the supremacy of tool-being would appear to be destroyed. The human entity now turns out to be the ground of possibility for all significance, and thus for the action or function of tool-beings as a whole. For this reason, it will be said that *Being and Time* is written from the standpoint of a latent subjectivism, and is therefore entirely at odds with the focus on equipment that I advocate. This subjectivist reading of Heidegger's most famous book remains surprisingly common. Even many of the philosopher's *admirers* are quick to concede this point, in spite of his own consistent denial of a human-centered bias in *Being and Time*.[22] Heidegger's sworn allies are heard to confess behind his back that their hero still has quite a ways to go ("I beg of you, just give him a few more years. By 1930, or 1936, everything will change for the better. Please be assured..."). The supposedly regrettable mistakes of the 1920s will later be overcome, as Heidegger moves on to the fertile territory of "truth" or *Ereignis*, or to some even more disembodied realm.

In chapter 2, these views will be discussed in some detail, but a preview is in order here. As a matter of fact, the tool-analysis does not rely in the least on any priority of the human standpoint. Heidegger's central insight is that the tool itself is bound up in a specific empire of functions, a system that takes its meaning from some particular projection, some final reference. Admittedly, the meaning of equipment is determined by that for the sake of which it acts. But I flatly contest the view that this *Worumwillen* is necessarily human. Tools execute their being "for the sake of" a reference, not because *people* run across them, but because they are utterly *determinate* in their referential function—that is, because they already stand at the mercy of innumerable terminal points of meaning.

To show this, I begin by asking the reader to note the obvious fact that the significance of pieces of equipment differs greatly between separate human beings. This requires no great leap of faith: it is a truism that every situation in human life presents vastly different aspects depending upon the specific hopes and fears of the observer. Moreover, it is a small step to extend this claim to the level of other mammals. Anyone can observe the confused misery of a dog in situations such as receiving a vaccine (torture-system), an ordeal that we ourselves know to be highly beneficial (health-system). Nor will it be hard to admit that *some* form of meaning must occur on the level of insects, or in the sphere inhabited by bacteria: "for the sake of" these smaller organisms, minor incidents that barely concern humans at all are frequently lethal (trace poisons, an early frost). On the bright side, beetles and microbes can discover marvelous environments in the tiniest spaces, sites too small to attract our notice. In sum, equipmental totalities undergo extensive alteration depending on what organism encounters them, in a way that does not yet touch on any supposed distinction between human and nonhuman creatures.

But it is necessary to go even further, to lengths that can only seem bizarre at first glance. Ultimately, the "for-the-sake-of" is a phenomenon that can be found even on the level of *inorganic matter*. We can bring to mind an Oriental paper screen of the type often used to divide fashionable rooms into sectors, filtering lamplight into a muted glow. Such a device offers a formidable barrier for the particles of dust that continually drift into it, or even for the gravel-chips that might accidentally be kicked up against it. But the soft light passing through the room encounters it as only a partial obstacle. At the same time, the screen is easily punctured by weightier or sharper objects: "for the sake of" a loose fan blade or carelessly handled machete, the paper screen is a nullity. While some might object to this use of anthropomorphic language for inanimate objects, I am actually making fewer arbitrary assumptions than Heidegger does. If I say that the light or the fan-blade "encounters" the paper screen, I am not claiming that material objects have souls; I simply lack a general term other than "encounter" that would not be painfully sterile. By contrast, Heidegger chooses to embezzle from the realm of common sense the ontic *assumption* that humans are very different from knives and paper. Although it seems reasonable that human awareness might be a different sort of reality from inanimate causation, Heidegger's analysis of the "for-the-sake-of" never brings us to anything uniquely human. Despite all his efforts to restrict its scope, his analysis of referentiality ultimately holds good for *everything*, even for mere flakes of dirt. The full argument for this claim will be developed gradually throughout the book. I mention it here only to preempt any dismissive objections.

The claim that the "for-the-sake-of-which" can be a visible thing pre-sent to a *human observer* turns out to be of derivative importance. More primary is that the being of the tool is utterly *determinate* in its specific relation to any entity it encounters, whether this be a person or animal "aware" of the screen, or a dazed block of matter ignorantly colliding with it. Thus, even amidst the sleek and unarticulated unity of an inanimate referential system, there is still a mutual reference of independent beings thoroughly capable of cutting, breaking, and burning each other. At this level, it is irrelevant that the knife does not seem to be consciously aware of the screen. The significance of the screen as a barrier is still something quite different for this dangerous knife from what it would be for, say, a ludicrous grain of sand. The screen exists "for the sake of" me, my pet Caribbean parrot, the knife, the light, *and* the pebble. If there is really a radical ontological difference between all of these entities, this is not the place to find it.

The basic dualism I defend is a familiar one, and will probably be endorsed by many readers of Heidegger. On the one hand, there is the world of tool-being, inaccessible to representation and existing only as the brute efficacy of a total system of equipment. On the other, there are the visible termini of that system, the various singular objects inhabiting the perceptible zone of life. These two realms are none other than those of Heidegger's *ready-to-hand* and *present-at-hand*. In turn, this opposition is precisely the same as that between *ontological* and *ontic*. Only the trivial misreading of tool-being as "useful human instrument" can permit the false objection that the tool is not yet anything ontological.

It might also be objected that readi*ness*-to-hand and pres*ence*-at-hand are actually both ontological determinations of *ontic* ready-to-hand and present-at-hand entities. I regard this as a fundamental misreading of Heidegger's distinction, one that results from two closely related errors: (1) the assumption that the ready-to-hand and the present-at-hand are two different *kinds* of beings, as if the first referred to hammers and chisels and the second only to *non*-handy entities. This is incorrect. *Das Zuhandene* and *das Vorhandene* are not two different types of entities, but two irreducible faces of the *same* entity. The hammer is ready-to-hand in one sense and present-at-hand in another. But the same is true for all entities, as will become clearer in the upcoming sections; (2) The assumption that specific entities are always ontic, and horizonal structures always ontological: as if adding the German suffix "-*heit*" to a word were the key to all profundity. This is equally incorrect. In fact, the notions of readi*ness*-to-hand and pres*ence*-at-hand are mere "things of reason," as Leibniz would put it. They do not really exist outside of the human mind. What *does* exist is a world packed full with hammers, roads, propane tanks, eagles, cobras, rolling woodlands, and countless other entities. If we consider any one of these entities—say, the propane tank—it can be regarded both as something ready-to-hand *and* as something present-at-hand. In the first case, it is a slumbering brute force irreducible to any experience we might have of it.

In the second case, it serves as the tangible object of some sort of perception or discussion, and is recognized by a specific shape and color and texture. The propane tank is both *zu-* and *vorhanden*, both ontological and ontic. In either case, it is always an *entity*, never a *horizon*. The two dimensions of the propane tank begin by standing in unbridged opposition, so that to describe their relation presents a genuine philosophical problem. The metaphysical aspects of this problem will be addressed at length in chapter 3.

The second, more unusual strand in my argument will probably seem less convincing at the outset. This is the just-cited observation that there is a crude sort of singularity even on the level of tools themselves, a presence of individual entities to one another as *specific* individuals. I freely admit that there is a sense in which the paper screen is unable to encounter dust *as* dust, since it lacks the consciousness of sentient beings. This issue will soon return to the forefront in my discussion of the as-structure in Heidegger's popular 1929/30 lecture course. But in a rudimentary way, if paper did not somehow encounter knife "as" knife, it could never be damaged by that knife. That is to say, the special kind of damage it undergoes shows that it *does* encounter the knife *as a knife*, rather than as a flame or harmless pebble. Note that no distinction between human and nonhuman forms of the as-structure should be smuggled into this discussion from the assumptions of daily life. If Heidegger wants to draw such a distinction, he will have to earn it through hard ontological work, and in my opinion he never even makes a serious attempt to do so. The celebrated distinction between the "in-order-to" of inanimate tools and the "for-the-sake-of" of human Dasein does not achieve what Heidegger wants it to achieve. It is meant to demarcate two distinct *kinds* of entities (human and nonhuman), and actually ends up defining two modes of *every* entity. Against all expectations, it will turn out that the structure known as the "for-the-sake-of" occurs even on the level of soulless matter.

This can be explained briefly as follows. If it is true that tool-beings are characterized by their function "in order to" do something else, it is also true that many such functions occur simultaneously for every entity. The *Um-zu* is what plugs one entity into another, undermining its claim to be a present-at-hand substance by swallowing it up into some larger system. The hammer is assigned to the nail, the nail to the board, the board to the house, and so on. In any instant, all of these entities are affixed to one another in an all-embracing totality of significance; to speak individually of the hammer or nail in isolation is always a derivative step in Heidegger's eyes. What is primary is the equipmental totality.

But in the strict sense, there is no way to limit this totality to the items in a single region of the universe, such as a single construction site. All of these objects are embedded in even remoter references, such as the specific gravitational field of the earth. The design of the house also refers to the presumed seismic stability of the land where it sits, since the architect has taken no special precautions against earthquakes, unlike in the doomed city of Los Angeles, where he would have been required by law to do so. In the strict sense, all objects in the universe refer to one another. If one of them changes, however slightly, the entire interlaced system of meaning has shifted in some minute but undeniable way. This is one of the famous claims of Alfred North Whitehead, but it can be found in Heidegger as well; in chapter 3, I will compare them on precisely this point. The important thing for now is to see that in the strict sense, the "in-order-to" must be *global*—and therefore *single*. To speak of the *Um-zu* of a *particular* hammer can only succeed as a sort of intellectual slang, since the interwoven strands of the world-machine supposedly precede any specific individual object. Hence, the "in-order-to" is a totalizing force. It creates a homogeneous empire, an oppressive universal regime with no room for distinct local segments such as hammer or knife or fire. In the end, there is only one "in-order-to," and Heidegger calls it *world*.

How is it, then, that local regions and specific districts can exist at all amidst the infinite empire of being? For Heidegger, the production of specific termini within the empire seems to be the privilege of human Dasein alone (for now, I will ignore the problem of animals). Consider what happens at the construction site when no humans are in the vicinity, as at 3 A.M. on a national holiday. There are moments when Heidegger seems to think that all of the objects on the site *are* nothing more than independent physical masses until Dasein arrives on the scene. But this is clearly impossible, since all of the objects in question affect each other in very specific ways regardless of whether or not anyone is present—each object gains its "force" with respect to the others. If a welding torch has stupidly been left blazing in the vicinity of some kerosene tanks, if fifty semi-trailers have been idiotically parked on top of a flimsy wooden grate, these entities will soon find themselves drawn into some sort of horrific disaster even if all humans are miles away from the scene.

But even so, it would seem that none of these objects can be individuals without the presence of a human being to *identify* them as such. Until I appear at the construction site to inspect the catastrophe the next morning, all of the objects are plugged into a single all-embracing unity, each of them embedded in the mighty whole. It is only I, almighty Dasein, who am able to insinuate cracks into this totalizing machinery, liberating specific fragments from what would otherwise have been a single homogeneous effect. What produces all of the local termini is the structure of the "for-the-sake-of," which frees up each of these elements in terms of how it can be projected for the potential of my own being. When the human being arrives, there is no longer just a single instantaneous effect. Here is a hammer, which has a certain significance for me; here is an empty paper sack, which also has its significance, however minor; here is a pile of scorched rubble, which frightens me. It is "for the sake of" my being that all of these things become visible to me as specific opportunities or threats. This "for-the-sake-of" is the only medicine able to counter the invisible, totalizing empire of the "in-order-to." It is the *only* thing that prevents all entities from being swallowed up into a global system devoid of any parts. And for Heidegger, it is only human beings who possess this magical antidote.

I answer that this cannot possibly be the case. The world cannot be thought of as a total empire of meaning that only humans would be able to break up into individual zones. If this were the case, physical causation could never occur, since there would be no individual objects, but only a single system, with no explanation for why this system should ever alter in the absence of human Dasein. As we all know, the inanimate world does *not* rest in static equilibrium, as it would have to if it were only a unified totality without parts. Instead, it is made of pieces that resist one another, that forever caress each other or wage war with one another. An entity does not run up against a single system of meaning, but against various *distinct entities*. The world is not just one; it is also many. It is not made up solely of pieces that push beyond themselves and lose their identity in a cosmic meaning-contexture; rather, its pieces are also *terminal points*, closed-off neighborhoods that retain their local identity despite the broader systems into which they are partly absorbed. But we have seen that our only protection from the hegemony of the "in-order-to" is the "for-the-sake-of." Heidegger may *want* to use these two phrases to refer to the difference between the inanimate and human spheres. Unfortunately, this wish remains unfulfilled, as both structures are found to an equal degree in *all* entities.

My claim is that Heidegger's account of the for-the-sake-of never reaches any specifically human features, except perhaps in a loose sort of literary way. What *does* emerge quite strongly from his account of the *Um-willen* is a deep-seated contrast between the global machinery of the world and the specific territories that erupt in the midst of it. Resisting the one empire of unified force, the "for-the-sake-of" frees up the world into a menagerie of specific hammers and windows and blades of grass. Now, it may or may not be true that only human Dasein can be fully *aware* of all of these entities, but no humans need exist in order for the paper screen to resist dust or perish by fire. And when this happens, the paper is involved in relations with *specific* entities, not with the world as a whole. There were territories and local governments in the world long before the human entity emerged. Our everyday prejudices about the human/inhuman rift carry no ontological weight whatsoever. For this reason, it must be said that *all* objects have the status of being-in-the-world, in spite of Heidegger's explicit statements to the contrary.[23]

As will be seen later, this also means that the much-discussed "priority of the future" in *Being and Time* has nothing to do with a bias in favor of one temporal dimension, nor does it result from an overestimation of human freedom against the withdrawal of being. Rather, the futural emphasis is simply a powerful strategy for demonstrating the countless layers of reciprocal projection that determine the reality of *every* entity, and thus for undermining any kind of mere presence—certainly in the human sphere, but ultimately even at the level of icicles, wheat, and coins. No more outlandish than any of the other monadic theories that have surfaced from time to time in the history of philosophy, this initial claim regarding tool-being has behind it the entire weight of Heidegger's analysis. In this way, it draws its energy not from some gullible cosmological impulse, but from the height of the times.

§3. Equipment Is Global

In a certain sense, the full subject matter of this book has already come into view. We have already encountered Heidegger's initial version of a two-world theory (tool-being vs. its presence to us). Further, we have even gained a limited sense of the drama at work in the heart of tools themselves (the example of the paper screen struck by dust and knives). Since any talk of an ontological interplay at the level of inanimate objects will initially strike many readers of Heidegger as bohemian, if not downright grotesque, I temporarily put this theme aside. The reader can safely forget the discussion of rock and paper until I reintroduce it later along a rather different path. For the moment, I will continue to speak only in human terms, referring to the difference between "tool in action" and "tool as present for us." This section and the next one will make a second examination of the tool and its reversal, clarifying and amplifying the basic features of the problem.

So far, I have described the simplest characteristics of the tool in its readiness-to-hand. These were summarized under the convenient heading of "reference," a term Heidegger endows with an equipmental rather than a semiological sense. As remarked briefly in the previous section, it should be obvious that this referentiality of tools is not just the property of certain narrow classes of entities. Whatever the usual view of the matter, it is clear that Heidegger's analysis of *Zu-* and *Vorhandenheit* has no validity as a classification of different object-types. It is not a choice between handy wagons or shovels on the one hand and amorphous globules of present-at-hand substance on the other. Instead, the execution and the presence of a thing refer to *two separate modes of being*, each of them at work in the case of *every* object. Consider any entity, and you will find that it does not escape the latent duality found in what Heidegger calls "reference." The referential being is *every* being, presenting itself *as* something even as it cryptically deploys its most invisible energies.

Any child can be taught to grasp this insight in the case of the hammer. But it extends equally well to such objects as "useless" chunks of dirt, which exemplify tool-being to no less an extent than do today's cutting-edge inventions. Whether we like it or not, even these wretched masses of soil are embedded in a referential contexture, soaking moisture from the air and inflicting themselves upon other beings in very specific ways. Nor can immaterial entities such as numbers escape the status of readiness-to-hand. After all, it is quite possible to discuss the meaning of "number" and to make new discoveries about mathematical entities—the simplest conceivable proof that the properties of numbers are not visible at a glance, not merely *vorhanden*. It is in this sense that even ideas must be regarded as real entities.

In short, Heidegger's so-called "tool-analysis" yields insights so fundamental that they cannot be confined to officially sanctioned tool-items such as picks, drills, and chains. The famous description of the tool turns out to be applicable to all entities. *Equipment is global; beings are tool-beings.* This is not to be confused with the superficial hypothesis that "everything is a tool," a phrase that fails to appreciate the depth of Heidegger's breakthrough. As I have argued, the point is not that everything can be "used" in some way, but rather that all entities are saddled with the duplicitous character of tool-being, an ontological fissure detectable in stars and angels and melons no less than in common utensils. This Heideggerian concept is so overwhelmingly *broad* that we are still not even remotely close to being able to talk about the special features of human activity, the Greek conception of *praxis*, or the fateful importance of the hand or opposable thumb for human thought—let alone about the specific character of modern technology. In brief: Heidegger has told us something quite important about beings in general, but *nothing at all* about tools in particular. In fact, it would be possible from here on out to discard the word "tool" from this discussion altogether. I retain it mostly for reasons of vividness, but also to emphasize that the reversal in being discovered by Heidegger plays itself out nowhere else than on the local level of specific objects. To avoid misunderstanding, I repeat the point: Heidegger's tool-analysis has no more to do with "tools" than with anything else.

The next step is equally obvious, although probably doomed to give rise to heated opposition. For if the structure of tool-being can be found in any entity whatsoever, then even *animals and human beings* must have the mode of being of equipment. Any objections to this claim cannot be based on appeals to the special abilities of Dasein, since this is precisely the point now under dispute. It would first have to be shown that the tool-analysis offers an account of "tools" as opposed to "nontools," which the present book flatly denies. The reference or action of entities in no way signifies that they are "only means to an end," such that the human kingdom would have to demand a nobler status than hammers. Readiness-to-hand does not describe a special kind of exploitation to which inanimate objects are subjected by work crews. Instead, *Zuhandensein* is the action of *beings themselves*.[24] We have not yet reached the moment when entities drift apart into distinct sets of the living and the dead; the referential persona of beings is something far more deeply rooted than any possible difference between man and machine. Thus, it is necessary to spy tool-being at work even in the entity called Dasein. This should no longer be controversial once all the connotations of useful hammers have been stripped from the concept of tool-being. Forget for a moment everything you think you know about the differences between people and utensils, and it is not so far-fetched to say that Dasein is caught up in the same ontological reversal as all other entities. On the one hand, both hammers and Dasein are involved in the sheer execution of their respective realities; however different these realities may be from one another, both unleash their forces amidst the world. On the other hand, both hammers and Dasein can be viewed *from the outside*. Even Dasein reverses into something *vorhanden*, which is precisely why it has been defined throughout history by all manner of present-at-hand properties—rational animal, laughing animal, tool-maker. Like all other entities, Dasein turns out to be *both* present-at-hand and ready-to-hand. This follows directly from my claim that these two terms signify modes of being rather than kinds of beings.

In this connection, it is also important to criticize Heidegger's distinction between "categories" (applicable only to present-at-hand objects) and the "existentiales" (like categories but reserved for Dasein alone. Regardless of the trivial fact that hammers do not seem to die, gossip, or have a conscience, it must be acknowledged that even inanimate objects require an *existential* consideration of their own. Among other passages, Heidegger employs this famous distinction when attempting to clarify the sense of "being-in." Wine is said to be "in" a bottle differently from the way in which Dasein is "in" the world. With respect to the former sort, we read: "All entities whose being 'in' one another can thus be described have the same kind of being—that of being-present-at-hand—as things occurring 'within' the world."[25] Being "in" qua present-at-hand is one of those "ontological characteristics which we call 'categorial': they are of such a sort as to belong to entities whose kind of being is not of the character of

Dasein."[26] Heidegger sharply contrasts this with the sort of "in" that is experienced by Dasein itself: "Being-in, on the other hand, is a state of Dasein's being; it is an existentiale. So one cannot think of it as the being-present-at-hand of some corporeal thing (such as a human body) 'in' an entity which is present-at-hand."[27] Heidegger could hardly make the opposing sets of terms any clearer than this. In one corner, we have entities other than Dasein, which have spatial reality only in a present-at-hand sense, and which we can describe by means of categories. In the other corner we have Dasein, which is *not* spatial in any present-at-hand sense; it cannot be described by categories, but only by existentiales.

The distinction is familiar to every reader of Heidegger. But it only repeats a mistake that was already criticized above. Here as before, there is a tendency to take two modes of being that can actually be found everywhere at all times, and to try to segregate them from one another in two distinct *types* of beings. We have already seen that present-at-hand and ready-to-hand cannot refer to two distinct kinds of objects, but mark the two irreducible aspects of *every* object. Of the same order as this is Heidegger's claim that being-in always belongs to Dasein, and spatial presence-at-hand always to non-Dasein. As usual, what serves to anchor this rigid opposition is not anything that emerges from the analysis itself, but only the common-sense prejudice that there is some sort of golden schism between the human and nonhuman realms. While this may prove to be the case, it does not mean that Heidegger has sufficiently accounted for any such opposition in *ontological* terms. The most damaging assumption here is that the primary rift lies between entities present-at-hand and entities for whom their own being is an issue. I contend that the *real* primary opposition is the one between present-at-hand and ready-to-hand, the latter term duly stripped of all overtones of "usefulness." In fact, all entities can be approached *either* categorically or existentially, just as all entities are both executant (*zuhanden*) and present to us (*vorhanden*).

This can be clarified as follows. To treat an entity as present-at-hand does *not* mean to treat it as a stupefied inanimate mass just lying around. The social scientist is fully aware that human life is a trickier matter than rocks piled up in physical space. But this does not stop him or her from describing the behavior of people in terms of categories (or would Heidegger claim that all sociologists are actually employing existentiales rather than categories in their work?). I know quite well that my closest friend is a creature who enjoys and suffers in a way that no mere piece of chemical matter ever will. But this does not stop me from being able to describe him to strangers in terms of hair color, eye color, height, age, and other fully tangible properties. In this way, it should be clear enough that Dasein is no less categorial than existential. As special as human Dasein may prove to be (and this has not yet been proven), we are often perfectly justified in describing it by external qualities rather than trying heroically to refer to the elusive depths of its being.

But by the same token, we have already seen that equipment cannot be viewed solely from an external standpoint any more than human beings can; this was already the keynote of Heidegger's tool-analysis. The special virtue of his analysis of the hammer is that it exhibits with unusual clarity the derivative character of the hammer's presence-at-hand, a tattooed surface beneath which it harbors its cryptic dynamism, its *vis viva*.[28] Like Dasein, the tool *is* in the mode of executing itself. *Equipment itself is existential.* It is not merely spatially located in some present-at-hand way, but is actually *in* the world; it does not merely have some neutral presence that could be viewed from the outside, but actually exists *in* a network of forces and meanings that determine its reality. As argued earlier, it is arbitrary to identify being-in with the special consciousness of human Dasein. What emerges from Heidegger's analysis is not a real difference between human and inhuman, but only his old obsessive dualism between presence-at-hand and the subterranean reality that lies concealed beneath it.

But insofar as *all* beings are tool-beings, not just hammers and their cousins, it immediately follows that *all* beings have an existential character. Contrary to what Heidegger implies, "categories" cannot be used to refer to the specific properties of physical nature, since mindless nature (be it of the lowliest order of dirt) *never* has only the mode of presence-at-hand. Thanks to Heidegger's theory of equipment, the possibility that nature might be made of stiff material blocks adequately describable by extant categories has been pulverized forever. To repeat: the distinction between existentiale and category cannot really serve to delimit human from inhuman, since it only repeats the primal dualism between ready-to-hand and present-at-hand.

Even in the wider analytic of Dasein, despite all its poetry and grandeur, what is central are not the "human" aspects. Rather, the distinctive feature of all the analyses of human being is only the subversion of presence-at-hand that they set in motion. That is to say, the cardinal error that Heidegger tries to combat in the analytic of Dasein is the view of moods or of being-towards-death as "extant psychological occurrences," since Dasein really exists only by executing the disclosure that it actually is, only by *in fact* revealing being in such and such a way. It is not that Dasein is existential because it has special experiences and moods not shared by machines or animals. Rather, Heidegger's excessively admired concrete analyses of Dasein (Max Scheler is far more stimulating on these themes) serve only to establish that human life is irreducible to anything present-at-hand in a psyche. As I will discuss shortly, Dasein does not first gain an existential status through its relation to its own being. Rather, this entity is existential only because it *is* its "there," *is what it is* rather than a sheer representation or definition of what it is. No mere rational animal, Dasein is captured *in the act* of its chatter, rumor-mongering, and guiltiness. Far from an attempt to expand raw ontology into a sensitive treatment of priceless human detail, the analytic of Dasein undertakes the merciless compression of all such detail down to a minute *punctum*—the point at which the presence-at-hand of any experience is shown to be derivative. Just when the reader thinks that Heidegger is about to *expand* his ontology to cover important themes of human existence, he is actually reducing these themes to his familiar repetitive dualism.

We have now gained a sense of the untenable character of any supposed special status for Dasein in *Being and Time*. This is especially necessary given that most of the summaries of Heidegger's thought tend to repeat claims of the following kind: "Dasein enjoys priority over other entities insofar as it is the entity posing the question of being; thus, in order to develop this question further, the conditions of the entity placing the question will have to be analyzed." Here is the point at which Heidegger is frequently accused of repeating the gesture of a "transcendental argument," a sterile academic term that I have been unable to locate in Kant's own works. With respect to Heidegger there could hardly be a more irrelevant notion, since the important point is not that *humans* pose the question of being. The crucial factor is not that "questioning" is a people-centered lens that conditions Heidegger's subject matter. The key is not the being of the *question*, but rather the *being* of the question.

The key is that the act of questioning is no mere mental incident (here I slip into Heidegger's tone of voice); rather, the question is executed rather than merely represented to some observer, which is to say that it has the mode of *existence*. It will be readily admitted that Dasein's pursuit of the *Seinsfrage* is necessarily an attempt to clarify being *as* being. And all would be lost if this "as" were not shown in its emergence from being itself, if it were taken as some kind of present-at-hand immediacy rather than as the equipmental derivative that Heidegger shows it to be. But it follows from this that the question of being cannot be elucidated until the meaning of being itself has already somehow been clarified, prior to any special description of Dasein. And in *Being and Time*, this clarification occurs in the disavowal of all *Vorhandenheit*—an oath sworn for the first time in the analysis of equipment.

The real reason that Dasein makes for an effective starting point for Heidegger is that human action simply offers the clearest possible case of the ineptitude of presence-at-hand as an absolute philosophical solution. Human Dasein is obviously an entity, but it is not the kind of entity that one would lightly regard as an "object" (in Heidegger's pejorative sense of the word, which I do not follow in the rest of this book). But it is all too easy to misconstrue wood or chemicals as present-at-hand materials, even if wrongly so. Entities are never merely fact, but also reality; even Heidegger's most vehement enemies might admit this where human beings are concerned. But as I have argued, the same holds true of hand-tools, and probably in an even more transparent way. As a result, asking about "the structure of the question," or asking about human Dasein at all, is only one way of rousing the question of being to life. In principle, even marginal objects such as rocks could have been the subject of Heidegger's analysis in *Being and Time*, and with equally fruitful results.[29] Even in this case, the question of the *being* of the rock would have thrown the dictatorship of physical categories into irresolvable crisis.

Whatever the usual view of the matter, it is untrue that anything is gained for the question of being by elaborating the faculties of the questioner. Note that to do this effectively, it is necessary to make a preliminary refusal of any *present-at-hand* human faculties, a critique performed even more smoothly by focusing on the subterranean reality of simple matter than by dredging up complex analyses of human moods. Certainly, recent scholarship has begun to prove the extent to which Heidegger in the *Being and Time* years suddenly begins to remold his favorite insights using the language of transcendental philosophy.[30] And quite apart from any archival research on this topic, one has to admit that Heidegger in this period really does behave as if the "conditions of possibility" of the question of being were a central concern for him. But for the present book this is quite beside the point, since my primary aim is not to recount the genesis of Heidegger's self-understanding. My goal is simply to clarify the internal mechanism of his central discovery, a discovery that *has no need* for any special human entity at this stage of the argument.[31]

Hovering in the background of these remarks is a startling realization: it must be acknowledged that Heidegger consistently mixes and even *confuses* two distinct senses of Dasein. A full consideration of this issue must wait until the following chapter, but we can summarize the two senses briefly as follows: (1) Dasein is the entity whose "essence" is that it *exists*. In this respect, it is the pure enactment of its "there," undercutting any present-at-hand determination that might be offered of it. But we have seen repeatedly that this is the basic feature of equipment as well. In this first sense, then—*every* entity is Dasein! For an entity to *be* its there, it does not also need to *see* it. Inanimate tools are every bit as irreducible to their *Vorhandenheit* as humans, meaning that in this first sense, bolts of silk and xylophones turn out to be Dasein every bit as much as people are. (2) In a second sense, Dasein is defined as the entity concerned with its own being, the entity that has an *understanding* of being. This more usual definition of Dasein obviously has a far more restricted scope. Ignoring for now the thorny problem of animals, it does seem to refer to human beings alone.

But *to be* is not the same as to *understand* being. We can begin by regarding this second, narrower sense of Dasein (understanding) as the distinguishing trait of the human entity. To understand being is to be stationed at a distance from it, to transcend it to some degree rather than simply coincide with it; it is to grasp being "as" being. But we know that for Heidegger, everything that appears "as" what it is emerges only from the prior reality of its equipmental being. The as-structure is derivative of the tool.[32] The objects of Dasein's understanding cannot be regarded as mere extant appearances: the "as" necessarily arises from some prethematic reference, from the sphere of *world*, the occluded underground zone of execution or tool-being. But for this reason, *any theory of the as-structure is automatically subordinated to a general theory of equipment.* I deliberately say "equipment" rather than "equipmentality" for the reasons mentioned earlier: what is at issue is the reality of entities or objects, not some disembodied horizon that would be more clever than all specific beings. There should be nothing controversial about the claim that the presence-at-hand of a thing can be understood only in terms of its prior equipmental character, which belongs to the most recognizable circuit of basic Heideggerian insights. The upshot is that the second, more widely recognized sense of Dasein (Dasein as the special entity which has an understanding of being) is only intelligible in light of the first (Dasein as actual existence in the world prior to any presence-at-hand). Then far from requiring human Dasein as its basis, the question of being can arise only from themes aired most clearly in the analysis of tool-being.

Throughout this section, I have tried to show that the description of equipment quickly expands to an infinite scope. No entity lies outside of tool-being; equally, no object has a privileged status with respect to it, whether it be Dasein or well-known devices such as lanterns. In this respect, the title of this book could just as easily have been "*Existenz*" or "Dasein" rather than "Tool-Being"; in that case, however, the usual human-centered biases would have lingered too long in the reader's mind. In order to counter such prejudices, it was important to show that the key Heideggerian themes are at work in even the most trifling material objects. Along this path, I have described the sense in which *all* objects must be regarded as forms of tool-being.

It can now be seen that every entity is a tool-being in the broadest sense of the term: even animals, even human beings. But this statement is about to appear in a new and somewhat paradoxical light. Equipment is also global in a second and more powerful sense, a sense suggested as early as the end of §1. There, it was mentioned that tools always belong to a referential contexture: in each case, the entities are swallowed up into some sort of "in order to," passing beyond themselves to some further reference-point, as when the hammer gives way to the house or the eyeglasses disappear in favor of the distant view that they enable. But as also mentioned earlier, even visible finalities of this kind remain relative, merely provisional. The alert reader will have noticed that I was speaking rather loosely when employing phrases such as "ultimate effect" to describe the "final" reference of a system of tools, or by speaking of an "individual tool" when describing a single implement's retreat into the system of meaning. In fact, if we follow Heidegger's reasoning to its logical conclusion, there should never be any genuine end-point involved.

I mentioned earlier that even a bridge does not stand as a simple finality, but gains its meaning only from an ulterior series of possibilities upon which it is projected. The bridge turns out to be only a partial component of further systems used for the sake of transportation, or for the sake of military operations. "Taken strictly, there 'is' no such thing as *an* equipment." This maxim ultimately asserts that there is only *one* system of equipment, the totality known as world. Every being is entirely absorbed into this world-system, assigned to further possibilities in such a way that there could never be any singular end-point within the contexture of reference. *In the strict sense, the world has no parts.* Beings are not only tool-beings in some limited private way; rather, they should be utterly swallowed up into a *single* system of tool-being, a total empire of equipment.

But the reader will remember that the tool is not only *total*, but also *invisible*. Thus, if the existence of the single world-system were the full story about reality, we would reside in a universe of absolutely simple action, thoroughly devoid of individual beings. The global carnival of entities would already have been reduced to a grey homogeneity of being-as-a-whole. All of the relative finalities (bridge, house, rail platform) would withdraw into the silent darkness of the tool-system encompassing them. Naturally, I say this only in a spirit of *reductio ad absurdum*: there is obviously a wide variety of objects arrayed before us at all times. Life expends its energy in taking them seriously: moon-ray, wish, puppet, number. As Levinas puts it, life is a *sincerity*, contending not just with a total equipmental system, but with an innumerable variety of distinct elements. The problem is that, for now, we can only concede this existence of individual objects as a glaring experiential fact—no room has been found for it yet in the context of Heidegger's theory. So far, we know only the referential system and its unified invisible deed; all presence-at-hand still enjoys a merely derivative status. The single network of tools, with its "parts" fused into a colossal world-machine, remains the single genuine item.

But the pressure of reality now forces the theme of individual entities upon us, since it is these objects alone that entertain, bewitch, and torment human life. The supposedly unified contexture of meaning is actually riddled with stumbling-blocks and barricades; the invisible unity of being is splintered apart by countless maverick entities, by hordes of defiant objects entering the fray of the world and impacting all that they touch. In the end, we are forced to reflect on the status of these individual beings in contrast to the world-machine that would claim to devour them. We are compelled to rescue presence-at-hand from the one-sided slander of "derivative."

During several earlier public discussions of these issues, I have twice been criticized for wanting to take this step into the sphere of individual beings. On both occasions, it was argued that such a strategy entails a hypostasis, a naively "static" conception of entities that cannot be reconciled with a supposedly insurmountable "play of difference." But objections of this kind fail to grasp the full danger of what Heidegger has shown. His referential contexture does not just lead objects into some innocuous parade of difference, nor does it merely de-absolutize them by "putting them in context." The system of equipment is no afternoon picnic; it is as violent as a ruinous hailstorm. If given free rein, it would altogether *bury* objects in anonymous tool-being, unreservedly harnessing them for some indefinite further purpose, even fusing the entire universe into a single undifferentiated piece. In short, I am not cooking up some reactionary's dream of stasis in order to combat difference. The difficulty against which I argue is only this: in the immediate wake of Heidegger's discovery, individual entities should vanish altogether.

If we take the first part of the tool-analysis at face value, beings are swallowed alive by being, vaporized and emptied into the ether, electrified within a homogeneous referential circuit. "There is no such thing as *an* equipment"—a stronger statement is hardly possible. Obviously, Heidegger recognizes as well as the rest of us that things do not happen in quite this way, that innumerable specific entities surround us at all times. For whatever reason, he never invests much energy in attacking this problem. But the central theme of the present book is precisely this event—the reversal by which concrete entities tear away from the shapeless totality of equipment, the stance in which *specific* beings take up a relation to their own being.[33] My approach is based neither on a credulous realism nor on some devious taste for substance abstracted from all relation. It relies only on a single, undeniable fact: *the fact that there are discernible individual entities at all.* The event in which these arise provides the topic of Heidegger's central philosophical breakthrough; we find its most famous presentation in his discussion of broken equipment.

§4. Reversal: Broken Tools

Up till now, I have discussed beings predominantly from the side of their readiness-to-hand. Tool-beings (namely, *all* beings) recede into the work of an unnoticed background; their sensible facade is not what is primary.

Insofar as the referential contexture dominates, being has no regions. Dissolved into a general equipmental effect, entities vanish into a unique system of reference, losing their singularity. The tool-system is a totality, the totality known as world. But we now recall that this accounts for only half of the story. In spite of the system of reference, individual objects erupt into view, compelling us to take stock of them, to settle our accounts with them, even if each should prove to be only a delusion or a mirage. Life contends with objects, concerns itself with a panorama of specific things.

We have seen that Heidegger's first step is to revoke the traditional prestige of present-at-hand entities in favor of the system of reference that absorbs them. Nevertheless, these very entities enjoy an immediate rebirth at the very root of his theory of tools. This can be seen most clearly in the description of malfunctioning equipment, which, for simplicity's sake, we can refer to under the blanket name of "broken tool," whether or not the entity in question is really a "tool," and whether or not it is really "broken."

Equipment in action operates in an inconspicuous usefulness, doing its work without our noticing it. When the tool fails, its unobtrusive quality is ruined. There occurs a jarring of reference, so that the tool becomes visible *as* what it is: "The contexture of reference and thus the referential totality undergoes a distinctive disturbance which forces us to pause."[34] There is thus a double life of equipment—tool in action, tool in disrepair. These two planes would seem never to intersect, since the visibility of the tool immediately marks its cessation as equipment. But in fact, their point of intersection provides what amounts to the central theme for Heidegger's career: namely, the as-structure. Through the "as," the two worlds actually turn out to exist *only* in communion, in constant intersection with one another. I have been describing these two realms separately up till now only for the purposes of exposition.

In the first instance, every object is obliterated, withdrawing into its tool-being in the contexture of the world. In this way, individual objects are smothered and enslaved, emerging into the sun only in the moment of their breakdown. I fully realize that it is possible to sit back and point to countless visible tools and machines that actually *work*, that are not broken in the least. But the visibility of Heidegger's "broken tool" has nothing to do with equipment not being in top working order. Even the most masterfully constructed, prize-winning tools have to be regarded as "broken" as soon as we consider them directly; the broken/unbroken distinction does not function as an ontic rift between two different sorts of entities. Thus, as ought to have been expected, Heidegger teaches us not about smashed-up blades and chisels, but only about beings in general. As mentioned earlier, the point is that the tool-being of a thing is invisible *in principle*, that whatever comes into view belongs to an entirely different realm from the execution comprising a tool's reality. Whether it is "out of order" or not, the visible tool is simply *not* the tool in its being; in this way, insofar as they are ever encountered, *all* beings are broken equipment.

In this way, Heidegger's thought starts from a *universal* dualism between tool and broken tool: "*every* alteration of the world, up to reversal and simple turnover [*Umschlag*] from something to something, is first experienced in this kind of encounter."[35] Any being that is encountered at all must share in this structure of the broken tool. Of all the trillions of entities each of us has ever run across, there has never been one that cannot be regarded as a specific "disturbance of reference." Put as sharply as possible, there are only two principles at work in the cosmos: *Zu-* and *Vorhandenheit*, tool and broken tool. These never exist in isolation, but compose two dimensions in every object. It will gradually become clear that Heidegger makes no further discoveries than this.

Any philosophy tends to do two different sorts of things. First, there is an *expanding* movement in which certain basic principles are exported to fresh fields, increasing the amount of territory covered by the philosophy. But second, and usually earlier, there is a *contracting* movement that attempts to show that numerous far-flung entities are merely special cases of a single basic principle. My claim is that Heidegger's philosophy is entirely of the *contractive* type. This will be the argument of the upcoming three sections, likely to be the least favorite part of the book for most confirmed Heideggerians. For now, the important thing is only to insist that Heidegger's voluminous written output not be mistaken for an actual plurality of central concepts in his career. As of this writing (January 2001), the Klostermann *Gesamtausgabe* runs to 18,649 published pages. Of these pages, the vast majority prove utterly predictable to anyone familiar with five or six key Heideggerian texts. Indeed, one searches the recent history of philosophy in vain for a more single-minded, repetitive thinker; if Heidegger had lived in a more taciturn age, it is easy to imagine his life's work confined to a single papyrus manuscript.

The genuine subject matter of this book is now on the table. It has been shown that the world is made up entirely of two distinct continents, island republics situated at an immeasurable distance from one another. But Heidegger is not satisfied to posit these two realms situated in abstract opposition. For him, there is a relation between these two domains, and it is found in the as-structure. The broken hammer is indeed no longer effective, but we can see from its failure that it once worked "as" a hammer, as an entity with special hammer-effects. But the same is true of *all* that is visible to us. Inspecting a length of unbroken pipeline, we do not merge into mystic union with its secluded function: we already rise above the contexture and see it as a pipeline rather than as something else. Objects do not unleash their forces upon us unnoticed. Rather, we encounter them as what they are—not running up against concealed dog-effects, but rather dog-as-dog, tree-as-tree, heat-as-heat, even while something forever withdraws behind these phantasms. Individual entities represent the appearance of tool-being *as* tool-being, no longer simply sheltered in its silent activity, but now explicitly on display. This dimension of the "as," rising from the depths of tool-being, is the plane on which life runs its course. Our awareness does not penetrate back behind objects into the system of tools, but lingers in the sensuous zone of raindrops and handshakes and bright colors. In each instant, we contend with a set of irreducible elements or stock characters, with objects populating the earth.

We have already reached the great paradox that is the central topic of Heidegger's thought. In one respect, *no* beings are present-at-hand, not even chunks of featureless limestone, since all entities in their being retreat into a withdrawn execution. At the same time, *every* entity is present-at-hand; otherwise, there would be an instantaneous global system, an oppressive totality withdrawn from view and devoid of particular beings. How does an object unify these two distinct strata of its being? We obviously cannot attempt to elude the riddle by saying that the entity is "a bit of each." Such a claim would have to seek its unitary term in an ontic theory of natural objects approachable from several different "points of view," a theory of the kind that Heidegger rightly condemns. Nor does it help if we try to argue that one of the two dimensions is "primary" over the other. Whether we claim that tool-being comes before presence, or make the contrary claim that only a present-at-hand substratum can enable manifold possible uses, in neither case have we raised the crucial problem: how is that which one takes to be secondary *inscribed in the things?*[36]

From this it becomes clear how the analysis of equipment ultimately demands a more concrete theory of objects. We began by considering the simple, homogeneous contexture of meaning, all-encompassing and devoid of any parts. But for Heidegger, there is already an uprising of distinct elements from this all-devouring context, a surge of minerals and battle flags and tropical cats into the field of life, where each object bears a certain demeanor and seduces us in a specific way, bombarding us with its energies like a miniature neutron star. Later, I will argue that no abstract reflections on the as-structure are rich enough to do justice to the distinctive force of these specific objects, to the eruption of personalities from the empire of being. Drifting over the earth, we encounter a crystallization of parrot-event and glacier-event, each of them defining a fateful tear in the contexture of meaning, the birth of an individual power to be reckoned with. There is far more to be said on this subject than might first be imagined. Too faithful to Heidegger's own procedures, those who follow have abandoned the inevitable reflection on objects in favor of an endless rehashing of the perils faced by famous books. Heidegger may have drawn our attention to the many fateful decisions at play in the history of ontology, but there are incomparably more to be found in the stance of distinct objects amidst the *limitless fate* of being.

Someone might now object that Heidegger gradually drops the theme of the tool altogether, even belittles it, except in the course of cameo roles or in connection with the more elaborate theme of technology. In response to this, I would point to Heidegger's lifelong obsession with attacking the illusory schemes of presence-at-hand, the lurking villain who haunts every corner of his work, and his corresponding appeal to precisely those virtues that belong to equipment itself. Again, even if Heidegger had begun to explicitly *ridicule* the theme of tool-being (and it will be shown that the usual examples that are offered hardly qualify as ridicule), it should always be remembered that we owe no loyalty to Heidegger's own self-interpretation. With the tool-analysis, we are confronted with a conceptual revolution far bigger than the author who introduced it. To remain true to Heidegger's insights may well require that we turn our backs on him. But as luck would have it, there is no great need to cut against the grain of Heidegger's self-understanding when it comes to the theme of presence-at-hand. For there is scarcely a new idea introduced in any year of his career that does not employ some version of *Vorhandenheit* as its municipal whipping-boy. Indeed, none of Heidegger's major concepts make sense without this implied polemic. In *Being and Time*, for example, we are told that things "never show themselves proximally as they are for themselves, so as to add up as a sum of *realia* and fill up a room."[37] (It would be entertaining to argue that things *are* a mere sum of *realia* that serve to fill up a room.) Much later, in a famous discussion of the *Antigone* chorus, we hear that "*polla ta deina* in no way means merely that there is a great range of uncanny things in terms of number. The uncanny is not 'given' at all in the sense of being merely present-at-hand."[38] (It would be equally enjoyable to insist that Sophocles *is* simply referring to a massive quantity of present-at-hand uncanny things: skulls, eclipses, the Cyclops, unexplained northern lights, the riddle of the pyramids, and so forth.)

Rather than burden the current discussion with dozens of further examples, I will begin each section of chapter 2 with a similar Heideggerian epigraph. God knows they are not hard to come by. This recurrent rhetorical gesture ("but *x* is no mere present-at-hand *y*") poses the most serious empirical challenge to any developmentalist reading of Heidegger's works, insofar as some version of this phrase can be found in *any* Heideggerian text. Even writings that contain neither "being" nor "*Ereignis*" nor "ecstasis" nor "concealment" nor "Dasein" inevitably appeal to some permutation of the simple word *bloß* ("mere" or "merely"). No entity is "mere presence-at-hand": not Dasein, not the tool, not language, not *hypsipolis apolis*, not the fourfold.[39] In fact, the shadow of the word "mere" is so ubiquitous in Heidegger that its wild overuse tends to become a stylistic tic among his admirers, a fact nicely exploited by several comic parodies of his thought.[40]

The result of this fourth section is as follows: when searching for the appearance of individual objects in Heidegger, there is no need to wait for the arrival of the assorted jugs and rivers of the later work, although these too can add weight to my claims. In fact, individual objects already hold center stage through the sheer universality of broken tools—for like the word "tool" itself, "broken tool" is a name applicable to all beings. For this reason, it obviously applies to far more than rusted drills and damaged houkas. The process of rupture that Heidegger defines as the "broken tool" can also be found in what he calls "theory" (which transcends the system of reference) and in his conception of "spatiality" (which has already risen beyond reference by splitting it up into individual territories). As a general term for entities considered in their liberation from the contexture, I have chosen the simple word "objects." The idea of an object-oriented philosophy is the idea of an ontology that would retain the structure of Heidegger's fundamental dualism, but would develop it to the point where concrete entities again become a central philosophical problem. Although Heidegger brushes up against the important theme of singular objects in their eruption from the system of the world, he turns out to be uniquely incapable of telling us much about any particular entities. His insight into broken tools remains only a global proclamation pertaining to beings as a whole. In §5 and §6 this lament continues, as it is shown that neither "spatiality" nor "theory" can be distinguished in any way from the theme of the tool and its reversal.

§5. Space

The broken tool counts as the first way in which the entity is freed from its contexture, released from the dimension of reference. Here, the tool is encountered *as* a tool rather than only quietly functioning as one. Fractured equipment emerges as a determinate entity, torn loose from the totality; to this extent, it attains a kind of presence *in spite* of the system that tries to consume it.

Heidegger takes pains to point out that broken equipment appears as bound up with a particular set of purposes that it once served, and does not become visible in a "mere staring." This denunciation is correct if his aim is to prevent broken tools from being regarded solely as present-at-hand materials. But it is misleading if he hopes to distinguish "mere staring" from a more savvy kind of encounter with the broken tool, that of the philosopher or engineer. In fact, even a fool or drunkard, or even a *reptile* gazing at broken circuitry encounters it on some primitive level *as* something, even if they haven't the slightest idea that it ever had a useful function. What I am contesting is Heidegger's ability to distinguish between any sorts of gradation in presence. For now, we still find a world made up only of a universal dualism between tool and broken tool, in the widest possible sense of these terms. Hence, for an entity such as a crocodile, the only alternative to the as-structure would be to encounter the contexture and nothing else; in that case, the crocodile would perceive nothing at all, or at best a blinding sheet of referential totality. Mere staring is always a staring *at* something, however vaguely we run across it, however dimly illumined it stands at the periphery of our awareness. So far, there is only one kind of as-structure, and it is a very basic kind: *anything* that has broken away from the invisible contexture and thereby entered into view is encountered *as* what it is. It is not yet possible to describe any distinction between an awkward or stupefied encounter with broken tools and an enlightened insight into them.

This is important, since it is all too easy to overlook the highly *primitive* sense of the as-structure that emerges from the tool-analysis. Many observers are tempted to rush ahead to an enhanced or turbocharged version of the as-structure, one capable of distinguishing between human and animal life, or even between theoretical and nontheoretical human comportment. I will address this issue in §7 below; here, it is important only to establish a point of terminology. So far, I have used the term "as" to refer exclusively to entities considered in their phenomenal appearance. But Heidegger sometimes also uses it to refer to our relation to the invisible realm of tools themselves. For example, we read that even the unthematic use of solid earth somehow understands this tool circumspectively as what it is, securely walking along it rather than feeling endangered or saddened by it. Thus, unconscious activity itself rests upon entities of a determinate character. This interesting discrepancy will force us to take a surprising cosmological turn in chapter 3. But for the sake of clarity, I propose *for now* to restrict the term "as" to the domain of tools in their manifest visibility. This is the usage that will be followed until further notice.

It was already evident that the phenomenon of broken tools extended far beyond the scope of failed hammers, since *every* entity can be defined by its reversal from sheer execution into a sort of tangible aura. On top of this, it also becomes increasingly clear that Heidegger never discovers any court of appeal beyond this rudimentary *Kehre* between the entity and its being. As a first example, it can be shown that his term "spatiality" acquires *precisely* the same determinations as broken equipment. This occurs through his sharp objection to the traditional way of conceiving space—predictably enough, he complains that the tradition regards space as "a set of present-at-hand locations." Against this custom, Heidegger proposes to consider space by way of a treatment of "place." This tactic apparently escapes the clutches of *Vorhandenheit* to the extent that the *place* of beings is always derived from the contexture of serviceability: "Such a place and such and such a multiplicity of places are not to be interpreted as the 'where' of some random being-present-at-hand of things."[41] The fact that entities are placed in the environment means that they are stationed somewhere within the connected texture of reference. Inasmuch as entities belong to a determinate point in this system, they inhabit particular regions. Even the most formidable entity (a black hole, a miracle drug) only commands a specific, limited place in the contexture. The tool is not infinite, but confined to a *particular* efficacy. Spatial distinctiveness arises only from out of this way of belonging to a region; with the advent of space, the region to which an entity belongs is simply unveiled *as* what it is.

If Heidegger offers anything like a philosophy of space, it is only in this limited sense: as yet another counter-concept to equipment, as just a further instance of the broken tool. Any possibility of additional concrete description soon implodes into the same inexhaustible dualism I have been describing from the start. For example, we might consider Heidegger's claim that space is determined by its "de-distancing" [*Ent-fernung*] and "directionality" [*Ausrichtung*]. Spatial objects encounter us at a determinate distance as well as from a certain specific direction. This distinction has a certain appeal for common sense, insofar as objects do seem to have both direction and distance as separate components. But even this tiniest concreteness in Heidegger's theory of space instantly breaks down: the separation is smuggled in from our ontic prejudices, and cannot even survive the analysis that supposedly gives rise to it.

To show this, we can consider the concept of directionality. If someone suffers from a phobia regarding water, this presents only one specific threat among others. It does not assault the entire basis of personal security, but only a particular part of it. One still trusts close friends, and does not also fear being poisoned; the phobia is finite. In this way, even non-spatial entities (in this case, fears) affect us from a particular "direction" in the contexture of meaning. If we somehow know that the outer world's compass-directions are different from inner mental regions, if we realize that the up and down of space is of a different order from the "place" of feelings in our spirit, this still does not prove that the difference can be adequately accounted for in Heidegger's philosophy. Space in the usual sense has no more intimate relation with the system of place than do the least spatial entities imaginable. Numbers have a "direction" too, even if they do not come from the North or West like breezes: they belong specifically to the mathematical sphere, as opposed to that of bicycling or medicinal herbs. Whether located in space or not, every entity has a distinct *place* in the contexture. Thus, nothing in the analysis of directionality enlightens us as to how spatial direction is different from any *other* kind of placement in the tool-system. Then far from clarifying the specific features of direction-ality, Heidegger simply collapses this theme back into a more general the-ory of the tool and its reversal. His loose talk about directionality is valid only in connection with equipmental place, and *never advances at all* into the specific arena of space.

It is even easier to show that "de-distancing" has nothing inherently spatial about it. After all, even on Heidegger's own terms, we cannot accept the notion of enduring substantial entities that would move, unal-tered, along a continuum of near and far. His theory of the tool-contex-ture makes this impossible. Although Heidegger never spells this out to the same degree as his distant intellectual cousin Whitehead, there is no possibility in the Heideggerian philosophy that the "same" object could ever move between two places. This would imply some sort of substance-theory, a theory of the kind that Heidegger forever mocks from the stand-point of a sum total of worldly interconnections and projections precedes any integrity of independent things. For this reason, he would *have* to say that the same object at different points in the tool-system is actually a dif-ferent object in each case, since it acquires a completely different equip-mental effect if it moves the least millimeter. A single length of pipe suddenly hooked up to a new acqueduct suddenly acquires an utterly dif-ferent place in the contexture of the world, a different relational stand-point with respect to everything else in the cosmos. Any attempt to identify it as the "same" length of pipe would have to occur on the deriv-ative level of presence-at-hand. Nor do we even need Heidegger to prove any of these points, since Bergson's 1888 dissertation had already attacked the possibility of any merely quantitative change in the "same" sensa-tion.[42] Just as a pin-prick and a harder pin-prick awaken utterly different strata of nervous reactions and fill up reality in incommensurable ways, the encounter with a dangerous animal at four hundred feet, seventy feet, and at grappling distance all present qualitatively distinct equipmental threats. This tells us only what we could have guessed in advance—that de-dis-tancing cannot refer to any measurable distance, but only to an object's actual *place* in the system of equipment.

Then both directionality and de-distancing refer to precisely the same phenomenon: the absolutely specific site of all entities in the world-system, *whether they are spatial or not*. The number 7, for instance, has a certain "proximity" to the number 12; these entities can exert their forces upon one another in the course of various mathematical operations. But the rela-tion between 7 and other entities (jewelry, the word "Cuba") is unlikely to be meaningful in any context other than that of a general philosophical discussion. Numbers, no less than hammers and ghosts and angels, belong to the contexture of meaning, and thereby share in the system of "distances" which this context inscribes. It is useless to object that ontological place *is* spatial insofar as it makes up the "ground" of ontic space. For as we have seen, ontological place is the ground of *everything*. Space simply has no privileged relation to it.

But this means that Heidegger's distinction between direction and distance has now fallen apart in *two* important ways, for: (1) What does "direction" mean? Only that a thing is harbored in a specific place in our concern. And what does "distance" mean? Again, only that a thing is harbored in a specific place in our concern. But this means that de-distancing and directionality are *one and the same*, both terms referring only to the specific place of a being in the tool-system. Although there is an obvious difference between the real-life phenomena of direction and distance, Heidegger has not accounted for this difference. His *Entfernung* and *Ausrichtung* turn out to be utterly identical. (2) Furthermore, the phenomenon of place is also not even spatial to begin with, since even the most incorporeal entities must be lodged at some place in the meaning-contexture. So far, Heidegger has only offered us yet another repetition of his theory of the hidden equipmental totality and its emergence into the daylight. The dual monarchy of tool and broken tool haunts us once again.

If even this bare and lukewarm split between distance and direction cannot get off the ground, there is little chance of Heidegger ever being able to elaborate anything remotely resembling a theory of space. With his "space," just as with his concept of "mood," we begin by imagining that we have encountered a rich existential philosophy capable of polishing all the diamond-like surfaces of life. But what we find is only an austere dualism, remote from all tangible concreteness. We had expected Goethe or Leonardo, and are disappointed to meet Parmenides instead. I am unable to find any doctrine of spatiality in Heidegger's writings, but only the usual theory of tools and broken tools: a reversal between "place" and "place *as* place."

This theme is thrown into relief by the hyphenated ambivalence of the term *Ent-fernung* itself. De-distancing, whether spatial or not, puts things at a specific distance from us and by the same stroke lets us come into contact with them *at* such and such a distance. This holds good not just for spatial objects, but for the entire field of entities, which is why Heidegger's earliest terminology identifies de-distancing (*Ent-fernen*) with the de-living (*Ent-leben*) that frees *any* object from its lived serviceability.[43] In this way, the broken tool is something transcended and at a distance, but is also something near, insofar as it thereby brushes up against our concern. Then the broken tool is *both near and far*. Conversely, the executant tool-being itself is utterly close to us as something immediately relied upon, but also far away to the extent that its existence is thereby obscured. Then the tool itself is also *both near and far*. In keeping with this unreadability of far and near, Heidegger sometimes tells us that Dasein has a tendency toward nearness,[44] and on other occasions prefers to call it a "creature of distance."[45] While this riddle of distance and nearness does possess a certain degree of depth, it is not nearly as subtle or complicated as is often insinuated. Heidegger enjoys returning us repeatedly to this distance/nearness between beings and their being, a duplicitous relation that the word *Entfernung* highlights no more and no less effectively than fifty or sixty other Heideggerian terms.[46]

Perhaps the most frequently cited index of Dasein's drive toward nearness is Heidegger's claim that human language is dominated by spatial metaphors. In the language of space, it is said, we encounter Dasein's habit of speaking in terms of the "fallen" understanding of beings as present-at-hand. But this criticism is misdirected. It is not space that should be blamed for the dominance of spatial metaphors, as if to the greater glory of *time*. Rather, space is only the villain *insofar as it is conceived as present-at-hand*. After all, would metaphors drawn from present-at-hand clock-time be preferable for Heidegger? Obviously not. And by the same token, metaphors drawn from Heidegger's own *ontological* conception of space would presumably avoid the temptations of fallen nearness. But this means that the fallenness of everyday language cannot be blamed on the evil djinni of space. Instead, this fallenness is to be blamed on the misconception of space as *vorhanden*, a misconception that can arise just as easily with respect to time. In short, language is not so much dominated by spatial metaphors as it is by metaphors of *presence-at-hand*.

On the whole, commentators too often take Heidegger at his word when he disdains space in favor of time in *Being and Time*. This only paves the way for a confusing spectacle of repentance, played out through an appeal to Heidegger's later "retraction" of his earlier theory[47] ("How wrong I was. I now admit that space is irreducible to time. Such foolishness in my youth . . ."). Here as always, the best procedure is to keep our eye on the topic rather than on what Heidegger *says* about the topic.[48] If we follow this procedure, we will see that space was never reducible to time in the early Heidegger in the first place, never subordinate to it at all. In *Being and Time* it is only in a *figurative* way that time can hold pre-eminence—that is, only when "space" is used as an alias for *Vorhandenheit* and "time" as a pen name for the rupturing ecstasis of the things themselves. I will raise this issue again in the following section. But space as a *specific* reality has already failed to stay afloat for Heidegger, since he is unable to distinguish it from any other instance of the reversal between tool and broken tool. And the same fate soon awaits the revered concept of "time." Taken in themselves, space and time have already jointly collapsed into what Heidegger will later call *Zeit-Spiel-Raum*, a temporal "leeway" of encounter in which individual entities emerge into view from the system of equipment.[49]

It is now useful to summarize the full contents of this section before moving on. First, we should recall that space is defined as a freeing of entities from the single referential totality into distinct regions. To live in the world is to encounter beings, to run across totalities of involvement that have already been liberated into specific districts. Deployed in space, objects occupy unique sites in reality. They appear to us as belonging here or there, and no longer just vanish from view into the global tool-empire: "...this amounts to freeing the spatial belonging-somewhere of the ready-to-hand."[50] But the same holds true even for the most incorporeal fears and wishes that emerge into our minds—even these *non*-spatial entities are freed from their unthematic effect upon us, released into a kind of explicit encounter. In short, space turns out to have precisely the same structure as the broken tool. It is nothing more and nothing less than this: spatiality and failed equipment both make entities present *as* what they are, delivering them into freedom from their referential oblivion. To repeat, I do not claim that there is actually no difference between space and broken hammers—far from it. My question is only whether *Heidegger* is able to shed any light on the difference between them. And for now, the answer remains a clear "No."

Earlier, I characterized Heidegger's analysis as leading to a global "theory of tools and broken tools." Given what has happened to his supposed analysis of spatiality, we can enrich our vocabulary further by referring to his thought as a "philosophy of tools and space." If terms of this kind sound counterintuitive at first, it need only be remembered that for Heidegger, failed equipment is not really failed equipment, nor does his "space" resemble anything that usually goes by that name. I will continue to use all such terms in absolutely interchangeable fashion, freely shifting between them for the sole purpose of freshness and vitality.

The lesson of this section is that for Heidegger, both spatiality and broken equipment allow us to encounter objects "as" what they are, as singularities somehow derivative of the referential contexture. And this is the central issue of the present book: *the relation between contexture and singularity in the entity*. It is not enough to be satisfied with talk of a "play" between the dual facets, not enough to show how they implicate or contaminate each other at every step, which is the point at which contemporary continental philosophy is apparently satisfied to remain. Instead, the interaction of these dual facets must be made into an explicit theme and described in its various forms—displayed in all its circus costumes rather than simply hunted down wherever it hides. In short, it must be shown how this relation comes into play in *specific* objects. Otherwise, we will remain in the same predicament as Heidegger, who attains unprecedented insight into concreteness "as such" only at the cost of packing vast realms of the world under a single roof.

There will be more to say about this problem as the book continues. But for now, there can be no doubt that both space and ruined hacksaws have been reduced to precisely the same structure. It remains impossible to free ourselves from this position if we do no more than defer to Heidegger's findings on the genesis of exteriority from depth.

§6. Theory

In this section, I will show that spatiality is far from the *final* case in which Heidegger's efforts at concreteness remain locked in the obsessive reversal that typifies the drama of tool and broken tool. An identical process occurs in theoretical comportment: theory, like space, proves to have the familiar structure of failed equipment. The key passages on this topic come from §69 of *Being and Time*, the section entitled "The Temporality of Transcendence." The usual disclaimer should be repeated here: I am not arguing that theory is *truly* indistinguishable in the real world from equipment and space. My point is only that *Heidegger* provides for no real distinction between them; he cannot be allowed to let our everyday familiarity with these issues create an ontological diversity where no such variety has actually been established. With theory, as with failed implements and with space, yet another region of reality is explained by invoking the simple drama of the tool-system and its "deficient mode." In this way, Heidegger's concept of theoretical transcendence only replicates the familiar basic duality unearthed in his first analysis of tool-being. And insofar as he proceeds to argue that such transcendence is grounded in temporality, it is also possible to place the strife of tool and broken tool at the heart of *time itself.*

I turn immediately to the famous section on "The Temporality of Transcendence."[51] Heidegger begins by referring to what was learned about tool-beings in the earlier analysis of worldhood: "we have already made an essential gain for the analysis of those entities which we encounter as closest to us, if their specific character as equipment does not get passed over."[52] The importance of equipment is that it establishes a pivotal role for our *pre*-theoretical encounter with beings. And in the course of his exceptionally long career, how often it happens that Heidegger blames virtually *every* failing of the tradition on the inflated status of the theoretical standpoint and its intellectual cousins—representation of objects by a subject, idealization in an *eidos*, or enslavement of beings to the "visual" model of production by a craftsman or deity.[53] With its simple allusion to what lies prior to all such visibility, the analysis of the tool contains in germ the entire destruction of the history of ontology, too often praised in isolation from the discovery that makes it possible.

In his discussion of theoretical comportment, Heidegger proceeds from an account of temporality to a reflection on transcendence; for the purposes of this book, it is preferable to treat these themes in reverse order. We can recall the basic situation of being-in-the-world: "When, in one's concern, one lets something be involved, one's doing so . . . amounts to an altogether pre-ontological and non-thematic way of understanding involvement and readiness-to-hand."[54] To encounter objects pretheoretically means that they do not continually obtrude upon us; it implies a sort of "forgetting": "The self must forget itself if, lost in the world of equipment, it is to be able to 'actually' go to work and manipulate something."[55] But it is important to note that not only the "self" is forgotten. The use of nails or asphalt indicates that these objects *themselves* are suppressed from view.

Not surprisingly, Heidegger reminds us here that theory is not to be attained by a mere gazing at present-at-hand objects. The truth is found in the alternative: that theory emerges *from out of* being-in-the-world, that it *arises* from this prior dimension. But the importance of such a statement is not that it tells us about the chronological order in which human experiences occur—instead, the crucial insight occurs once again *on the side of the things*. That is to say, the object as grasped in theory is possible only on the basis of that same object in its prior reality, its tool-being, its being just what it is. As we have already seen, this primary reality does not consist in "being used," which is at best a secondary phenomenon. It must always be remembered that an object can be manipulated only because it executes its own reality, because it exerts some sort of impact upon the world. Without this primal effectiveness, it could never possibly be useful for a human being. For any entity, "to be" means "to be embedded in the contexture of equipment." To display such an entity by developing a theory about it means to somehow illuminate it in its *being*. In Heidegger's view, science at its finest refuses to operate within the confines of the traditional definitions or properties ascribed to its object. Instead, it leaps ahead and discloses this object in its being, in the work it performs in the midst of reality—the labor that would have gone undone if the thing had not existed. In this way, Heidegger wants to show that science arises from the pretheoretical shadows.[56]

In the midst of these shadows, a raw form of temporality can already be recognized, a fabric woven of the "awaiting" and "retaining" that are jointly manifested in a "making-present": "Even if concern remains restricted to the urgency of everyday needs, it is never a pure making-present, but arises from a retention which awaits . . ."[57] This notion is already familiar to us in a different guise. We can imagine that Dasein is involved, for instance, with a shovel. It does not run across such an object in a vacuum, as if it were some sort of drifting sensory irritant. In the first place, Dasein finds the shovel already available, makes use of or *retains* this object as something "alongside which" it exists. Second, the shovel-object is not encountered as a neutral datum divorced from the situation in which it is inscribed. The shovel used in slave labor and that of the amateur gardener's pleasure-dig are vastly different objects for Dasein, and display different sorts of *awaiting*. This dual unity of awaiting and retaining lies at the heart of all that is present, and points to the error of any notion of sheer making-present (*Gegenwärtigen*), any concept of equipment divorced from the two-faced status of the tool-system. But still, making-present is not a distinct moment with respect to the others—together, these *are* the making-present. Then the apparent threefold of temporal concern is actually only a *two*, a fact relevant to all of Heidegger's claims regarding what he will call "time," but which actually has nothing more to do with time than with anything else in the universe.

Already, it can be seen that awaiting and retaining are irreducible to any ontic, common-sense version of these terms. After all, even the amnesia patient "retains": she does not just hover in the world as in an emptiness devoid of equipment, but is already immersed in a viscous atmosphere of floor, telephone, and clothing, even if she fails to remember what purpose these serve. By the same token, "awaiting" can still be detected even when Dasein is without a thought for the morrow, as occurs in certain cases of psychotic depression. Here too, the lost soul who endures such an illness does not encounter the world directly in its naked truth, but only in a specific way, one that might eventually be altered. Then as is usual throughout Heidegger's philosophy, awaiting and retaining are ubiquitous structures that enjoy no special link with what we know ontically as "remembering" and "expecting." From this, we can gather that they are already *ontological* structures, even if Heidegger wishes to denigrate them as inauthentic forms of temporality.

Simply put, since all experience *is*, all experience has an ontological character. The term "ontic" cannot be employed to belittle the use of tools as opposed to moments of profound resolution; there can be no moralizing split between distracting specific objects and solemn ontological structures. The ontic realm only presents a problem if we approach it uncritically, in a mood of satisfaction with the one-sided claims of *Vorhandenheit*. But the hammer itself is neither ontic nor ontological; or rather, it is always *both*. Hammer-being enacts its infernal executant being while *also* emerging to light as something present-at-hand. It would be an error to flee from this concrete tool toward some loftier realm, as when following the typical line of retreat from the use of hammers into the ground of this use, over to the possibility of the ground, and finally on up to the "granting" of the clearing/lightening appropriating play of the possibility of possibility. Serial disembodiment will get us nowhere. In fact, the humble example of the worker's shovel already displays the fissure between awaiting and retaining that permeates all reality, revealing the contours of Heidegger's first and only subject matter: the mutual compression between a being and its being. It is sometimes claimed that this ontological difference "collapses" at a certain point in his career, forcing him to leave it behind for a more sophisticated subject matter. In fact, the only collapse that occurs is the one that has *already* occurred—the reciprocal implosion of beings into the tool-system and of this same tool-system into concrete elements.

To speak of the different ways in which an observer can disclose a shovel or telephone in different ways already indicates how science arises from the obscurity of the world-system. Still, "a fully adequate existential interpretation of science cannot be carried out until the meaning of being and the 'connection' between being and truth have been clarified in terms of the temporality of existence."[58] Heidegger is already far closer to attaining this goal than might be imagined. But before entering into the problems of truth and time, it is important to review in more detail the way in which Heidegger's view of theory remains insufficient.

In the first instance, he tells us, it might be thought that what allows theory to arise is an abstention from handling. Instead of our usual unnoticed reliance upon implements, we now step back and rise above any immediate action. Thus, the genesis of theory requires a sort of "disappearance of praxis." But far from endorsing this view, Heidegger says that abstaining from praxis is not enough to result in true theoretical comportment: "Holding back from the use of equipment is so far from sheer 'theory' that the kind of circumspection which tarries and 'considers,' remains wholly in the grip of the ready-to-hand equipment with which one is concerned."[59]

My view is that this distinction between theory and the simplest forms of broken tool cannot be maintained at the level on which Heidegger attempts it. Certainly, the "tarrying" that Heidegger ridicules does remain caught up in an unthematic relation to the equipment it uses, even if the observant loiterer reaches a certain degree of transcendence beyond the equipment that absorbs his hard-working neighbors. But herein lies the problem—even *theory* is unable to free us entirely from the unthematic contexture; there will always remain a depth to the entity that eludes any theoretical view. The tools themselves, enacting their own reality, remain aloof from any possible visibility. Thus, no pure seeing is possible, just as there cannot be a completely unthematic form of acting. As *Being and Time* puts it: even praxis has its sight, and even theory has its praxis.[60] The boundary between theory and nontheory is anything but clear.[61]

At this point, we are still concerned only with the most austere form of the as-structure, the "as" of the most minimal visibility. It is true that theory does seem superior to all "empty staring"; the philosopher does appear "more" capable of grasping an entity as what it is than any aimless lounger ever will. Nonetheless, Heidegger remains unable to clarify the ontological root of any such difference, since he offers no explanation that would allow for degrees of reality in the as-structure. As a result, there are still only two clear-cut modes of being: (1) the tool withdrawn and effective in its tool-being, and (2) the tool viewed *as* tool. In short, there are only tool and broken tool, or tool and space. Considered purely in terms of the as-structure, theory is no better at freeing objects from the contexture than is the most glazed or zombie-like staring and tarrying. Both attitudes present us with tools *as* tools; both transcend the sort of praxis that unobtrusively relies upon objects.

Admittedly, theory must somehow be able to modify our relation to the system of tools: "The understanding of being by which our concernful dealings with entities within-the world has been guided has changed over."[62] But whatever Heidegger's views may be, such modification hardly requires anything like theory. Since *all* awareness is built upon the as-structure, the 'as' must be present even in states of the most unremitting idiocy, and ultimately in animal perception itself (unless we follow Descartes in his baseless claim that monkeys are automata, which Heidegger does not). Like so many philosophers when it comes to such themes, Heidegger is distressingly impatient. He wants to jump the gun and fence off humans from the animal kingdom before he has acquired the conceptual resources to do so. But surely, even he would admit that a newborn puppy is not simply plugged into the contexture of tools like a piece of electrical wiring. Instead, the puppy encounters food as a specific beneficial entity, vaguely interprets a warm blanket as "resting-zone" rather than as "water" or "mother." To argue that dogs cannot encounter food *as* food is simply to *assert* a difference between forms of the as-structure that has yet to be demonstrated. I hereby challenge the reader to establish a way for Heidegger to introduce further gradations in the as-structure without illicitly importing any number of ontic prejudices. At this point in our discussion, theory cannot claim any special status; there are still only the tool and the ever-present as-structure (the broken tool). Thus, "we must again make the phenomenon of the 'as' a theme . . ."[63] But to follow Heidegger's next step along this path, it is necessary to refer to *time*, that most prestigious concept of his thought.

What I wish to address here is Heidegger's claim that time is the "horizon" of being-in-the-world: "Like understanding and interpretation in general, the 'as' is grounded in the ecstatico-horizonal unity of temporality."[64] We have seen that the "as" interprets (or "retains") that which it is already alongside of, and that it does so by projecting this reality ("await-ing") upon some possibility of its own being. In this way, the as-structure is *geworfener Entwurf*, "thrown projection." Heidegger wants to make the further claim that the unity of ecstatic temporality is the horizon of this thrown projection. But I have already mentioned the difficulties faced by any notion of a horizon as something distinct from the elements that pop-ulate it. After all, what could the relation between equipment and a remote temporal horizon possibly be? Any difference between them obviously can-not have the mode of presence-at-hand, since this would undermine every-thing that Heidegger has worked for. Hence, their separation cannot be absolute: they necessarily have *some* kind of ontological connection, a link by way of the totality of meaning. Pushing the issue further, it is clear that the horizon of tools must either be found in the tools themselves, or some-where else. If the horizon lies in the tools themselves, then my point has already been conceded. If it lies elsewhere, this can only mean "elsewhere in the contexture of meaning": after all, there *is* no other place for Heidegger. And I have already argued that this system of meaning is not the "horizon" of the system of tools, but is identical to this system itself.

Any objection to this claim can be based only on a fear of identifying the referential contexture with the sum of *ontic* tools (hammer + board + window . . .). But this possibility was eliminated by my claim that readi-ness-to-hand has no especial connection with everyday hardware. In short, tool-beings are *themselves* partly horizonal. On the one hand, entities are present-at-hand phantasms; on the other, they retreat into a horizonal depth whose secrets can never fully be mined. The horizon is not some-thing distinct from individual tool-beings, but makes up a full half of their reality. Even the horizon cannot exist outside of the system of equipment and its inherent reversal from totality into specific elements. In sum, thing and horizon *cannot be distinguished at all*, except for the purposes of a pedagogical strategy designed to suppress all pre-Heideggerian notions of independently existing substances. In this latter role, the term "horizon" can be quite effective; extended any further, it becomes a red herring.

At any rate, the temporal ecstases do correspond, respectively, to the three familiar dimensions of everyday time. Immersed in its world, Dasein finds itself "thrown" amidst beings already on hand; here, we glimpse the moment of "having-been." Equally, there is a "futural" ecstasis corre-sponding to the "for-the-sake-of." But we have already encountered *both* of these dimensions in the simplest shovel, which can be projected in var-ious possible ways. Dasein's involvement with this shovel is *already* an ek-stasis, an event that stands outside of itself along two distinct fronts. It is not as if there were a kind of incorporeal ecstatic time, a separate structure that would lie even further back behind the mere manipulation of gear. There is no need to fear such manipulation: any possibility of an isolated present-at-hand shovel is already dead from the opening pages of *Being and Time*, from the very moment that the contexture of tools is discovered. Thus, Heidegger's "ecstatic" temporality demonstrates nothing but the reality of a single system of equipment, viewed in its simultaneous reversal into distinct objects. Deployed outside of itself in its own *metabole*, the system of tools in which Dasein is immersed *is* the ecstasis.

Soon enough, I will address the question of whether this ecstatic structure of the world can exist apart from an observer *for whom* it exists. But it should already be clear that there are no grounds for considering the *human* observer as the subject matter of the temporal analysis, Heidegger's own opinions notwithstanding. To emphasize this, we can envision a situation similar to that of Plato's cave. Imagine that an unintelligent but exceedingly tranquil person is chained to a pillar somewhere on the earth, motionless. Placed before him is an immense but well-camouflaged machine, a device that controls all aspects of his environment—the unchanging temperature and scent of the air, the uniform amount of light that shines on him from a fixed angle, the constant sonorous drone that he hears, the steady infusions of intravenous liquid that provide his nourishment. Furthermore, we can assume that a second blend of chemicals introduced into his veins keeps his moods at an optimum level of stability.

Imagine that it goes on in this way for years, until suddenly, the machine enters an era of gradual decay. Each day, two or three of its thousands of functions cease to operate, leading to various failures in its workings. Only now will the drugged man begin to notice the "temporal" structure of the machine and of his world. That is to say, only through this passive observation of the suddenly collapsing terrain does he perhaps become aware of an inherent reversal of execution into tangible landscape, an *Umschlag* that had already characterized the stable machine-world from the outset. Put more simply, *only now* does the ever-present phenomenon of equipment and its breakdown come to light. My question about this scenario is as follows: would it ever occur to such a person to consider *himself* as the *source* of the ecstatic-temporal nature of this environment? Not at all. By hypothesis, his vantage point has never shifted in the least, and his mood has remained entirely unaltered. Obviously, faced with the sudden decay of his environment, he would have to regard the machine's *own* degradation as the source of all temporal ecstasis.

Imagine further that the machine finally breaks down to such an extent that the prisoner becomes wracked by inner turmoil. Now undergoing violent mood-swings, he breaks loose from his chains and stands on his own feet. Locating the machine itself after a brief search, he deliberately begins to dismantle its gears one by one, ruining its various functions as he goes. Only at *this* point in the story would the prisoner be tempted to regard *himself* as the key to all ecstasis, only after realizing that his willpower and manual activities and even his own crazed, turbulent moods can lead to changes in the total environmental effect of the machine.

The point of citing these images is to suggest that only common-sense prejudice leads us to regard Dasein, rather than the things themselves, as the site of temporal ecstasy. In everyday life, we tend to conceive of the world as a relatively stable landscape that we ourselves can personally reorganize as thinking, acting, transcending animals. This encourages the faulty ontological inference that the world's ecstatic structure results from a sort of human mental-physical kinesis, a subjective *Bewegtheit* that resolutely goes to work in a theater made up of bland solid blocks. But although the ecstatic environment is indeed conditioned by our own projections, it is still the ecstasis *of the things*: it is still the machine itself that either functions quietly or falls into ruin.

The effect of the machine is, of course, co-determined by the standpoint of the entity who is affected by it: in this case, the drugged man. But the observer need not be a human being for the ecstatic analysis to function properly. We could also imagine certain animals trapped in horrific situations of precisely the kind described above. A blue jay, for instance, could easily be restrained in a cage governed by a similar environmental stabilizer. But there is no need for further examples here. It is already evident that temporal ecstasis also belongs to *objects themselves* in their encounter with sentient observers. It takes two to generate an ecstasis, and it ought to be reemphasized that inanimate objects also play a role in this drama. Whether this remains the case in the absence of all sentient observers is a question to be addressed in chapter 3. (The answer will be yes.)

I have contended that the temporal ecstasis takes place neither in some distant horizon nor in our own psyches—rather, it is an ecstasis *of the things*. As a result, ecstatic temporality turns out to be nothing but another name for the global tool-system and its reversal into distinct elements. The greatest obstacle to accepting this claim is nothing but the stubborn connotations of the word "time" itself. For this reason, I will now argue briefly that Heidegger *never* discusses time in the strict sense at all.

To this end, I ask the reader to perform a second thought experiment: imagine that the flow of time is suddenly halted, whether through witchcraft or by other means. Even if time cannot *really* be stopped in this way, there is nothing to prevent our *imagining* it (the notion that time cannot be built out of isolated cinematic frames does not come from Heidegger, but from the Bergsonism he condemns).[65] Strangely enough, if we picture this freezing of the universe by a wizard's wand, we find that Heidegger's ecstatic temporality is still perfectly applicable. The bewitched cosmos is now petrified; Dasein is locked forever in a statuesque pose with the mallet it is using. But note that this cessation of time's flow *does not* reduce the

mallet to a present-at-hand substance. Dasein is still "thrown" into the situation that contains its utensil; there is a "retaining" even here. Nor is this
item of gear a straightforward piece of equipment free of all projection,
since the mallet is still determined by Dasein's "awaiting" of the end to
which it is assigned, even if the halt of time forever prevents it from
approaching this goal.

For Heidegger, then, *each instant* is already a self-contained ecstasis.
Presence-at-hand does not require any *actual* future in order to be
dethroned. Most readers of Heidegger make an unjustified leap from the
valid insight that all presence is intertwined with a past and a future to the
invalid assumption that there is no such thing as a present instant in time.
This misses the point of the analysis in a way that would be inconceivable
if it were not so widespread. The result of Heidegger's ecstatic analysis of
time is that there is no such thing as an innocent presence not composed
of an ambiguous interplay of pregiven reality and futural projection. But
it does not follow from this that we cannot isolate a single frame of time
in the world, for such an isolated frame by no means violates the rules of
the ecstasis: even a frozen moment of time can be formed of two opposed
but interlocked dimensions. Here as elsewhere, many readers draw a baseless ontic consequence (irreducibility of time to instants) from an ontological breakthrough (irreducibility of instants to simple one-dimensional
presence).

In all likelihood, it will still be objected that Heidegger forbids the
reduction of temporality to "a sequence of now-points," with the implication that my thought experiment lapses into the most discredited traditional
theory of time. I answer this complaint as follows: no matter what
Heidegger may say, his objection to the sequence of now-points is effective
not against the *now-points*, but against the *sequence*. For Heidegger, the traditional view of time appeals to a simple flow in which the present-at-hand
instant finds a dialectic only *outside* of itself, only by way of contrast with
other present-at-hand moments that are coming to be or have passed away.
In opposition to this model, Heidegger shows that *even the single instant* is
already outside of itself, torn between an awaiting and retaining that have
no contact with any *real* past or future. In other words, the detested now-
point is not a problem as long as it is not naively construed as *vorhanden*,
as long as we recognize that even the "now" is torn between the two irreducible facets of its being (tool, broken tool). The ecstasis is never some
horizonal structure off in the distance, but is the very ambivalence of an
instant, an inner turbulence that trumps its own external posture.

In lieu of a concept of time that would measure changes in present-at-
hand states, Heidegger presents us with a temporality that is imploded into
stasis itself: in this philosophy, every stasis is already an ek-stasis. To argue
otherwise is to imply that Heidegger is *unable* to rupture the presence-at-

hand of the simple now-point without additional help, that he somehow *needs* the idea of an actual temporal flux for his concept of ecstasy to hold good. But Heidegger neither requires nor elaborates any such claim. Instead, he remains content to undercut the *present-at-hand* now-point, without bothering to dethrone the now-point *as such*. To repeat what was said earlier, the argument that no distinct "now" can ever be isolated from a future and a past is the argument of *Bergson*.[66] It has absolutely nothing to do with the writings of Heidegger, who simply ignores this additional theme.

An even clearer way of stating the point would be as follows. Both Heidegger and Bergson would enthusiastically agree with the following statement: "time cannot be viewed as a sequence of now-points." But the motive for agreement would be different in each case. The problem according to Bergson is that duration is intrinsically irreducible to any series of frozen cinematic poses; the *élan* of time and motion cannot be reconstructed from out of discrete fragments, even if only a millisecond should separate any two frames. But there is no such worry for Heidegger, who is interested only in showing that even the supposed static instant is not really static at all, but rather *ek-static*— already torn apart by its own incurable ambiguity. In short, Bergson never addresses Heidegger's problem at all, since the stream of *durée* teaches us nothing about the internal strife between an entity's subterranean force and its seductive facade. But by the same token, Heidegger never discusses Bergson's theme, since he adds nothing to our knowledge of what movement and duration really are. Instead, he simply provides us with the most diligent theory of statuesque being ever devised: a doctrine so fixated on the duality of the absolute instant that it misreads Bergson's groundbreaking conception of temporal flux as trivial.[67]

In fact, the difference between these thinkers sheds such obvious light on Heidegger's avoidance of temporality in the genuine sense that only the obstinate tendency to take his word "time" at face value can continue to cloud the issue. You can say what you like, but *Heidegger has no theory of time.* This statement is not motivated by the desire to valorize Bergson, who is equally guilty of overlooking the issue that Heidegger addresses. I only wish to insist that the everyday overtones of the word "temporality" not be allowed to interfere with a clear-sighted inventory of which features belong to ecstasis and which do not. For these reasons, I regard Levinas' claim of an analogy between Heidegger's thought and Occasionalism on this topic (repeat: on *this* topic) as irrefutable.[68] Obviously, Heidegger does not follow Malebranche in advocating a Cartesian theory of substance. Nor does he appeal to God as the medium of relation between successive instants—but he *might as well* have done so. Like his seventeenth-century forerunner, Heidegger deliberately excludes any account of a real relation between instants, except *possibly* through a vague insinuation that the emergent future can arise only from previous states of cryptic potentiality. But this hardly qualifies as a detailed theory of time.

Here, I repeat the bluntly paradoxical conclusion of the preceding discussion: Heidegger, the famous philosopher of time, has nothing to tell us about time. As was true with space, it is futile to object that Heidegger's ecstatic temporality is temporal by virtue of serving as the "ground" of everyday clock-time—his "time" is the ground of *everything*, and has no closer intimacy with real duration than with the frozen world of my thought experiment. In sum, whatever treasures may be contained in Heidegger's innovative concept of time are already fully accessible in the simplest form of the as-structure: namely, in the ubiquitous interplay of tool and broken tool. But this means that "time" is nothing more than an additional alias for the theme of the tool and its reversal. Indeed, Heidegger places so much weight on the ambivalence of the single instant that any concept of time is effectively *excluded* from his thought as tacitly vulgar. For this reason, a genuine theory of time even becomes a *glaring need* in the wake of Heidegger's philosophy.

In this connection, it can also be seen that the phrase "temporality of transcendence" is redundant. Even in the least clear-sighted situation, Dasein has already transcended the system of equipment: "one's 'practical' being alongside the ready-to-hand is something which a transcendence of Dasein must already underlie."[69] Equally so, even the most opaque form of praxis is temporalized, torn between the environment that already greets it and the possibility upon which these surroundings are projected. However hopeless our stupor in any given situation, we never encounter neutral object-bulks, but already somehow understand the *being* of these entities: "if Dasein is able to have any dealings with a context of equipment, it must understand something like an involvement . . . *a world must have been disclosed to it*."[70] With the awaiting that belongs to transcendence or time, this world is unveiled in its truth: "[the] awaiting of discoveredness has its existentiell basis in a resoluteness by which Dasein projects itself towards its potentiality-for-being in the 'truth'."[71] In other words, "the entity which bears the title Da-sein is one that has been '*cleared*' [*gelichtet*]."[72]

Earlier, I cited Heidegger's statement that the meaning of being and the relation of being and truth need to be clarified in terms of the temporality of existence. In fact, this clarification was already achieved rather early, by the first analysis of equipment. The "temporality of existence" is nothing other than the transcendence that "clears" Dasein above and beyond its immersion in the equipmental system, the "time" that shatters this empire into districts. And it is also temporality that immediately clarifies the relation between truth and being: Dasein is not merely a part of the tool-system, but transcends or "clears" the being of equipment in its "truth." This event of *aletheia* was already evident as soon as the broken hammer was freed or unveiled from the global system of meaning. But this means that two new pairs of synonyms arise for our previous phrases "tool and broken tool" and "tool and space." We can also call them "being and truth"—or"being and time"!

At work in all of these relations is an even more provocative claim: the tool-system is the meaning of being; *being itself is tool-being*. There are good reasons not to be surprised by this apparently delinquent result. It was shown earlier that the tool can be used only because it *already exists* in the total execution of itself, in an action irreducible to present-at-hand properties. Therefore, it is not at all my claim that forks and saws are the meaning of being. To speak of the ready-to-hand in the sense of recognizable tool-items is already to operate on a derivative level—namely, that of broken tools, space, theory, time, beings. But I have already shown that, for Heidegger, readiness-to-hand is not itself a single being in each case. Instead, it is the total system of equipment, the unitary system of reference that Heidegger calls "world," and which forever withdraws behind any present-at-hand property. Accordingly, we can add another synonym to the mix by saying that *world* is the meaning of "being."

But it was shown early in this book that the first sense of "to mean" is to exist as what is meant, to *be* this reality, to execute it. Then being doesn't simply "mean" world: it *is* world, *is* the ready-to-hand. This is not to make the ludicrous boast that *Sein* is only a socket wrench, or that "being is extremely useful." Rather, it is to say that being is the concealed underground execution withdrawn from all presence-at-hand, just as the being of the hammer is withdrawn from any possible list of its properties. Further, we can also recall the second sense of "to mean": namely, to exist as the *terminus* of a concealed action, to be that which comes into view as a result of the withdrawn work of equipment. In this second sense, tools are the meaning of being in a different respect, as the distinct fragments that have somehow emerged into view from the single empire of reality. In the first respect, the meaning of being is a hidden *Vollzug*; in the second respect, the meaning of being is *beings*. This second point does not imply that being is itself a being. Rather, it says that the meaning of being is *metabole*, *Umschlag*, the very *reversal* into beings.

Broken tool, space, theory, and even time itself have now all been identified as cases of the simple structure of failed equipment. Wherever we look, Heidegger tells us no more and no less than this: "all reality has the structure of the tool and its breakdown." But this results in a highly unsatisfying situation, since we now find it impossible to discuss any concrete subject matter in particular. With this section now drawing to a close, I would like to suggest that a new way of talking about specific entities is precisely what Heidegger had in mind when he briefly introduced his famous term "metontology."[73]

It seems clear to me that this theme never really disappears from his thought, even if the word itself quickly vanishes. I have already argued that *Being and Time*, far from establishing any subjectivist priority of human Dasein, repeatedly breaks down into a simple reversal between "tool" and "as," between being and beings. Metontology is not a theory of being carried out on the "meta-level," but is rather an ontology fueled by the constant *metabolism* between being and beings. Whenever this theme is mentioned, a single famous Heideggerian claim is tediously cited: namely, that metontology alone is where philosophy would be able to work out the possibility of an ethics.[74] True enough. But if we continue to refer only to this possibility, then we rely too heavily on the accident of what Heidegger himself *mentions*.[75] In fact, the reversal of being provides us not only with the ontological basis for an ethics or a gender theory, but is also the necessary basis for a psychology, a poetics, a historiography, a dynamics, a speculative cosmology, a theory of birds and minerals, or even a concept of time. Indeed, it is metontology alone that offers the hope of an ontological discourse about *anything* other than the pale structural coupling of tool and broken tool.

§7. The As-Structure

We have now examined four important Heideggerian concepts—broken tool, space, theory, and time. Surprisingly, each of these turns out to be nothing other than a code name for the simple as-structure that arises from out of the prior system of equipment. I would remind the reader that *all* beings must be regarded as falling under the heading of "equipment." Every entity is a tool, not as a luckless material abused for remote technical purposes, but as an actual reality not to be equated with any manifestation of its presentable form. All individual beings withdraw into the contexture of equipment, where they execute their cryptic reality; whatever emerges into view from this prior dimension is no longer the tool itself. To run across any particular object is already to encounter a "deficient" mode of the system: tool *as* tool rather than tool pure and simple. I have tried to suggest that Heidegger remains locked in permanent orbit around this single event, this ubiquitous reversal between concealed and revealed equipment. The analysis of tool-being becomes the headquarters for Heidegger's assault upon every form of presence-at-hand, a polemic that dominates all of his various historical discussions.

But it was also mentioned that the critique of *Vorhandenheit* only accounts for half of the story. Obviously, individual beings *do* somehow appear from amidst the contexture. A thing appears as what it is; entities are encountered on the plane of the as-structure. Phenomenology has long focused our attention on this basic appearance-character of reality, which precedes any distinction between correctness, semblance, and falsity. Every phenomenon is necessarily an appearance taken "as" something, whether it be empty hallucination or unshakeable fact. But the thing "as" thing is not the same as the thing itself, which can *never* be openly encountered. The broken hammer never offers direct revelation of its own being, but exhibits this being only within the theater of the *as*. In short, Heidegger's as-structure marks an event of *simulation*; to paraphrase Levinas once again, beings resemble themselves.[76]

For this reason, at the risk of appearing to ally myself with passing fashion, I would suggest that genuine progress in Heidegger studies requires nothing so much as a detailed *geographic atlas of the simulacrum*, replacing his bare formal duality (tool/broken tool) with a catalog of those fault lines along which being is articulated into specific elements. In any case, the sort of simulation at issue points to a *real relation* between the object and itself—between what this book has called tool and space, or being and time.

Before introducing any further complications into this picture of the as-structure, it will be useful to show one final time that the "as" has no aptitude whatsoever for distinguishing between different *kinds* of comportment. The ideal place to do this is in Heidegger's famous 1929/30 Lecture Course. This intriguing work has often been described in shorthand as Heidegger's reflections on life-philosophy, or as his notes for a philosophical biology. While not entirely erroneous, these characterizations are seriously misleading. In fact, 1929/30 *does not* offer us a general philosophy of life. Nor *could* it do so, for precisely the same reasons that render Heidegger incapable of giving us any insight into space or theory or time as specific sorts of subject matter. On the contrary, this magnificent series of lectures actually touches on the theme of life *only in its relation to the as-structure*. It should be noted that Heidegger tells us nothing about nutrition or reproduction or self-induced motion, despite his fascinating examples drawn from insect research. Still less do we hear anything about the life of plants—further proof of his lingering inability to escape the dual bondage of the as-structure and its shadow. Of the several features of life discussed in Aristotle's *De Anima*, Heidegger focuses on perception alone. On the whole, 1929/30 is not a life-philosophy at all, but a philosophy of the as-structure, which is not at all the same as a genuine discussion of bodily organs.[77]

For the purposes of this book a brief treatment of the 1929/30 course will suffice. My theme so far has been the all-embracing status of the as-structure for Heidegger. The question that now arises is whether the com-

parative analysis of humans and animals in 1929/30 provides for any interesting new gradations within this structure. I have already argued that the
"as" that emerges from *Being and Time* cannot be restricted to human
beings alone. In the context of the tool-analysis, the as-structure simply
marks a primitive reversal of the system of equipment, a sort of rudimentary awareness that would have to be granted to even the most reviled spi-
der or bacterium. For this reason, it might be expected that Heidegger
would devote the 1929/30 course to developing a theory of specifically
human comportment, something genuinely lacking in his earlier works.
And at first, he would seem to be doing just that. It has occasionally been
noted that the term "benumbedness" (*Benommenheit*) is already used to
characterize human Dasein in 1927: "Dasein is thus benumbed by its
world . . ."[78] In 1930, this word is suddenly redeployed as a description
for *animal* perception, perhaps leading Heidegger's readers to anticipate
that he is finally on the verge of developing a special theory of human
being, one that would go beyond the all-embracing "broken tool" permutations of a few years earlier.

But at this point, Heidegger adopts precisely the *opposite* procedure.
Instead of beginning with the rudimentary as-structure and working
upward toward a more intricate vision of human life, he instead works
downward from primitive *aisthesis* toward an even deeper cellar of being in
which animals will now be confined. Against what should have been
hoped, Heidegger wrongly conceives of the primitive as-structure of *Being
and Time* as something already exclusively human. The strongest evidence
for this lies in the fact that virtually all of the new terminology in 1929/30
is introduced on the side of the animals rather than in connection with
human beings. For example, we hear that the animal does not comport
itself toward present-at-hand entities, but only "eliminates" them (*beseit-
igt*). Further, the animal operates within a "ring of disinhibitions"
(*Enthemmungsring*), another term unfamiliar to readers of Heidegger's
earlier works. Additional coinages can be found in his brief discussion of
the role of bodily organs.

All of this indicates a belief on Heidegger's part that the *impoverished*
form of the as-structure is what is novel here, and that the special features
of human reality were already sufficiently described in *Being and Time*. In
my view, the problem is quite the opposite. Animals obviously *do*
encounter present-at-hand entities: stick, river, stormy day. To object that
they do not run up against these objects *as* what they are is to presuppose
exactly what is still in question, contaminating the ontology of the human-
animal divide with illicit contraband from the realm of common sense. As
argued repeatedly, without this crude form of transcendence, animals
would perceive *nothing at all*. Hence, even rats and mosquitoes must rise
above the sheer invisibility of the tool-system, unless we wish to accept the

Cartesian dogma of animal-as-mechanism, a principle as much at odds with reality as with Heidegger's own views. In conclusion, while 1929/30's account of animal life is a pleasure to read, it provides no *philosophical* insight into the as-structure that was not available in section 69 of *Being and Time* at the very latest.

Certainly, there are numerous passages in which Heidegger refers to a more rudimentary form of life, a just-plain-life (*nur-noch-Leben*) obtainable from Dasein by way of subtraction. But even if this subtractive method were practical, it would never yield any knowledge about the biology of organs: it would provide us with nothing more than an impoverished form of the "as." The 1929/30 course actually contains no unexpected ontological insight into the netherworld of lower life forms, despite Heidegger's prolific generation of animal-related terminology. His treatment of organisms simply repeats the account of transcendence beyond the tool that already provided the central theme for *Being and Time*.

It will be generally admitted that there is a sense in which even rocks confront other entities, whether by smashing or discoloring them. But it will also be widely pointed out that the sentient organism seems to go further, confronting them *as* specific entities, meeting up with them in some overt form of encounter. While this obviously points to some sort of important distinction, I deny that it has much to tell us about specifically *biological* reality. It would hold true even for disembodied, nonbiological ghosts, provided these ghosts were able to perceive the world in some minimal way. It is still a remark about *aisthesis*, not about biology. In the event of further objections, the reader is referred to Bergson's strangely neglected *Creative Evolution* as a model for what it would take for philosophy to seize this bull by the horns. Heidegger's virtues lie elsewhere.

We should now turn briefly to Heidegger's discussion of the difference between tools and organs, since at first glance this distinction might appear to throw the present book into disarray. Up till now, I have been arguing that the tool is an utterly universal phenomenon in Heidegger, one capable of accounting for all possible entities. But there would now seem to be a striking counterexample in the case of the organism and its organs. After all, Heidegger declares explicitly that the organ is *not* equipment: whereas the tool is ready (*fertig*) for some end, an organ is capable (*fähig*) of it.[79] It would seem that the organ is not a tool-being, and the present book's claim that equipment is global would seem to be permanently damaged.

But in fact, this supposed distinction between tool and organ does not challenge the primacy of tool-being in the least. There are two reasons for this. First and most fundamentally, I have *never* claimed that a brain or lung is no different from a power saw. The argument of this book is not that "all entities are just as useful as tools," an empty claim deservedly

ridiculed by Heidegger.[80] It is not my purpose to grant preeminence to the
list of common handyman's gear over all other beings. This would be
"metaphysics" in the pejorative sense, and in a highly eccentric form. My
point is simply as follows: in the wake of Heidegger's analysis, neither mallets nor arteries, silk nor crickets, monocles nor chunks of dirt, can be
regarded any longer as merely present-at-hand entities. The being of these
objects *and all others* is shown to consist in the execution of their reality
prior to any coming-to-presence. The hammer must be *Vollzug* before it
can be *fertig*; equally, the eyeball is *Vollzug* before it is *fähig*. Or rather,
both *Fertigkeit* and *Fähigkeit* consist in a primordial execution of their
being. In this sense, there is no difference between tool and organ at all.

Second, and more ironically, the distinction between tool and organ
that Heidegger *does* offer only results in yet another repetition of the
tool/broken tool rift. The 1929/30 course tells us that a tool is "serviceable" for some end (*dienlich*), while an organ stands "subservient" to this
end (*diensthaftig*). In other words, the tool functions instantaneously,
plugged directly into the homogeneous system that terminates at some
remote point, its singularity dissolved into some sort of systematic action-
at-a-distance. In this way, the tool is the very embodiment of *speed*. By contrast, an organ stands at the service of the organism, opened onto a leeway
of possibilities at its disposal. Instead of being an immediate conductor of
world-force as the girder or pipeline are, the organ has already stepped
beyond this force, and compelled being to divide into specific regions of
fluids or chemicals to be acted upon. Ultimately, Heidegger insists that the
organ is not an isolated finger or kidney, but rather *the organism itself*: a
body part removed from its body would no longer be a functioning organ,
but only a kind of grotesque remainder. From all of this, we learn only that
the organism as a whole is characterized by *aisthesis*, and that consequently
the organ does not reside solely in the realm of tools, but in that of tools
"as" tools. Otherwise, there would be no leeway of action for it; it would
be a simple piece of equipment devoured by a wider system. It would not
be a specific organ at all, but would be vaporized into the system of the
world. If the tool is the principle of speed, the organ would be a principle
of individual integrity, a singular being that cannot be defined as a
Fertigkeit. But this simply means that *Fertigkeit* belongs to tool, and
Fähigkeit to perception or "broken tool"! The reader will recall that we
have been down this road numerous times already, and that it leads us
nowhere near the biological and visceral realm for which the 1929/30 lecture course is often mistaken.

But this is always Heidegger's hidden fate as a thinker. His most daring forays into concrete problems inevitably come to rest in this simple
notion of the as-structure. None of these attempts is more daring than
that of 1929/30. But as if he were sensing the very inadequacy I have

described, Heidegger never again attempts anything so bold. Perhaps beginning his career with encyclopedic aspirations, he soon finds himself locked into the repeated discovery of an awesomely radical first principle. Unfortunately, his attempted distinction between human and animal reality remains a placeholder for differentiations that never clearly emerge. Little wonder that in the years immediately following the obvious failure of the 1929/30 course, Heidegger begins to retreat into the innermost shell of his thought. If the writings on "freedom" and "truth" of the early 1930s are uniformly excellent, they are also carried out on terrain that is anything but risky for Heidegger. His contentment in those years with the play of veiling and unveiling, far from overcoming anything naively metaphysical in the period of *Being and Time*, represents a predictable recap of what could already be learned from the drama of tool-being itself. This ambivalence of "concealed" and "revealed" forever endures as the landscape where Heidegger feels most at home, the province in which he prefers to remain.

But we should return briefly to the supposed human/animal chasm. We have seen that some rudimentary form of the as-structure must belong even to animals, given that Heidegger does not appear to regard them as machines. Otherwise, just like worldless minerals, they would be no more than another inanimate locus where the forces of reality immediately exert themselves. There is no other alternative, no third way distinct from tool and broken tool. In 1929/30, Heidegger first tries to attain animal perception by way of *subtracting* from transcendence. So little content was inherent in transcendence to begin with that this procedure was bound to fail. But if one door closes, another opens: for Heidegger, a more promising account of human being appears at the very moment that the as-structure is flattened into useless generality. I refer to the "forming" [*bilden*] of "world-forming," a feature that Heidegger *also* seems to regard as the exclusive domain of the human animal. Still, even this restriction is observed somewhat loosely, since he tells us that the merest parasite *forms* its organ,[81] and in a later essay it is said that even the inanimate jug "*forms* an emptiness."[82]

For the moment, however, we can leave this inconsistency in peace. As a general rule, Heidegger does reserve the term "forming" to refer to the specifically human faculty of language: "On the basis of agreement with beings, man can and must come to utter his understanding, *form* those alliances of sounds which are the coining of meanings, utterances that we call words and vocabulary."[83] In this way, Dasein is suddenly redefined in terms of *symbolizing*: "*All* discourse is determined by this genesis of *symbolon*."[84] Pursuing the issue further, it becomes necessary to address the supposed difference between the "semantic" and "apophantic" types of *logos*:

If a discourse becomes *apophantic*, then this *semantikos* must become transformed in the manner indicated, i.e., what happens is *not simply* an agreement
in general between the meaning and what is intended, rather the meaning and
the meaningful content of the *logos apophantikos* agrees with what is meant in
such a way that this *logos* as discourse and in its discursivity seeks *to point out*
what is meant itself. Discourse now has the tendency *to let* whatever the discourse is about *be seen*—to let it be seen, and this alone.[85]

As always, everything hinges on the as-structure. Heidegger tells us
that whereas the semantic logos simply refers to the object, the apophantic kind makes this referent present *as* what it is. We encountered this claim
already when discussing the role of theory in *Being and Time*, and it falls
short now for the same reason as before. Since *every* instant is irreducibly
torn between the "as" and its dark twin, there can be no exemplary status
for theory—Socrates in his prime was "not without [his] *praxis*," and the
village idiot not without a full dose of transcendence.[86] There was an identical claim in connection with the 'sign' in *Being and Time*: "Signs always
indicate primarily 'wherein' one lives, where one's concern dwells, what
sort of involvement there is with something."[87] But this is not an especially
helpful remark, since even a situation devoid of signs in the usual sense still
manifests to us "that wherein which we live." A barren nonsemiotic island
of coconuts and sand still manifests these objects to us as *specific* features
of the landscape—the coconut appearing "as" coconut rather than as
grapes, and not simply retreating into the silent execution of its coconut-
effect. Pointing to this object *explicitly* may well change our relation to it,
but it brings us not one inch closer to the subterranean reality of coconut-
being.

This should leave us disappointed in at least two ways. First, the distinction between the semantic and apophantic logos tells us nothing new
about the split between human and animal. Why not? Because Heidegger
tells us that animals are *without any logos at all*: "Discourse and word are
to be found only in the occurrence of the symbol . . . Such an occurrence
is lacking in the case of the animal . . ."[88] Thus, the semantic/apophantic
divide is a distinction that claims to lie in the camp of human beings alone.
But if even the *semantic logos* contains something beyond simple animal
perception, I have no idea what this could be. After all, this kind of *logos* is
so completely primitive that it should already belong to any situation characterized by the merest broken tool, including that of animal life.

This leads to the second disappointment: the distinction between
semantic and apophantic cannot even serve to distinguish between different kinds of *human* experience. If we say the word "sun" (a semantic act),
our attention is directed toward the sun itself, a result accomplished just as
easily by a simple glance at this object. But even a rigorously theoretical,

"apophantic" discourse about this sun *also* only makes it visible, as opposed to tacitly effective—even if science gives us "more" information about it than any pretheoretical basking or sunbathing. We can *never* arrive at a "simple seeing" of the sun that would free us from every form of dark, withdrawn residue in its being, concealed behind all of our efforts to penetrate its mysteries.

Nor can the distinction between semantic and apophantic be saved if we imagine the difference to lie in the apophansis somehow pointing to *itself* "as" pointing. While this step would be fully in keeping with the high regard in which all forms of self-referential discourse are held today, it would also be irrelevant. To follow a sign to where it points is *already* to become aware of what it points at, even if we do this in a merely half-hearted or lazy fashion. It is difficult to see what is gained *ontologically* if we suddenly become aware of this pointing "as" pointing ("How strange, my friend... The mere color and shape of that sign are enough to deflect my attention toward the danger ahead."—"You are right, it is indeed uncanny . . ."). The problem is that we will *never* be able to retreat to a point at which the apophantic logos would make its own activity utterly transparent at a glance. As we have repeatedly seen, no entity can ever become present in its executant being; the as-structure is always a simulacrum from the start. But this means that theory cannot be distinguished from other experience by appeal to the as-structure, since the "as" can never bring us the least bit closer to the things themselves than we already were.

This issue deserves further attention insofar as it haunts Heidegger's own view of literature. At the close of a century notable for its ceaseless critical pose, there are many who reserve their deepest admiration only for self-reflexive gestures: for theories about theorizing and literature about literature. Even in nonacademic life, there are those who remain especially intrigued by artworks about art, films about filming, self-referential cabaret shows, fireworks that explode into shapes of themselves, dog biscuits in the form of dogs, and drummers who drum songs *about* drumming—a kind of "drumming at the limit." In each case, the supposed cleverness comes from the fact that the activity in question not only *happens*, but also refers to *itself* "as" what it is. But this fashionable trend only represents the worst of metaphysics in the old-fashioned sense, since it declares self-reflexivity to be a privileged moment in the relation between the two faces of being.

In the opening pages of his "Hölderlin and the Essence of Poetry," Heidegger himself reveals a taste for this prejudice. Conceding that Hölderlin may well not be as great a poet as Homer, Sophocles, Virgil, Dante, Shakespeare, or Goethe, Heidegger still decides to give Hölderlin center stage. Why? Because Hölderlin is the poet who "expressly [poetizes] the essence of poetry."[89] For this reason, we learn very little from

Heidegger about what makes Hölderlin an effective *poet* rather than an explicit poetic *theorist*—whatever the philosopher's protests to the contrary, and whatever his attempts to disarm in advance any critique of this procedure.[90] And indeed, it is very difficult to imagine the Heidegger of the *Andenken* Course ever giving us much insight into the works of a Dante or a Baudelaire. Where could he possibly begin?

We have seen that the as-structure is capable only of accounting for the merest boundary between the world of the rock and that of borderline creatures such as plankton and viruses. Even animals encounter entities *as* entities, and thereby engage in dealings with meaningful signs, however blurrily or inadequately. Further up the scale, it is even clearer that the as-structure cannot distinguish between the laziest human comportment and the heights of theoretic genius. The fool and the inventor clearly stand in different positions with respect to the same objects; nonetheless, the as-structure cannot possibly account for this difference. The planet Neptune in its tool-being remains every bit as hidden from the astronomer as from the idle skygazer; the execution of its planetary reality is forever revoked from the sphere of visibility. Thus, whatever is special about theory, or poetry, or jokes or threats or songs, cannot emerge on the level of the transparent *exhibition* of signs. Rather, the distinction between them can only be deciphered on the level of their *forming* or *creation*.

Ultimately, the same is true of the difference between humans, animals, and soulless matter. "*Bilden*" cannot explain human uniqueness by serving as an exclusive property that no other type of entity could possess. As mentioned earlier, there is also a sense in which even an animal forms its organs, and a ceramic jug forms its interior. But unlike the as-structure, "forming" *is* capable, in principle, of distinct gradations and utterly specific incarnations, since it always involves the formation of a *specific* entity. This points to a domain within which we might be able to articulate specific objects in the midst of Heidegger's thought. Since the as-structure remains everywhere and always exactly the same, the metontology of life must unfold on the level of *bilden*, and cannot earn its living on the back of the as-structure. The as/non-as opposition only provides a sort of unvarying structural skeleton for reality, while any real concreteness must be found in the sphere of *bilden* alone. Although Heidegger never does much to develop this notion, it is worthy of some reflection. For stylistic reasons, I would like to momentarily abandon the literal translation of *bilden* as "forming" and replace it with the related English homonym "building," a term equally familiar to readers of Heidegger.

The process described in the 1929/30 course as the forming or building of signs is described elsewhere in Heidegger as a *stiften*, an "instituting." This can be as simple as the familiar "knot in the handkerchief."[91] In other passages, instituting is referred to as the special gift of the poet as opposed to the "grounding" achieved by the thinker.[92] But in a postscript to the 1929/30 course (made up of a 1966 letter to Eugen Fink), we find a uniquely interesting suggestion concerning these issues. Heidegger's fascinating claim is that the traditional roles of *Gründen* and *Stiften* are now in the process of being reversed, such that the building of signs becomes the aim of philosophy itself: "The commencement of Western thinking in the Greeks was prepared by poetry. Perhaps thinking must in the future first open the time-play-space [*Zeit-Spiel-Raum*] for poetizing, so that through the poetizing word there may again be a wording world."[93] The best way to clarify this suggestion is to ask further about building or instituting, about the *distinct* ways in which it might be able to deploy the strife between the object's dual facets, and about the various possibilities of human and animal "symbolizing" that thereby arise. Only in this way can we learn anything about how the organism forms its organs, and about how even the plant forms its various miniature parts; Heidegger's "philosophical biology" has little future as long as it attempts to root itself in the as-structure.

I have now discussed at length the inability of this structure to provide any concrete account of time, space, theoretic knowledge, or animal organisms. But this lead to other, parallel realizations. If theory cannot be explained by appeal to the as-structure, then for precisely the same reasons technology cannot be viewed as the boundless reign of presence-at-hand. Technology is inadequately understood if we view it as a sheer agent of "standing reserve," as a stockpile of visibility brutally ignorant of all that withdraws from its grasp. To view the matter in terms of as and non-as is to miss the point, here as everywhere else. For technology is not just a *gründen* or even *ent-gründen*—it is a *stiften* or *bauen*, a "building," and needs to be treated as such. Since everything that is built is different, and *concretely* different, it is in no way true that the atom bomb exploded long before Hiroshima, or that mass murder is the equivalent of corporate farming.[94] Nor is the outlook for Heidegger any better if we move *forward* in time: he could only regard the future of germ-weaponry, fusion reactors, cruiser-blimps, and bionic implants as the fleeting surface of an ancient destiny, the playing out of a story preordained from the Greek beginning. But in fact, these phantoms of cybernetic fantasy are every bit as self-contained and unique as the toucans or wild boars of the Amazon, and just as deserving of a diligent taxonomy as these animals.

It is easy enough to criticize Heidegger's meditations on technology; many commentators have done so already, and not always in a way that does him justice. But far worse than such criticism is the dishonest practice of immediately ambushing all critics with ninety-nine academic gunmen, all of them shouting aloud that "Heidegger is not anti-technology in any straightforward sense," perhaps with the added insinuation that any

definite statement at all about Heidegger's technological views is inherently superficial. The fact that even some of the philosopher's worst enemies are often willing to go to bat for him on such occasions is an
astonishing testament to his skills of persuasion. And while Heidegger's
anti-technological biases should be clear enough for anyone to see, this is
not even the point, as will be seen from the following scenario.

Consider an alternative life in which Heidegger's basic philosophical
outlook was largely the same, but in which his temperament was that of a
vehement pro-technology agitator. Instead of playing the Allemanic peas-
ant clad in *Lederhosen*, he might have been a pioneering aviator, a famous
confidant of Henry Ford and Frank Lloyd Wright, and an early advocate
of electronic music. Under these circumstances, it is possible to imagine a
cheerful inversion of *The Question Concerning Technology*. In this imagi-
nary mirror-text, instead of simply making obscure appeal to "the saving
power" emerging from every danger, Heidegger might have downplayed
the danger altogether, and prophesied an epoch of technological salvation
lurking just a few decades away. At last, instead of the being of things
remaining cloaked from view and unconsciously manipulated, the grand
contours of these entities themselves would soon be revealed. Perhaps
Heidegger would have fled Hitler's Germany for an endowed chair at
UCLA, later spearheading Walt Disney's efforts to construct a park where
the forms of the things themselves might finally be mirrored.

I offer this scenario not for entertainment's sake, but only to show that
it would not alter my criticisms of Heidegger in the least. The problem
with his view of technology lies not in the excess of pessimism over opti-
mism—but in his attempt to understand technology *by means of the as-
structure*. Among other difficulties, this procedure is utterly incapable of
distinguishing between the effects of different *kinds* of machinery.
Heidegger's defenders might reply that he was never interested in doing
such a thing, that a general survey of gadgets belongs more to anthropol-
ogy or social history than to ontology. But this would be a weak alibi, given
how *ontologically* different a CD-ROM must be from a smallpox vaccine or
a flint axe. The most insightful remarks on specific technologies of philosophically powerful authors such as McLuhan and Latour put Heidegger's
aloof reflections on hydroelectric dams to shame, revealing them by contrast to be both painfully abstract and insufficiently useful.[95]

Again, there is nothing new about criticizing Heidegger's views on technology, a process as easy as it is necessary. What *is* new is my claim that the
failure of the technology essays stems from the same structural problem that
also undermines every one of Heidegger's various claims about space and
time and theory. In all such cases, Heidegger tries to use the as-structure
simultaneously in two incompatible ways. As shown earlier, the "as" is
exhibited on the one hand as a universal structure present in all experience,

an ambiguous counterpoint in which the subterranean reality of an object and its visible facade are locked in unending strife. At the same time, the "as" is also illegitimately employed in what might be called "normative" fashion, as a criterion for differentiating and even *ranking* specific beings. Although even nontheory grasps its objects as what they are, theory is supposed to see them "even more" *as* what they are. But given the absolutely unpresentable character of tool-beings themselves, such gradations are impossible. *Then the key to theoretical comportment must be found elsewhere than in the as-structure.* Precisely the same difficulty undercuts Heidegger's technology writings, which culminate in the untenable claim that the technological world strips all reality down to its bare visibility or manipulability. Just as theory ultimately cannot be understood as the making-present of thing "as" thing, technology cannot adequately be grasped if we regard it only as the univocal stripping away of secrets. The usual tedious and annoying caveat about the "saving power" is not enough. Where technology is concerned, Heidegger's grouchiness is louder than his words.

It follows for *precisely the same reasons* that the history of metaphysics cannot be viewed as the boundless and fateful evolution of presence-at-hand. A metaphysical concept is understood only sketchily if we view it simply as the over-reaching attempt to bring the being of beings to presence. There is a substantial grain of truth to this view, as Heidegger has worked so hard to demonstrate. But even if it could be shown that in each era the concepts of *eidos* or monad or absolute spirit have deemed *themselves* to be the very incarnation of the being of beings, there is no reason to reduce them to this self-image alone. A new idea is never just the latest installment in a crushing historical sequence, nor simply the further unveiling of a long-decreed destiny. Like a new invention, a new philosophical idea is always both liberating and dangerous in an unprecedented way. Like a new flag, it rallies previously unknown comrades to action. Like a giant mythological bird, it protects numerous territories even while abandoning others to the flames.

Likewise, a coal-burning furnace is not merely the naked expression of planetary manipulation: its creation marks the birth of an actual concrete power amidst the cosmos, the *Vollzug* of an independent force whose true value and true danger is hidden even from its creators. Whether dimly or lucidly, all of reality takes up some kind of stance toward this furnace-object. The air it blackens lives in reaction to it, as do the fish poisoned by it, the workers employed by it, and the stadiums powered by it. These same vectors of relation can be found in the case of every object: a wooden cup, a religious icon, a firearm. Additionally, they are fully operative in the case of philosophical concepts ("*energeia*," "intentionality," "condition of possibility"), stars around which entire systems of thought revolve. These concepts, too, must be regarded as species of wild animal, as machines unleashing their energies into the world in a much more complicated and interesting way than as agents of forgetfulness. In conclusion, neither technical objects nor intellectual concepts can possibly be assessed by means of the as-structure, an omnipresent structural relation ill-equipped to also be used as a measuring stick.

We began by recalling that the tool in Heidegger's analysis is not a simple present-at-hand object. Instead, the hammer and bridge turn out to be concealed agents in the world, real objects that build or institute their forces into the fabric of the cosmos rather than simply *unveiling* these forces (which in the strict sense was shown to be impossible). Additionally, since Heidegger's tool-being must be interpreted in the broadest possible way, the same necessarily holds good for everything from sharks to rubies. In the end, even the most dubious creations of global technology have to be looked at in precisely the same way, no less subtly than we would reflect on a beautiful piece of crystal. However dubious the uses to which an atomic energy plant might be put, this facility is still an object stationed in the midst of reality, no less than any maple tree or thistle. Ontologically speaking, the energy plant is a distinct event in the universe, one that cannot be understood solely by saying that it cruelly suppresses the mystery of the world. To say such a thing is nothing more than to say that technology ratchets up the dominance of *Vorhandenheit* to previously unknown levels. But we have already seen that the *amount* of presence-at-hand in the world never increases or decreases at all, since at each moment it makes up a full half of reality.

I also suggested that a metaphysical concept cannot be understood solely through the fact that it falsely claims to take the whole of being under its wing, to reduce the secret of *Sein* to some form of presence-at-hand. The history of philosophy is not only, as Heidegger implies, a standing reserve of onto-theological presence. Like the tool, like theory, like the organs of an animal, metaphysical concepts are *instituted* or *built*. Even when such concepts forget the roots from which they emerge, they are still fresh powers released into the world, stock characters varying in prestige and impact as much as the various plants and musical instruments that duel for supremacy across the earth.[96]

It is now time to discuss the *second* Heideggerian theme, the sole problem known to Heidegger other than his well-known play of light and shadow: his elusive second axis of reality.

§8. A Second Axis

Only by acknowledging the most extreme dominance of the tool–broken tool opposition in Heidegger's thought do we gain a genuine thirst for anything that might escape it. This is the reason that previous commentators have overlooked the theme that will now be discussed. So far, I have presented Heidegger as unable to break the stifling monopoly of the as-structure. It has been shown repeatedly that all entities are "tools" in the broadest sense of the term. In turn, these tool-beings become visible, break away from the contexture as individual entities, only insofar as they experience a kind of "failure" in their activity.

In the strict sense, any individual piece of equipment is untenable in Heidegger's philosophy, as in any philosophy that grants such overwhelming dominance to the network over the individual object. As an instantaneous and unitary event, the contexture has no parts: *being should have no beings*. But in spite of this, experience obviously testifies that there *are* individual entities, a fact that highlights the reversal or metabolism by which such objects arise. The present section will add a new spice to this discussion. For it turns out that, quite apart from his unworkable distinction between the perceptual and theoretical versions of the "as," Heidegger still refers to the as-structure in *two distinct senses*. In addition to the ubiquitous opposition between concealed and revealed, or tool and broken tool, a second axis of division can be found, one so elusive that in the present book we can only begin to explore its mysteries. Conveniently enough, this new principle is already at work in Heidegger's earliest published lecture course, the Freiburg Emergency War Semester of 1919.[97] Moreover, it appears in the midst of a full-blown analysis of equipment. Even better, it does so in a form that simultaneously demystifies the vaunted term *Ereignis*.[98]

I now turn directly to this enchanting series of lectures, delivered by Heidegger at the age of twenty-nine. His discussion here of the emergence of theory should present few surprises for readers of *Being and Time*. All experience, he tells us, occurs in a setting populated with various sorts of objects—lectern, book, blackboard. Immersed in this environment, Dasein does not run across isolated substances which it would then endow with meaning only after the fact. Rather, "the meaningful is what is primary; it is immediately given to me..."[99] The same thing is said often enough in Heidegger's better-known writings. The unique ingredient in the 1919 presentation of "environment" is its connection with the fact that entities simply *are*, that "*es gibt*" beings at all: "There are [*es gibt*] numbers, there are triangles, there are pictures by Rembrandt, there are U-boats . . ."[100]

This listing of various objects that exist might seem to lead nowhere. But as Heidegger adds, "even this completely colorless 'there are,' emptied as it were of determinate significations, contains a manifold riddle precisely because of its simplicity."[101] The fact that there is a mystery surrounding even the emptiest *es gibt* indicates that the simple presence-at-hand of

being has already been denied. In other words, the question of the meaning of being has already been posed. But this indicates that the shadowy *es
gibt* and the famously coy *Seinsfrage*, far from requiring some sort of complicated retreat into ineffable themes, already emerge into view in the consideration of the dullest everyday utensils. For this reason, it is regrettable
that so many interpreters strike out in precisely the opposite direction, creating a developmental mythology in which we find Heidegger in increasingly hot pursuit of an "it" that "gives," while supposedly fleeing ever
further from the realm of concrete objects.

Any entity, says the young Heidegger, emerges only from out of a
familiar context. We can imagine the dispersal of various items in a room
filled with typical academic equipment, most of it already understood, even
taken for granted. As we already know, this set of gear can easily experience
a disruption. But the scenario offered in 1919 is not that of the well-known
malfunction of the tool; instead, Heidegger approaches the familiar system
of objects through the eyes of a disoriented stranger. In an illuminating but
deplorable example, he asks us to imagine the sudden appearance of a
"Senegal Negro" [*Senegalneger*] amidst the items in the hall. This embarrassing occurrence of a minstrel show in the heart of the *Gesamtausgabe*
goes a long way toward ruining an otherwise masterful analysis.

Most observers would immediately recognize a professor's lectern.
Having seen it dozens of times in this particular room, we fail to take it
seriously, or overlook it altogether. But Heidegger suggests that the native
of Senegal, freshly emerged from his "hut" [*Hütte!*], might regard it as a
piece of magical paraphernalia, or as a barrier behind which to hide from
arrows and sling-stones. An even more likely result, according to
Heidegger, is that he would fail to understand this object at all. Even so,
the man from Senegal would never encounter the lectern as raw sense-data,
as something present-at-hand prior to all interpretation. Whereas most of
us encounter the lectern as equipment for educating, this stranger could
only be perplexed by a sheer form of equipmental strangeness: "In the kernel of their essence, what is meaningful in 'equipmental strangeness' and
the 'meaningful' lectern are not identical."[102] Immersed in this environment, everything is laced with significance, everything is *welthaft*, laden
with world. Everywhere, "*es weltet*"—the celebrated "it's worlding" that
delights every reader of these early lectures.

Heidegger's lifelong fascination with the impersonal propositional
form has often been noted. But the value of this observation tends to be
diluted by the usual approach to the problem, as reflected in the common
corny wisecrack about the proposition "It's raining." Poking holes in the
subject of the sentence is too predictably smug ("... but what, after all, is
this 'it' that supposedly rains?"). Among other drawbacks, such irony fails
by assuming that it already knows what rain is. So, too, with respect to

Heidegger's phrase. The real mystery does not arise from the phantom "It." Instead, the true puzzle unfolds in the sphere of the "worlding" itself.[103] It's raining a rainstorm; it's worlding tools.

The 1919 account of the genesis of theory also has a familiar ring. Here as later, we are told that theory rips us away from the interior of the world and somehow *de-worlds* the thing that is theorized about. The environment is made up of objects and actions—of *situations*. In an essay appended to the text of the course itself,[104] Heidegger speaks of knowledge as extinguishing the situation-character of experience, transforming it into an objective datum at the cost of cutting it off at the knees. Life is not a set of present-at-hand occurrences, but an *event* (*Ereignis*). As Heidegger puts it, in his already familiar tone of voice: "The relation to life of the situation-I is no mere directedness toward mere objects."[105] Life is always some actual state of things, some *scenario*. We could easily say that it is made up of what the old Italian comedy called *lazzi*, stock gags or lived situations of an immediate and irreducible force ("Colombine flirts with the Spanish pirate"; "Pierrot chews on holy wafers").[106] The main difference is that these comic scenarios are already openly visible to the theatergoer, whereas in the first instance, life is delivered over to a situation without even knowing that this is the case.

Life is pure event; *Erlebnis* is *Ereignis*, fully invested with significance. Knowledge halts this event and converts it into mere *Vorgang*, best translated here as "occurrence" rather than the usual "process": "Objectified happening, happening as something objective or something known, we will call by the name *occurrence*."[107] Viewed as such an occurrence, life is always only a shadow of *Ereignis*. To encounter an entity as the represented object of knowledge requires a kind of de-living, a de-distancing or de-severing: "The objective, the known, is as such de-severed [*ent-fernt*], lifted away from authentic lived experience."[108]

Clearly, the stranger from Senegal's basic experience of the professor's lectern is not that of a mere occurrence, but rather "something completely new,"[109] a startling kind of *Ereignis*. Viewed as occurrence, life is already reduced to a form of mere representation (*Vorgang* = *Vorstellen*). But life in the truest sense is actually an *Ereignis*. This leads Heidegger to make a word-play requiring that we momentarily translate *Ereignis* with the cumbersome phrase "event of appropriation": "Lived experiences are events of appropriation, insofar as they live from out of what is proper [*eigen*] and live life only in this way."[110] The "proper" in this context is the near, what the world itself really is—a nearness in the *authentic* sense. Thus, there is hardly any need to jump ahead to Heidegger's technology essays for examples of false versions of nearness (for instance, radio or film or rocket). Already in 1919, we have been told that theory itself is unable to grasp lived experience in its most proper or nearest character: "A science of lived experiences, then, would have to objectify them; that is, it would have to strip them of their non-objectlike character as lived experience and event."[111] The *Ereignis* of our environment is opposed by the theoretical attitude, "which in accordance with its sense is only possible as a destruction of the lived experience of the environment."[112] Thus, theory works by ripping asunder the connectedness of the *Umwelt*. This process is given several names: it is a *de-living* or *de-signifying*. Even more innovatively, Heidegger calls it a *de-historizing* [*ent-geschichtlichen*].

I have summarized these passages to solidify my earlier claims as to the abiding importance of the tool-analysis at all points of Heidegger's career. But what is most interesting about 1919 is still to come. So far, we have followed the young Heidegger's account of the emergence of objects from the concrete system of life, an emergence which this talented student of Husserl regards as the hidden key to his teacher's method. Knowing how to disclose entities from out of the sphere of the life-world, he tells us, is the basic principle of phenomenology.[113] But it is here that something completely unexpected happens. Heidegger tells us that there are *two* kinds of such theorizing.[114]

On the one hand, he says, we can exhibit entities in a way that is concerned with their bondedness to a particular level of reference. Let's say that from amidst the global empire of reference, I encounter a colored object. I begin by having a sort of blurred, unthematic relation to it. But after a certain amount of reflection, I become explicitly aware that the object is brown. Upon further abstraction, I realize that brown is a color, so that the category of "color" was already applicable to that blurry object that crawled into my view from out of the life-world. Color, in turn, can give way to the even deeper categories that encompass it: "perception," "experience," "reality," and so on. In each case, there are discernible grounds in the situation at hand for thematizing things in such a way: "I call this the specific bondedness to levels [*spezifische Stufengebundenheit*] of the steps in the de-living process."[115] Later in the same lecture course, the thing viewed as a *specific* something will be referred to as the "object-type something" [*objektartiges Etwas*].

But on the other hand, there is another kind of theorizing that has nothing to do with this step-by-step uncovering of levels. At any moment in the process, whether at the level of "blur" or "brown" or "color" or "perception," we can also stop and note that any of these things is at least *something* rather than nothing. We can say "the blur *is*," "the brown *is*," "the color *is*," "the perception *is*." This possibility belongs to *any* part of the environment that we might be discussing at *any* moment. Then, not only do tool-beings have a double nature as effect and appearance: in addition to this, *appearance itself* has a twofold character. And with this, we encounter a truly fresh philosophical theme, however arid it may seem at first glance. For the first time, the single repetitive axis of fundamental ontology gains a second dimension.

Of the two types of theory described by Heidegger, the one that pertains to "something in general" is said to be connected with "the highest principle of referentiality." The fact that a thing is anything at all rather than nothing is deemed its ultimate significance, the bedrock reality that shadows any of the *specific* qualities it might manifest. This "highest potentiality for life," as Heidegger puts it, this "something at all," is also referred to as "the thing *formaliter*" (or as the *formallogisches gegenständliches Etwas*). It should come as no shock to admirers of *Being and Time* when the young Heidegger tells us that this "*formaliter*" is no simple genus, no empty present-at-hand designation: "In the 'something' as that which can be experienced at all, we should not see something radically subjected to theory and de-lived, but rather an essential moment of life in and for itself, one that stands in close connection with the event-character of lived experiences as such."[116]

The "something in general" is not a concept at all, but rather an *Ereignis*. It is nothing less than the *being* of the thing: "It is a basic phenomenon that can be experienced in an understanding way, e.g., in the experienced situation of sliding from one life-world into one that is genuinely different, or in moments of especially intense life . . ."[117] This stunning remark of 1919 is an unexpected precursor of some of the most beautiful passages of 1935: "The question ['Why is there something rather than nothing?'] looms in moments of great despair, when things tend to lose all their weight and all meaning becomes obscured. . . . It is present in moments of rejoicing. . . . The question is upon us in boredom . . . ."[118]

But I argued earlier that theoretical comportment could never be regarded as an especially pure manifestation of the as-structure. The thing revealed by theory always recedes behind any possible objectification of it. Now, the same thing must hold true of exemplary disclosive moods (despair, rejoicing, Angst). The "something in general" might *loosely* be said to appear with especial clarity in moods of this kind—but it is neither *identical* with these moods, nor can it become bodily present in them. The "something in general" is not only something that is not primarily *seen*, but also something that is not primarily felt, such as in an *attunement*. Far more than something seen or felt, it is something that *is*, whatever our mood might happen to be at any given moment. Neither Heidegger's second kind of theory nor Angst itself has any exemplary ability to present the simple something *as* that simple something in all its purity, to present *Sein* to us in person. But this means that the "something in general" must somehow *always* be present: not only in anxiety or boredom, but also in stupefaction, in drunkenness, and in the rage of a madman. Since it inherently belongs even to the most primitive sorts of perception, it must be there too for the rabid coyote and the wounded butterfly.

We have already seen that the as-structure is incapable of distinguishing between human theory and the most dazed perception found in insects. But the same is equally true for moods or attunements. No kind of mood has a privileged ontological access to the being of things. Theory and mood alike are caught up in the same unshakeable dualism of tool and broken tool. Both of them come to birth in a world already strangled by this duality, such that the most daring theory and the most extreme attunement are equally incapable of providing us with the things themselves. If Angst or being toward death have some sort of special status, this certainly cannot be for any reason pertaining to the as-structure. They may be *distinctive* moods, in the sense that they are different from sadness or confusion or vengefulness. But we cannot follow Heidegger in granting them the special capability of accessing being *as* being.

As a consequence, even moods must be regarded as a form of building or instituting, rather than as any exemplary sort of unveiling disclosure. A mood has less in common with pure unveiling than it does with the formation of a jug or a bridge (and ultimately, the same is true of theory itself). Theory and Angst are simply incapable of taking us on a magical voyage outside the permanent civil war of tool and broken tool. Even anxiety must belong to the level that Heidegger usually designates as "derivative"—that of appearance, presence-at-hand, broken tool.[119] Hence, the duality between thing as specific something and thing *formaliter* marks a duality in the appearances themselves, and is not something that simply appears to us in a certain mood, or at the dawn of a special "Greek beginning." For this reason, the reality previously described under the name of "broken tool" (or "space" or "theory") no longer forms a simple unity over against the withdrawn contexture. *Appearance itself has become duplicitous.*

But perhaps even more disturbingly, this same duality is already operative at the pretheoretical level of tool-being itself. For even as the system of the world tries to behave as a single unified empire, it also exists in each case in the form of distinct objects such as seashells, trumpets, glass, or hammers, regardless of whether these are explicitly present to us or not. Indeed, even the *concealed* tool is marked by the two moments of "specific something" and "something at all." The ground supporting our feet is at least *something*, but it is also a something marked by specific and limited features: it supports us rather than laughing at us or irradiating us with lethal energies, whether we notice any of this or not.

In short, the duality within appearance is not an *ad hoc* schism generated only in rare moments of theoretical inquiry or intense moods. Rather, both sides of the appearing thing serve only to objectify a kind of being in which we are already immersed, two halves of a world that exist prior to all theory. This too is already clear in 1919, when the two sectors of the invisible realm of Ereignis appear under two distinct names: "preworldly something" [*vorweltliches Etwas*] and "world-laden something" [*welthaftes Etwas*]: "the preworldly and world-laden functions of meaning have in themselves the essential feature of expressing event-characters [*Ereignischaraktere*]. . . ."[120] The consequence of this for the present book is as follows. I have been arguing all along that reality in Heidegger's eyes turns out to be nothing but a monotonous interplay between *Ereignis* (tool) and *Vorgang* (broken tool). But it now turns out that *Ereignis* has two faces, and *Vorgang* has two faces. This is something absolutely new, something never mentioned before either in the present book or in any other work on Heidegger: his term "ontological difference" is ambivalent, as it is employed simultaneously to describe two altogether separate distinctions.

As concerns this unexpected new theme, I will try to show only that it is the direct source for Heidegger's later theme of "the fourfold," which is usually viewed as an arbitrary flight of poetry on the philosopher's part. Against this view, I will maintain that *das Geviert* is nothing more than the dry logical outcome of Heidegger's philosophy of tool and broken tool. To this extent, I will only be making a claim about the internal relations among several Heideggerian concepts. A further question is whether his notion of reality as quadruple in structure can be of any further use to us in the year 2002 and beyond. The important thing for now is only to see that an alien force has somehow crept into the dualism that otherwise dominates Heidegger's works; tool and broken tool are both exactly *twice* as complicated as they first seemed to be. The formerly unlimited dominance of the as/non-as axis is now crossed by a power of equal rank. Instead of facing our previous repetitive twofold, we are confronted with the number *four*.

*   *   *

A traditional Zen story speaks of a temple novice who hoped to attain enlightenment by chopping a cat in half with a sword. Witnessing the preparations for this atrocity, the head monk cried out and asked the newcomer to explain himself.

"I am cutting the cat *in two* with *one* sword," was the young man's reply.

Outdoing this supposed paradox of duality and unity, the monk countered with the following remark: "It is easy to cut the cat in two with one sword. What is difficult is to cut the cat *in one* with one sword."

"But what is 'cutting the cat in one'?"

"The cat itself."
Hearing this reply from his master, the novice attained enlightenment.

*   *   *

As if to one-up the Zen master in this anecdote, Heidegger cuts the cat in one with *two* swords. The first weapon, the reversal between tool and broken tool, has been the primary focus of this book from the start. The second blade is none other than the newly uncovered difference between the thing regarded as something *in particular* and as something *at all*.

So much for the appearance of this second and widely ignored theme in the lecture course of 1919. Following an equally lively treatment in the 1920/21 course, the matter is largely dropped. However, it seems to survive as a kind of suppressed genotype, for it reappears in explicit form in the twin treatises of 1929: "What is Metaphysics?" and "On the Essence of Ground." But before discussing these fascinating and central works, another brief historical remark is in order. In 1949, a new foreword was added to "On the Essence of Ground," a page-long declaration in which Heidegger scolds his readers for two decades of indifference to none other than the mysterious second axis I have just described. This will be a key topic for the next section.

Furthermore, 1949 is an interesting year for Heidegger to be pressing the point, since this is the time of the ghostly Bremen lecture "Einblick in das, was ist,"[121] in which the two distinct axes of his thought openly cross for the first time. As I will continue to argue from time to time throughout this book, their intersection is the true source of the baffling fourfold of that lecture and its spin-off texts, a theme that has frustrated interpreters for over fifty years. At any rate, the familiar dualism of tool and broken tool has now been crossed by a new divide between "specific something" and "something at all." If these oppositions seem impossibly barren at first glance, they are still fertile enough to give birth to a tetrad of mythic proportions: earth, sky, gods, mortals. And there will be no further zones of the world for Heidegger: the untapped enigma of his thought is that of the quadrants of reality.

§9. The Duel in Appearance

This final section of chapter 1 seeks only to review and clarify the basic features of what has already been shown. I began with an epigraph from Deleuze referring to philosophical commentary as a form of "slow motion." It should now be clear what was meant by this remark. Whatever else I have attempted to say so far, my strategic objective has been to redirect the reader's attention from the unruly multitude of popular Heideggerian themes toward a single structural enigma—that of the relation between tool and broken tool. Now as always, I take these terms in the broadest possible sense, as referring to the dual life of *every* entity.

But the general status of this theme has just undergone a significant modification. For most of this book, reality appeared to us in a double guise. It now turns out that, in some elusive way, the world has been *quadrupled*. I began by arguing that all of Heidegger's attempts to elaborate some concrete reality (broken tool, theory, space, animal life) soon implode into the opposition between the absolute and concealed power of the tool-system, and the visibly fragmented landscape of specific objects. But this opposition between "non-as" and "as" has now been complicated by a second principle, and *only* by this second principle. It was seen from the 1919 lectures that all appearance can be considered under a further twofold perspective: the thing exists both in the specific form of "loud," "sour," "ice cube," or "wood," and in the simple aspect of "something at all."

In the preceding section, it was shown how this second topic is introduced in Heidegger's earliest surviving lecture course, the Emergency War Semester of 1919. But as already mentioned, the same theme reappears nine years later, as the explicitly emphasized bond between a pair of magnificent essays: "What is Metaphysics?" and "On the Essence of Ground." For decades, these two related works have met with vastly different fates. The first is universally regarded as one of Heidegger's masterpieces, and is often familiar even to beginners in philosophy. The second essay, although composed on the pivotal occasion of a *Festschrift* for the aging Husserl, has been less widely appreciated.

But the new foreword to this latter work, a prefatory remark dating from 1949, openly describes the way in which these two texts belong together. Heidegger tells us that the first treatise is concerned with the "not" of nothingness, and the second with the "not" between being and beings. These "are indeed not identical, but are *the same* insofar as they belong to the coming-to-presence of the being of beings."[122] These moments, the same without being identical, are none other than *nothingness* and *the ontological difference*: "What if reflective people would finally begin to enter thoughtfully into this sameness, which has lain in waiting for two decades?"[123] Since the appearance of this remark, five additional decades have elapsed, and the command to read these works in unison has still rarely if ever been obeyed.

The likely reason for this oversight has already been mentioned, but bears repeating here. As Heidegger's foreword testifies, his two essays develop the theme of a rift *within* appearance itself (nothingness and the ontological difference), thereby reintroducing 1919's dual principle of reality. From the standpoint of mainstream readings of Heidegger, such a principle can only seem like one new bibliographical detail among others, an interesting connection discovered between essays written a decade apart. Accordingly, if noticed at all, it is filed away and quickly forgotten. It is really possible to see the second axis as *decisive* only if we submit to the sort of ascetic deprivation that the present book has advocated, offering an interpretation of Heidegger in which all concrete detail continually implodes into the simple repetitive dualism of the tool and its breakdown. Only under these circumstances can such an apparently dry distinction as that between "something specific" and "something at all" come to seem pivotal.

A joint consideration of Heidegger's two essays provides an optimal chance to refine the description of the duel within appearance, thereby clarifying this second theme to the reader to as great an extent as its shadowy austerity allows. I should begin by pointing out that each essay marks out its subject matter on the level of the as-structure rather than that of the things themselves. Put differently, both of them unfold on the plane of what has been termed the "broken tool." "What is Metaphysics?" is dominated by its account of the nothing *as* nothing, as openly revealed the experience of *Angst*. Likewise, "On the Essence of Ground" refers to the encounter with the specific beings that are explicitly visible for Dasein in *any* instant of its transcendence, and makes no attempt to address the secret life of objects themselves. The latter essay, while less widely known than its counterpart, offers a better starting point due to its greater simplicity and closer relation to themes discussed so far in the present book.

The essay on ground is sometimes described as the place where Heidegger fully settles his accounts with Husserl. While this probably occurs more explicitly elsewhere (namely, in the 1925 *History of the Concept of Time*), the ground essay does proceed in explicit counterpoint to Husserl's theme of intentionality. Famously enough, Heidegger tells us that the fact of such intentionality, the presence of an object to thought, is only possible on the basis of a prior state of *transcendence*. Several years earlier, he had criticized his teacher for halting phenomenological inquiry prematurely, for not examining further the *being* of intentionality.[124] For Husserl, or so Heidegger says, the fact of intentional reality is mistakenly regarded as a final all-encompassing datum immune from further inquiry; in this way, it remains nothing more than a sophisticated representative of presence-at-hand. In the 1929 *Festschrift*, this criticism continues: "The subject never exists beforehand as 'subject,' in order then to transcend *in case* objects are present-at-hand. . . ."[125] Rather, consciousness exists only in the mode of *always* outstripping the world that is given. In an important footnote, Heidegger even tells us that the whole of *Being and Time* might be read *exclusively* as a meditation on transcendence.[126] Simply put, the virtue of such transcendence is to undermine the presence-at-hand of the phenomena that appear to consciousness. That which is intended never reposes in a state of sheer presence—instead, it is forever torn apart by the innate duality of its own being.

Like intentionality, transcendence can always be found at the core of human comportment. But *unlike* intentionality, it cannot possibly be regarded as a simple vision in which things become present for an observer. Instead, Heidegger says just what we would expect him to say: that the beings that emerge in our transcendence are born from the robust power of a hidden depth, unearthed from the dark empire of a prior execution. Transcendence is a "not" that surpasses the anonymous realm of tool-being: "*That which* is surpassed, is precisely only beings themselves, i.e., every being that can be unconcealed and become unconcealed to Dasein, and thus *even and precisely* that being as which 'it itself' exists."[127] At no time do we encounter isolated present-at-hand phenomena, not even if the things we encounter are mere illusory phantoms or direct observations of our own mental life. Instead, even these apparitions must arise from the "nihilation" that characterizes our transcendence. Already more than sheer appearances from the very moment they are encountered, phenomena are partly liberated from their occluded action into some sort of tangible form.

Another name for this surpassing is "outstripping" (*Überschwung*), a freeing of entities into the clearing where they are encountered. But predictably enough, Heidegger also tells us that beings are never *completely* transcended, as if they were somehow able to become transparent at a glance: "The projection of possibilities is in each case richer than that which already rests in the possession of the one projecting them."[128] Thus, whatever contours of objects may be illuminated through Dasein's transcendence, other possibilities remain forever withdrawn. The objectification of things *never* offers the full monetary equivalent of their dark and silent labor, since no such objectifying can exhaust their reality: "In accordance with both ways of grounding, transcendence outstrips and withdraws at the same time."[129] This means that transcendence is torn by an inescapable duality, a schism we have already dealt with quite thoroughly: "non-as" and "as," tool and broken tool. The luminous figure of the transcended entity and its indomitable underground reality *both* collapse into the ambiguity of a single transcendent state.

As a related theme in the ground essay, we find that Dasein's transcendence is cited as the root of all *questioning*. Only the fact that entities are surpassed in the first place allows them to be disclosed, thereby enabling us to probe into the possibilities locked within their hidden reality. But here, recalling the myth of the drugged man offered in §6 above, it should be reemphasized that Heidegger is in no position to identify Dasein as the *source* of transcendence. What is primarily given is the unity of a transcendent state, a state in which we encounter *objects of a transcendental char-acter*. This dolphin and this Bible and that emerald are manifest only *in transcendence*, flickering with the irreducible duality that sparkles at their core. Heidegger's repeated claims that only Dasein can be regarded as transcendent are not relevant here, since such remarks are clearly designed only to subvert the notion of entities that would stand "beyond" us in a merely present-at-hand way (for example, an invisible god or impercepti-ble universe-as-a-whole).

As was also discussed in connection with the drugged man, the claim that it is *we* rather than *objects* that transcend makes illicit appeal to an ontic prejudice—the everyday fact that we human beings are able by force of will and muscle to alter the details of our world, whether by moving objects around or simply viewing them in a different light. But this does not prove that only human beings transcend, as if the objects surrounding us were only dreary present-at-hand lumps that needed a "human touch" to come to life. It might even be the case that, like the menacing toys prowling in some depraved Gepetto's workshop, objects truly flourish only in that mid-night reality that shields them from our view. Perhaps entities are actually rendered bland or uni-dimensional only *through* their contact with humans. Perhaps instead of *liberating* objects into a clearing, Dasein is actually guilty of *chloroforming* the things, of pinning them down like the exterminated moths that bulk up an amateur's private collection.

To repeat, the sand and diamonds and cloth that surround us must obviously exist *in transcendence*. They cannot possibly be regarded as *vorhanden*, but must be grasped as ambivalent disclosures of the diamond-being and sand-being that lie forever beyond our reach. The fact that these objects are unable to sweep *us* aside in the same way that we can banish them from *our* awareness has, for the moment, a merely ontic status, and cannot be smuggled into the question at hand. Berries and falafel, bulldogs and quicksand—all of these things exist as *transcendental* realities. Thus, the term "transcendence" can only be used for the purpose of further obliterating the notion of present-at-hand beings; it cannot also serve to distinguish between human beings and lifeless hulks of granite, not even in a rough preliminary way. Heidegger's vague attempts to develop such dis-tinctions simply repeat one of the most consistent errors found in his writ-ings: the tendency to wrongly identify being-in-the-world with Dasein's *awareness* of the world.

It should be noted briefly that Heidegger likes to describe transcen-dence by yet another alias that might easily lead us astray: "the surpassing toward world is *freedom itself*."[130] The problem with the word "freedom" is that it involves us in precisely the same difficulty that already ship-wrecked so many of Heidegger's other key terms. In the first place, there is the obvious and oft-cited difficulty that his concept of freedom would be applicable even in the case of a shackled prisoner or a slave, so that "freedom itself" might just as easily be known as "*bondage itself.*" Not surprisingly, Heidegger's notion of freedom turns out to be politically and ethically useless. But there is also the further, familiar problem already cited numerous times throughout this book with respect to other terms—namely, freedom is not defined in any way that could possibly distinguish it from temporality, theory, space, or broken equipment. Now as always, Heidegger only takes us on a return visit to the well-worn kingdom of tool and broken tool. The already massive Heideggerian thesaurus continues to expand. But the philosopher has gone no further toward working out a possible "philosophy of freedom" than he did for any of the other key terms mentioned above. In every case (time, space, theory), the term in question collapses into a single-minded insight concerning the dual facets of reality. And we meet with the identical problem here (not just the "same" problem): to call transcendence "freedom" is simply to muddy the stream. As will be discussed in §14 below, similar charges are sometimes justifiably leveled against Heidegger's conception of "truth." For in the first place, his famous "unconcealment" is present even in the case of malicious lies and gross hallucination, so that Heidegger's "originary truth" could just as easily be called "originary falsity." And in the second place, "truth," like "freedom," turns out to be just another alias for the strife between the visceral darkness of equipment and the dazzling luster of its surface.

To sum up, the account of ontological difference in "On the Essence of Ground" serves as nothing more than another compact summary of the tension between veiled and unveiled reality, a dual situation which it chooses to describe as "transcendence." This transcendence, a fundamental trait of human Dasein, is always related to a prior being of the things in their executant reality. Heidegger would be the first to admit that a full dose of concealment is intrinsic to every surpassing; as a result, the being of the things themselves can *never* be brought to view for transcendent Dasein. Hammers or melons or crystals become visible to us only in the ambivalent state of transcendence, and not "in themselves," which would be impossible in principle. The time has come to transpose the discussion into Heidegger's *second* quadrant of appearance: not the zone inhabited by a menagerie of colorful specific beings, but that of being itself. This theme is touched upon in Heidegger's famous discussion of Angst.

In the triple structure of transcendence, the observer "nihilates" the things in the world, outstripping the taciturn action of the tool and bringing it to explicit presence. This gulf or negation between concealed tool-being and specific projections of it is more widely known as the ontological difference, the "nihilating 'not' between being and beings." The more famous essay "What is Metaphysics?" points to a kind of nothingness that is quite distinct from any such combat between being and beings. Even so, it begins with a quick return to the threefold structure of the ontological difference. All science, all projection of beings, has a threefold configuration: (1) it is characterized by a "relation to world," a *Weltbezug*; (2) its relation to this world necessarily assumes a determinate stance or attitude, a *Haltung*; (3) as such, science is a particular kind of "irruption" marked by a distinctive transcendence of beings, a specific *Einbruch*.[131] This list offers a clear summation of the same trio of terms that we have encountered at *every step* of Heidegger's numerous analyses. But here, by means of what looks at first like a distracting word-play, Heidegger negates this triple unity at a stroke: each of these three moments of knowledge pertains to beings themselves, and aside from this—*nothing*. Thus, in addition to the strife between the world and the various stances of Dasein that confront it, there is the additional fact that the entire structure is finite—that it is something at all, that it exists against the background of a void which alone reveals its contours to view.

To clarify this new theme, it is necessary to consider the nothingness that accompanies the reality of transcendence of a whole. Obviously, this nothingness must be described in its *being*: after all, it is not some definition or appearance of transcendence that is now negated, but rather transcendence in its *reality*, in its *actual labor* of existence. Just as it was not permissible to define the hammer or bridge by their visible material shape, equally little can we reduce nothingness to an idea or representation; this would amount to treating it as something present-at-hand, a move opposed by the most rudimentary tenets of Heidegger's thought. In any event, the general features of his reflections on nothingness are well-known: the nothingness of being is said to be encountered in the fundamental mood of Angst. In this basic state of attunement, it is not just one or two possibilities among others that slip away. Instead, *beings as a whole* are exhibited as the pure and featureless realities that they are, as sheer "something at all" rather than nothing. As far as Angst is concerned, there is no distinction between paper, steam, radios, canaries, and tar. All of these entities are now exhibited only in a single respect: that of their sheer *reality*. In this distinction between the always *specific* objects of transcendence and the all-encompassing *unity* displayed in Angst, we encounter once more Heidegger's 1919 distinction between "specific something" and "formal-logical something." If the sensitive literary overtones of the later treatments of nothingness are mostly lacking in the 1919 text, they are hardly necessary. For even in 1919, it is impossible for the formal-logical term to be defined as any sort of present-at-hand term. Here already, the young Heidegger is readily alert to the fact of the thing's being *something* rather than nothing at all. Hence, the later distinction we are now tracing between the difference of being from beings and the nothingness of being itself, was already to be found in the young Heidegger's two kinds of theory, even if he arrived at this notion by means of a dry ontological distinction rather than through a stirring description of anxiety.

Anxiety's revelation of the world as a whole is also familiar to readers of *Being and Time* under another name: "being-towards-death," one of the most enduringly popular themes of that work. Heidegger's discussions of death hold an understandable appeal for the philosophically inclined reader; dark reflections of this kind tend to occur with especial frequency in theoretically acute souls. And when comportment toward death breaks free inside of us, it *does* seem to offer a moment of rare insight. But in fact, any focus on exemplary moods of this kind is bound to mislead us. The main problem with privileging fundamental moods is that something like Angst *always* occurs. This supposedly rare exemplary mood actually never leaves us at all: "Holding itself over into the nothing, Dasein is *always already* beyond beings as a whole."[132] And again, "this originary Angst is mostly suppressed in Dasein. *Angst is there*; it is only sleeping."[133] By the same token, we could also say in reference to Heidegger's other famous examples that "being-towards death is always there; it is only sleeping," or "boredom is always there; it is only sleeping," or "joy at the presence of a loved one is always there; it is only sleeping" or "theoretical comportment is always there; it is only sleeping." Each of these shining examples really serves only to unveil a state of transcendence that was already in operation from the first. The implications of this are significant. "Sleeping Angst" must somehow already exist in *all* comportment, and to exactly the same degree no matter whether in cases of somber theoretical commitment or careless idling. It follows that, *at most*, Angst or being-towards-death display nothingness "as" nothingness, bringing to explicit view a negativity that could already be found anyway. But in that case, Heidegger would only find himself derailed once again by his continual unjustified extension of the as-structure to serve as a measuring-stick for judging special occasions, rather than simply as a universal opposition.

I say that Angst can do this "at most" for a very good reason: for in fact, such moods cannot possibly have the function of revealing the whole *as* whole. We already know why not—the as-character of the whole is already there in *all* transcendence, even in the *absence* of such extreme forms of attunement, even in a waster or slacker who ignores the fundamental attunements on those few occasions when they do arise in his life. This becomes even clearer if we review the outline of Angst-ridden moods that has emerged so far. Recall that it began with Heidegger pointing to the crucial importance of experiencing *nothingness itself*, the whole of being *itself*, rather than a representation or definition of this whole. The pre-eminent means of access to this whole turned out to be the mood of Angst. But the puzzle has just been modified by Heidegger's admission that this experience of being as a whole is *always* present. The altered situation would have to run as follows: *any* comportment contains the whole, while only Angst and its variants are able to manifest this whole "*as*" whole.

The error lies in assuming that comportments such as Angst reveal being as a whole *in person*, as if it were somehow accessible outside the concealing mediation of the as-structure. But how could this possibly be the case? We have seen repeatedly that hammer-being and bridge-being withdraw behind every silhouette of hammer and bridge that has ever emerged into our awareness. Are we now to think that even the lowliest tools conceal themselves from view in this way, while *being itself* is open at a glance to anyone undergoing a flash of resoluteness or boredom? The notion is implausible, even if Heidegger himself does seem to believe that being itself does not "temporalize," that it does not withdraw behind the experience of Angst in the same way that the tool-being of objects hides behind their luminous profiles. In short, what becomes visible in Angst is always being "as" being, *which is very different from being itself.* Nor does this do much credit to Angst in the first place, since being "as" being is present not only in anxiety, but *at all times.* Despite Heidegger's reputation as a skilled interpreter of ominous moods, he does very little to elucidate them at all in any strict philosophical sense, and only foists upon them his typically deep but raw insights into the as-structure.

Heidegger's ground essay recalls the way in which Dasein renders objects visible by "outstripping" them, transcending them as immediate forces and thereby casting them into tangible but shadowy outline. But the two poles of this transcendence are *permanently incommensurable* with one another. To take an example, if we explicitly study a broken piece of wire that was functioning invisibly just a few moments ago, this is still not enough to bring the previous tool-being of the wire into view (an impossible hope). The wire in its executant reality and the piece of wire now lying openly before us could hardly have less in common. While the broken wire-piece has a shape and a color, a definite weight, and a specific angular profile, the wire as tool-being could not possibly have *any* such traits. For it is nothing but the concealed center of some indeterminate kind of being, the headquarters of a certain real entity. Yes, it might be defined or described *ad nauseum*, but all such description belongs to an utterly different plane of reality from that at which it aims. The wire will always exceed any such descriptions. Even if there were an *infinite* number of such descriptions in the mind of God, these would not be able to stand in as the understudy for this piece of wire or replace it in its unique existence, its impact upon the world.

Admittedly, it is quite possible to undertake a full investigation into the failure of the wire, an inquiry which would presumably leave us better informed than we were at the start. But such detective work can never be characterized as a quantitative improvement in transcendence, as if we were somehow drawing "closer" to the thing in its being. Let's suppose that observer Abelard simply notices the broken wire, while observer Baker roughly identifies the specific kind of failure that has occurred, observer Celarent recognizes this failure as having a very special type, and observer Dolon goes so far as to formulate a revolutionary new electromagnetic theory to describe this event. Now, can it really be said that Dolon and Celarent are any "closer" to the tool-being of the wire than their less talented friends? By no means. Even here, the far-ranging theory of the scientist is only one objectification of the cryptic tool-system among others. In other words, the invisibility of the tool does not just mean that it happens to be unseen now and can be summoned before us at any moment we choose. Instead, whatever emerges into view in the successive "breakdowns" or theoretical elaborations of equipment lies at an *equally* unbridgeable distance from tool-being.

I do not make this claim in the name of a relativism that would liquidate all existing distinctions between beings, so that all interpretations of any entity become "equally true." Far from it. What is actually needed is the opposite—a more overwhelming survey of the differences between objects and perception than has ever been known. But to this end, we need a very different understanding of theory than the one that would like to use "unveiling" as its meal ticket.

From this brief detour into the impossibility of full transcendence, two conclusions can be drawn. Conclusion Number One: it is *not true* that the relation between visible tool and concealed tool-being is one of negation. The observer does not stand beyond the things, seeing them for what they really are, as if thanks to a background of nothingness against which they might be impeccably contrasted. Even in the midst of the most intense theoretical labor, the tool-being of the things continues to work upon us no less than it ever did. Most importantly for the present book, this must be true even of Angst, which is supposedly the experience of being as a whole. In Angst, we do not actually stand *beyond* being so as to encounter it directly in the flesh. Rather, we encounter nothing more and nothing less than being *as* being. But we do this to precisely the same degree in *all* comportments. Being itself, just like rock-being and moon-being, necessarily exceeds any encounter we might have with it, untouched and untouchable by the as-structure. In this way, the key problem for Heidegger is no different from what it always is: the relation between the realm of the as-structure and that of the tool. We can call this relation "transcendence" if we wish, but to regard it as any form of "nihilation" is to neglect the fact that tool-being cannot be halted in its tracks simply by making it visible. To bring the hammer to light is not to negate it. The hammer continues to sustain its hammer-effect, no matter how obtrusively analyzed or how directly perceived it might be in any specific case. In short, to engage in ever more explicit encounters with specific objects (or even with being itself) does not entail *negating* or *rising beyond* the cryptic tool-being of these things.

Conclusion Number Two: it follows as a corollary that truth cannot possibly be regarded as *aletheia*. To speak the truth of something cannot be to unveil it, since this would imply that the being of the thing *really can be unveiled*, or given some sort of representation. The problem remains even if we confess up front, as Heidegger always does, that the being of the thing can never *really* be brought into view, that there will always be *some* unthematized residue behind any apparition of the tool. It is not enough to say that reality itself can never be exhausted by any "adequation" in the mind; it's too easy to score points in this way, given the current unpopularity of correspondence theories of truth. It must *also* be said that we cannot even approach the reality of the things by way of gradations. As the privative formation of *a-letheia* indicates, Heidegger's theory of truth is closely bound up with his reading of transcendence as nihilation, and is thus every bit as inadequate as his theory of transcendence.

But if truth cannot be regarded as an outstripping or transcendence of the things, then what is it? If truth is not an unveiling, then it must be a sort of *unlocking* of beings, one that does not "reveal" them in the strict sense. How this unlocking might occur is anything but clear. What should already be clear is the dissatisfying character of Heidegger's famous theory of truth as unveiling.

The resulting status of Angst is also somewhat disappointing: this fundamental mood has been pushed yet another step further from being itself, since the interplay between being and being *as* being turns out to have no need for Heidegger's exemplary moods. *All* comportment is pervaded by this interplay. The relation between being experienced *as* being (e.g., in Angst) and being itself has precisely the same bond of *simulation* that marks the link between any *specific* object and its own being. As a result, Angst has no special status in connection with the as-structure. Anxiety must lose the pampered position it enjoys in Heidegger's writings, and be thrown back into the chaotic democracy of moods, tinged with the same triple structure that defines *all* behavior toward beings. Angst is no different from any other attunement: it is *gestiftet* or fabricated, forced to come to birth *within* the fourfold skeleton of the world rather than offering us any unique adventure outside of it. The same holds true for the related mood of being-towards-death, whose treatment by Heidegger is closely related to the treatment given to Angst.

This final section of chapter 1 now draws to a close.[134] My purpose here was to show that for Heidegger, the as-structure is broken up into two distinct modes: (1) the specific character of any comportment (its encounter with this or that set of distinct objects); (2) its actuality plain and simple (the sheer fact of its simple existence, no matter what traits it might possess). I have argued that both of these modes can be found at *all* times, in all perception and in every possible mood. It is a further ubiquitous dualism about which Angst has nothing special to teach us. Whether this new duality is decisively important or nothing but a pedantic triviality can only be determined by whether Heidegger's fourfold proves to be philosophically useful for those of us who are still alive today.

The next chapter will consolidate what has already been learned about tool-being, by testing the strength of this concept against the vastly different concerns of mainstream Heidegger scholarship. With the reader having been further oriented in this way, the third and final chapter will press forward into fresh territory. Already, we have seen that the depth of Heidegger's tool-analysis is matched only by its startling austerity. But it may be that with this anchoring of ontology in a single ascetic dualism, thousands of gods are released into the woods, unnoticed.

Chapter Two

Between Being and Time

Why does being get 'conceived' 'proximally' in terms of the present-at-hand and not in terms of the ready-to-hand, which indeed lies closer to us?

—MARTIN HEIDEGGER,
from the final page of *Being and Time*

§10. Concerning *Poiesis, Praxis*

Sheer number, says Duns Scotus, does not have unity and determinacy through mere accumulation, as in a pile of stones. (Heidegger, 1915)[1]

The initial claim of this book was that the key to a fresh interpretation of Heidegger's thought lies in his famous but underestimated theory of equipment. I have argued that this theory has a far broader scope than is commonly believed; it cannot possibly be limited, as is often imagined, to the human use of carpenters' and plumbers' gear. In chapter 1 I argued that the tool-analysis already pushes us much further than this, even while restricting our philosophical activities to the confines of a single recurring dualism between tool and broken tool. As a result, we are poised to enter still further into the implications of this theme. But in the interest of consolidating what has already been gained, I propose a pause of one full chapter, so as to contrast the central claims of this book with those of some of the better-known figures in Heidegger studies. In addition to preparing the reader more fully for the unorthodox speculations of my final chapter, I hope that this survey of the secondary literature will demonstrate what is lacking in the current approaches to Heidegger, so that my own more speculative strategy will not seem like a pointless gamble. By the end of this chapter, it should be clear why I am happy to take full responsibility for pushing Heidegger in a highly surprising direction.

The best place to start is with a discussion of human Dasein, the dominant concept in most interpretations of Heidegger's best-known book. Against my claim that tool-being marks his central discovery, it is often objected that the tool is really only one passing example among others, a fleeting scenario designed only to illuminate the most fundamental structures of human being. What is always at stake, the critics say, is Dasein itself: Dasein in its practical life. The silent assumption underlying this view is the strange notion that objects themselves are nothing but a simple pile of dull material blocks, like the stones mentioned in the epigraph to this section. As Heidegger himself seems to suggest, it is only with the human *use* of these dead masses that any ambiguity arises; only then are these torpid clods of atoms swept up into a fascinating existential drama, a People's Republic of Ontology. *Being and Time* would thus amount to a kind of especially profound human autobiography, the heartwarming story of Dasein superimposing a grid of human transcendence and temporality onto a colorless plateau of drowsy physical bulks.

In my view, this widespread interpretation abandons everything that is revolutionary in Heidegger. It lacks the courage to venture beyond the details of Heidegger's own self-assessment, which already displays mixed or even contradictory aspects in the texts themselves. For the apparently over-

whelming role of human Dasein in Heidegger's most famous book are easily countered by even more frequent statements that it is *being* that interests Heidegger rather than narrowly *human* being. The usual method of
removing this tension is to locate it in the movement of Heidegger's own
curriculum vita, as if focusing on an evolution between "early" and "late"
career were the best way to hash out the details of a supposed man-
being/being-man reversal. But whatever the shifting opinions of Martin
Heidegger may have been at various dates in the past century, this must
remain a secondary theme for any commentary other than the purely
philological kind. The important thing is not what the author tells us about
his book *Being and Time*, but rather the new reality that this book helps to
reveal. Heidegger's philosophy, like any other, is poorly understood if we
regard it primarily as a series of inner meditations to which he himself
would have exclusive access. If Heidegger is an unusually *interesting* expert
witness on the meaning of his discoveries, he is by no means an infallible
one. As mentioned in the introduction, we cannot assume that Heidegger
foresaw every implication of tool-being, any more than we can expect
Luther to have predicted the Thirty Years' War that his reforms would one
day unleash.

My central dispute with mainstream Heidegger studies may have been
evident to some readers even in the preceding chapter. My argument has
always been that Heidegger's discovery of equipment presses us toward a
philosophy of objects themselves, rather than to any theory of human
praxis or philosophy of language. Luckily, to base one's reading of
Heidegger on tool-being already means that one is not abandoned to
monastic solitude—some of the most influential analytic and continental
interpretations of Heidegger have long been converging on precisely this
point. The analytic group is perhaps typified by Richard Rorty, Hubert
Dreyfus, Mark Okrent, and the rising star Robert Brandom, who see in
Heidegger's equipment the gateway to something resembling pragmatism.
An analogous group of continental readers, while presumably uneasy about
this analytic trend, have far more in common with the pragmatists than
they realize. These authors, among them Robert Bernasconi, Jacques
Taminiaux, and Franco Volpi, might roughly be termed the "Aristotelo-
Heideggerians," given their assertion of a strong link between Heidegger's
tool-analysis and Aristotle's *poiesis/praxis* distinction. While quick to insist
that Heidegger focuses on the use of tools only in order to pass on to the
more fundamental themes of "time" or "freedom," this latter group
heartily endorses the central assumption of the pragmatists: the very notion
that tool-being is a matter of human praxis.

In this way, both camps reinforce one of the leading traits of most
forms of contemporary philosophy, analytic and continental alike: a deep
suspicion of any attempt to philosophize about anything beyond the pale

of human experience. While anchored reasonably enough in Kant's Copernican Revolution, this assumption has gradually taken on the character of an invisible dogma, to the point where present-day philosophy is beginning to suffocate from it. Why is nobody tired of being frozen in place on Kant's petrifying landscape? The reason is simple: many people have convinced themselves that a major revolution is already afoot, one that replaces the notion of an aloof Cartesian consciousness with a form of human being that is enmeshed in linguistic signs and practical contexts. But the supposed transition from philosophy of consciousness to pragmatism or philosophy of language is not enough; neither is the parallel continental shift from phenomenology to hermeneutics. These supposed paradigm shifts are really only changes of residence within the same neighborhood. To congratulate Heidegger for passing beyond the "foundationalism" of *Being and Time* (as is done, for instance, by the otherwise unlikely pair of Rorty and Taminiaux) is only to salute the replacement of a lucid intuiting subject by a Dasein irreducibly entangled in its shadowy context. And this is not enough.

As radical as this change may seem, philosophy continues to renounce all claims on the world of rocks, stars, and trees, except insofar as these are treated as linguistic utterances, semiotic tokens, objects of practical manipulation, loci of human power, or flowery literary figures for otherwise formalistic insights. Philosophers are so worried by the possible encroachments of physics or cognitive sciences on their domain that they have locked themselves away in a linguistic-pragmatic ghetto, afraid to fight for philosophy's eternal homeland—reality itself. The guerilla metaphysics that emerges from Heidegger's tool-analysis aims to liberate this homeland as quickly as possible. But that is a subject for chapter 3. The present chapter will only prepare the way through a survey of some of the major figures in the secondary literature.

In some respects, it is hard to disagree with the reading of the continental group. The deep influence of Aristotle on Heidegger's education is beyond dispute, and presumably our awareness of this influence will continue to grow as additional documents surface from the archive in Marbach. Perhaps even more importantly, prolonged contact with Aristotle is perhaps *the* time-honored recipe for deepening one's own philosophical speculation—as shown in the striking cases of Ibn Sina, Aquinas, Leibniz, and Hegel, as well as in the humbler biographies of many present-day figures. Even so, it is never enough to note a link of influence between two philosophers. The key problem always lies in finding the most effective *point* of intersection between whatever thinkers are being considered. And it is on this decisive point where the Aristotelian reading of Heidegger is unconvincing, and even turns out to have very little to do with Aristotle at all. The existing analogies between the

Nicomachean Ethics and *Being and Time* fail to do justice to Heidegger's discoveries. Above all else, such comparisons are grievously weakened by the fact that tool-being has no special relation to human productive activity at all. The growing prestige of the scholarship linking Heidegger to the *Nicomachean Ethics* is built on sand, since it owes its existence to an overly literal and overly narrow interpretation of tool-being.

For reasons of brevity, I have chosen to confine the present discussion to Bernasconi's influential article on the link between Heidegger and the *poiesis/praxis* distinction.[2] The lengthier arguments of Taminiaux and Volpi require more work to place the meaning of their claims in context, and for this reason I will not address them in this section.[3] As might be expected from the sober and clear-headed Bernasconi, the point of his article is stated openly at the outset. As he sees it, Heidegger's concept of equipment cannot be read simply as an innovative phenomenological description. Nor can it be thought that Heidegger means to *reverse* the traditional priority of presence-at-hand, as if he were offering a more primordial "readiness-to-hand" to replace it. Instead, the theme of the tool can be understood only by approaching it historically. More specifically, it is necessary to interpret Heideggerian tool-being with one eye fixed on Aristotle. On the whole, Bernasconi's article is serious and well-focused. Even so, for the reasons outlined above, it is necessary to reject his starting point no less than his conclusions.

Bernasconi gets off to an excellent start, quickly evoking the futility of any attempt to define presence-at-hand and readiness-to-hand as mutually isolated realms. The relation between these two dimensions is not one of two independent domains sitting side by side, but is rather that of an "exchange of presence."[4] Tool and broken tool are caught up in a metabolic reversal. They are inseparable poles that never refer to discrete ontic families of objects. This insight can hardly be contested. But just one page earlier in his article, Bernasconi had already managed to neglect the real power of this "exchange." There, he criticized the frequent assumption that readiness-to-hand is meant as a replacement for the traditional privilege of presence and intuition: "in referring *Vorhandenheit* to *Zuhandenheit* Heidegger does not attempt to offer an alternative foundation for ontology. It is not the task of so-called fundamental ontology to offer a rival thesis to that which has been maintained by the tradition."[5] In support of this claim, Bernasconi offers two pieces of evidence, neither of them convincing.

(1) Bernasconi reminds us of Heidegger's warning not to attempt to derive everything from a single primordial ground. But in this respect, the passage Bernasconi cites in his own favor (from page 170 of *Being and Time*) is not a good one. In the passage in question, Heidegger tells us that the phenomenon of "being-in" is not to be derived from some other term,

not explained away via some sort of "solution." But it is hard to see how this warning can cast suspicion on readiness-to-hand. Whatever Bernasconi might say, the method of grounding is employed in *Being and Time* almost *constantly*, far more frequently than I myself would wish. Throughout that work, one term after another appears at first to be fundamental to the analysis, only to be unmasked a few pages later as dependent on the deeper strata of "care" or "transcendence" or "time." While I have argued against this method for other reasons, there is certainly nothing wrong with singling out certain explanatory terms as being more fundamental than others: no mainstream Heideggerian would have any problem, for instance, with saying that ecstatic temporality is more fundamental than pounding a piece of wood. When Heidegger unleashes his famous attack on grounds or foundations, this is obviously only meant to combat the "metaphysical" attempt to establish one kind of entity as a present-at-hand explanation for all others.

But by definition, tool-being cannot be a present-at-hand cause or ground of this kind. In fact, it is only by *introducing* the concept of tool-being that Heidegger ruptures the metaphysical notion of ground—only then does the dominance of presence-at-hand come under serious attack. In this sense, readiness-to-hand clearly *does* serve as a new foundation for ontology, as Heidegger's repeated diatribes against the tradition of *Vorhandenheit* show. Here, one senses that Bernasconi is already beginning to read tool-being once more in terms of practical physical gadgets, as if he were opposing the possible "metaphysical" claim that hammers and saws and bridges are more fundamental than theoretical comportment. Clearly, Heidegger would never want to replace the dominance of presence-at-hand with the dominance of wooden and metallic utensils. But just as clearly, his concept of tool-being *is* meant as an alternative to the history of metaphysics as presence. Just what this tool-being is remains the central puzzle of Heidegger's philosophy, but it is simply an error to jump the gun and identify it with construction equipment.

Furthermore, it is not even my claim that readiness-to-hand is introduced as a new basis for ontology, as if the realm of presence were reduced to the status of mere disposable illusion. Rather, the new ontology must be rooted in the *Umschlag* between tool and broken tool, the very "exchange of presence" that Bernasconi points to so aptly on his very next page. In short, the half-truth that Heidegger opposes "foundations" does nothing to alter the fundamental status of tool-being. Tool-being *is* a fundamental concept for Heidegger, which does not make it a "foundational" one at all.

(2) Bernasconi claims that Heidegger's *Zuhandenheit* cannot be intended as a radical challenge to Greek philosophy. For Heidegger himself tells us that "neither 'being' nor 'time' needs to give up its previous meaning, but it is true that a more original interpretation of their justification

and their limits must be established."[6] But to cite this remark as evidence is to mix two distinct senses of Greek philosophy in Heidegger's thought. On the one hand, there is Greek philosophy, a datable tradition that for Heidegger extends from Plato up through Medieval thought and possibly up to Husserl and beyond. On the other hand, there is "Greek philosophy," code name for a traditional privileging of vision, production, theoretical comportment, and presence-at-hand in general. There can be little doubt that this latter series of terms is one that Heidegger not only challenges, but simply *reviles*. The question of whether Heidegger believes that Plato and Aristotle are *reducible* to defenders of presence-at-hand is Heidegger's own business; we are not now obliged to take a position on this vast historical claim. What is decisive is that Heidegger has neither patience nor mercy for *Vorhandenheit*, which in his eyes deserves far rougher treatment than "a more original interpretation of [its] justification and [its] limits." I showed in chapter 1 that his philosophy makes sense only as a brutal *coup d'état* against presence-at-hand. Whatever it may be in the history of philosophy that Heidegger aims to "repeat" or "retrieve" (to use Bernasconi's words), it certainly cannot result in the retention of *Vorhandenheit* as an adequate concept of being. Precisely this concept is what Heidegger aims to *annihilate*—or better yet, *enslave*, by showing that it is forever bound to the "exchange of presence" between *Zu-* and *Vorhandenheit*.

In other words, the retrieval of the tradition that Bernasconi calls for can escape *blind* repetition only through a critique of presence-at-hand, the very engine that powers such a repetition in the first place. As Bernasconi would no doubt agree, the destruction of the history of ontology does not proceed by way of reading hundreds of canonical works and then drawing conclusions as to their fateful similarities. Rather, it is guided in advance by a central idea capable of illuminating key points or "failings" in the tradition it examines. There is little of the empirical in Heidegger's history of being; it owes its existence not primarily to library work, but to the intuition that *Vorhandenheit* is on shaky footing. And this intuition stems from the analysis of tool-being, not from philology.

So much for Bernasconi's two major objections to the ontological preeminence of the tool. There is also a third, which I reproduce here only because it surfaces repeatedly even among the best-informed Heideggerians. The objection stems from the well-known witticism in which Heidegger seems to poke fun at his own tool-analysis: "the existential analytic of everydayness does not want to describe how we use a knife and fork."[7] I have personally been ambushed with this objection on some half-dozen public occasions, and not always in a friendly and joking spirit. The main problem with this jest is that it proves most effective against a *pragmatist* reading of Heidegger, and not the kind offered in the present book—which has argued from the start that the tool-analysis is *not* about the human use of equipment! Granted that the point of the existential analytic is not to show how we use a knife and fork, what *is* the point? Until this question is answered, to cite Heidegger's remark is to do only half the work required.

And this is the point at which every form of *non sequitur* creeps in, among them Bernasconi's odd claim that Heidegger's insult against knives and forks means that only a historical approach to equipment is possible. His tacit syllogism runs roughly as follows: (1) the tool-analysis must be understood either phenomenologically or historically; (2) Heidegger's "knife and fork" remark subverts the phenomenological approach, and therefore, (3) we cannot understand tool-being except by way of Aristotle. The biggest problem with this logic is that Heidegger's jest does not attack the phenomenological approach to equipment, but the *ontic* approach, the assumption that the tool-analysis is about "tools" in the limited everyday sense. The reason the tool-analysis is not about how we use knives and forks is because it is about the *being* of these knives and forks. Between kitchen utensils on one side and Aristotle's *Ethics* on the other, there lies a decisive alternative overlooked by Bernasconi and others: the fundamental metabolism between readiness-to-hand and presence-at-hand, whether this occurs in the heart of knives, toys, apples, human beings, or time itself.

But all of this only shows that Bernasconi is unable to establish the superiority of a historical approach to equipment on *a priori* grounds. So far, he has been wrong that *Zuhandenheit* cannot serve as a new foundation for ontology, wrong to deny to this concept any critical force, and wrong to hold that Heidegger's "knife and fork" wisecrack undercuts the status of tool-being. This might also suggest that he is wrong in believing that appeals to the history of philosophy are the only way to understand equipment. But it may be unfair to hold Bernasconi's introductory remarks against him. Perhaps the only fair test of his claim is to examine his comparison of Heidegger with Aristotle and see whether it unearths anything of decisive importance for the tool-analysis. But Bernasconi is wrong here as well, and for reasons pertaining directly to the equipmental "phenomenology" he so quickly dismisses.

It is in Heidegger's 1924/25 *Sophist* lecture course that we find his most detailed discussion of *poiesis* and *praxis*. Here, *poiesis* is said to aim at an end that is distinct from its activity, while *praxis* is an end in itself. For now, let's set aside any doubts we might have about the possibility of directly translating Heideggerian concepts into Aristotelian terms. Let's assume for the sake of argument that this is unambiguously possible. The question now will only be whether it is done in the right way, or whether Heidegger's equipment is understood in an improper sense from the outset.

As Bernasconi sees it, Aristotle tries to subordinate *poiesis* to *praxis*, but stumbles in this effort insofar as he makes *praxis* the *hou heneka* of *poiesis*, that for the sake of which the *poiesis* occurs. As a result, the subordination that Aristotle desires is actually reversed. Converted into the distinct goal or terminus of a production, *praxis* ceases to be an end in itself.[8] According to Bernasconi, this insubordination of *poiesis* is one that Heidegger, unlike Aristotle, manages to avoid. This happens insofar as Heidegger's own "for-the-sake-of-which" is inverted with respect to Aristotle's *hou heneka*; it lies *prior* to everything that is understood, thereby undercutting any teleology that would turn it into a disposable present-at-hand product.[9] In this way, it is Heidegger who understands better than anyone else that *praxis* can never become present in its own right. Lying hidden from view, it comes to light only as a "trace."

All of this is convincing enough. The problem comes from Bernasconi's wish to identify equipment with *poiesis*, an identification explicitly rejected throughout chapter 1 of this book. On page 6 of Bernasconi's book, we read the following: "The account of equipmentality in *Being and Time* is not an account of production as such, but of our relation with things which have been produced." In fact, I have argued that it is neither of these. Bernasconi continues: "Nevertheless, these two are not so very different, given the way that our relation with what has been made exhibits the goals which already control production." Herein lies the cardinal error of his article, a mistake in which he is far from alone. Seduced by the ontic connotations of the word "equipment," Bernasconi imagines that hammers belong solely to the side of *poiesis*—after all, hammers are used to make things, and making is what *poiesis* is all about. The further implication (more explicit in Taminiaux's book) is that the neglected *praxis* is to be found on the side of human Dasein rather than that of tools.

But this is untenable. As we have seen often enough, readiness-to-hand has nothing to do with hand tools in the narrow sense, and therefore has no special relationship with productive activity. A hammer in action is certainly tool-being, but so are a fragrant meadow and an Attic temple. Moreover, insofar as a tool is a tool, it has no visible teleological surface—any *telos* already lies in the realm of what I have called "broken equipment." (It is precisely this concealed reality that Bernasconi implicitly wants to deny to the tools themselves, while fully ascribing it to the "Humans Only" structure of *hou heneka*.) The conclusion, while seemingly paradoxical, is inescapable: tool-being actually has less to do with *poiesis* than with *praxis*. If our goal were to interpret Heidegger in terms of the *Nicomachean Ethics*, this might be more effective if it were done in precisely the *opposite* way. But in fact, it is not my complaint that Bernasconi has it backwards. What I am really claiming is that *poiesis* and *praxis* are two dimensions of *every* entity, and thus cannot possibly be apportioned among distinct sorts of beings. On the one hand, both humans and screwdrivers recede into their concealed reality, existing as ends in themselves without ulterior finality. On the other hand, both come to explicit view, whether they have been "produced" or not (their causal origin is simply not the point).

The danger of overidentifying *Zuhandenheit* with some particular class of entities (namely, tinkerer's gear) is avoided more cleanly by John Sallis, who makes the following excellent point: "One could say, then, that in the strict sense everything is ready-to-hand; or, alternatively, that there is nothing purely present at hand. In what one might take as present-at-hand— that is, the hammer merely stared at—there is always something else operative yet repressed. . . ."[10] As the first part of this statement clearly implies, it is not only productive "tools" that are ready-to-hand, but everything under the sun. In fact, had Bernasconi only approached *Zuhandenheit* from this direction, he would never have been so skeptical about attempts to establish readiness-to-hand as a new foundation for ontology. But given his interpretation of tool-being as production, it is little wonder that he was so harsh at the beginning of his article: clearly, only a fool would assert that Heidegger wants to lionize *productive activity* as a new foundation for ontology. But this has nothing to do with the claim of the present book, since tool-being has nothing to do with productive activity, all etymology aside.

From here, Bernasconi goes on to describe a new relation between *theoria* and *poiesis*, and assigns tool-being to the latter domain. As he sees it, the consequences for Heidegger are momentous: "In finding support for [the priority of production] in the form of the priority of readiness to hand, Heidegger remains within the confines of Greek ontology."[11] Bernasconi's "distinction" here between production and theory serves only to cast a wider net. It amounts to saying: "certainly the use of hammers is vastly different from theory, but both are united as forms of presence-at-hand; therefore, *praxis* or *phronesis* are our only escape from the limits of Greek ontology." Just as Aristotle ends up granting priority to *poiesis* in spite of himself, so does Heidegger lapse into yielding top-dog status to productivity. According to Bernasconi and others, this mimics a similar event in the development of technology and that of metaphysics as a whole, both of which reduce reality to a presence-at-hand surface.

In short, Bernasconi believes that both terms of the opposition— *Vorhandenheit* and *Zuhandenheit*—belong on the side of presence, and that both must be opposed by *praxis/phronesis*. In support of this supposed brotherhood between ready-to-hand and present-at-hand, Bernasconi offers the fashionable but shaky etymological argument that both terms contain the word "hand," the organ which is traditionally regarded as the instrument of production.[12] My objection is simple enough. Bernasconi wants to say that tool-being is just one more concept living on the wrong side of the tracks: *Zuhandenheit* is production, production is teleology, teleology is presence-at-hand, and presence-at-hand is metaphysics. His mistake is no less clear than it is common—namely, the assumption that equipment means "productive device." And this is a mistake that cannot possibly be remedied by reading Aristotle, but only through minute attention to the phenomenology of equipment that Bernasconi disdains.

As an unfortunate side-effect of his mistaken interpretation of tool-being, Bernasconi feels compelled to move to the later Heidegger in his efforts to find anything like *praxis*. From this point forward in his article, he aims to show that through Heidegger's "dwelling" and Aristotle's *phronesis*, something is retrieved from beyond the zone of mere productive and theoretical activity. Beginning with the interesting suggestion that the terms "building, dwelling, thinking" are a translation of Aristotle's "productive, practical, theoretical,"[13] Bernasconi zeros in on "dwelling" (and to a lesser extent on "building") as a way to overcome the metaphysical residue that plagues both *theoria* and the traditional sense of production.

This seems feasible enough, even when he justifiably wonders whether Heidegger confuses thinking with dwelling in his infamous statement about overcoming homelessness.[14] But while Bernasconi accurately notes that technology's annihilation of the thing makes it analogous to *broken* equipment,[15] he fails to see the other side of the coin—namely, that the *praxis* that would elude the desolation of technicism is analogous to *unbroken* equipment, to tool-being. And if "building" (*poiesis*) is analogous to broken tool and "dwelling" (*praxis*) to tool, that would leave thinking (*theoria*) as the "between" that listens to what is granted in dwelling, and unveils it in the thoughtful word of the thinker. In other words, Bernasconi's building/dwelling/thinking schema, which he insists can be understood only by means of a historical comparison with Aristotle, actually has a cash value *identical* to that of Heidegger's familiar account of "temporality." And I have already argued that this temporal schema is really nothing more than a simple code word for the recurrent duel between tool and broken tool.

In other words, Bernasconi's appeal to the history of philosophy has only served to return us to Square One of the present book. On the one hand there is the domain in which entities are released into tangible presence ("building"), and on the other the opaque dimension of tool-being itself ("dwelling"). To describe this relation in further detail is the goal of this book; strangely enough, it sometimes appears to be Bernasconi's goal as well. What I disagree with in his approach is as follows: (1) The implicit retention of a human-centered standpoint. Nowhere does Bernasconi consider the possibility that what he terms *praxis* could belong to the things themselves. Throughout his article, it is clear that tool-being is regarded as the specific layer of human comportments, and not as the structure of reality itself. (2) His jabs at "phenomenological" description, with the corresponding assertion that the tool-analysis makes sense only within a historical analysis. I have already objected to this procedure in the case at hand, but it might be helpful to express my objection in more general terms.

Bernasconi's claim of priority for a historical approach seems to result from a typical misapplication of Heidegger's insights into the "historicity" of Dasein. True enough, it may be Heidegger more than all other philosophers who alerts us to our thrownness, our inevitable rootedness in a tradition. But this rootedness is an ontological structure of Dasein, present *everywhere and at all times,* completely independent of how deep or facile Dasein's grasp of the history of philosophy may be. The historicity of Dasein refers to *all* that withdraws from view in any situation, and grants no special license to those who wish to subordinate phenomenology to historical comparisons. My thrownness as an American certainly has plenty to do with Aristotle, but it has just as much to do with Gettysburg, gypsy moths, oxygen, and supermarkets. We find the same problem here as arose with the as-structure: history cannot serve as *both* a ubiquitous ontological structure *and* an exemplary *portion* of this structure. You cannot say "Dasein is always rooted in a tradition at any moment" and then also say "but anyone who retrieves Aristotle is *really, really* rooted in a tradition." The historicity of Dasein has no more to do with history than does tool-being with tools or "temporality" with time. But there is no point in blaming Bernasconi for thinking otherwise, since Heidegger himself seems strangely convinced that the practice of the history of philosophy has some *special* relationship with the ubiquitous historicity that characterizes all Dasein.

In general, the question of how much history to bring into philosophy is a far more *ad hoc* or *practical* question than Bernasconi believes. The importance of history for formulating any given philosophical problem can never be dictated *a priori;* like everything else that exists, the historical method must earn its living one battle at a time. The insight that Dasein is thrown into the world does not prove that philosophers must now make as many references to ancient classics as possible. Indeed, everything covered under Bernasconi's term "phenomenology" *also* belongs to thrownness, a term that applies to the concealed backsides of cola cans as much as it does to the *Nicomachean Ethics.* Perhaps we need to strike a better balance between phenomenological and historical approaches to Heidegger. But if so, it seems clear that the balance has already swung much too far to the side of the history of philosophy. The evidence is clear enough: thousands of books and articles are available that consider Heidegger's relation to various historical figures, but to my knowledge not a single book before the present one has been devoted solely to a patient exposition of all the stated and unstated consequences of tool-being.

It is possible, even *likely*, that Aristotle will continue to provide unparalleled inspiration for philosophers of the future. Even so, this process can never be any better than hit or miss. Millions of readers still unborn will someday master the *Ethics* and the *Metaphysics*, even in the original Greek, without being able to shed more than a conventional light on the issues described in those texts. Meanwhile, for every great philosopher steeped in the Archives of the West, there will be additional future cases like those of Husserl or Wittgenstein: figures who revolutionized philosophy despite significantly less historical knowledge than that of a solid graduate student.

While praising Bernasconi for the seriousness of his approach, I have also wanted to show that his impatient appeal to the history of philosophy leaves him trapped in a series of conventional prejudices regarding the meaning of Heidegger's "equipment." The supposed link between Heidegger's *Zuhandenheit* and Aristotle's *poiesis* is based entirely on a misreading of the tool-analysis. To interpret tool-being as practical production, and to look for the saving power of *praxis* only in human Dasein, is simply to follow Heidegger at his weakest—namely, in his rather traditional split between intraworldly entities and human *access* to these entities. There has never been a better case for continuing the phenomenology of tool-being in spite of every call for its dismissal.

§11. Not Pragmatism

Even for Idealism, the world is not mere representation...

The relation to life of the situation-I is no mere directedness toward mere objects. (Heidegger, 1919)[16]

Alongside the usual continental interpreters of Heidegger, there have appeared in recent years a growing number of analytic commentators. It would be hard to say which of these groups disdains the other more intensely ("you are sterile and lacking in subtlety, and ought to learn more foreign languages"; "yes, but you are fuzzy and precious, never make any arguments, and are also afraid of math"). Despite the tendency of these two groups of authors not to read each other's books, their basic similarities are overwhelming. Both groups have something to say about Heidegger's tool-analysis, and both regard it as primarily a human affair.

Bernasconi provided an excellent model of the continental approach, which in keeping with the historical spirit of this movement likes to trace Heidegger's tool-being back to a specific birthplace in ancient Greece. Likewise, following their own most typical instincts, the heirs of Anglo-American thought prefer to rework Heidegger's insights into a series of propositions and arguments, translating his notoriously difficult style into plain American English and "mainstream" philosophical terminology. This procedure usually leads to a familiar verdict: Heidegger is a pragmatist. While numerous authors seem to have reached this same assessment, the most systematic account of this reading is *Heidegger's Pragmatism*, by Mark Okrent. For reasons of space, I will have to focus on Okrent here, to the exclusion of Hubert Dreyfus' influential book *Being-in-the-World*, as well as assorted writings by Brandom, Haugeland, Blattner, and others.

For anyone concerned with the fate of Heidegger in the United States, the appearance of Okrent's admirable book in 1988 was a welcome event. As one of the founding heroes of continental philosophy in the English-speaking world, Heidegger has been the focus of decades' worth of intensive discussion. But in terms of institutional prestige and access to a large academic audience, continental Heideggerians remain in very bad shape, partly through their own shortcomings and partly through the analytic stranglehold on the top universities. The best way to remedy this situation is to cheer Heidegger's growing stature in analytic philosophy rather than making fun of it, and simply to have enough faith in reality to believe that the power of his work will transform whatever it touches. Put negatively, there is no good reason for my colleagues to sneer at those who describe Heidegger by means of unfamiliar terminology such as "nonmentalist" or "verificationist" (which is not to say that one actually ought to *adopt* such terminology).

For Okrent, the key to Heidegger's philosophy is the term "understanding," a term which his subtitle places on equal footing with "being." Laying out his argument with admirable clarity, Okrent begins by isolating three key premises of Heidegger's analytic of Dasein: (1) It is Dasein and only Dasein which "understands"; (2) Dasein *always* understands, since understanding is an omnipresent category rather than an ontic event that only occurs every now and then; (3) What Dasein primarily understands is its *own* being.[17] Despite my arguments so far against the priority of Dasein, Okrent can easily make a good case for all three of these points. Heidegger does say such things much of the time, perhaps *most* of the time. Even so, Premise 3 is already enough to lock Okrent into a set of assumptions that strip the tool-analysis of its true value.

According to this third premise, Dasein's great distinction is not just understanding, but the understanding *of itself*: "Dasein is distinguished from everything else not by its essential property but by its kind of being, existence; and existence consists in self-intending."[18] As he himself points out, such understanding or self-intending occurs *at all times*. As a result, self-understanding is obviously not a matter of introspection *as opposed to* those outgoing moments when we are fixated on the world of external things. Both scenarios would be cases of "self-understanding" to an equal degree. Thus, if I look at a hammer or a grassy field or the sun, these are all really forms of comportment toward myself. Okrent spells this out with a refreshingly concrete example of Dasein's comportment toward a car. To understand an object such as a car is not to have explicit knowledge about it, but to understand *how to use it*; this seems to follow directly from the priority of understanding over theoretical knowledge. But what about a case in which someone does not know how to use the car? Does this mean that they fail to intend the car altogether? Obviously not. From this puzzle, Okrent draws an unusual conclusion: "Heidegger doesn't claim that there can be no intentions directed toward a thing unless we understand *it*. Rather, he asserts that one can't intend oneself, *and that one can't intend anything else unless one understands oneself.*"[19]

But this is the wrong way to interpret the example now on the table. Okrent's supposed paradox of how someone can intend a car without understanding how to use it arises only because understanding is taken too specifically as "know-how," as a practical competence of the kind that the later Wittgenstein esteems so highly. It is only for *this* reason that the case of a mechanical ignoramus poses a momentary threat to Okrent's reading, and that he is forced to answer this threat with yet another variant of the erroneous Dasein-centered standpoint. If we imagine a fool who knows nothing about cars but is still somehow able to *see* a car, Okrent concludes that the necessary *savoir faire* must come from the fool's *self*-understanding. The mistake lies in assuming that Heidegger's "understanding" has anything to do with practical ability at all, when it is really far more general than this. *Verstehen* or *Verständnis* do not mean "knowing how to do something" as opposed to explicit theoretical knowledge. Instead, they refer only to the unthematic "being-with" that occurs in *every* moment for Dasein, an existing-alongside-the-car that is inevitable no matter *how* ignorant the observer may be. We might consider the limit-case of a human being locked in a permanent stupor, with no understanding of his self or of anything else. *Here too*, "understanding" is present. This term has no more applicability to situations of competence than to cases of the most deplorable ineptitude—it is an *ontological* term. Okrent seems to realize this, since he grasps better than others that understanding occurs *constantly* in Dasein. But since he interprets understanding as competence, and since we are often *incompetent* in our dealings with things, he is forced to claim that the only permanent source of understanding is our self-knowledge.

But if we simply abandon the definition of understanding as "competence" (and it *deserves* to be abandoned) the supposed difficulty immediately vanishes. And with it, Okrent's forced retreat into the competent self disappears. For there is no paradox at all in saying that the fool exists alongside the car or relies on its reality without knowing how to use it in any sense. If I walk along the ground, I already "understand" the ground, whether I am aware of it or not. The fact that the word "understanding" often connotes a sort of dim half-conscious awareness does not alter the fact that Heidegger's actual *use* of the term implies nothing of the kind. When Heidegger opposes implicit understanding to explicit interpretation, he does not thereby define it as know-how in opposition to theory. In a far broader way, he simply uses the term "understanding" to refer to that concealed layer of reality that underlies all conscious theory or conscious manipulation. But this has nothing to do with practical know-how: it is nothing human at all.

Indeed, we never know *what* it is exactly. This is precisely the point of the tool-analysis, since whatever lies behind theory partially withdraws from all of our attempts to clarify it. To define it as competence is to misread Heidegger as saying that practice is the root of theory, a proposal that does no justice to the dark underground being of hammers, apples, and volcanoes which exceeds any theoretical understanding, and *also* exceeds any pretheoretical *use*. Being is being, not "use." Whether we relate to objects theoretically or practically, in both cases we are *relating* to it, and this relating is something quite different from the tool-beings themselves.

Thus, from the moment we join Okrent in considering an example about the car and our human use of it, we have immediately entered the realm of presence-at-hand, and thereby completely misread tool-being. The subterranean reality of the car belongs on an utterly different plane from that of all use-value. In a Heideggerian context, it is certainly true that in any situation I have some understanding of *myself*, since every entity emerges into view only in accordance with my projection of that "for-the-sake-of-which" it appears. But this is no better than half of the story. For it is also true that such projection is a projection *of the car*, and not just of a driver-competence or mechanic-competence that would somehow be lodged in my Dasein.

Since this supposed priority of self-understanding serves as the foundation for the rest of Okrent's book, he is on thin ice from the start, and his remaining analyses suffer accordingly. This is emphasized when he repeats the usual assertion that no entity other than human Dasein escapes the sphere of presence-at-hand, as if the rest of the cosmos were nothing but joyless slabs of dismal matter: "what it is to have properties . . . is different for substances than it is for existing beings [i.e., Dasein]."[20] But in defense of Okrent, he backs up this claim with a clear citation. And true enough,

Heidegger does say quite often that Dasein alone escapes the dreary fate of vacuous substance. But I have argued that Heidegger must not be regarded as an absolute authority on such matters. In each case, the proper question is not "what did Heidegger think?" but "what does his analysis *require?*" There is nothing more presumptuous in this claim than in Heidegger's own violent historical readings (including his attempt to read Kant by way of the temporality of imagination, an emphasis Kant may well have ridiculed just as he dismissed Fichte with a wave of the hand[21]).

Okrent's consistent reliance on a limited notion of "understanding" should prompt us to look ahead to the consequences. We know that he regards competence as central: "to understand x (for example, a hammer) is primarily to understand how to do y with x (to hammer) or how to use x (to use x as a hammer)."[22] For Okrent, there is an unbreakable bond between this practical knowledge and knowledge of the self: "Self-understanding as purpose and practical understanding of the capabilities of things are just two sides of the same coin, a coin that consists in the ability to use things to bring about ends."[23] In the same vein, Okrent holds that "world" can only be understood by way of human "being-in-the-world,"[24] and it is the teleology of human purposes that defines the equipmental whole.[25] These are standard, respectable views among Heidegger scholars; there is certainly no trace of crankishness or whimsy about them. But they are based, as I have argued, on the faulty assumption that the tool-analysis is concerned with the human *use* of tools, with the tale of a competent human agent who grasps otherwise dead objects, jazzing them up with ambiguity by lifting them into a pragmatic gridwork of goals and wishes. Taking this reading of Heidegger at face value, he would be what is known as a "relativist."

But this relativism, says Okrent, is precisely what makes Heidegger a pragmatist. Or rather, he is a pragmatist only *half* the time—for here, we find another strange paradox. Heidegger is defined as a pragmatist insofar as he holds that there is no objective access to absolute things independent of us. The thing is always defined by many possible uses, and is therefore dependent upon my own self-understanding.[26] But there also seems to be something that escapes this "pragmatic" viewpoint. As Okrent puts it, Heidegger is not just a pragmatist, but a *transcendental* pragmatist.[27] For it is not the case that *everything* is capable of multiple interpretation and use. There is one exception: namely, the conditions of possibility of intentionality itself. In Okrent's view, this allows Heidegger to escape the usual pitfalls of transcendental thinking. By restricting his "conditions of possibility" to the immanent sphere of Dasein, Heidegger retains a multifaceted pragmatic view of the conditions of being and of particular beings. Old-style transcendental philosophizing will still hold good for inner, human reality. But it has been made safer through its state of house arrest in the Halls of Dasein; when it comes to objects in the world, or to being itself, these things must always appear in the light of perspective and interpretation.

But all of this requires several untenable assumptions. First, who says that I have an immediate, context-free and perspective-free understanding of *myself*? If my understanding of a popsicle or a zebra is inherently temporal, perspectival, based on a network of interpretations, the same is equally true of my understanding of myself as a concrete individual, and even of my understanding of the conditions of human being *as such*. Even Heidegger realizes this, as shown by his numerous analyses of moods. Self-understanding is not a magical cruise outside the temporal structure of the world; it too is temporal. Whereas Krell merely wants Angst to be an exception to this rule, Okrent wants to obtain a waiver for self-understanding as a whole. But it should be crystal clear that self-understanding is every bit as "temporal," every bit as determined by projection and concealment, as any of our dealings with hammers. The practice of psychotherapy would go bankrupt overnight if not for the often impenetrable fog through which all human introspection must pass.

But if Okrent is referring not just to self-understanding in a limited sense, but to the extremely *broad* form of this concept that appeared in his example of the car, then he is saying something he certainly does not want to say. For in that case he would not only be saying that we can grasp the transcendental conditions of our human selves as one part of the world among others. Instead, the very same transcendental permission slip would have to be granted to our understanding of the full run of hammers and cars and sidewalks, which Okrent seems to views as proxy cases of "self-understanding." Such a ballooning of the transcendental sphere, while not inconceivable, would not leave very much room for pragmatism. Hence, it seems clear that Okrent wants to restrict perspective-free transcendental knowledge to our knowledge of Dasein alone, Dasein in the limited sense of human entities. Pragmatic contextuality seems to be the name of the game when we try to understand entities, or even being itself.

For this reason, it comes as no surprise when Okrent concludes that the contrast between subjectivity and being disappears for Heidegger. Since the understanding of the world is irreducibly temporal, *everything* (with the strange exception of self-knowledge in the limited sense) can be understood only in terms of Dasein's purposive activity. All hope of a reality principle is doomed. As a result, Heidegger is termed a "verificationist." Roughly speaking, this means that he reduces any entity to the way in which that entity manifests itself to Dasein at any given set of moments. The supposed "things themselves" would not exceed the evidence we are able to obtain about them, and it would be naive to think that anything might be lying behind the veil of appearances. In other words, Heidegger would be a "pragmatic anti-realist."[28] This would mean that he regards being as nothing beyond all the various incarnations in which it is successively represented to humans. Being is never anything more than what we represent of it in some "purposive" way, which is always some configuration of presence-at-hand.

But in fact, there is nothing even remotely "verificationist" about the tool-analysis, an analysis which is absolute *poison* for any attempt to reduce entities to their current manifestation in the sphere of perception or purposive action. *In no way* does the description of the hammer reduce the hammer to what my self-competencies can tell me about it. Rather, it teaches us precisely the opposite lesson: namely, any tool-being is something vastly different from any of the simulacra of it that emerge into Dasein's view. If Heidegger really were a verificationist, his critique of presence-at-hand would simply be impossible. Both *Zu-* and *Vorhandenheit* would be subordinated to a general pragmatic realm in which nothing had any sort of reality outside of the transcendental conditions of our own intentionality. Objects would not have that dark, secluded power which the tool-analysis clearly grants them. Heidegger would not be Heidegger, but only an unnatural mating of Dewey with a vulgarized Descartes, giving birth to a kind of ghastly "instrumental solipsism." In short, far from *eliminating* the contrast between subjectivity and being, Heidegger *increases* their separation to the most astonishing degree ever known in the history of philosophy.

For Heidegger, there is certainly no simple objective world to which the mind can "adequate" with relative ease, but neither is there a subjective sphere for which the outside is irrelevant to the point of being nonexistent. Instead of these options, he gives us a world of visible broken equipment, which in its visibility is utterly incommensurable with the real effect of *equipment in action*. "Realism" will probably always be a loaded term that awakens dozens of misconceptions; for this reason, it should be avoided whenever possible. But if there were ever a philosopher who respected the force of a reality absolutely distinct from its conditions of being perceived, Martin Heidegger is that philosopher. At least classical realism believed that the things themselves could be adequately copied by human knowledge. But for Heidegger, no such adequation is possible, since the tools themselves forever elude any attempt to represent them in the flesh; the tool-analysis has no other result than this. And whereas Platonism made an equally absolute division between what is real and what is seen, it placed this division only at the single point where human meets nonhuman. But according to my interpretation of tool-being, Heidegger is forced to admit a similar unbridgeable gulf even into the causal interaction between inanimate things. The difference between things in themselves and any presentation of them is an ontological gap that haunts causality itself, and not just a predicament faced by human beings in their efforts to know the world.

In general, Okrent misses the point when he reads equipment in terms of human usefulness. This fateful misstep is what leads to his indefensible claim that the conditions of the self are transcendentally accessible in a way that other entities are not. As we have already seen, Okrent is not alone in viewing tool-being through the lens of a human bias. Given this bias, we can see why he follows Rorty's lead in questioning the uniqueness of Heidegger's achievement:[29] "With the possible exception of the emphasis on temporality, the principal doctrines of the early Heidegger concerning the primarily practical character of intentionality are hardly unique in the twentieth century. A whole series of philosophers, including John Dewey, the late Wittgenstein, and the contemporary American neo-pragmatists... have made very similar points."[30] True enough, with the possible exception of temporality, Heidegger may not be all that different from Dewey and the late Wittgenstein. But by the same token, with the possible exception of the emphasis on relativity, Einstein's universe is not all that different from Newton's. Although I do not wish to contribute further to continental philosophy's gross underestimation of Dewey, a perfectly interesting thinker, what Dewey misses with "temporality" makes up the very heart of Heidegger's uniqueness. The same is even more true of Wittgenstein, who lacks even Dewey's occasional cosmological bent. The question is only: "what exactly is implied by Heidegger's 'temporality'?" My answer, expressed earlier, is that it implies nothing other than the global reversal between tool and broken tool. And these terms cannot be taken as handy human devices, as the correlates of "know-how," but must be regarded as the two faces of beings themselves.

But at this point, I worry that some of my continental readers will be too harsh in their assessment of what Okrent is doing. There is an unfortunate tendency among Heideggerians to dismiss the pragmatist interpretation *even while repeating its central mistake.* One common criticism of the pragmatists runs as follows: "Heidegger is not interested in equipment as anything more than a means to describe 'transcendence'." Fair enough. But those who make this objection join the pragmatists in regarding transcendence as something specific to Dasein, rather than as an index of the duel at the heart of all human and nonhuman entities. An equally common remark has it that "the analysis of tools is only a way for Heidegger to arrive at temporality." But here too, ecstatic time is immediately interpreted as belonging *only to Dasein.* No differently from the analytic pragmatists, the dismissive continental anti-pragmatists base their entire interpretation of Heidegger on a supposed special distinctive status of Dasein. The only difference is that the continental Heideggerians show greater scorn for specific *cases* of practice, and are always quick to try to pass beyond the pragmatic trivialities of knives and forks into the deeper structures that make them possible. This sort of approach assumes that the best way to solve a philosophical problem is to disembody it, to remove it as far as possible from specific objects themselves. I have argued that precisely the opposite approach is required. Until this happens, even the continental readers who smirk at Okrent's terminology will themselves remain trapped in a "non-mentalist verificationist anti-realism." This phrase is as apt a description for the dominant views at SPEP and Perugia as it is for much Anglo-American philosophy of language.

An interesting alternative to these views is provided by the account of Heidegger developed by Dreyfus, which deserves to be mentioned briefly here. Given the surprising similarities between the continental readings of Heidegger via Aristotle's *poiesis* and the analytic interpretations of *Being and Time* as pragmatism, the realist vision of Dreyfus comes as a breath of fresh air. I will refer to an especially concise version of his reading found in his on-line article "Coping with Things in Themselves: Heidegger's Robust Realism." This article begins with a wonderfully clear statement of what Dreyfus opposes: "Science has long claimed to discover the relations among the natural kinds of the universe that exist independently of our minds or ways of coping. Today, most philosophers adopt an antirealism that consists in rejecting this thesis."[31] For the view that any reference to a world-in-itself independent of human access is "incoherent," Dreyfus uses the term "deflationary realism." Against this standpoint, Dreyfus proposes a "robust realism," and claims to find traces of it in Heidegger himself. Like Cristina Lafont, Dreyfus reads Heidegger against the background of the theory of direct reference developed by Kripke and others; unlike Lafont, he sees Heidegger as an *ally* of this theory.[32]

Against the Cartesian concept of the human subject as a lucid observer standing over against the world, Heidegger is famous for saying that Dasein exists *in* the world. Human being is always enmeshed in a network of things, people, institutions, customs, and values. Naturally, Heidegger is not alone in this view. As Dreyfus observes: "Both Heidegger and Donald Davidson, a leading antirealist, reject [the Cartesian] view and substitute for it an account of human beings as inextricably involved with things and people." This delightful parallel with Davidson, which would be scandalous for most continental philosophers if they were to learn of it, does have some convincing features. Since both Heidegger and Davidson regard meaning as inseparable from its total context, Dreyfus refers to both of them as "practical holists." According to deflationary realism, the inseparability of reality and context means that there is no coherent way to talk about things in themselves apart from human practices. By the same token, it is said, there is also no way to talk about these practices apart from the things. Deflationary realism claims to loathe both extremes, and believes that it has settled into a necessary middle ground that "repudiates both metaphysical realism and transcendental idealism." The alternative to realism and idealism is a focus on "ordinary practices" that makes no sweeping claims about the absolute status of the world.

In passing, I would like to say that deflationary realism occupies no middle ground whatsoever. To champion "ordinary practices" as the home terrain of philosophy is by no means to stay neutral in the debate between realism and its enemies. All the deflationary realist does is abandon the transcendental standpoint in favor of a holistic immersion in the world in which perspective is king, and no result ever absolute. Fair enough. But by quarantining the cosmos within a network of human significance, deflationary realism weighs in quite decisively on the side of idealism. If one insists that metaphysical realism is incoherent (because we cannot even *discuss* realism outside of language or outside our context of practices), then one is openly stating that philosophy can be concerned only with our *access* to things. And this is idealism pure and simple, whether "transcendental" or not. The same false neutral ground is occupied today by hermeneutics, which if it makes no sweeping idealistic claims about the cosmos, still focuses only on reality *qua* accessible to human interpreters. It is occupied by deconstruction, which even while snarling at the cliché that it "reduces everything to language" basically does *just that*, allowing for the minimal existence of traces from the otherworld, but still harnessing these traces within a theory of human meaning rather than letting them battle it out amongst themselves in the caverns below. It is occupied by the Lacanian standpoint of the brilliant Slavoj Žižek,[33] which considers itself beyond the old-time dispute over realism, but still views the real as something retroactively produced by the fantasy life of the subject. And above all, this false neutral ground is occupied by every form of dialectical philosophy, which tries to undercut any subterranean power of the things by calling this power an "essence," then claiming that essence is a naive abstraction unless it finds its proper place in the drama of human *knowledge* about the world. In short, the position that Dreyfus calls "deflationary realism" is really the central philosophical dogma of our time. In each of its forms, it continues to wring its hands over the single gap between humans and the world, even when it replaces the mighty Cartesian subject with a more troubled, ambiguous human. Deflationary realism is nothing more than idealism in less absolutist guise, and in this way it lacks even the illuminating courage of the extremist.

As Dreyfus admits, there are numerous vestiges of deflationary realism in the writings of Heidegger. Given Heidegger's commitment to the power of contexts and networks over present-at-hand things, there would seem to be little opening for him to talk about things *outside* of such contexts. But Dreyfus sees that there is another side to the coin: "as

I will now seek to show, in *Being and Time* Heidegger describes phenomena that enable him to distinguish between the everyday world and
the universe and so claim to be a robust realist about the entities discovered by natural science." His strategy is simple: by alerting us to
Heidegger's early concern with "formal indication" [*formales Anzeigen*],
Dreyfus reminds us that this philosopher held that we can *point* to the
things lying outside direct human awareness without being committed to
any particular *descriptions* of those things, descriptions which by definition can appear only *within* the human context. In this way, Heidegger's
"formal indication" is linked with Kripke's notion of a "rigid designator,"[34] in my opinion quite convincingly. Through our experiences of
what Dreyfus calls "the strange," science is able to gain a scent of what
lies beyond the human system of practices, and which from time to time
is capable of resisting or disrupting that system. Referring directly to the
world in this way, we become "robust realists."

All of this is quite fine. My objection is to Dreyfus' interpretation of
tool-being, which pushes us in precisely the wrong direction. Like all
readers of Heidegger, Dreyfus is charmed by the memorable figure of the
tool: "[Heidegger] points out that normally we deal with things as
equipment. Equipment gets its intelligibility from its relation to other
equipment, human roles, and social goals." From the start, Dreyfus forgets that equipment is what always *hides* from view and is *irreducible* to
any sort of presence, that it is no longer equipment as soon as it lies
explicitly before us. For this reason, it cannot possibly be identified with
contexts, roles, or social goals. Heidegger says only that the hammer is
not a piece of wood that has contexts and goals projected upon it *after
the fact*; he never says that it exists *only* in a context. The first mistake
made by Dreyfus lies in is his assumption that tool-being always exists
only in connection with humans. This explains his horrible mistranslation
of *Zuhandenheit* as "availability"; the problem is not the level of his
German ("availability" is not bad as a literal translation), but rather his
mistaken reading of equipment. Dreyfus would admit that we cannot
reduce the tool to whatever me might notice about it in any given
moment. This is the whole point of the analysis—equipment is a direct
challenge to every form of "verificationism." But the tool is equally irreducible to whatever *unconscious* use is being made of it at any given
moment. If we could total up all the "contexts, roles, and social goals"
in which a specific bridge or flagpole are currently embedded, this would
still not give us the being of these objects. In short, Dreyfus' biggest mistake is to think the difference between tool-being and the as-structure is
the difference between unconscious practices and explicit awareness. In
fact, tool-being goes far deeper than praxis, because even praxis does not
exhaust it.

Dreyfus inevitably makes a strange inversion in his reading of equipment. Once the tool is defined as "availability," presence-at-hand receives surprising praise as that which exists *independently* of all human contact: "we sometimes experience entities as independent of our instrumental coping practices. This happens in cases of equipmental breakdown. Heidegger calls the mode of being of entities so encountered, *occurrentness* [*Vorhandenheit*]." Since tool-being has been reduced to a matter of "instrumental coping practices," the only exit to the real world will be presence-at-hand. There are at least two forms of occurrentness for Dreyfus: "Occurrent beings are not only revealed in breakdown but also revealed when we take a detached attitude towards things that decontextualizes or—in Heidegger's terms—deworlds them. In this detached attitude, we encounter occurrent entities as substances with properties."

The mistake that Dreyfus makes is in large part Heidegger's fault, but is a mistake nonetheless. In defense of Dreyfus, it must be said that Heidegger *does* refer to the breakdown of the tool as a kind of "deworlding." This tends to give the impression that whereas tool-being belongs to the great world-context, occurrentness is what exists *apart* from that context. But this is simply not the case. If I have an explicit encounter with an entity, whether through breakdown or through my taking a distance from it, it cannot have any independence at all. Here am I, and here is the object. I have *objectified* it in a very specific way, "cutting it off at the knees," as the young Heidegger puts it. Occurrentness or presence-at-hand is not what *truly* exists in isolation from me, but only what falsely *seems* to be independent. Presence-at-hand refers to what is manifested in my *encounter* with a thing, not to its reality *prior* to that encounter. If I stare at a bridge, this bridge-appearance is a parasite off of my Dasein, and could hardly be less independent. If not for me, this appearance could not exist. What is truly independent of me is not the *occurrent* bridge, but the *executant* bridge, the bridge that is hard at work in enacting its own reality and all that this entails.

At the same time, as Dreyfus himself realizes, the bridge that I encounter in my unconscious "instrumental coping practices" is *also* not independent, since it is obviously a useful instrument only insofar as it belongs to an interlocking system of significance, with one tool gaining its meaning from all the rest. What Dreyfus and all other commentators (and perhaps Heidegger himself) have failed to grasp is the following: no real difference exists between theory, broken equipment, and practical "coping." There is no ontological fissure between conscious and unconscious human experience. When I encounter an object, I reduce its being to a small set of features out of all its grand, dark abundance—whether these features be theoretically observed or practically used. In both cases, my encounter with the object is *relational*, and does not touch what is independently *substantial* in the things. It does not touch that in the things which both resists my coping practices *and* eludes my attempts at theory.

And here is where Heidegger must be blamed for two sloppy abuses of terminology, both of which fuel understandable misreadings by Dreyfus and others: (1) Heidegger does sometimes seem to criticize presence-at-hand precisely for its claim to be independent of human contexts. For this reason, when he attacks the scientific concept of present-at-hand chunks of matter, he is taken by some to be a strong anti-realist, someone who denies the existence of entities outside of all holistic systems of meaning. But in truth, Heidegger is doing just the opposite. For him, the problem with presence-at-hand is not that it claims to exist outside of human contexts. The problem is that what exists outside of human contexts *does not have the mode of being of presence-at-hand.* Occurrentness falsely degrades the entity from a rumbling withdrawn action down to a single pale facade, and it does this through the inescapable fault of human beings: we cannot encounter another entity, whether consciously *or* unconsciously, without cutting it off at the knees, "de-living" it, transforming it from *Ereignis* into *Vorgang.* An entity becomes present-at-hand when we relate to it, *not* when it is independent of us. All of Dreyfus' examples of strange occurrentness are examples of situations *encountered by humans.* These cases, much like Kripke's "rigid designator," are able to *point* to the veiled underworld of objects, but they are never its equivalent. Certain things that happen within the zone of presence-at-hand may be able to *alert* us to a region of independence lying elsewhere, but they can never inhabit this region themselves. Dreyfus is simply wrong to define *Vorhandenheit* as independence from context. Quite the contrary.

(2) But Heidegger also makes the related and converse mistake: he also seems to identify *tool-being* with *world.* I won't deny it—whereas present-at-hand objects *seem* to exist as independent blocks of matter, tool-beings *seem* to emerge from a set of relations with other objects, discourses, practices, and goals. There is no point blaming Dreyfus for seeing it this way. Whereas the first case of sloppiness by Heidegger had to do only with misleading terminology, this second case arises from a basic ambiguity at the heart of his philosophy. On the one hand, equipment is said to withdraw from all human view; on the other, it is said to belong to a system of meaning that seems imbued with all kinds of human hopes, projects, and wishes. The usual way of resolving this ambiguity is the Dreyfus way—namely, to treat it as a distinction between explicit awareness (which grasps objects as *independent*) and unconscious practice (which relies on them as mutually *dependent*).

But in chapter 3 I will propose a bolder solution, one that pushes us in the direction of a full-blown object-oriented philosophy. The difference between tool and broken tool is not between unconscious and conscious, but between *substance and relation*. And if my perception of a bridge reduces its bridge-being to a mere caricature, the same is equally true for the pigeon that lands on it, the hailstones that strike it, and the military satellites that spy on it prior to a bombing. Yes, tool-beings withdraw *from each other* no less than they withdraw from us. This has fateful consequences for Heidegger, because it means that tool-being does not belong on the side of "world" at all. If world has to do with context, then it has to do with relation. And if world has to do with relation, then it is *sheer presence-at-hand*, no matter how "invisible" it may be. Whereas Heidegger tries to distinguish the occluded network of world from the sparkling arena of present-at-hand perception, these two domains turn out to be *ontologically equivalent*. Yes, the first is unconscious and the second is conscious, but this is of psychological rather than ontological interest. To repeat: Heidegger's concept of "world" belongs to *Vorhandenheit*, not *Zuhandenheit*.

But this means that the true nature of tool-being is somehow extra-worldly, or unearthly. And with this result, his analysis of equipment has pushed us yet another step in the direction of a speculative metaphysics.

§12. The Being in Phenomena

The appearance of the Antichrist is no mere transient happening . . . (Heidegger, 1920/21)[35]

The goal of the previous two sections was to reinforce my earlier claim that human Dasein is not an adequate starting point for the interpretation of tool-being. As already mentioned in chapter 1, the term "Dasein" has two related but *distinct* senses in Heidegger, senses which are often wrongly mixed: (1) Dasein is that entity whose essence consists solely in its existence; (2) Dasein is the entity with an understanding of its own being. It should be clear by now that the *first* sense of Dasein cannot be confined to humans. A chisel or a tree cannot be regarded as present-at-hand any more or any less than a person can. But in a strange unexpected way, even the *second* sense of Dasein turns out to hold good for all entities. For Dasein's understanding of its own being occurs only through the lens of the as-structure: it does not have direct contact with its own being, but can understand it only "as" this being. But the as-structure can be clarified only through an analysis of equipment, for unless it is regarded as emerging from a prior equipmental realm, the "as" will be viewed in the traditional way—as some sort of present-at-hand representation. For these reasons, the real action in Heidegger studies is not to be found in the concept of Dasein, but in the reversal between tool and "as," tool and broken tool, tool and space, being and time (all such pairings have proven to be completely synonymous).

In short, the theme of Dasein is subordinate to the analysis of tool-being rather than the reverse. But to repeat the warning sounded in §10, this does not mean that Dasein is subordinate to "knives and forks"—it means that the being of an entity makes sense only in terms of the general strife between its concealed execution and its luminous surface. The special features of human uniqueness not shared by birds and rocks, whatever these features may be, *have not yet come into play.* Heidegger's "fundamental ontology," widely regarded as an existential theory of Dasein, actually has nothing special to tell us about human reality at all.

In the present section, I intend to show that the question of being itself is dependent on the theory of tool-being. While this might sound like a colossal task, the arguments here are much the same as those that asserted the secondary status of human Dasein; accordingly, there will actually be *less* space required to prove the point than was needed in the previous case. The result of the brief analysis that follows can be stated in advance: *being itself is readiness-to-hand.* Although some conservative readers of Heidegger will regard this statement as ridiculous, this would be the case only if "equipment" were wrongly taken to mean useful hand-tools, which is no longer a serious option after all that has been said. In other words, I am *not* saying anything of the following kind: "I hereby salute being as the most useful of all tools. For without being, there would *be* no other tools; indeed, there would be nothing at all. Throughout the ages, being has served us well. May it long continue to do so." Obviously, this is not what is meant.

What *is* meant becomes clear through an examination of Heidegger's famous criticism of Husserl in the 1925 *History of the Concept of Time.* While often used as ammunition in a cruel campaign against the already beleaguered Husserlians, the passage in question is actually less dangerous for Husserl than for certain readings of *Heidegger.* For there is a continued tendency among Heideggerians to want to disembody the *Seinsfrage* beyond all reasonable limits. The question of being is widely abused in such a way as to try to one-up *any* specific philosophical question asked by anyone about anything at any time. It is employed as a permanent ace in the hole, or rather, its increasingly chic successor concepts are used in this way. For given the perplexing general consensus that *Being and Time* is still trapped in a "metaphysical standpoint," most readers of this type try to be more sophisticated and claim that it is not *being* that should be regarded as superior to any specific theme that might be raised, but rather *Ereignis,* or the granting of the "*es gibt,*" or some equally prestigious phantom. Instead of this procedure, what if we were to discuss all key Heideggerian concepts in the most tangible way, with almost *tactile* concreteness? To mystify "being," to make it always one step more clever than anything that can be said about it, is only to surrender the most potent forces of Heidegger's philosophy.

As already suggested, the 1925 lecture course is less interesting as a critique of Husserl than as the most illuminating discussion of being that Heidegger ever provides. For my purposes, Heidegger's argument can be rephrased in two simple steps: (1) the phenomenological model of consciousness is based on intentionality as a form of *representation*; (2) such a model cannot possibly address consciousness in its *being*. That is to say, Heidegger believes that Husserl ultimately regards both consciousness and the phenomena it intends as merely present-at-hand. Heidegger claims that this is an invalid procedure, that intentionality must have some mode of being other than that of representation. But here, his own human-centered bias subtly announces itself. For as we have seen, it is not only human intentionality that cannot be reduced to a representation. The same is true for this green ball that I throw, and that shiny mailbox directly in front of you. Objects themselves are not mere targets of human representing. For this reason, a "hermeneutic" criticism of Husserl is not what is really at stake, since any hermeneutic strategy only replaces the lucid observing *cogito* with a historically rooted, "thrown" Dasein. Whatever the supposed revolutionary importance of this shift, it still cedes a good portion of Heidegger's ontological gains, taking inanimate objects for nothing more than the pale accessories of a strictly human drama. In fact, the tool-analysis is already a full step further down the path than this, even if Heidegger does not seem to recognize the deeper tendency of his own breakthrough. *The critique of Husserl is a critique of presence-at-hand in general, and not just of the presence-at-hand of intentionality.* Although Heidegger confines his protest to the realm of human being, I hold that it can be extended to cover the full scope of the things themselves.[36]

One evening, no more or less self-absorbed than most people at most times, I take my habitual stroll down Oakley Avenue to buy a newspaper and a bottle of water. Trapped in that half-living state that benumbs most of our mortal hours, I continue with my earlier train of thought—wondering how to address the typical difficulties that have arisen during the day, looking forward to the routine or extraordinary pleasures of the hours to come, and perhaps drifting back through many years of memories. Even if these thoughts vacillate wildly, they unfold against the stable background of this street, which is familiar enough to me that I ignore it altogether. But suddenly, it occurs to me that everything has taken on an unusually magical cast, and the situation is revealed in all its detail. For this is no usual evening, and I have now grasped several important factors that had been conditioning my mood in a very unique way all along. Walking along in the gathering dusk, I had only vaguely noticed the harvest moon emerging from near the shore of the lake. Tonight this moon is of a very peculiar quality, bathing the city with a fiendish light: part halo and part funeral pyre. It suddenly occurs to me that a writer such as Proust would be able to describe the modulations of this moonlight at almost infinite length; the phenomenon is essentially inexhaustible.

But additional elements of the night also come quickly to mind. The faint music in the background, which I had lazily assumed to be coming from a passing car, is actually growing louder. It is soon recognizable as a popular song that debuted in the summer of 1988, one of the most memorable of my life. This fact had obviously been altering my mood for the better all these past minutes. Even so, the resulting good feelings are simultaneously dampened: for unfortunately enough, the song is coming from the apartment of a bitter neighborhood enemy, a foul-mouthed braggart whose pampered and vicious Doberman had once charged a favorite visiting cousin of mine. This also instantly brings to mind a memory of T. J. "Stonewall" Jackson, whom my cousin had been researching at the time; as a result, Jackson's eerie personality, while never the object of my explicit thoughts until now, had been silently unleashing strange feelings in the back of my mind all this time. Suddenly, I also notice that there are faintly perceptible ice crystals on the wind, and I am reminded that it is late October, a thought which puts everything in a new and refreshing light. Then, in a flash of insight, my vague mood of ill-defined surprise and relief is explained—two strange remarks made by separate acquaintances many weeks ago suddenly combine before the mind's eye, immediately explaining a bizarre series of events that had previously resisted all comprehension. In all of these ways, a situation that had seemed to be simple and integral had actually been saturated all along with the ferment of minor submoods and hazy intentions. In my typical human stupor, I had been alert to practically none of it, and had recognized only the single deadening errand of walking to the store.

Even if only a small number of our moments are as dramatic as this one, all are *at least* this complicated. In any experience, there are countless layers of background perceptions and muffled syllogisms that can gradually be unearthed—whether they be unnoticed sounds and colors and memories, or raw categorial structures. This insight is nothing less than *the fundamental contribution of phenomenology* (and in a somewhat different way, of psychoanalysis), though it is usually expressed in technical terminology of a kind that I have purposely avoided. Husserl's proverbial mailbox-analysis demonstrates above all that the mailbox is not a simple and obvious natural unit that accidentally happens to get colored by personal psychological bias. Rather, our perception of the mailbox is deeply woven into a tapestry of meanings and associations. Countless previously unknown facts about it can be elaborated by the patient observer ("we only see its front but *assume* that it has a back as well," "it reflects more light from the left than the right side," and so on).

In one sense, there seems to be no reason that Husserl could not have been the discoverer of Heidegger's tool-being. After all, Husserl is perhaps the greatest pioneer of those shadowy background realms of perception, those horizonal fringes that precede all explicit theoretical awareness. It is for this reason that Burt Hopkins[37] is justified in defending him against the excessively loud claims of Heidegger's originality, especially in an era when Husserl has become unjustly marginalized by the mainstream of continental thought, having been indicted as a member of the outlawed Cartesian Brotherhood. Nonetheless, my own claim is that there *is* something unique about Heidegger's tool-analysis, something that Husserl was in no position to discover for himself. However, the unique point has nothing to do with Heidegger's supposed "hermeneutic" revolution, an aspect of the Heideggerian philosophy that contains little to nothing not already found in Husserl (as Hopkins observes with moving vehemence).

In the meantime, my example of the moonlit evening on Oakley Avenue was meant as a simple reminder of how much phenomenological material is available in every instant. There is no limit to the possible number of analyses that can be performed, however bizarre or trivial. Whatever the subject matter, phenomenology functions by liberating the elements of a situation from the murky lived blend in which they are forever obscured. Countering our natural tendency to suppress the objects in our surroundings in favor of a vague and unified experience, phenomenology tries to step back from the "use" that obscures most objects most of the time. The light of the harvest moon, the memory of General Jackson—these are transformed from tacit environmental overtones into explicit perceptions easily "bracketed" and explored in as deep or flippant a manner as we wish.

This entire method is already marked by that passage from implicit to explicit, that absolute rootedness of the human observer in a *factical* situation that is often regarded as foreign to Husserl and his "philosophy of consciousness." By abstaining from direct engagement with a phenomenon, we should be able to bring it to some sort of presence, even if further unspoken aspects of it can always be added to our ongoing census of its properties. All in all, this sounds quite similar to the usual interpretation of *Heidegger*, who was of course steeped in his teacher's vision of the world for a full decade. Even so, it is on this question of implicit and explicit perception that Heidegger will try to fire his heaviest weaponry against the phenomenologists. For we know that in his view, phenomenology wrongly adopts *perception* as its basic model of reality: "Thus every act of directing oneself toward something receives the characteristic of knowing, for example, in Husserl, who describes the basic structure of all intentionality as

noesis . . ."[38] Indeed, Heidegger suggests that it may be Max Scheler alone
who has heralded Heidegger's own advances beyond this model of reality
as intuition.[39] For it is not only Husserl who is accused of privileging intuitive consciousness over any alternatives, but the philosophical tradition
as a whole: "Primordial and genuine truth lies in pure beholding. This thesis has remained the foundation of Western philosophy ever since
[Parmenides]."[40] Among dozens of other examples, Hegel is accused of
following this same timeworn path: "[Hegel's] argument, that to know the
limits is to be *beyond* them, has meaning only on the basis of the thesis that
the essence of the I is *consciousness. The fundamental question concerning
being itself is not posed at all.*"[41]

I deliberately italicize so much of this passage for the reason that it
repeats almost word-for-word Heidegger's attack on Husserlian intentionality. In both cases, consciousness or representation takes the blame for
covering up the question of being: "in the consideration of pure consciousness, merely the *what-content* is brought to the fore, without any
inquiry into the being of acts in the sense of their existence."[42] The real
problem with consciousness is that it is taken as a neutral container for representations, and both container and contained are regarded solely as
something present-at-hand: "The being of the intentional, the being of
acts, the being of the psychic is thus fixed as a real worldly occurrence just
like any natural process."[43] To repeat, Heidegger holds that phenomenology is undermined by its focus on the representational *content* of consciousness, a fixation that suppresses the theme of the *being* of Dasein and
of the phenomena—their "*Wie*" or *Vollzug* or action or reality.
Unfortunately, as is too often the case, he regards human Dasein as especially well-equipped to bail philosophy out of this situation: "But what if
there were an entity *whose 'what' is precisely to be and nothing but to be*, then
this ideative regard of such an entity would be the most fundamental misunderstanding."[44] As Heidegger sees it, Western philosophy has not yet
done justice to this special entity, Dasein: "the being of acts is in advance
theoretically and dogmatically defined by the sense of being which is taken
from the reality of nature. *The question of being itself is left undiscussed.*"[45]

My objection to Heidegger, of course, is that Dasein *does not* have any
special status with respect to this issue. I have argued repeatedly that it is
not only Dasein that should not be regarded as a "natural occurrence" in
the world—instead, *no* entity should be viewed primarily in this way. When
Heidegger says that human beings cannot be reduced to representational
content, but that wood and metal *can* be, he misses the full scope of what
his tool-analysis grants to the future of philosophy. For the analysis of
equipment should already have taught us something unexpected about
Husserl's mailbox: the point is not just that certain features of the mailbox
are visible to me on the basis of my private hopes and goals, while other

features are concealed and may someday be made visible with a bit of hard work. Rather, the point is that the mailbox itself is a subterranean creature. It is the performance of a reality that cannot be reduced to properties at all, no matter how many billions of them might eventually be enumerated. Let this serve as a *first* distinction between Husserl and the best tendencies of Heidegger, a distinction whose features will be elaborated only in chapter 3 below.

What Heidegger attacks in Husserl is his assumption that representations can ever tell the full story about the world, that to abstain from acting upon a thing and thereby to free it in its various categorial structures is already to reveal its being. But the problem with this view is different from what it is usually believed to be. It is not just that we can never exhaust the horizons of our awareness, and not just that we always confront the world from the stance of a particular historical project. A good case can be made that Husserl already knows this, even if he fails to emphasize it. What has really emerged from Heidegger's kitchen is a world that cannot even be *partially* brought to view, a world of *things* rather than of phenomena. True enough, these cannot be substantial things in the old sense: "It is *not things but references* which have the primary function in the structure of encounter belonging to the world, not *substances but functions*, to express this state of affairs by a formula of the '*Marburg School*'."[46] But by the same token, it is not acceptable to think of these references as something human, as if they were easily explained in terms of language or practical competence. The fact of the matter is that we never gain a direct view of these underground functions; as soon as we do, they have already been converted into something else, translated into a foreign tongue. The understandable fear of traditional substance theories is no excuse for claiming that everything in philosophy must be confined to the immanent human sphere.

The basic point of this discussion should be clear enough: Heidegger's famous critique of Husserl is nothing more than a critique of presence-at-hand. Heidegger tells us openly that Dasein can never be understood as the "representing animal." But by the same token, it is also true that no object can be understood as *something that Dasein represents*. Although Husserl is said to come up short on these questions, Heidegger offers a ringing final compliment to his teacher: "Phenomenological questioning in its innermost tendency itself leads to the question of the being of the intentional and before anything else to the question of being as such."[47] By discrediting the naturalist prejudice that objects are preexistent units that drift accidentally into conscious view, Husserl isolates them in no other mode than that of their intentional *givenness*.

It is here that we find Husserl's "tendency" to raise the question of being. The error of phenomenology would lie only in the additional assumption that intuitive *givenness* is the genuine being of entities. In this respect, Heidegger believes, phenomenology remains within a long tradition that interprets being only as simple presence: "*existentia* according to the tradition is tantamount to *being-present-at-hand.* . . ."[48] Against this tradition, we hear complaints of the following kind: "The 'that it is and has to be' which is disclosed in Dasein's state-of-mind is not the same 'that-it-is' which expresses ontologico-categorially the factuality belonging to presence-at-hand."[49] The strategic enemy of Heidegger's thought is always and everywhere *Vorhandenheit*, and nothing but *Vorhandenheit*.

This is a good moment to revive one of the more unorthodox claims from earlier in this book—namely, that the primary alternative to presence-at-hand is not human Dasein, but *tool-being itself*. The usual view is that *Vor-* and *Zuhandenheit*, as "intraworldly" terms, are merely two sides of the same coin. It is believed that both concepts refer only to entities, and that as a result they fall short of the true protagonist: human Dasein. Bernasconi believes it; Taminiaux believes it; Okrent believes it; many others believe it. The problem with this belief is that Dasein does not really stand outside the opposition between tool and broken tool, but oscillates between these two poles as much as any hammer ever did. On the one hand, Dasein executes [*vollzieht*] its own existence no less than drills and bridges do; its essence is nothing more than to exist, to exist as a factical reality. On the other hand, Dasein is just as present-at-hand as anything else, with its face and body and family name and register of good and evil deeds. This means that Dasein is no better than one entity among others, and therefore cannot provide the unique key to understanding those others. But unlike Dasein or birds or paper, presence-at-hand and readiness-to-hand are *not* specific entities among others, since tool-being is a universal mode of all entities rather than some sort of limited category of patented gadgets.

In sum, *Vor-* and *Zuhandenheit* are less "two sides of the same coin" than they are two mutually unexchangeable currencies. And these currencies are none other than those that circulate in Heidegger's famed "ontological difference." There is a big difference between being and beings, and that difference is *identical* to the difference between tool and broken tool. Readiness-to-hand is nothing less than *being itself*. This last statement will be jarring for many readers. To forestall any potential objections, I ask only that our everyday associations of the word "tool" be momentarily abandoned. This having been done, we can examine the properties ascribed by Heidegger to equipment, and ask whether they are any different from those he would ascribe to being itself: absolute unity, absolute totality, and absolute withdrawal from every inquiring glance. Note that there is no difference between the characteristics of the tool-system and those of being itself, at least for Heidegger (I will argue later that unity and totality *do not* really belong to being or to the tool-system). The proper-ties of *Sein* and those of tool-being are one and the same for Heidegger. Given the rather austere list of ontological traits that belong to both, it would make little sense to denounce my equation of being with tool-being as if I were reducing reality to a giant set of steel girders.

A more interesting objection would come from the following ques-tion: "if this is all you mean by 'tools,' then why focus on the tool-analy-sis at all?" The objection is relevant, but the answer is simple: it is only in the theory of equipment that Heidegger fully liberates us from the oppressive *junta* of human Dasein. Only the analysis of tool-being fully pushes us beyond the human sphere, pointing to an ontological fissure in the heart of all entities in the world, which are not mere gravel to be tram-pled upon by the sensitive ambiguities of Dasein. The drama of philoso-phy plays out in *all objects*, and not just in the human entity. If we interpret Heidegger by way of the analytic of Dasein, we are left thinking that only human *access* to the world ruptures the dominance of presence-at-hand. If we claim to find liberation in some "later" phase of Heidegger's career, in some supposed reversal in which being itself takes priority over human being, then we are still focused on nothing more than our own neighborhood dualism—the split between human being and the world. Only the theme of tool-being reverses the tide and sabotages the emphasis on Dasein from within. Otherwise, as mentioned already, we do nothing more than replace the old free-thinking transcendental subject with a pragmatically involved, linguistically determined, or "de-centered" subject, while still leaving the rest of the world in impenetrable mist. I insist that there is a pivotal ontological battle underway in every tiniest stick and mulberry tree, and only the tool-analysis allows us to approach this drama. Being *is* tool-being.

But all of this is Heidegger, and has nothing to do with Husserl. Let me say that I loathe the neglect into which Husserl has fallen in many camps of continental philosophy, and believe that there is a Husserl renais-sance yet to come. Nonetheless, I have been unconvinced by the usual attempts to show that Heidegger is only hijacking insights pioneered by Husserl himself. In addition to the interesting book by Hopkins (which I cannot discuss in more detail for reasons of space), the views of Rudolf Bernet have been influential among many defenders of Husserl. Although Hopkins seems to regard Bernet as a kind of Heideggerian Trojan Horse among the phenomenologists, I will discuss an article by Bernet that is hardly flattering to Heidegger's claim to have superseded his teacher. A brief summary of this article should be enough to establish two points: (1) Bernet is correct that Heidegger as he is *usually* understood is not all that different from Husserl; but (2) Heidegger *is* quite different from Husserl anyway, though for reasons other than those advanced by Bernet himself.

While there are several places to look for Bernet's intelligent account of
the being in phenomena, I will confine my attention to one relevant article.[50] Beginning with an account of Dasein's use of equipment, Bernet
draws a clear and legitimate parallel between Heidegger and Husserl, referring to the broken tool as a kind of revelatory 'reduction': "Exactly as in
Husserl and Fink, this first reduction, by making manifest the equipment's
intraworldly being in its relation to the being-in-the-world of concernful
Dasein, reveals the hidden being of the world and of Dasein, their difference and their bond."[51] In an equally convincing analogy, Bernet finds that
Heidegger also retains Husserl's *second* phenomenological reduction, the
stance in which the phenomenological spectator-subject views at a distance
the very *relation* between constituting subject and constituted world, quite
apart from what the specific intraworldly beings may be. For Heidegger,
this occurs in the experience of Angst: "Like the phenomenological reduction in Husserl and Fink, anxiety therefore sees to it that Dasein, when
confronting itself and alone with itself, meets for the first time not only a
new self, but also the phenomenon of its own authentic or proper
being."[52]
Here Bernet hints that, in spite of these similarities, it will turn out that
there are important differences between the two thinkers. We will soon see
what he believes these differences to be, but it is clear that he thinks they
have nothing to do with the tool-analysis:

> In *Being and Time* Heidegger develops and illustrates [the] Husserlian con-
> ception of natural life without adding much that is very new. Besides, the dis-
> tinction between things that manifest themselves as being ready-to-hand or as
> being present-at-hand was already sketched within the second book of
> [Husserl's] *Ideas*, whose manuscript Heidegger had consulted as early as
> 1925.[53]

This last statement shows a rare lapse in scholarship on Bernet's part:
the phrase "as early as 1925" could hardly be more irrelevant, since
Heidegger's first tool-analysis belongs not to *History of the Concept of
Time*, but to the 1919 Emergency War Semester. It is far more likely that
the influence went in the other direction. But forgetting about this for the
moment, we should take seriously Bernet's claim that the world of equipment can already be found in Husserl, and see what follows from this.
What follows most immediately is an identification of Heidegger's
Umwelt with Husserl's term "horizon": "As with 'horizon' in Husserl, this
environment is never taken into account for itself in the course of daily life,
even though it underlies and makes possible circumspective concern for
things."[54] For this reason, Bernet claims, Heidegger's originality cannot be
found in his "description of natural, daily, or ordinary life." But Bernet

makes an even bolder claim: Heidegger's originality cannot even be found in his posing of the question of being! For the *Seinsfrage*, he says, comes from the contrast between the being of the things within-the-world and that of the Dasein able to be concerned with them at all—a difference already found in Husserl's transcendental reduction. Whereas Heidegger was willing to concede that the question of being exists in Husserl as a "tendency," Bernet holds that the genuine item was already on the table.[55]

With Husserl having discovered so much already, one may wonder whether Bernet is willing to credit Heidegger with any breakthroughs at all. The answer is "yes." But the primary spark of innovation that Bernet concedes to Heidegger is not especially flattering: "If there is a radical difference between Heidegger and Husserl, then it involves . . . the phenomenological *access* to the disclosure of these different modes of being and their specific sense."[56] Although Bernet holds that a process of "reduction" can be found in both philosophers, there is a difference in the *attitude* by which this reduction takes place. For Husserl, the phenomenological spectator *wants* the reduction to happen, *wants* to rise above the everyday sphere to gain scientific insight into the constituted character of the phenomena. Quite the opposite for Heidegger, whose examples of reduction come less from theoretical activity than from the experience of malfunctioning equipment: "Far from wanting this reduction and its countless revelations, Dasein would much rather avoid having to undergo its unexpected occurrence again."[57]

In this way, Heidegger is converted by Bernet into Husserl's melancholic apprentice, a phenomenologist with less faith in the sciences than his teacher, but a more sensitive literary soul better attuned to the various malfunctions and failures that plague our lives. To phrase the problem in terms of "wanting" versus "not wanting" seems not only strange, but utterly untenable, since Heidegger's examples clearly do not *have* to be negative in character. Along with the unwanted trauma of a broken hammer, it can also happen that I lose a tooth in a car accident, suddenly curing a three-year migraine whose causes had previously been undiagnosed. But let's grant Bernet the apparently stronger case that if Husserl is *primarily* concerned with voluntary acts of bracketing the natural world, Heidegger focuses *mainly* on the involuntary situations in which this occurs. If the "involuntary" happens in the case of broken tools, it certainly happens all the more in Angst: "Whereas in the disturbance of usage, equipment alone loses its purposiveness and thus becomes 'unemployable', anxiety, on the contrary, brings about the collapse of all significance in the familiar world."[58]

Thus, Dasein is lodged in something of a double life, torn between *inauthentic* absorption in the tool-pieces of its world and the *authentic* moment of vision that is typical of anxiety. But this too, Bernet reminds us, is something that Husserl had already seen: "Phenomenological reduction, which makes Dasein's being manifest, presents it as torn between truth and untruth. . . . Dasein's life, *much like that of the transcendental subject*, is a life both in authenticity and in inauthenticity, in the care of the self and in the concern for the world."[59] And now, Bernet's distinction between "wanted" and "unwanted" reductions is drafted into service for an interesting final argument. Both Husserl and Heidegger point to the life of a divided human, torn between light and shadow. But for Husserl, there is always a *potentially* lucid representation lurking about:

> Regardless of whether the being of constituting consciousness, the being of the phenomenological spectator, or else the difference between the transcendental subject's two modes of being is at stake, their manifestation always consists in presenting themselves before the intentional gaze of a 'supervisor.'[60]

By contrast, Heidegger's Dasein is beyond hope of ever finding such a supervisor: "Regardless of whether it concerns the being of a tool, of the world, or of Dasein, the manifestation of being is inseparable from the way in which Dasein's existence is carried out."[61]

The argument is clear and appealing, but not at all convincing. Bernet begins by showing that Husserl and Heidegger both employ a reduction that disentangles objects from the natural attitude; in its different second form, such reduction allows the observer to step back from objects altogether. The only difference between the two thinkers turns out to be that whereas Husserl's consciousness is always a potentially luminous intentional agent, Dasein is always enmeshed in a world with hidden depth. It is interesting that in his concluding description of this difference between the two thinkers, Bernet explicitly stresses the example of the *second* reduction, in which the human observer observes *itself*. This is especially intriguing insofar as Bernet had denied any such difference in Husserl's and Heidegger's accounts of the environing world—that is, in the *first* reduction. In that case, Bernet apparently finds a close resemblance between the two thinkers, in spite of the fact that for Heidegger there is as much concealed depth to Dasein's perception of a hammer as to a perception of its own being. To repeat: why is it only in the *second* reduction that Bernet is willing to see a difference between the lucid transcendental subject and the Dasein haunted by a surplus of unknown residues?

Here as in the previous cases, I sense that we are dealing with a first-rate commentator who remains too infatuated with the "self," with the ontological preeminence of human entities over all others. As far as the *first* reduction goes, Bernet seems to think that Husserl and Heidegger might as well be the same person. Indeed, he goes so far as to make the ungenerous claim that Heidegger's tool-analysis is directly cribbed from

Husserl's *Ideas II*. But Bernet's account of the *second* reduction also does not go very far in drawing any distinctions between the teacher and his student. All talk of a "supervisor consciousness" aside, there is no reason to say that Husserl claims any more immediate access to the self than Heidegger does. Angst is indeed a "mood" rather than a dry philosophical act, but Heidegger at least *argues* that it is a very *special sort* of mood—one that is free from the usual concealment that plagues temporal Dasein. Anxiety is at least *supposed* to be every bit as exemplary as the knowledge gained by Husserl's transcendental super-observer. Angst too is supposed to provide Dasein with a vacation beyond the bounds of everyday horizons. Even so, Bernet holds that this supposed second reduction would provide both Husserl and Heidegger with a privileged outlook only on *human* being, and not the being of other objects. With this single stroke, Bernet's interpretation becomes surprisingly reminiscent of Okrent's, since the author of *Heidegger's Pragmatism* also holds that there is a duality between the knowable conditions of the transcendental self and the conditions of other entities. Bernet, too, can be said to read Heidegger as a "transcendental pragmatist," even if he would be likely to resist such terminology.

My conclusion is that the difference between Husserl and Heidegger cannot be seen in "hermeneutic" terms at all. It is not enough to say, as per custom, that Husserl's subject *knows* and Heidegger's Dasein *projects* or *interprets*. For as described in my example of the moonlit walk, even the Husserlian subject never succeeds in thematizing every last horizon in a situation. The argument could be made that Husserl's second reduction succeeds in doing this where the first reduction fails, but in that case the same thing could be said of Heidegger's Angst. If it turns out that anxiety never fully succeeds in transcending all of its horizons (which Heidegger unfortunately denies), this is true of the phenomenological reduction as well, as has been noted by critics of Husserl since Ortega y Gasset in 1912.[62]

As with any other comparison in the history of philosophy, we should not concern ourselves primarily with Husserl's and Heidegger's own stated opinions about their achievements. What must be done is to contrast what is *actually accomplished* in their respective writings. And when it comes to the supposed difference between the lucid voluntary consciousness and the thrown Dasein, it is hard to see as big a difference as most commentators see. As concerns the first reduction, both thinkers leave room for a hidden depth in the phenomena, even if Heidegger seems to emphasize this more. As concerns the second reduction, both *try* to speak of a privileged experience in which the world as a whole becomes visible, but both fail to make a convincing case. In sum, both Husserl and Heidegger describe the same double life of human being—partly standing in the light, partly enveloped by a dark horizon. Then contra Bernet, the difference between Husserl and Heidegger is precisely *not* to be found in their respective views of our "access" to reality. No, any differences must be found in their views on *reality itself.* But this means that the *first* reduction is a better place than the second to search for a contrast between Husserl and Heidegger. Turning our back on the recent dogma that only human being can rescue us from philosophic peril, we need to ask about the differences between Husserl and Heidegger as concerns the ontological status of pine cones or sand. This is by far the more revealing disagreement.

As mentioned previously, the so-called hermeneutic circle turns out to be a terrible place to look for Heidegger's innovation beyond Husserl. For we have seen that even in Husserl's case, consciousness intends its objects against a horizonal background of limitless shadow. Husserl realizes that in human beings we will always find the same inseparable mixture of light and dusk (just as the crusading Hopkins rightly insists). To be sure, Husserl usually sounds a more cheerful tone about the possibility of bringing the things themselves to view. But Heidegger too, at least in *Being and Time,* is often optimistic about the chances of a theoretical standpoint that would reveal the object just as it is, free from any projection based upon its usefulness. The irreducible interplay between light and darkness, then, never really changes for either philosopher, no matter how theoretical or how untheoretical we may be at any given moment. There is always an unsounded surplus in the things. Hence, the "hermeneutic" label cannot serve to distinguish the student from his teacher. There is nearly as much horizon in Husserl as there is historicity in Heidegger.

What *does* distinguish these thinkers is their views on the relation between the phenomenon and its very being. Put differently, the distinction between how Husserl and Heidegger regard the hammer has nothing at all to do with their respective modes of "access" to this hammer. The "access" is identical for both—one minute, I am using the hammer, the next minute it has become broken or obtrusive. Who cares if for Husserl this usually occurs voluntarily and for Heidegger involuntarily? If confronted with sudden ruptures and unforeseen breakdowns, Husserl would surely have been intelligent enough to perform phenomenological analyses of these events on the fly. By the same token, Heidegger's works are *packed* with references to the voluntary breakdown of tool-being: he calls it "theory."

The real difference between these philosophers can be stated clearly as follows. For Husserl, the relation between the appearance of the hammer and its still-unexhausted horizonal reality is only a relation of *two representations,* one of them currently in consciousness and the other *potentially* so, whether minutes or decades from now. For Heidegger, hammer and hammer-being are *not* both representations: *only the former* is something that can ever be intended. By contrast, he holds that the hammer-being is not just "withdrawn" (for even Husserl's horizons withdraw), but withdrawn into a *real effect* amidst the cosmos, as an autonomous reality unleashing its forces upon the world quite apart from any of Dasein's projections.

In other words, Husserl is interested in the things themselves *as potential targets of consciousness*, while Heidegger is interested in the things themselves *for themselves*. The "hermeneutic" reading of equipment, remaining as it does within the sphere of human reality, yields only a darker, historicized version of Husserl. The step beyond Husserlian phenomenology takes place not as a theory of unseen horizons, but as a theory of real equipment, tool-being in action. What turns out to be primary for Heidegger is not the hermeneutic structure of expression or language, but rather the hidden *infrastructure* of tool-being. The crucial difference between these will become clear once the nonhuman standpoint of this book receives more concrete development, which will occur in chapter 3.

But Bernet's article also points to a further interesting connection between Husserl and Heidegger, one that I have avoided mentioning until now. By explicitly linking Husserl's two primary reductions to Heidegger's intraworldly comportment and experience of Angst, Bernet links Husserl with my argument about the "quadrants of reality" at the end of chapter 1. For Husserl's two reductions, latter-day heirs of the essence/existence split, seem to be the direct source for the second axis of division in Heidegger. The first reduction frees up beings in their essence, as *something specific*, as described most clearly in "On the Essence of Ground." The second reduction reveals the entire field of consciousness as *something at all*, irrespective of its content, much like Heidegger's Angst. This second reduction gives us Heidegger's *nothingness* or *being*, depending on which of these reciprocal terms the reader prefers to emphasize. It could be said that the preface to "On the Essence of Ground," with its discussion of two differences that are the "same" without being "identical," is Heidegger's appropriation of the two famous Husserlian reductions. By doubling these two reductions, so that they hold good for the subterranean world of tool-being no less than for the visible world of phenomena, Heidegger generates a reality that is split into four modes. I mention this so as to give added historical weight to Heidegger's 1919 distinction between "something specific" and "something at all," a distinction otherwise more difficult to grasp than that between the tool and its breakdown.

§13. The Threefold

Substantiality means presence-at-hand, which as such is in need of no other entity. The reality of a *res*, the substantiality of a substance, the being of an entity, taken in a strict sense means presence-at-hand in the sense of not being in need of anything, not needing a producer. . . . (Heidegger, 1925)[63]

Before discussing the views of Bernet, I showed that Heidegger's critique of Husserl arises as a direct consequence of the tool-analysis. Heidegger's complaint about Husserl overlooking the question of being turns out to be, more generally, a slap at the presence-at-hand of phenomena and of the transcendental subject who intends them. But in Heidegger's works, the original and unsurpassable antidote to presence-at-hand is always nothing other than *Zuhandenheit*. The alternative to presence-at-hand is not to be found in the hermeneutic insight that Dasein is always thrown into a context, but in the withdrawn actuality of *the things themselves*. The attempt to distinguish between Heidegger and Husserl by contrasting interpretation with direct vision (a distinction that Bernet, like most readers, endorses) is only partly successful. I have suggested that if we take human being as the pivot-point of the issue, these two philosophers can be distinguished only in *relative* terms, only by pointing to a difference in emphasis and in tone. But this means that Heidegger's objections to intentionality make little sense if they are read only as a fifteen-round title bout between Subject and Dasein.

The real difference, I suggested, lies in these philosophers' respective views on the being of *the things*. For Husserl, the relation between tool and broken tool is never more than the relation between two successive representations: "View A," in which the hammer is present only in a tacit background, and "View B," in which the hammer has emerged from ground into figure. For Heidegger it is quite otherwise. He reads hammer-being *not* as a representation waiting to happen, but as a real being that supports or hinders both our own labors and the deeds of other objects. No mere horizonal fringe of Dasein's awareness, equipment is an autonomous province that could hardly care less about Dasein. Until this is realized, Heidegger's thought will continue to be interpreted as a philosophy about *people*, whether they be called subject, Dasein, or any other new alias that might emerge. Heidegger will be read simply as a hypercontextualized phenomenologist who still views rocks as dead matter, thereby ceding most of the pre-Socratic landscape to the heirs of Democritus. As Hopkins rightly implies, Heidegger would be little more than a romanticized double of Husserl; as Rorty openly asserts, he would be nothing but Dewey plus ten thousand pages of historical writings.[64] But neither of these views is correct. The full originality of the question of being appears as soon as we take our bearings from the things themselves. If for Husserl these are phenomena, for Heidegger they are *tool-beings*. For this reason, the question of being is best addressed by way of Heidegger's analysis of equipment.

But perhaps there are still other themes that might prove to be more important than equipment. One serious candidate would be the all-important concept of "time," which can be discussed more rapidly than one might think. In chapter 1, I argued that "time" in Heidegger has nothing to do with time; this word itself is already highly misleading, and causes needless confusion for generation after generation of young Heideggerians. In support of this claim, I offered the thought-experiment of a world in which time as we know it were suddenly to be stopped. Under these circumstances, every last feature of Heidegger's analysis of time still held good. I also noted the irrelevance of the usual response by Heideggerians, that ecstatic temporality can still be called "time" insofar as it is the *basis* for so-called vulgar clock-time. After all, Heidegger's temporality is the basis for *everything*: for space no less than time, theory no less than time, moods no less than time, hammers no less than time. This vast metaphor ("time") serves only as a trap for the reader; originary time could just as easily have been termed "originary mood" or "ecstatic *spatiality*" and the results would have been the same. In addition to all of this, I claimed that Heidegger's concept of temporality was already fully visible in the simplest analysis of the tool. Withdrawn into an unthematized background ("having-been"), the system of equipment gains its configuration from the observer encountering it ("futural projection"), thereby forming the ambivalent present.

The likely objection to this claim would be that this triplicity of tool-being is only a starting point, and that one must pass beyond these concepts into a series of increasingly deeper temporal conditions. Indeed, many interpreters claim that Heidegger's intellectual biography is *nothing but* such a passage. Starting from the tool-temporality of the mid-1920s, the deepening movement would run through the following stages: (1) the "ecstatic" temporality of *Being and Time*; (2) the "*Temporalität*" beyond "*Zeitlichkeit*," as discussed in the 1925/26 *Logik* course and *The Basic Problems of Phenomenology*; (3) the "*Zeit-Spiel-Raum*" of the 1936-38 *Beiträge zur Philosophie*; and (4) the "deepest" theory of them all, that of the celebrated "On Time and Being" in *Zur Sache des Denkens*. Rather than spend ninety pages covering this entire list, the present section will focus exclusively on Stage 1. The stages that follow only repeat this initial move while trying to one-up it by going even "deeper." If this strategy can be shown to fail in the first case, the burden of proof will have shifted to those who want to champion one of the later theories of time as being different from and superior to the others.

My claim that the ecstatic analysis does not significantly further Heidegger's earlier concept of time draws unexpected support from a commentary by Krell, who along with his unlikely bedfellow Kisiel is one of the more effective critics of the developmentalist approach to Heidegger. Attempting to retrace the stages of the time-concept as listed above, Krell suddenly has second thoughts:

Yet after reading the text of Heidegger's 1925 lecture course, "History of the Concept of Time," I wonder whether these attempts of mine are not misconceived. For in that lecture course much of what in *Being and Time* becomes the "preparatory fundamental analysis of Dasein" appears in fully developed form, while *nothing at all* of the analysis of ecstatic temporality appears there, not even the word *Ekstase*. Nevertheless, the temporal quality of Being in general is *already known*. . . .[65]

From this, Krell concludes that "the crucial problem is therefore not the movement from *Zeitlichkeit* to *Temporalität* but precisely the reverse; the crucial problem is the *original advance* in Heidegger's thought *from* the temporal quality of Being in general to the temporality of Dasein as revealed in *ecstatic analysis*."[66] This refreshing inversion echoes the commentator's preceding chapter, in which he makes short work of the usual cliché about Heidegger's golden path from *Dasein* in the early work to *being* in the late:

> Phrased more crudely, [it is held that] Heidegger's is a turn from Man to Being. Such a turn ostensibly accomplishes the move from mere ontic investigation (into Man) to ontological inquiry (into Being). It is essential that we loosen the grip such developmentalist theories of the "turn" have had on us. For the sake of such a loosening, let me propose a thesis: *If* there were a dramatic "turn" of this sort in Heidegger's career of thought . . . then it would be a turn, not from man to Being, but from the neutral designation *Da-sein* to *homo humanus*, to *der Mensch, die Sterblichen*; in other words, a turn from Being to Man. If the developmentalist theory of the "turn" is helpful at all, it is only because it speaks precisely contrary to the case.[67]

It would be difficult to improve on this formulation. Far from a limited meditation on human Dasein, *Being and Time* is already involved in a far wider adventure. It is only *later* that Heidegger might be able to offer a specific theory of human reality, and I contend that he never makes it very far down that road. But it is necessary to push the issue even further than Krell's two passages, both of which refer only to a gradual turn by Heidegger toward *human* being. For in my view, it is not just *der Mensch* that could be discussed for the first time only in Heidegger's reversal, but any *specific entities at all*. Like Krell, I hold that the *Kehre* is not a turn in Heidegger's career that can be dated on a calendar, but a turn that is already in play from the start. But whatever this turn may be, it is not simply one "from being to man," but more generally from "being to beings."

For the moment, however, my primary theme is "time." Whenever this word is mentioned, all kinds of connotations and biases easily drift into the mind. But the austere rigor of Heidegger's term "temporality" is more easily discerned if we focus on its impact in a specific situation. It is 1865, and Lincoln is gunned down in the theater. This is a fact, a reality that cannot be reversed and into which every contemporary Dasein is "thrown." But it is also not the *same* fact for everyone. For the typical Northerner, it is the tragic slaying of a visionary leader; for Mrs. Lincoln, a final personal blow destined to send her to the madhouse. For Booth and his co-conspirators, it is death to a tyrant—revenge is served. Although the attempt is often made to place "temporality" at a distance from all concrete examples, it is really nothing more than this very interplay of reality and projection. A specific hammer is regarded by one Dasein as just another hammer, while for others it is merchandise to be stolen or sold. For yet another Dasein, it is the precious *memento* of a deceased grandfather. Clearly, none of these examples have much to do with the time that ticks away on a clock. For this reason, the word "time" ought to be handled with a very light touch whenever newcomers to Heidegger are in the room; instead, Heideggerians seem to love brandishing this word.

But here is the first and final reality of Heidegger's "time": every situation is defined by a *pregiven* system of equipment, but only *as projected* by some individual Dasein. (In chapter 3, it will turn out that even inorganic beings "project.") This thorough duality of every situation, this interplay of equipment and observer, shadow and light, is the specific *chiaroscuro* of every moment. No abstruse terminology is needed to explain "time" in Heidegger's philosophy, which may well be the simplest concept of them all. Like the theme of equipment itself, "temporality" is designed only to shatter any notion of reality as present-at-hand. And this mission is already accomplished as soon as we point to the permanent dualism of: (a) the withdrawn and inescapable reality in which we are always tacitly stationed, and (b) the specific manner in which this reality appears to me, a specific Dasein.

We can now ask whether the "ecstatic" model of time adds anything to the account of the Lincoln assassination. As we can read in one of Heidegger's later musings on *Being and Time*, "time 'is' time insofar as it temporalizes itself ecstatically, and the unity of time is in each case an ecstatic unity."[68] In that book, this unity was regarded as the condition of possibility for a familiar triple set of terms: "Temporality makes possible the unity of existence, facticity, and falling, and in this way constitutes primordially the totality of the structure of care."[69] And further: "The phenomena of the 'towards . . .,' the 'to . . .,' and the 'alongside . . .,' make temporality manifest as the *ekstatikon* pure and simple. *Temporality is the primordial 'outside of itself' in and for itself.*"[70] Here, we encounter the two main features of ecstatic temporality: (1) ecstasis is inherently *outside* of itself; (2) ecstasis also serves as the unifying condition for at least one other triple manifold in Heidegger's writings (existence, facticity, and falling), with the strong implication that it is responsible for all the rest as well. But we must ask whether these two points add anything to what we already knew from the tool-analysis.

With respect to point 1, the answer is certainly no. The tool-analysis already showed that entities are stationed partly beyond their own presence (at least insofar as Dasein encounters them), suspended between a pole of obscurity and another of light. To say that ecstatic time is outside of itself is only to say that it is not present-at-hand. As Heidegger puts it: "[Temporality] is not, prior to this, an entity which first emerges from *itself*. . . ."[71] That is to say, time is not some independently extant reality that would relate to Dasein only after the fact. But this merely echoes what we already knew about hammers and other tool-beings, which were also not discrete, independent substances that entered into functional systems only accidentally. In Dasein's merest encounter with a hammer, the hammer is already outside of itself: it is not a pregiven wooden and metallic hulk, but is swept away into the contexture of meanings and projections.

Point 2 seems more decisive, but even here the uniqueness of the ecstatic analysis turns out not to be very strong. It is easy enough to say that the use of equipment depends on a deeper structure that makes it possible. But I already criticized this strategy in the earlier reference to a slumber party chant.[72] In that connection, it was pointed out that Heidegger cannot regard grounds as something *actually distinct* from that which they ground, since this would involve an ontic or even causal relation of the kind he despises. If care is the ground of concern, for instance, this obviously does not mean that there is something called care that mentally generates concern by means of neurotransmitters or psychological associations. The grounding relation between them can only mean that care is *already there*, in the heart of all concern, as its unthematized background reality. Analogously, if ecstatic time is the ground for our use of a hammer, this does not refer to any sort of remote and disembodied relation, as if ecstatic time were somehow *outside* of the hammer. Rather, it means that temporality permeates all such practical activity. In other words, time is not an *isolated* ground; it has no discrete existence in some place apart from particular objects or events.

Then the appeal to time does not cause entities to vanish from the scene, but is useful only insofar as it prevents their being treated as obvious, present-at-hand masses. *But the tool-analysis already does this.* As a result, anyone who gives the tool a fair hearing from the start will find the entire "grounding" aspect of *Being and Time* quite tedious ("On the dark, dark planet, there's a dark, dark nation . . .") Once our ontic prejudices about hammers have been jettisoned, there is nothing at all to distinguish the ecstatic rapture of Dasein from the simple shadowy reversal between wrench and broken wrench. To repeat what was said in chapter 1, there is no such creature in the universe as a "ground," but only being and beings. If Heidegger's claim that the use of tools is grounded in care or ecstatic time helps to disrupt the misunderstanding of tool-being as ontic hardware, so much the better. But once the discussion of grounding becomes a free-floating meditation, remote from the concreteness of the ontological difference itself, it does far more harm than good. It is important to remember that Heidegger's various ground/grounding discussions are possibly useful even when they refer to structures that are not actually distinct. When I stroll across a bridge, care is already there, time is already there, being is already there, and Ereignis is already there. I will never be able to approach these terms by abstracting from the bridge and my act of strolling. Each of these structures exists only in *concrete form*.

So much for the first two features that were supposedly unique to ecstatic time. But there is a third feature that is said to be unique to ecstatic temporality. For, at least at this stage, Heidegger seems to regard *one* of the three moments of ecstasis as dominant: "Temporality temporalizes itself primarily out of the future."[73] This famous claim has led to a wide-ranging debate on what the futural priority could mean, and whether Heidegger retains or abandons it in his later career. But now as always, I propose to ignore the question of Heidegger's development, and ask instead whether this dominance of the future has any discernible *effect* on the analysis of time. And I see only one such effect: namely, the continued flattery of the human entity as a philosophical superhero. The supposed priority of the future is not a true ontological priority, but has a merely rhetorical priority for Heidegger's own exposition. In this limited sense, as a *practical* strategy, arguing for a futural priority makes a great deal of sense. Heidegger's goal is to undermine presence-at-hand, and it would be strategically difficult to do this by beginning with the moments of present or past, both of which have the *connotations* of self-evident, preexistent objects available for subsequent use.

Accordingly, Heidegger's exposition needs to start from the most obviously volatile of the three temporal ecstases: the future, that free projection that openly subverts the presence-at-hand of entities by rapidly shifting them between different situations or viewing them in terms of different possibilities. But this does not mean that the future is *truly* more important than the past within the ecstatic regime. If numerical measures were in order here (and why not?), each of these ecstases would have to receive a round 50 percent of the glory. (The "present," I have argued, is nothing more than the composite unity of the two dimensions, so that we are really dealing with a twofold rather than a threefold.) To repeat, equipment is *already* outside of itself, already "ecstatic." The vaunted ecstatic analysis of Dasein adds nothing more to the problem than the usual unfortunate human-centered twist to the problem. The answer to Krell's question about why ecstasis is missing in the mid-1920s would appear to be simple: the ecstatic terminology was never necessary in the first place. Nor does Heidegger succeed, once he *does* introduce the ecstases, in carrying out that turning movement from being to man that Krell too generously ascribes to him. In the aftermath of Heidegger's triple horizon of rapture, we have still learned very little about Dasein that is not equally true of the simplest hammer and its malfunction.

Heidegger purists might also demand a full account of his later conceptions of time, later visions of temporality that might yet be able to cut tool-being down to size. One such revamped time-concept appears in the mid-1920s with the emergence of the terms "*Temporalität*" and "*Praesenz*." We might begin with the latter term: "Praesenz is not identical with the present, but, as *basic determination of the horizonal schema* of this ecstasis, it joins in constituting the complete time-structure of the present. Corresponding remarks apply to the other two ecstases, future and past. . . ."[74] It is in this return to the "horizon" of ecstasy that the concept of *Temporalität* consists: "*Temporality* [Temporalität] *is temporality* [Zeitlichkeit] *with regard to the unity of the horizontal schemata belonging to it*, in our case the present with regard to presence."[75] As he does all too often, Heidegger seems to be implying that we previously stood at an insufficiently fundamental level of analysis, and must now free ourselves from our prior state of being duped by retreating into even remoter horizons. In this sense, "*Temporalität*" is somehow supposed to be distinct from "*Zeitlichkeit*." It is often suggested that this shift in terminology during the later Marburg years indicates Heidegger's first glimpse of the "finitude" of time itself, and therefore an initial step toward his supposed later period. It is easy to see why some commentators find this suggestion appealing. By returning the ecstases of Dasein to a primary unity that binds them, it might seem that we advance at least *one* step away from a Dasein-centered view of time. Now, perhaps, we have arrived at what sustains time ontologically, what harbors its reality or "grants" it to Dasein. Time itself has become finite.

But this view is artificial, since time is *already* finite from the moment that the sheer presence of the hammer is abandoned. Without this simple step, there could be no book called *Being and Time*. The limits of Heidegger's various time-concepts cannot be found by scouring through his elderly writings for some supposed Rosetta stone, but only by looking outside of Heidegger altogether. The ecstases of Dasein can be "radicalized" not by reading about what happens in Heidegger's life history a few years later, but by keeping the ecstatic model so firmly in view that it can be constantly measured against reality, and thereby subjected to whatever modifications are necessary. In short, to pass through layer upon layer of ever-deepening terminology is a less effective strategy than to look as closely as possible at temporality itself. Consider it this way. If *Praesenz* is real, then it is real in the world now lying before us, and in that sense the objects in the world must be imbued with it like a blanket with blue dye.

The simple reversal between hammer and broken hammer contains every possible measure of finitude, concealment, temporality, and being that one could ask for. It is not the *hammer* that is insufficiently fundamental, but our ontic *view* of the hammer as a present-at-hand conglomerate of physical parts. There is no temporality outside of the relation between specific beings and their being; indeed, outside of this relation there is nothing at all. It is the Alpha and Omega of philosophy.

As concerns the *Zeit-Spiel-Raum* that appears repeatedly throughout the *Beiträge*, I have already argued that Heidegger provides for no *genuine* distinction between space and time. Both of these concepts collapse into the same *Spielraum* ("leeway") as everything else—the reversal between tool and broken tool. While the resulting discussions in the *Beiträge* have a certain appealing darkness, they do not really mark an evolution beyond the same interplay of tool and space that already captured Heidegger's heart in 1919 (as shown by the explicit connection of theory with *Ent-fernung* in that early text). I say this only as a rough indication of my views on this aspect of the *Beiträge*; a far lengthier discussion would be possible under different circumstances.

The same is true for the celebrated treatise "On Time and Being." While a point-by-point discussion of this text might be of interest to many readers, I would personally find it monotonous, since no Heideggerian text more openly champions the methods that I have criticized repeatedly. In this work, Heidegger's general strategy (a terrible one) is to elaborate an expanding set of terms that might be called "horizonal," terms that wish to take us deeper than Heidegger has ever taken us before. In "On Time and Being," these terms become sufficiently numerous as to reach almost encyclopedic proportions. There is the clearing-concealing *Reichen*, the "giving" that exceeds any particular gift. There is the prespatial *Ortschaft*, without which no space can be a space. And as opposed to any specific presencing, there is now a *letting*-presence that exceeds any tangible reality. It should be clear that this is nothing more than a sophisticated version of the "grounding" tactics that I have already frequently decried. ("The dark, dark gift is grounded in a dark, dark giving. The dark, dark giving is grounded in a dark, dark *Reichen*. . . .") It is regrettable that this method retains such overwhelming prestige among interpreters of Heidegger, even the most recent among them.

§14. Truth and its Double

Ousia is being in the sense of *modus existendi*, of presence-at-hand. . . . But time is regarded as something present-at-hand, which is present at hand somehow in the soul. (Heidegger, 1927)[76]

In §10, John Sallis was commended in passing for his willingness to grant an unusual scope to readiness-to-hand. Whereas the majority of commentators still read tool-being as a limited class of familiar pieces of hardware, Sallis noted that in the strict sense *everything* is ready-to-hand. In this way, he seems to recognize that tool-being is more than a question of usefulness, though without granting the tool a major role in his own interpretation of Heidegger. Most readers familiar with Sallis would agree that his reading of Heidegger is centered in the concept of "truth," a theme that he has been pursuing closely for a number of years. What needs to be asked is whether "truth" adds anything to our understanding of Heidegger that tool-being does not already teach us.

Sallis' high regard for the Heideggerian notion of truth is reflected in most of his books and essays, as well as in a popular critical interchange with Walter Biemel. Here I will confine myself to a discussion of Sallis' *Double Truth*. Like the majority of commentators, Sallis is interested in tracing an *evolution* in Heidegger's thought, a development that he finds to reach its initial climax in the reflections on truth of the early 1930s. In order to set the stage for the high drama of "On the Essence of Truth," which appears to be his favorite Heideggerian work, Sallis follows the useful procedure of backing up a few steps and referring to the still untranslated 1925/26 lecture course—*Logik: Die Frage nach der Wahrheit*.[77] In this lecture course, Sallis tells us, "the bonds are still in place, those that bind truth to knowledge and knowledge to intuition and presence."[78] Although the draft of *Being and Time* was nearing completion as this course was delivered, Sallis still contends that Heidegger remains partly caught up in a Husserlian model of knowledge. As a result, he still views knowledge to some degree as a sort of intentional representation: "he is no less insistent than was Husserl that only a psychology based on an understanding of the psychic as intentional could succeed in rigorously determining the basic concepts of logic and thus preparing the field of pure logic."[79]

This is one possible reading of the relationship between Heidegger and Husserl in the mid-1920s; I prefer others. But what is most important here is Sallis' claim as to *how* Heidegger frees himself from his teacher: the analysis of equipment. Unlike Bernet, who goes so far as to claim that the tool-analysis was actually *invented* by Husserl, Sallis regards tool-being as a genuine Heideggerian breakthrough (though for reasons different from those I have advocated). While the concept of intentionality requires the bodily presence of what is intended, "Heidegger mentions that the concept of bodily presence, of *Leibhaftigkeit*, is oriented to theoretical knowledge. . . . Thus does Heidegger broach . . . the radical divergence from presence that *Being and Time* will produce through its orientation to the most proximate surrounding world."[80]

With the analysis of equipment, Heidegger begins to "stretch and twist the bonds"[81] that hold knowledge to intuition. But there is a problem with this. If the bonds are really still in place in 1925/26, Sallis will have to make this claim not only despite the impending completion of *Being and Time*, but also despite the lecture course of the *preceding* summer: *History of the Concept of Time*, where the tool-analysis is already there for the taking (to say nothing of 1919). If Sallis claims that the tool-analysis is what stretches and twists the bonds of truth, and *also* claims that the 1925/26 *Logic* course still operates entirely within this bond, then he will have to argue that Heidegger has suffered some sort of intellectual relapse between July and October of 1925. Although conflicted retreats of this kind are not unheard of in intellectual history, it would require a very subtle analysis to argue for any such thing in the present case. What seems clear is that the "stretching and twisting" begins far earlier than Sallis wants to acknowledge. I have already cited some fascinating passages from the 1919 lecture course that are *easily* recognizable as the later tool-analysis. On this point, Sallis repeats one of Bernet's crucial errors, misreading the birth certificate of tool-being by a good six or seven years, a widespread error that only Kisiel seems to avoid. If Sallis wants to credit the tool-analysis with the stretching and twisting of intuitional truth, he will have a hard time also claiming that the 1925/26 course still labors under Husserl's thumb.

But this is only a minor objection. So far, I still agree with Sallis on the main question: "For when Dasein comes to present things so as to objectify and thematize them, it will have done so only by modifying the comportment that it will have already had to them in its circumspective concern, its dealings with them as *zuhanden*."[82] Sallis knows that there is far more than "pragmatism" at stake: "The field will thus have been cleared for a radical redetermination of truth."[83] I would also applaud Sallis' uncommon alertness to the direct link between the tool-analysis and Heidegger's 1925 complaint that Husserl never asks about the *being* of intentionality.[84] Whenever Heidegger opens up his heavy artillery against "presence" or "intuition" or "the neglect of the question of being," the shock troops of readiness-to-hand are not far behind. Unlike many commentators, Sallis is not afraid to insist on the decisive role played by hammers in Heidegger's campaign against the forgetting of being. So far, so good. The problem is that Sallis falls into the usual pattern of believing that the tool-analysis is still not enough, that it is only the foreshadowing of a deeper discovery yet to come.

Before assessing this supposed deeper discovery, I would like to point to the reemergence of a familiar bias in Sallis' reading of *Zuhandenheit*. In §10 above, I praised him for noting that in a certain sense, *everything* is ready-to-hand, since everything partially recedes into the contexture of meaning. In *Double Truth*, however, there is little evidence that Sallis places sufficient value on his earlier remark. Here, he once again seems to hold in a tacit way that the ready-to-hand consists solely of *human devices*, for the examples of tool-being that he chooses display a strictly artificial character: table, chair, lamp, door. This restriction of the analysis to well-known "tools" suggests that, for all his uncommonly broad intuitions regarding the theme of equipment, deep down Sallis is still thinking of tool-being in the sense of "usefulness." That is to say, he apparently continues to presume that the difference between *Zu-* and *Vorhandenheit* is equivalent to a difference between unconscious handling and conscious theorizing.

In my discussion of Dreyfus,[85] I argued that this is not a sufficiently radical split, that both of these poles (handling and theorizing) are merely *human-centered*. The related view is that all entities other than people are simple, unproblematic lumps of matter, and that the duplicitous drama of being occurs only in some moody human oscillation between practical action and aloof observation. Given this Dasein-centered view of equipment, currently accepted by almost everyone, it is little wonder that *Being and Time* continues to be read as a work stained with residues of subjectivism, as a mere rough draft of better insights that will come only in later years.

If we adopt this as our standpoint, it is then all too easy to hold that the radical relation between tool and broken tool is something belonging only to the sphere of human Dasein. Inevitably, we will have to leave the human world of tools so as to advance on the truth of being itself. But the fact that *Heidegger* generally aims his tool-analysis only at lamps and tables and other human products is irrelevant. Whatever his own examples may be, we can speak of the readiness-to-hand even of dead moths and of tremors on a distant sun. As "useless" as these things may be, they still exert their reality within the total system of entities. Any measurement or direct vision of them, along with any bizarre *use* of them that might be imagined, will always be dependent on their primary reality as tool-beings. In this respect, objects of such an outlandish kind are no different from any shovel.

Here, Sallis takes a different approach to the issue, an approach from which the book *Double Truth* takes its name. The author recounts Heidegger's summary of Husserlian intuition, referring to the famous example of a person who is told that a picture on the wall is hanging askew, and who then turns around to verify this fact. Sallis points out that this discussion of Husserl could easily have been improved by an example drawn from *circumspective concern*, in which the object in question is never encountered visibly. The absence of such an example, he claims, is due to a far more decisive move on Heidegger's part: "a regress from truth to its ontological condition of possibility."[86] This is precisely the kind of horizonal strategy that the present book has opposed from the start. For this reason, my objections to this new claim by Sallis will have a familiar ring.

From truth as being-uncovering, we are told, Heidegger makes a decisive step into the very *condition* of such uncovering. That is to say, he enters the hidden realm of being-in-the-world, of that *disclosedness* of Dasein which alone makes any intuition possible: "The move is a doubling of *truth*, doubling truth as a being-uncovering, doubling it with the originary phenomenon of truth, which is the ontological condition of possibility of truth as being-uncovering."[87] With this entry into the *condition* of all *particular* truths, the subject matter of Sallis' book is fully established. And it is here that he finds the decisive break between Heidegger and the previous tradition: "It is this doubling that decisively breaks the bind of truth to knowledge in its traditional determination as intuition. For disclosedness is a matter neither *of* intuition nor *for* intuition. The originary phenomenon of truth, truth as disclosedness, is a truth that is not of knowledge."[88]

Given the context of these remarks, and given their obviously important role in Sallis' interpretation of Heidegger, his terminology is insufficiently distinct. For by his own admission, it was already true that the *circumspective concern* that deals with equipment was a "truth that [was] not of knowledge"; here already, the primacy of intuitive knowledge was ruptured. What, then, is supposedly gained by this notion of the very *possibility* of truth that was not already attained in the account of our dealings with the environment? With no direct explanation available, I am forced to conclude that Sallis simply wants to move beyond the uncoveredness of *particular* lamps or tables into the more all-embracing disclosedness in which all of these concrete things can possibly appear. This seems all the more likely given Sallis' next chapter, where he reverts to telling us that Heidegger's analysis of the worldhood of the world had already carried out precisely the move that he himself now recommends.[89] Even so, there is a supposed advance beyond tool-being, and it seems to have the following character: specific cases of uncoveredness are now "doubled" by a deeper *condition* of disclosedness. But I have argued numerous times against this appeal to "grounds" or "conditions of possibility" in opposition to specific entities, and will not repeat the argument here.

Whatever the process by which he reaches the notion of "originary truth," Sallis regards it as the key to interpreting Heidegger: the question of truth is not just one question among others.[90] Here I must disagree yet again, having seen no convincing evidence from Sallis that "truth" is any more important in this regard than are "time," "freedom," "ontological difference," or any of a hundred other Janus-headed expressions used in Heidegger's career. Nowhere does Sallis demonstrate that the theme of "truth" is able to take us to a new level of analysis; nor does he even show us that truth alone is uniquely "doubled." Why not call the book *Double Time*, for instance, and argue for a two-sided relation between everyday clock-time and its "condition of possibility"? Heidegger raises these sorts of questions on a regular basis. In defense of Sallis, he does make clear throughout his book that such doubling is pervasive in Heidegger. In principle, then, he would willingly acknowledge that time has a double, space has a double, moods have a double, and so forth.

The present book largely agrees with this notion, but I have added an all-important twist: *the "doubled" forms of all such entities are exactly the same for Heidegger.* If truth in the everyday sense is doubled by a ground, this ground is none other than the interplay of light and shadow, of tool and broken tool. But this deeper *Doppelgänger* turns out to be *one and the same* for all regions of reality. Although truth in the everyday sense is something quite different from time in the everyday sense, the doubled versions of these are strictly identical: in each case, the double that is "not of knowledge" turns out to be nothing more than a new nickname for the tool and its reversal. But one forgets too quickly that it is only a nickname, and begins to imagine that Heidegger has provided us with genuine theories of "truth," "time," "tools," "space," "theory," and other specific forms of reality. In this way, Sallis pursues the usual regressive horizonal movement, at the expense of his unusually clear grasp of the boundless scope of tool-being.

§15. The Event

> Being appears as "something" which man either approaches or not, which he either procures for himself via representation (and even forms) or not, just as if being came to presence like something in itself present at hand. (Heidegger, 1938/39)[91]

Theodor Nelson, the brilliant writer on the history of computers, makes striking use of a concept he entitles "ideas once but no longer liberating."[92] With this label, Nelson refers to ideas that begin as innovative breakthroughs, but which soon fossilize into needless bureaucratic obsessions. In every sphere where human intelligence exerts itself, the glory of old victories easily leads to continued warfare against enemies that no longer exist, while new and pressing threats are left unaddressed—just as the Pentagon is often accused of "planning for the last war." The same mistake infects philosophical critique just as readily; Heidegger studies is no exception. One of the "last wars" that continues to be fought by Heideggerians is that of the famous "verbalization" of substances advocated by Heidegger himself. The present book acknowledges the lasting service to philosophy of Heidegger's criticism of present-at-hand entities, a critique that paved the way for his probing (if monotonous) survey of technology and positive science no less than for his destruction of the history of ontology. It was Heidegger above all others who taught us that the cups and dishes lying before us are not sheer blocks of porcelain, but have their being only within a dynamic totality of references, a system to be understood only as a totality of projections of meaning. Philosophers should forever be grateful for these insights. But at least in principle, *this battle has already been won.*

It is time for Heideggerians to move on to the future, to cease resting on the laurels of their dead master. I have already suggested what it is in the master that ought to be abandoned. The analyses of *Being and Time* serve wonderfully to undermine the pretensions of present-at-hand entities, advancing beyond the visible horde of chainsaws and refrigerators into the depth-dimension that makes these possible. Unfortunately, Heidegger also tends to argue that it is the structures of *human Dasein* that accomplish this grounding: insofar as everyday natural objects seem to be merely *vorhanden*, they turn out to be secondary, and deserve to be left in the dust.

Even so, we must also stress the following: what Heidegger leaves behind with all of this is not *objects*, but *presence-at-hand*. There is nothing inherently unphilosophical about a screwdriver or a grain of dust, as the tool-analysis already demonstrates. Feel free to retreat into the deepest horizons you can find, scorn specific entities in favor of the "play" which alone makes them possible—indeed, do as many similar things as you wish. Even so, *you will never be able to think entities out of existence.* With his later treatment of the "fourfold" that haunts the lives of jugs and vases, Heidegger emphasizes to an especial degree the renewed dignity of *things* that begins to blossom in his writings. His justified attack on present-at-hand natural substances is too easily read as an unjustified distinction between the thing and its horizon or ground. As I have argued repeatedly, there is no such thing as a "horizon," but only a system of exchange between beings and their being. This system is also known as "world," a colossal infrastructure of humans, plants, sea mammals, gasoline, perfumes, rivers, pirate colonies, and opium. The primary dualism is not between the thing and its ground, which is Dasein's own personal problem (insofar as Dasein takes the things as simply present-at-hand) and does not concern the things themselves in the least. Rather, the key dualism is the one between the tangible contours of all such entities and the mute system of actuality into which they withdraw. Heidegger's single referential contexture is always *concrete*, always exists nowhere else than in the here and now. There is already plenty of tension and plenty of shadow in this system at any given moment. Therefore, it is too hasty to want to press beyond the limits of the moment toward some "dynamic process," some overarching and disembodied principle of "play" that would exceed the untapped riches of any instant.

The point of these preliminary remarks is to deny Sallis' claim that any particular being needs to be doubled with a horizon. In fact, the only doubling that occurs is the one that has *already* occurred from the first pages of Heidegger's career—the ubiquitous reversal between beings and their being. But I prefer not to develop this criticism any further in connection with Sallis, since his focus on truth does not offer a sufficiently broad target. What is needed is a commentator who offers a much more *sweeping* account of the play beyond all concrete objects, one who thereby proclaims a comprehensive manifesto on behalf of the "horizon" in opposition to distinct entities. The person I have in mind is the late Reiner Schürmann, justly regarded as one of the most influential commentators on Heidegger in any language.

In Schürmann's book *Heidegger on Being and Acting*, the reader can find a vast meditation on virtually every key Heideggerian theme. But far from offering a bean-counting survey of details, Schürmann has a very clear idea of how to integrate all these themes, an idea easily discernible in the book's subtitle—"From Principles to Anarchy." If Heidegger abandons the metaphysical notion of a highest entity or ruling principle in the cosmos, it is Schürmann's view that he means to replace it with a foundationless zone of ceaseless transitions: "a cessation of principles, a deposing of the very principle of epochal principles, and the beginning of an economy of passage, that is, of anarchy."[93] While more colorfully expressed than most commentaries, and far more systematic in its execution, the book's most general views are actually fairly mainstream among continental philosophers. In spite of the overall excellence of this work, it advocates virtually every method that I have claimed to be harmful to Heidegger studies; it is an encyclopedia of all that is opposed by object-oriented philosophy. Accordingly, the summary that follows must adopt a largely critical attitude, which I hope will be interpreted as respect for the seriousness of what Schürmann has to say.

All the complexities of Schürmann's argument are neatly concentrated in his chapter 12, which begins with a useful (though indefensible) contrast between Kant and Heidegger. Kant, we are told, jettisoned the ontological question altogether, replacing it with a merely formal concern: "how is *experience* possible?" In contrast, a reading of Heidegger shows the ontological theme to be fully intact, "at least if it is understood that 'being' designates neither some noumenal in-itself nor the mass of raw sense data, but the event of presencing."[94] More is said here than meets the eye. Schürmann is not just attacking Kant's own specific conception of the noumenal. As indicated by the added jab at "raw sense data," Schürmann is deeply skeptical of any transcendent realm at all. His views are an excellent example of what Dreyfus calls "deflationary realism." Schürmann's Heidegger confines the full ontological problem to the phenomenal sphere, even if, redefined as a dynamic "event," being seems to be stationed beyond any *particular* concrete situation. To use Caputo's phrase from *Heidegger and Aquinas*, being is an "emergent process" rather than a discrete set of phenomena. Here already, Schürmann has begun the search for a "non-principial play of presencing."[95] By deserting the world itself in favor of the guiding *process* that unfolds the world, Schürmann hopes to carry out his turn from principles to anarchy. It will be seen in the next section that this vehement rejection of anything transcendent links Schürmann directly to the views of Richard Rorty, to float just one possible eclectic marriage. Such an unlikely comparison, not the first in this chapter, provides another useful reminder that the analytic/continental rivalry is entering a new phase. The philosophical content of these movements increasingly overlaps to such an extent that their remaining differences are primarily of a terminological and even *institutional* character.

For Schürmann as for those already discussed, the movement from metaphysics to the event of presencing results in a "doubling" of Heidegger's conceptual arsenal. Living in an age of transition, we are forced to speak in a double vocabulary; each doubled conceptual pair must contain one "title of closure" and one "title of opening." This allows us to pass beyond all particular epochs of the history of being into the clearing play that vaults beyond any specific epoch: "In epochal history, the hypertrophy of one arch-present entity allows being only to be thematized as *chiefly* (literally) the entity's being. In the play of clearings, on the other hand, what will have to be treated as 'being' is an ever-shifting, event-like network of relations."[96]

As Schürmann sees it, this is not just an issue to be hashed out in the ivory tower: it has clear political implications. The present-day transition away from the ontological difference toward the "play of clearings," a purported historical shift that I will discuss shortly, is regarded by Schürmann as the very core of "the various breakdowns by which social scientists describe the twentieth century,"[97] an ominous list indeed. In even franker terms, Schürmann heralds "a modification in unconcealedness such that no standards are reliable any longer in private and public life—most of all, in public—and that life has nothing to conform itself to but the event of presencing."[98] It is not clear why Schürmann sees the standards of public life as being any more threatened than those of the private sphere. But be that as it may, his radical political claim is defended further by a more familiar notion, in my opinion a stale one: the double face of technology as both "danger" and "saving power."[99]

I would like to criticize all of these steps on several grounds. Most importantly, Schürmann seems to be repeating one of Heidegger's own

most illegitimate moves. It is no simple matter to claim that a collapse of
ontological principles can be the cause of a century-long political crisis, as
if metaphysics and genocide were the outcomes of one and the same history. Heidegger has deservedly come under fire in recent years for suggestions of this kind. Can mass murder really be explained by the historical
dominance of *Vorhandenheit*? Numerous immediate objections to this
claim come to mind ("it is not just *crops* or *oil* that were reduced to a stockpile, but *the Jews*," "the practice of genocide antedates even the pre-
Socratics," and so on). Furthermore, the application of the danger/saving
power theme to any concrete political question easily becomes disastrous;
any genuine political leader would have to regard this principle as useless.
The permanent ontological duel between sheer presence and that which
withdraws, their constant reversibility from one pole to the other, by no
means promises eventual good luck in the political arena. Often enough,
danger only multiplies danger: a society is permanently broken by the force
of events, ruined by betrayal, grief, and collective suicide. In a sense which
Heidegger fails to surmount, it is untrue that political danger and political
salvation go hand in hand. In other words, even if being does come to be
redefined as "an ever-shifting, event-like network of relations," this statement has no political value as anything more than an exploratory probe. It
does not prove that the age of dynastic monarchies is at an end; it does not
necessarily herald an era of confused civil turmoil; it does not serve as sufficient grounds for anti-Vietnam War protests; it justifies neither the majority nor the minority of the Supreme Court in *Roe v. Wade;* it does not
prove that Baptist fundamentalism is not the sole true path.

In short, any form of "anarchy" that emerges from Heidegger's
thought is useful neither as an instrument of social reform nor as a tool of
historical prediction: *no sufficient metontology of history or politics ever
appears in his works.* As a result, if we were to work as Heideggerian political analysts, we would be able to say only that Biblical Nazareth, Hapsburg
Prague, 1790s Shanghai, and 1990s techno capital Detroit are equally governed by a "play of light and shadow." We cannot say that present-day Las
Vegas profanes the mystery of being any more than do the huts of the
Black Forest, since there are no genuine resources in Heidegger's thought
to measure *specific* forms of political anarchy in terms of the ubiquitous
anarchy at the heart of being itself. Seen from the standpoint of ontology,
the Summer of Love and a dreary police state are equally "anarchic"
situations. There are no more *ontological* obstacles to Schürmann having
been a far-right politician than for Heidegger to have been a Maoist
guerilla. Political philosophy plays out on a level very different from that
of ontology. It is always strange when Heideggerians employ their master's
work for the purpose of generating political pronouncements, as this has
never been their strong suit—let alone his. Vague assumptions about the

reversibility of danger and saving power only come off as amateurish in comparison with the detailed historical wisdom of such authors as Tacitus, Ibn Khaldun, Gibbon, Michelet, or Braudel. Are we to think that these are only "ontic" historians? It is unlikely that even Heidegger could make such a claim with a straight face.

Even so, the most objectionable features of Schürmann's argument lie elsewhere. Resuming a survey of the supposed passage from principles to anarchy, we soon encounter another familiar claim: "Dasein's three temporal modes of being 'outside itself' turn out to be derivative of 'the epochal essence of being,' which in turn is dependent on being as the event."[100] Here is the well-worn commentator's saga of the turn from man to being, already skillfully reversed by Krell in the passages cited earlier. Be that as it may, Schürmann at least recognizes that more than human being is at stake for Heidegger, even if the stakes are quite different from what Schürmann thinks them to be.

He begins with a plausible claim about a parallel anarchic shift: "the difference between being and entity turns into the difference between world and thing."[101] In chapter 1, I used these sets of terms interchangeably, and see no reason to cease doing so now. But the interesting point here is what *Schürmann* believes to be the difference between these two formulations. The answer is the one we might expect: the being/beings difference supposedly rests on a some notion of a transcendent being outside the sphere of Dasein, a notion that Schürmann believes to be permanently discredited. Meanwhile, "world and thing" escape this difficulty by collapsing or gathering together in a "process," which is nothing "in itself" but which still rises above the confines of any given moment: "Heidegger's entire effort here consists in trying to show that the world, or contextuality, announces itself in the 'as'—the thing 'as' thing. This deals a blow to transcendence, since the world is not elsewhere than the thing. . . ."[102]

There are two important mistakes in this passage. The first is Schürmann's assumption that the world/thing duality has a more intimate relationship with the as-structure than did the being/beings duality of the 1920s. For there already, being announced itself only in the "as"—the entity as entity. Indeed, Heidegger's whole theory of the concept-formation of theoretical comportment revolved around the attempt to disclose entities *in their being*. Hence, no shift away from earlier principles can be found in the world/thing dualism at all. On this count at least, there are no grounds for impeaching the ontological difference to make way for a new set of terms.

Second, Schürmann is grievously mistaken to suppose that the as-structure abolishes transcendence. Far from it! It is true that the broken hammer only comes to light through an appearance of hammer *as* hammer. No one will deny that the hammer can only *announce* itself by means of the as-structure. But this fails to justify Schürmann's claim that there is nothing *outside* such announcement. Put somewhat differently: hammer "as" hammer is by no means identical with hammer-being. This was the central argument of chapter 1 of the present book. Although the tool in its executant action never becomes visible, this does *not* mean that it has no reality. If it did, the tool-analysis could not possibly function, since the traditional treatment of entities as exclusively representations would *succeed*; the dynasty of presence-at-hand would never have fallen. All of this can be overlooked only as long as the tool/broken tool rift is trivialized into a psychological theory of the relation between automatic, unnoticed activities and conscious, explicit ones. In fact, there is an unbridgeable chasm between tool and broken tool which even the as-structure cannot cross. However the as-structure is supposed to function, it surely cannot bring the concealed contexture of the world into simple, transparent presence. There must be some sort of complicated way in which being announces itself *in* appearances; otherwise, even approximate forms of knowledge would be utterly impossible. Just how this happens remains unclear. But in negative terms, it cannot possibly be through an as-structure that would adequately mirror the things themselves, or even one that would give us a closer and closer but merely asymptotic approach to the things. The gap between the two dimensions remains absolute.

Just as matter cannot touch anti-matter without being destroyed, the as-structure cannot capture tool-being without killing it as tool-being. To this extent, the realm that Schürmann calls "transcendence" is not abolished in the least. If we read him in this way, Heidegger turns out to be *the* philosopher of the noumenal (a term I use here mostly for shock value, since there will turn out to be a crucial difference between Heidegger and Kant on this point; see §22 below). *Being and Time* would never reach Square One if not for the distinction between objects as explicitly encountered (*Vorhandenheit*) and these same objects in their withdrawn executant being (*Zuhandenheit*).

Wrongly believing that transcendence has been abolished, Schürmann now gazes upon the play of world and thing, a drama freed from any ulterior foundation. It is an "autonomous" play,[103] as well as a "self-regulating" play.[104] And it is here that Schürmann offers yet another synonym for his favored anarchic play: "the fourfold." This widely disdained Heideggerian term is one that Schürmann utilizes more eagerly than most interpreters, albeit in a neutered form that deprives it of most of its virtues. As Schürmann sees it, Heidegger introduces *das Geviert* as just another method for pluralizing the "One" of Greek philosophy, a pluralization that has always typified Heidegger's methods from the outset. I will discuss this claim of Schürmann's in a moment, but it should first be noted that he gets off to a very bad start in his interpretation of the four. Relating it to the purported Heideggerian shift from man to being, whose very existence I have already disputed, Schürmann assesses the resultant new status of human beings as follows: "The moment the world ceases to be seen as the structuring element of Dasein, men—'the mortals'—find themselves, as it were, marginalized. They only enter as one of the elements of the fourfold . . . ."[105] There is at least one obvious problem with this statement. Namely, Schürmann implies that the fourfold is referring to four *kinds* of entities, of which human beings would be one kind (mortals), Zeus and Shiva another (gods), mineral springs and apple trees yet another kind (earth), and stars and planets a final kind (sky).

But this is just as indefensible as holding that the distinction between tool-being and presence was meant as a taxonomy of hatchets and brushes. To think this way is to trivialize the fourfold from the start. Allow me to pose the following question: when was the last time that Heidegger actually drew up a classification-scheme of different *types* of beings? No strategy could be more foreign to Heidegger, more similar to what he always avoids. Anyone vaguely familiar with those texts in which the theme of *das Geviert* is developed will remember that it is described as a *global* mirroring relation, with all four terms mirrored in *every* entity. In fact, all connotations aside, "the mortals" cannot refer to Dasein as one specific sort of being in opposition to other sorts. The quadrants simply *do not serve* to name mutually exclusive sets of *particular* objects. If we fail to remember that the four of the fourfold are everywhere at all times, we have simply missed the point. Schürmann's implication that *die Sterblichen* represent one kind of entity among three others is especially strange given his remarks in an earlier footnote, where the luckless Walter Schulz is skewered for interpreting the four as "prototypes."[106] It would seem that Schürmann's only objection to the term "prototype" is its obvious incompatibility with the anarchic play that he champions; in all other respects, *he himself reads them as prototypes*!

The key transition in Schürmann's eyes is that between unity and plurality, whatever the number of this plurality may be. Had the fourfold instead been called the 17-fold or the 231-fold, Schürmann's interpretation of this concept would remain strangely unaffected. In his view, any conceptual shift in the direction of plurality is an admirable thing, and helps pave the way for "the possible transition to post-modernity."[107] It is for this reason that the fourness of the fourfold is studiously downplayed in his book: "Whether the new play is called 'the fourfold' or something else, what matters is that nearness has ceased to play."[108] Schürmann has little interest in the specific number four: throughout his book, the phrase "the onefold and the fourfold" is consistently glossed as "the one and the many." On one occasion, Schürmann even begins a sentence in the following way: "The four constituents, taken from

Hölderlin. . . ."[109] In context, the phrase "taken from Hölderlin" is not intended as well-known historical information, but obviously means to imply that the number four has no organic source in Heidegger's thought at all. Schürmann is trying to hint that the fourfold is merely a suggestive trope imported by Heidegger from his favorite poet to describe a sheer "multiple origin," à la Schürmann himself.

Indeed, Schürmann is so convinced of the unimportance of any quadruple reality that the already chastised Schulz soon has company in the Inferno of Heidegger commentators. This is none other than William Richardson, the dean of American Heidegger studies, who is taken to task in precisely the same footnote for offering a literal rendering of "*Geviert*" as "quadrate." Schürmann's objection runs as follows: "It is not the number four that is important, nor any hint at geometry."[110] This criticism is puzzling. Concerning the first part of the complaint, any scrupulous scholar has no choice but to side with Richardson. The ethics of translation obviously demand that the numerical meaning of "*Vier*" in the German original be preserved, and not jettisoned simply because Schürmann has an axe to grind about its irrelevance. In this sense, Richardson deserves our praise for faithfully transmitting a key term even when it baffles him as much as any other reader. Concerning the second part of the complaint, it is hard to understand Schürmann's objection to "geometry," since no concept in Heidegger's writings is displayed in diagram form more often than this one. If anything, the geometry of the mirror-play seems to be *decisive* for Heidegger.

Furthermore, if Heidegger were concerned only with pluralizing the One of the Greeks, why bother with anything so exotic and bizarre as the much-derided fourfold? All phases of Heidegger's thought are already saturated with numerous double and triple structures. Indeed, there is perhaps not a single page in the Heidegger *Gesamtausgabe* that fails to appeal to some dichotomy or trichotomy in order to break up the pretensions of simple presence. Why would Heidegger introduce new "fourfold" jargon if he had already made his point more clearly elsewhere? For this reason, it seems false to claim that Heidegger moves from two to four only for novelty's sake, or only as a tip of the hat to his favorite poet. The fact that Heidegger does a miserable job of explicating this concept (miserable enough that no convincing interpretation of it has ever been offered, and few even attempted), does not mean that it is truly indecipherable. It may simply mean that previous commentators have been looking in the wrong place, sticking the wrong key in the lock. But the evidence of its *uniqueness* in Heidegger's philosophy is too overwhelming to be ignored.

In the first place, it should never be forgotten that *das Geviert* appears for the first time as the central concept of an unusually decisive text: the long-withheld 1949 Bremen lecture, "Einblick in das, was ist."[111] This work is important not only due to its status as Heidegger's first substantial postwar composition; it is not only for circumstantial reasons that we can safely call this Bremen lecture the original source for most of the late Heidegger. After all, it is the sourcebook for many of the later works that have been familiar to readers for decades—from "Building Dwelling Thinking," "The Thing," and "The Question Concerning Technology," to large parts of *On the Way to Language*. In this sense, Heidegger's admirers were already familiar with the fruits of the 1949 lecture long before its belated publication forty-five years later.

Although I have been critical of Schürmann in the preceding pages, his book was chosen because it is the most masterful of its kind. My objection lies not with his execution of the work (which is commendable), but only with his guiding idea of anarchy. The foregoing criticisms are directed not just against Schürmann, but against the prevailing understanding of Heidegger's term "Ereignis." While for Schürmann this term is only one name among others for the anarchic play of reality, the usual interpretation of "the event" is a perfect match for Schürmann's preference for processes over single instants, for "emergence" over entities. It is widely believed that with Ereignis, Heidegger means to leave entities behind in favor of an anarchic process that would be more fundamental than any specific entity or set of entities. Further, it is assumed that Heidegger had to "work his way up" to this insight; accordingly, it is thought that *Being and Time* and other writings from the same period cannot possibly contain any foreshadowing of Ereignis. For this reason, even when confronted with Heidegger's explicit discussion of Ereignis as early as 1919, developmentalist readers of Heidegger are forced to claim that there is merely a "verbal similarity" in these terms. (As usual, Kisiel is a refreshing exception.)

In this way, the accepted evolutionary history of Heidegger is now so deeply entrenched that the comfortable legend of his Horatio Alger-like climb toward *Ereignis* has been allowed to take precedence over the weight of the texts themselves. But the truly interesting question is why this term disappears for so long in Heidegger's works, since it actually *does not* seem to have a different sense later from the one it already had in 1919. As I have argued at length, the notion that the first and second incarnations of Ereignis do not refer to the same subject matter can be defended only if it is *assumed* that Heidegger's general strategy is to move from specific events toward the ethereal conditions of the conditions of the conditions of these events. While not entirely lacking in support from Heidegger's own works, this method of successively retreating into conditions is found mostly in the secondary literature, where it has now taken on a life of its own. As Theodor Nelson might say, the dream of a movement away from objects toward a deeper "clearing play" is an idea once but no longer liberating.

§16. Language and the Thing

> But the counterposing of world and en-framing is not only a present-at-hand and therefore representable opposition between present-at-hand objects. (Heidegger, 1949)[112]

The surprising Alain Badiou, by no means a Heideggerian, fuels his vigorous book on Deleuze with the following remark: "When all is said and done, there is little doubt that the [twentieth] century has been ontological, and that this destiny is far more essential than the 'linguistic turn' with which it has been credited."[113] It is to be hoped that Badiou will seem increasingly clairvoyant in the decades to come. But he stands far from the mainstream, and the mainstream in both analytic and continental philosophy still regards "language" as Big Man on Campus. From Frege and Russell on one side of the tracks to Habermas and Derrida on the other, there is no denying that something resembling a "linguistic turn" has left a deep imprint on all of our recent major thinkers. Still, this is not to say that the linguistic paradigm deserves an infinite lifespan, nor even that the later Heidegger is best read as a philosopher of language. Indeed, the claim to be developed briefly at the end of this section is that Heidegger's theory of language is subordinate to a theory of *objects*, to a further articulation of the inner dynamics of tool-being.

Among those likely to disagree with this aspect of the present book, Richard Rorty is one of the most prominent. In his widely cited essay "Wittgenstein, Heidegger, and the Reification of Language,"[114] we find an entertaining summary of his reading of Heidegger's career. As usual when it comes to Rorty, the great value of this essay stems from its author's willingness to make bald-faced and daring assertions in clear English at precisely those points where others tend to hedge their bets behind tortured professional jargon.

In the case at hand, Rorty sets the table by criticizing some of the previous versions of the linguistic turn in analytic philosophy. As he sees it, the *ancien regime* in the philosophy of language was heir to a Kantian philosophical program: its mission was to mark off an *a priori* sphere of inquiry that would remain untouched by the monthly vacillations of empirical science. Simply put, it was an attempt to remodel transcendental philosophy into a philosophy of language.[115] Although Rorty himself was once a fire-breathing advocate of this very species of philosophy, he is so no longer, and it shows. Against any attempt at a transcendental philosophy, he now recommends a specific form of pragmatism; on the basis of this new standpoint, Rorty suggests a fresh interpretation of Heidegger and Wittgenstein. According to this interpretation, Heidegger began his career as a pragmatist but eventually lost his nerve, relapsing from *Being and*

Time into a philosophy that restores a concealed transcendent *reality* to the throne. The case of Wittgenstein, says Rorty, was just the opposite. Whereas the *Tractatus* appealed to a realm of ineffable atomic facts, divorced from all contaminating relations, the *Philosophical Investigations* came to recognize the pragmatic-relational character of meaning as "use." In this way, Heidegger and Wittgenstein seem to have passed each other in mid-career, heading in opposite directions.[116] Shortly, I will criticize this interpretation by suggesting that Rorty simply misses what is most important about *Being and Time*.

In the meantime, we can review in greater detail the parallels that he draws between the Kantian and linguistic versions of transcendental philosophy. His overarching claim is that "language" plays the same role in twentieth-century philosophy as "experience" does in the thought of Kant. The common features are every bit as striking as Rorty says they are. In each case, language and experience serve to delimit the *entire field* of philosophical inquiry. Just as Kant called a halt to all speculative adventures beyond the bounds of spatio-temporal appearance, the philosophy of language is keen to strip ontological assertions down to grammatically "meaningful" propositions (recall Carnap's attack on Heidegger). Furthermore, language and experience are held in each case to be immune to the blows of natural science. Since scientific knowledge is regarded by these philosophies as, respectively, dependent upon the conditions of experience, or meaningful only through mediation by the language through which it announces itself, experience and language are both employed as foundations for a full-blown "first philosophy."

For Rorty, this ambition is typical of Wittgenstein's *Tractatus*, and finds contemporary support in the molecular theory of meaning developed by authors such as Michael Dummett.[117] If Kant sought the conditions of "experienceability," then philosophy of language is in analogous pursuit of the conditions of "describability." But the naturalization of semantics in analytic philosophy eventually led to the death of "meaning" as a transcendental topic, a process set in motion by figures such as Davidson.[118] This, in a nutshell, is Rorty's refreshingly condensed view of post-Kantian philosophy.

While this historical argument is interesting enough in its own right, it is even more intriguing as a sample of Rorty's basic philosophical outlook. And true to form, he describes this outlook in the frankest possible terms. Specifically, Rorty says that much of the history of philosophy results from a prolonged dispute over what he calls "type A" and "type B" entities. As concerns the first of these: "Russell's logical objects, the Kantian categories, and the Platonic forms were all supposed to make another set of objects—the empirical objects, the Kantian intuitions, or the Platonic material particulars—knowable or describable."[119] These type A entities *are what they are*, apart from all relation with anything else: "These entities contextualize and explain but cannot, on pain of infinite regress, be contextualized or explained."[120] With their counterpart entities, it is just the opposite: "Call the lower-level entities, those which stand in need of being related in order to become available, entities of type B. These are entities which require relations but cannot themselves relate, require recontextualization and explanation but cannot themselves contextualize nor explain."[121] Anyone vaguely familiar with the spirit of Rorty's other recent books will not be shocked to hear that he sides with type B entities and is highly suspicious of those of type A. Against any such noncontextual type A entities, Rorty invokes the later Wittgenstein, who seemed to have realized in the end "that philosophy, like language, was just a set of indefinitely expansible social practices. . . ."[122] Put differently, Rorty sees the whole issue as a conflict between *atomism* and *holism,* viewed respectively as: "the assumption that there can be entities which are what they are totally independent of all relations between them, and the assumption that all entities are nodes in a set of relations."[123] Now we are getting somewhere! Although I strongly disagree with Rorty's interpretation of Heidegger, the conflict between atomism and holism is surely the source of the two leading dogmas of contemporary philosophy, both of which will be rejected in chapter 3 below.

But for now, we can move straight to the endgame of Rorty's argument. Given what we have already heard about type A and type B entities, it is easy to follow Rorty's conclusions:

> I interpret the pragmatism of the first Division of *Being and Time*—the insistence on the priority of the ready-to-hand, the *Zuhanden*, over the present-at-hand, the *Vorhanden*, and on the inseparability of Dasein from its projects and language—as . . . a holistic attempt to replace a distinction between entities of type A and those of type B with a seamless, indefinitely extensible web of relations.
>
> From the point of view of both *Philosophical Investigations* and *Being and Time*, the typical error of traditional philosophy is to imagine that there could be, indeed that there somehow *must* be, entities which are atomic in the sense of being what they are independent of their relation with other entities. . . .[124]

In these passages—an excellent summary of Rorty's version of Heidegger—it is possible to isolate three distinct and erroneous claims. I will address them point by point:

(1) "The priority of the ready-to-hand over the present-at-hand equals pragmatism." I already argued against this when discussing Okrent's book. By now, I hope the reader will be permanently convinced that Heidegger's analysis of equipment cannot be restricted to well-known "tools," and that it has nothing more to do with unconscious practice than it does with con-

scious theory. The tool-analysis describes the drama in the heart of objects themselves, not the purely anthropological shift from practical know-how to hyper-alert knowledge. Every last entity in the universe, whether "used" or not, is marked by the duality between its terminal effect and its silent withdrawal from presence. This is true of hammers, but equally true of plants, dogs, and steroids. It is also true of human beings, whose unique features (whatever they may be) have not yet come into play at this level of the debate.

In the spirit of fun, and to emphasize the point further, it might be noted that even *Richard Rorty himself* is simultaneously present-at-hand and ready-to-hand. We all know certain merely "extant," present-at-hand facts about him: that he wrote such and such books, that his hair and eyes are of a particular color, that he recently left Virginia for Stanford, and so forth. These are sheer present-at-hand properties, even if it can justly be claimed that Rorty the man will never be present-at-hand in quite the same *way* as a broken window or a piece of paper. But by the same token, Richard Rorty the man is also *ready-to-hand*. I say this not because he is useful for some devious person's aims, nor because he can be regarded as "equipment for teaching graduate students"; such remarks would reveal an overly literal view of *Zuhandenheit*. Instead, it means that prior to any list of properties that can be drawn up, Rorty *exists as a reality*. The world would be a different place if he did not exist: different for his vast network of readers, colleagues, family, friends, and even for the Charlottesville and Palo Alto merchants from whom he must have purchased thousands of goods over the years. Nor can the being of Richard Rorty be regarded as something subjective or internal in a *mental* sense, a being to which he would have direct or privileged access. If *his* knowledge of Rorty is better than ours, this difference is still only a matter of degree, not an ontological gulf. Rorty is presumably just as vulnerable as the rest of us to stunning self-discoveries and unexplained physical pains that arise from out of nowhere.

In short, the duel between the ready-to-hand and the present-at-hand is not some external classification of types of objects, but the very rift in which our lives and the lives of *other* objects all unfold. And wherever this Heideggerian insight may lead us, it can never lead us to pragmatism. For what is at stake in the dualism of tool and broken tool is not a simple distinction between practical and theoretical behavior, but a chasm between two modes of being. And this chasm is found in even the most pitiful inanimate entities.

(2) "Dasein is inseparable from its projects and language." True enough. But Rorty wants to imply much more than this. Along with this more limited claim, we find the insinuation that not only *Dasein*, but *the world as a whole* is inseparable from projects and language. In his ongoing

crusade against all transcendent type A entities, Rorty tries to draw not just humans, but *reality as a whole* into the linguistic-pragmatic orbit. But this cannot be done without serious violence to the facts. The root of the problem is Rorty's mistaken view of readiness-to-hand as "human interpretedness," a mistake he shares with Dreyfus and hundreds of other readers. The result of Heidegger's tool-contexture is *not* that "everything becomes relativized to human perspectives and social practices." Or rather, this is only *half* of the story. What the analysis of equipment shows is that individual entities are derivative of the total referential system. The exact status of this system remains, and must remain, *inaccessible*. Otherwise, it would revert to the conditions of presence-at-hand, resulting in instant contradiction. Hence, there are no grounds for identifying the equipmental contexture with "language": quite the contrary, since the tool is what *withdraws* from any particular expression or perception, including linguistic ones.

But Rorty wants more than a *human* pragmatism, one which would say only that theory always arises from practice. Beyond this, he explicitly champions a kind of ontological pragmatism in which *nothing* can meaningfully be said to exist outside of Dasein's "projects and language." But this is precisely what the tool-analysis *denies* (whether Heidegger denies it or not is a separate question). We simply cannot know what tool-being really is. To define it as "language" is to represent it, to construct a theory about it, and therefore to convert the world back into something present-at-hand—always the worst possible gaffe at Heidegger's dinner table. From all of this, we can see that Rorty is not opposed to the linguistic turn *per se*, as might have been supposed from his opening jab at Gustav Bergmann.[125] What he recommends is only a *pragmatist* version of the philosophy of language, a weapon designed to fight any theory of isolated atomic referents (such as those of Dummett or the early Wittgenstein). In short, Rorty opposes the priority of language only when it is treated as a sheer instrument of consciousness. Instead of abandoning the linguistic turn, he simply modifies it with the help of what might be called a standard "hermeneutic" view of language: language as forever entangled in a web of interpretations. Put differently, he advocates a typical shift from the philosophy of consciousness to philosophy of language, as long as language is understood as a pragmatic process of "getting things done" rather than as an antiseptic set of discrete signifiers and pointing arrows.

While this places Rorty squarely in the mainstream of contemporary philosophical trends (both analytic and continental), it does not go far enough. Indeed, it does not even go as far as Heidegger himself already goes: the analysis of tool-being as that which *slips away* from any practical or linguistic grasp already surpasses the people-centered holistic philosophy that Rorty imputes to *Being and Time*. I will say more about this below. But when Rorty accuses the later Heidegger of a "failure of nerve" in his appeal to a realm of being beyond social practice, he fails to see that the the hammer-being behind all broken hammers already has absolutely nothing to do with social practice. As unlikely as it may sound to Rorty, tool-being is *nothing but* an entity of type A—which is *not* to say that it is a present-at-hand atom that explains other beings while being inexplicable in its own right. A third alternative will be proposed in chapter 3. But a failure of nerve? Hardly. With nerves of steel, Heidegger presses his analysis to its staggering conclusion.

(3) "The distinction between type A and type B entities is replaced with a seamless web of relations. This remedies the error of traditional philosophy, which believes that there are atomic entities that exist independently of their relation with other entities." While Rorty packages together the seamless web of relations and the downfall of type A entities, these are actually rather different themes. Unlikely as it may appear, it is possible to replace the traditional theory of atomic entities with a doctrine of relations *without* thereby proving that type A entities do not exist. Heidegger himself provides the best possible example of this: after all, he does define the realm of tool-being as a giant *relational* system, but this by no means entails Rorty's brand of "anti-type A" linguistic pragmatism. Objects relate not just to human language, but also to *each other*. Rorty's holistic system of meanings and projects, whether "conscious" or not, is already a kind of transcendence which outstrips the tool-system in some way. As already mentioned apropos Dreyfus, meanings and projects are already relational, hence already belong to the as-structure, and hence cannot be identified with the tools themselves. The results of the present book can be stated in Rorty's terms as follows: tool-beings are emphatically *not* "type B" entities. Tools are *not* that which belongs to human practice, but that which always withdraws from such practice, and not just that which withdraws from explicit visibility. Tool-beings are by their very nature Rorty's nemesis: "type A" entities.

But this does not make them atomic, as if tool-beings were the present-at-hand final data of the world. The usual view is that the world itself would have to be made up of immediate givens, and that only human relationality can free us from the hegemony of solid type A billiard balls. I insist on the contrary: paradoxically enough, it is *relations* that turn objects into present-at-hand atoms. Throughout this book, I have tried to depict how the tool-being withdraws into its vast inner reality, which is irreducible to any of its negotiations with the world. Only in its relations with other entities is it caricatured, turned into a unitary profile—as if we fantasized about the sky that it is itself blue, while too stupefied to grasp its subtler electromagnetic realities; as if the paper fantasized about the fire that it is in its own true nature "Evil Burning Force," unable to appreciate the far richer inner life of the flame, as granite or salamanders may well do.[126]

In other words, the usual assumption is that the world in itself would be "immediate," and the world of human projects and practices would be "mediated" or relational. Strong anti-realists merely add the additional claim that immediate reality (type A) is impossible, and that everything is in fact mediated (type B). But here, three separate objections must be made:

1. Holism is responsible for *generating* presence-at-hand, not freeing us from it. If read properly, the tool-analysis shows us that equipment has nothing whatsoever to do with relationality. Tool-beings are utterly non-relational. In this sense, they are indeed "type A" entities. But they are by no means obvious atomic units that can be used to explain everything else. It is not that an "objective" hammer would be *vorhanden* and human praxis saves us from this fate. Rather, hammer-being withdraws from any presence or relation, and is converted into an atom, into an immediate datum with specific properties, by whatever other entity encounters it. This may be a nail; it may be theoretical comportment; it may be nothing more than a carpenter who grasps the hammer and pounds with it. But none of these situations have anything to do with the *being* of the hammer. All are relational through and through. In short, *it is actually the holistic context of the world that produces atoms*, reducing the murky depths of objects into limited and specific profiles, severely editing their realities by cutting away whatever part of their being has no relevance to the current situation. Paradoxically, holism does not free us from presence-at-hand, but enslaves us to it forever.[127]

2. It is not just human perception that does this, but any kind of relation whatsoever. Hence, it is not only humans who are to be blamed for the reduction of reality to presence. This is an essential feature of all kinds of relations, since no relation can ever fully harness the reality of its terms, including physical causality itself.

3. To withdraw from the context of the world is *not* to become an atom. The hammer is a dark reality far surpassing all current uses of it, indeed all *possible* uses of it. In this sense, it cannot be a "type B" entity, the kind that inhabit Rorty's holistic contexts. Thus, tool-beings are type A entities. But in another sense they are not: Rorty's "type A" cannot be contextualized or explained, whereas tool-beings *can*. The key to the difference is as follows. Traditional philosophies of substance split the world into parts. Certain entities (diamonds) may be substances, while others (pairs of diamonds) are merely relations (see §24 below). To stay with Rorty's terminology for the moment, the claim of the present book is that the world is not split up into type A and type B entities, but rather *every point of reality is both type A and type B*. If the being of the hammer withdraws from all of its relations, it is equally true that hammer-being is not a present-at-hand atom descended from the skies to breathe life into mere

derivative relations. Instead, tool-being is a *form*, a kind of formal cause that acts as substance with respect to its surroundings, but which is born only as a relational composite of its internal elements. On the one hand, the hammer is a vast surplus beyond human praxis no less than beyond human theory. On the other hand, hammer-being would vaporize if handle or head or gravity were to disappear. No doubt Rorty would condemn this theory as entailing an "infinite regress," since it replaces the human/world split with an endless layer of withdrawn forms wrapped inside of withdrawn forms—yes, perhaps *ad infinitum*. But for the moment, infinite regress is the least of three evils. The first evil is the traditional substance theory, which posits present-at-hand substances and reduces relational events to illusory nullities or "beings of reason." The second evil is the currently more fashionable theory, the context-ontology of Rorty, Whitehead, Heidegger, and others. This theory reduces the dark reality of things to a present-at-hand profile by saying that they exist only for each other. This second theory is unable to explain: (a) how an object can ever change if it has no surplus beyond its current set of relations, and (b) why we should speak of "individual" objects at all, since they seem to be devoured by the network of relations. However barbaric an infinite regress may sound, it is a small price to pay for avoiding both theories of presence-at-hand, whether they speak in the name of substance or relation.

We can review these problems in a slightly different way by considering the concerns of Heidegger and Rorty together. For there is one issue on which these two authors completely agree. When Rorty attacks type A entities, and when Heidegger disdains present-at-hand entities, both are trying to undercut the idea of independent slabs of stuff that would give rise to secondary realities but which would themselves be underivable from anything else. For Rorty, the only way to avoid positing such slabs is to say that the total network is the true reality, and he identifies this network as a seamless web of perspectives, human practices, and linguistic significances. To a large degree, Heidegger seems to agree with this priority of context over individual substances. But whatever he might think, the force of his tool-analysis itself pushes us in the *opposite* direction. For the real force of tool-being lies in its *resistance* to all holism, its withdrawal behind any seamless web of relations. During my discussion of Dreyfus, I observed that, paradoxically enough, presence-at-hand is actually *relational*—to perceive something as broken or as a theoretical object is for me to cut it down to size, to caricature its withdrawn being, even if the tendency of presence is to *claim* to be independent of my perceptions. But this means that the "seamless web of relations," a.k.a. "world," is not the hero who will rescue us from presence-at-hand, but just another turncoat who will sell us down the river, ever deeper into the empire of *Vorhandenheit*.

It is understandable why Rorty would champion the web of relations, the very strategy pursued by some of the most serious philosophers of the twentieth century. What he is trying to avoid is a theory of atomic type A entities that would leave an unsatisfying choice between either a Kantian theory of categories, a Russellian theory of logical objects, a Platonic doctrine of whistle-clean forms divorced from reality, an Aristotelian theory of primary substances that enter and exit countless relations without paying an ontological penalty, or a brute materialism of hard billiard balls. In any of these cases, we will have true atomic realities on the one side, and mere derivative accidents on the other. But these are not the only alternatives to Rorty's holistic empire of language and praxis. Even while the tool-being recedes from any human or nonhuman relation, it is not a simple present-at-hand atom, but is fully relational in a very different sense from that of *Vorhandenheit*.

I regret Rorty's excessive worries about positing any sort of "deeply hidden essence" in reality. He openly exults in the idea that we have finally been liberated from the deep and the hidden, so as to make room for a philosophy of social practices. As early saints of the new pragmatic religion, Rorty praises (along with Dewey) the early Heidegger and the later Wittgenstein, "both [of whom] set aside the assumption that philosophy might explain the unhidden on the basis of the hidden, and might explain availability and relationality on the basis of something intrinsically unavailable and nonrelational."[128] But even in *Being and Time*, Rorty asserts, Heidegger was already losing his grip on this insight: the notions of "authenticity" and "being-toward-death" seem to imply that our social practices are something finite, something to be rectified by appeal to a standard that would transcend such practices. Rorty regards this maneuver, which he sees as erupting in full form in the later Heidegger, as akin to "Kant's project of denying reason in order to make room for faith."[129]

Whatever one might think of the reason/faith distinction, this is clearly the wrong place to invoke it. As mentioned a short while ago, Rorty seems to think that the shift from *Vorhandenheit* to *Zuhandenheit* is merely a transition from rock-hard substances to silky-smooth human contextures and perspectives. But this is not the case. The readiness-to-hand of a bridge cannot be defined in terms of social/linguistic practices at all, and for numerous reasons. First of all, the bridge exerts a real effect upon the reality of frogs, trout, dragonflies, and ultimately even the wind. If Rorty wants to extend the term "social practices" to cover the lives of these entities too, it would be a bold move on his part, but I strongly doubt that he intends to do so. Second, our human lives stand at the disposal of far more than *linguistic* reality. The earth on which we stand is ready-to-hand, as are the nonlethal air we breathe and the tornado-free meadow through which we so obliviously stroll. These entities are not of human origin, nor are they "used" in the normal sense of the term. And even if our responses to such objects are inevitably "socialized" or "culturally coded," all of this touches only on the *Vorhandenheit* side of the equation. Whether we speak of shared social practices or lone-wolf theorizing, in both cases it is a question of what we graft onto the reality *in the midst of which* we already exist.

Unfortunately, the current fashion of bashing "deeply hidden essence" so often seems to be motivated by political concerns of a kind that have less to do with the essentialism debate than might be expected. Rorty openly states that any theory of type A entities inherently fuels the "logocentric" or "ontotheological" style of philosophy of the kind from which we have so recently been freed. I disagree entirely. The "logocentric" problem with deeply hidden essences was never that they were deep and hidden; the problem lay only in the assumption that they could somehow be delivered to us *in person* in order to serve as normative criteria. There is no obvious political problem with saying that the world has an essence; there is a *huge* problem as soon as we say that Germany rather than Russia, or the male rather than the female (or vice versa), or "the Greeks" rather than "the Senegal Negro," most fully *embody* this essence. In other words, present-day philosophy suffers from a deep and widespread confusion of two *different* kinds of essentialism. To criticize the ability of any essence to become present in the flesh in privileged objects *does not* entail that the world must be converted into sheer surface. The problem is not with the deeply hidden, but with the attempt to convert the deeply hidden into the perceptible and relational.

Be that as it may, Rorty seems convinced that by defending the claims of manifold interpretation against any deep essence, he helps to defend pluralism and democracy. But the opposite case can also be made, and *has* been made, by opponents of postmodernism running the gamut from arch-conservative Straussians to Marxist magazine columnists. It is far from clear that bad politics comes from deeply hidden essence and good politics from the "performative" contexts and perspectives that were so pleasing to Gorgias and Meno. The present fashion is for the Left to appeal to performative constructivism and the Right to invoke the majesty of nature. But who would be shocked if the fashion suddenly reverses, and the Right suddenly begins to defend the claims of historically evolved power structures while the Left reintroduces an appeal to the universal rights of the human essence? Who can predict which side of the opposition will *truly* prove most useful to feminists, emerging African nations, Arabs, the steel industry, genocidal dictators, or labor unions? Essentialism and constructivism will probably continue their endless flip-flop across the political spectrum for centuries to come. To try to correlate them directly with basic ontological positions is as disastrous for ontology as it is for political struggle.

But the relationship between hidden essence and political pluralism is not a central concern of the present book. What is more worrisome for the moment is that the present-day fashion of treating the deep and the hidden with suspicion always causes interpreters of Heidegger to denounce as retrograde an approach that may very well be *new*. For it is quite possible that Heidegger's tool-analysis provides us with the resources, not to reduce the things themselves to human linguistic practices, but to talk about these things themselves in a more rigorous way than has ever been done before. Perhaps Kant's revolution against dogmatism has really just paved the way for a Heideggerian revolution against Kant. Only time will tell.

But consider the issue in the following light. Much of the best twentieth-century philosophy, from whatever camp it has arisen, has gathered its greatest fruits through an attack on traditional substances and transcendent realities. This tendency can be found in authors as diverse as the later Wittgenstein, Davidson, Husserl, Whitehead, Heidegger, Habermas, Rorty, and Foucault. It might even be said that "contextualization" has been the intellectual mission of our time, that the destiny of the twentieth century was to champion the notion of *holism*. These days, holism tends to be a winning proposition in academic work, and on many days it does still feel like a refreshing sea-breeze in comparison with the tendency of common sense to break the world apart into independent chunks. I have even heard one of America's most prominent educators say that the very *meaning* of a college education is to teach the student that "everything is connected." But this abandonment of independent substance and essence in favor of contexts is another of those ideas once but no longer liberating. The paradigm of "contextuality" or "relationality" has now been stamped in our minds to the point that it dominates every corner of our thinking. The motto of "nothing without context" has proven extremely useful, providing innovative research paradigms for many fields of study. It has become a flag beneath which almost everyone can rally, a guiding model by which to structure research and arguably even to transform political awareness.

But it has now largely triumphed; the battle has largely been won. The revolution of "contexts" has been victorious to such an extent that anyone defending anything like a "type A" entity is immediately stamped as a fossilized reactionary. But this assumption is a product of the *last* war, the war against static present-at-hand substances that get known more or less adequately by a human subject who copies them like a wax tablet.

But what is the alternative? There is no need to speak in hypothetical terms: thanks to Heidegger's tool-analysis, *objects themselves are already back in town*. The force of Heidegger's tool-being is that it resists all possible practices, significations, and even inanimate contexts. For all his stimulating candor, I would like to suggest that Rorty is on the wrong side in this particular conflict.

But rather than simply deferring to Rorty's interpretation of the place of language in Heidegger's thought, it will be useful to refer directly to a specific Heideggerian discussion of this topic. I have already stated my belief that the role of "language" for Heidegger is vastly overrated. There are two reasons for saying so: (1) His meditations on language have the same difficulty as any of his *other* reflections on particular topics. In the first place, they tell us nothing about language that is not also true of that which is *not* language. In the second place, they turn out to make sense only as a further elaboration of the theme of the tool and its reversal. (2) To read Heidegger as a proponent of the "linguistic turn" is to smother the independent life of shadowy objects, which emerges directly from his philosophy whether he wishes this or not. To support these suggestions, I will refer briefly to his 1950 lecture, "Die Sprache."[130] From this lecture, it becomes quite clear that what is important for Heidegger is not "language" as a specific phenomenon, but rather the interplay between world and thing: a.k.a., the widely ridiculed *fourfold*. What looks at first like a classic text of the linguistic turn soon resembles instead a cryptic manifesto for an object-oriented philosophy.

Before telling us what language is, Heidegger invests some energy in telling us what it is not. Any reader who has followed me this far will not be shocked by what he says: *language is not present-at-hand*. Here as always, Heidegger displays an almost sensual pleasure in mocking the claims of *Vorhandenheit*. In a discussion of Trakl's "Winterabend" poem, we read that "The speaking names the time of a winter evening. What is this naming? Does it simply decorate the representable, well-known objects and occurrences—snow, bell, window, falling, sounding—with the words of a language? No."[131] In reference to two crucial lines of the poem, Heidegger says that "the two lines of the poem speak like propositional sentences, as if they noted something present at hand,"[132] with the phrase "as if" delivered with an obvious dose of irony. Meanwhile, we hear that the first stanza of the poem "summons things, calls them to come. To where? Not as present things among that which is present. . . ."[133] As might be expected, the usual Heideggerian punch line is not far behind: "The summoning that gathers is the sounding. In it, something happens that is other than the mere causing and the mere spreading out of a sound."[134] (Here again, one is tempted to play devil's advocate and perversely insist that sounding *is* the mere causing and mere spreading out of a sound.) In beginning his reflection on language with a denial that it can be conceived as present-at-hand, Heidegger sets out along the familiar path of the tool-analysis.

The most justly famous sentence of this lecture will immediately be recognized: "Language in its essence is neither expression nor a human deed.

Language speaks."[135] Language speaks. On the one hand this is good news for the present book, but on the other it is seriously misleading. To begin with the good, Heidegger seems to take language out of the sphere of the human subject and transform it into a wider event within being itself. Yet he only follows this procedure halfway. No matter what does the speaking, the speaking clearly occurs only within the realm of human Dasein, "the mortals." Whether Heidegger uses this term to include all humans or only specially attuned ones is still a widely debated question. In §18 below, I will argue that the mortals cannot be *either* of these, and must be one of four structural elements of the things themselves. But for Heidegger, there seems to be a sense in which language *is* still a specifically human event, however much he simultaneously denies this.

But given this overriding limitation, Heidegger pushes the scope of language very far indeed. Naming is not a narrowly linguistic act, but one intimately connected with the interpenetration of world and thing: "In naming, the things that are named are summoned in their thinging. Thinging, they un-fold world, in which the things abide and thus are in each case the abiding. The things, in their thinging, carry out [*austragen*] world."[136] And further, "summoned in this way, the things that are named gather among themselves sky and earth, the mortals and the gods. The four are an originary-unitary assembly. The things let the fourfold of the four tarry among them."[137] Although the inner dynamics of the infamous fourfold remain murky for now, I have already shown that its four terms derive directly from the first tool-analysis of 1919, whatever Hölderlinian mask they wear beginning in 1949. And regardless of their source, they refer to the structure of reality itself, and not to any structure of "language" in the narrower sense—just as the tool-analysis refers to a reversal within objects themselves, and not to some limited range of human practical activities. The language of mortals simply summons or gathers or calls world and thing in their interpenetration, in their tarrying amidst the four: "[Saying] pledges world to the things and at the same time preserves the things in the radiance of world. . . ."[138] Or in other words: "In the middle of the two, in the between of world and thing, in their *inter*, in this among [*Unter-*], there prevails the difference [*Unterschied*]. . . . The difference carries out world in its worlding, carries out things in thir thinging."[139]

Although it is common to throw around the notion of "language" as though it were as central to Heidegger's concerns as it is to so many other twentieth-century philosophers, there can be no question that language is a concern for Heidegger *only insofar as it relates to the central tension between world and thing*. But contrary to popular belief, this tension is fully available in *Being and Time* as soon as the contexture of equipment experiences a rupture. It is fruitless to artificially inject nonexistent naiveté back into the tool-analysis, claiming that *Being and Time* only spoke about humans using hammers and that Heidegger needs to discover "language" in order to transport the duel of world and thing from the sphere of human being over to that of being itself. What stands equally at the center of both *Being and Time* and the language essays is neither Dasein nor some fantastically disembodied sense of being or Ereignis or "Reichen," but rather the absolutely *concrete* interpenetration of world and thing. But this means that Heidegger's supposed philosophy of language is actually a philosophy of objects: "The speaking of mortals must above all have listened beforehand to the call in which the conciliation of the difference summons world and things in the rift of their simplicity."[140] The only trace here of anything like language in the sense of a "linguistic turn" is the talk of *mortals*, which seems to be pointing to a strictly human phenomenon. More about this in a moment. But first, it will be worthwhile to list some of the other prestigious code names that crop up in Heidegger's lecture for the same interpenetration of world and thing that we have been following from the opening pages of this book.

The duel of world and thing is sometimes called *Austrag*: "The third stanza [of Trakl's poem] welcomes the middle for world and thing: the carrying out of their intimacy."[141] The duel is also called *Riß, Fügen*, and even more strangely, *Auf-Heiterung*: "The rift of the difference lets the pure brilliance radiate. Its clearing jointure [*Fügen*] re-solves the lightening up [*Auf-heiterung*] of world in what is its own."[142] The bread and wine of the Trakl poem are granted control over an increasingly exotic range of technical terminology: "Bread and wine gather these four among themselves out of the simplicity of the quadration [*Vierung*]. The things that are called, bread and wine, are the simple, for their conducting [*Gebärden*] of world is immediately fulfilled out of the favor of the world."[143] And finally, for those who prefer images of peace to those of strife: "The difference expropriates [*enteignet*] the thing in the calm of the fourfold. Such expropriation does not steal from the thing. . . . To preserve in the calm is conciliation. The difference conciliates the thing as thing into the world."[144] And for those who prefer the fantasy of a rescue: "The difference conciliates in a twofold way: things into their thinging and world into its worlding. Conciliated in this way, thing and world never evade the the difference. Rather, they save it in the conciliation. . . ."[145]

While citing all of these terms, I want to avoid two possible unfortunate tendencies. The tendency of most analytic philosophers would be to smirk at the apparently excessive poetry of these passages, and to wonder whether they are not "meaningless." I cannot share this attitude, given that the pathos of these lines is not unmatched by a certain pathos in reality itself. Is the attitude of a sober tenure-track academic, speaking in clear propositional English during a faculty debate or in journal submissions, really the most appropriate mood in which to address the permanent dark strife at the heart of reality? Consider the following. All philosophers currently alive will someday be struck dead, each of us eventually reduced to dust in our graves. Distant stars bombard our planet with radiation, while our bodies constantly fight the growth of the cancer within. Moments of extreme euphoria and betrayal lie in waiting for us at least a few times per decade, much more in the case of the especially lucky or unlucky. All of our loved ones are potential victims of crime, and we are probably deceived by much of what we take to be our knowledge. Biological war or nerve gas terrorism could break out at any moment; innocent animals are constantly massacred across the globe. Contrariwise, the previous scenarios can all be reversed: all of our lives take an occasional glorious and unexpected turn in the direction of wealth, fame, virtue, and abiding friendship. Does this world of monumental good and bad fortune really justify the style of analytic philosophy of language as the highest type of human comportment? If there is a spark of poetry in Heidegger's mind, then this is not a signal of "fuzziness," but of a rare vocation for sounding out the depths of the world. The widespread lack of such a spark is perhaps the main reason why analytic philosophy has produced so few classic books, and why despite its abundance of sharp brains it is often viewed as an arid technical clique by that wider general readership which alone guarantees the long-term survival of written work. It is necessary to *combine* the emeralds and sphinxes of the poet with the iron fist of the logician, as most of the great philosophers in history have done. The current preference for "desert landscapes" in philosophy is without deep roots in history. It remains to be seen whether it even has deep roots in *reality*.

But there are plenty of problems in the other camp as well. While few continental philosophers would dismiss Heidegger's discussion of world and thing as "fuzzy," they can fall prey to different vices. One of these is the unfortunate tendency to leave as many of Heidegger's key terms as possible in the original foreign language, exaggerating their untranslatability, when the gap between German and English is actually far less interesting than the gap between reality and our ability to probe its secrets. Another unfortunate trend is to treat every piece of Heidegger's massive vocabulary with *excessive* respect, when even a cursory look at the language essays shows that he generates synonyms by the boxcarload for a frustratingly tiny number of basic concepts. Finally, and worst of all, there is the hereditary vice of every historical approach to philosophy (gleefully pointed out by so many analytic philosophers)—the assumption that Heidegger, as a classic figure, is so immeasurably deep as to have trumped in advance any "trivial" objections we might throw at him. Although there is no point in reducing Heidegger to platitudes, it is not too much to ask that he give us some definite *arguments* about the world. And in fact, he does so; they are simply much stranger arguments than those offered by more conventional minds.

Instead of ridiculing Heidegger's pathos, it is a more valuable use of time to sort through the menagerie of his basic terms and try to put them in some logical order, one that with a bit of luck might be pressed further than Heidegger himself managed to press it. In the present case, putting the concepts in order is not especially difficult, since all of the terms mentioned several paragraphs ago are *explicitly introduced* as aliases for the interpenetration or mirror-play of world and thing. Heidegger's philosophy of language is a philosophy of world and thing: that is, of tool and broken tool. I have already argued that every other version of this simple dualism simply repeats the others, and fails to secure any *specific* subject matter. Is it any different with language? The only way in which it *could* be different is if Heidegger were able to show that the "language" of the language essays had to be restricted to language in the narrower sense, or at least to the sphere of *human* reality in general.

But not surprisingly for anyone who has read this far, he is unable to pull it off, assuming he were even trying to do so in the first place (which hardly seems the case). Bit by bit, the reality that Heidegger calls "language" begins to shed any trace of language at all. Speaking collapses into a cor-responding to the differentiation of world and thing (*sprechen* as *entsprechen*). Hearing is no longer a mere listening, but rather a "belonging" to the stillness of the very same differentiation of world and thing (*hören* as *gehören*).[146] Instead of a discrete act of speaking, what we have is a concept of "language" that seems utterly indistinguishable from reality as a whole: "Language speaks. Its speaking welcomes the difference which expropriates world and things into the unity of their intimacy."[147] But when is this differentiation *not* summoned to come? In every instant, the play of world and thing is deployed, as already suggested by the double meaning of "heißt": not only does the speaking of language *summon* the differentiation, it itself *is* the differentiated onefold of world and thing. Language becomes just another name for world, for being, for the universal empire of tool and broken tool.

I have mentioned that the only way Heidegger can distinguish language from being as a whole is by restricting it to the sphere of human being. He tries to do precisely this with his constant invocation of "the mortals" throughout the essay. Clearly, no matter how broad Heidegger's concept of language has become, he would never be willing to grant it to chirping birds or to gorillas using sign-language, much less to the interplay of world and thing found in the collision of wood-chips with dry leaves and gravel. Indeed, given his invocation of Trakl's poem as an exemplary form of language, and given as well his rumored remarks about the superiority of German over French, Spanish, and other tongues, it would seem that Heidegger wants to have it both ways yet again. On the one hand, language is a universal structure that seems indistinguishable from anything else; on the other hand, certain languages deploy more fully that summoning of the unitary difference of world and thing that is also present everywhere and at all times. But this is nothing more than the same problem he faced with every aspect of the as-structure. And precisely this is his problem: even the term "mortals" cannot be restricted to human Dasein, as will be discussed in an upcoming section.

But given this, Heidegger's philosophy of language tells us no more about language than about dolphins or melting plastic. It cannot even be restricted to human *access* to the world, and permeates every crack in the nonhuman world as well. But this means that it is not a philosophy of language at all. (Now *this* is a version of the "linguistic turn" that I can live with.) It has no more to do with the language than the tool-analysis has to do with hammers and drills, and offers very little ammunition to the current defenders of the philosophy of language.

§17. Technology

> In *Being and Time*, the term "hermeneutics" is used in a *still* broader sense; "broader" meaning, however, not the mere extension of the same meaning over a still larger area of application. (Heidegger, 1959)[148]

Any attempt to convert the primacy of tool-being into the rule of language must have recourse to an impossible humanization of equipment. Here as elsewhere, by interpreting the ready-to-hand too narrowly as "practical devices," commentators take something that is by nature withdrawn from every view and imprison it in Dasein's front yard. But the focus on language is only one of many possible symptoms of this mistake. An even more dangerous temptation for interpreters of tool-being is to misinterpret readiness-to-hand as *technology*. In fact, it turns out that Heidegger's tool-being has no greater connection with planetary technology than with a rural flour-mill or immemorial redwood forest. Although I have already enumerated various reasons for this claim, a final survey will be helpful in driving the point home. To this end, I will discuss perhaps the finest general work on the topic: *Heidegger's Confrontation with Modernity*, by Michael Zimmerman. This thoroughly researched study, with its especially intriguing account of Heidegger's relation to Ernst Jünger, will be a widely cited reference for years to come. Even so, it is necessary to disagree with virtually the whole of its content.

My central objection to this book arises quite early in the game, since it immediately becomes clear that Zimmerman reads the tool-analysis as a limited description of practical instruments. As Zimmerman sees it, Heidegger is discussing "tools" as opposed to objects such as dirt and rainbows: "Heidegger had a lifelong concern with the nature of working and producing. He manifested this concern in what may be the most famous portion of *Being and Time*: the analysis of the workshop."[149] Zimmerman follows this up with a dubious political link—Heidegger, enthused by the pre-1936 Nazi critique of industrialism, is correspondingly fascinated with handicraft in *Being and Time*. This is incorrect for both factual and systematic reasons. *Factually* speaking, it is not even true that the analyses in *Being and Time* tell us more about countryside labor than about technological infrastructure. One need only recall Heidegger's numerous examples of light fixtures, rail platforms, and automobile turn-signals. We all know what Heidegger's anti-urban prejudices really were, but the tool-analysis is actually one of the places where those prejudices *do not* interfere with his reflections. And in *systematic* terms, even if *Being and Time* had been packed solely with examples of Neolithic flint-flaking, this would not demonstrate any real link between the tool-analysis and anti-technologism, given the fact that Heidegger's analysis is not inherently limited to "tools" at all. Perhaps it could still be argued that there was a psychological connection in Heidegger's own mind between his tool-analysis and handicraft, but this would only yield a point of biographical interest, and would not establish any innate conceptual link between the example of the workshop and the supposed confrontation of Nazism with Bolshevism and Americanism.

Like many commentators, Zimmerman adopts an overly specific approach to the theme of equipment, which leads him off the track from the outset: "Heidegger argued that even if I am in a workshop about whose products or procedures I am completely ignorant, I nevertheless recognize that it is a workshop."[150] This is too reminiscent of Okrent's discussion of auto repair. A statement of this kind can indeed be found in *Being and Time*—but not with the psychological, almost *anecdotal* twist provided by Zimmerman's reading. In the passage at issue, Heidegger is simply concerned to emphasize that our primary encounter with objects is not with sheer present-at-hand entities. He *never* makes the psychological claim that Dasein is always able to recognize a workshop as a workshop. This is clearly false, as numerous cases of extreme disorientation will attest. I myself have frequently entered workshops without immediately realizing that fact; on two occasions, the results have been disastrous. I trust that many readers would be able to provide similar tales if asked to do so. Once again, Zimmerman's analysis is unjustifiably humanized, and converts tool-being into an issue of Dasein's own understanding rather than of the tools themselves.

That Zimmerman does this becomes evident in still other ways: "My prior understanding of the being of tools enables me to use them appropriately."[151] Instead of saying that the "being" of the tools is what allows me to pick them up and employ them, Zimmerman follows a familiar pattern, reading the *Zu-/Vorhandenheit* pair not as kinds of *being*, but as kinds of *knowing*. The ramifications of this move are the same for Zimmerman as for everyone else: language, as the very medium of understanding, is now said to have primacy over tool-being. Zimmerman overlooks the ontological drama of *reality vs. presence* in favor of the less interesting pragmatic struggle of *using vs. seeing*. Here is another example:

> Consider the cobbler in his shop. He uses tools to make shoes. How is this possible? Because the cobbler understands in advance the equipment and supplies with which he works in terms of the network of relationships and possibilities that constitutes his world. He understands what his tools and his products "are for."[152]

Once again, Zimmerman follows the Okrent–Dreyfus-Rorty model of reading *Zuhandenheit* as practical know-how. But the key to producing shoes is not, as he suggests, the cobbler's "understanding" of how all his gadgets work. Rather, the key is the actual *reality* of the equipment, its real efficacy in sustaining his efforts. Much of this equipment is not "understood" by the cobbler in the least. For example, does the cobbler ever reflect on the law of gravitation, which prevents his shoes from sailing off into empty space? Does he often think about the currency system that allows him to offer the shoes at reasonable market prices? Does he ever ponder the unusual political stability of the region in which he lives, which prevents Frankish raiders from pillaging his shop and murdering him? *All of this* is equipment too, and it cannot be understood in the narrow sense of tool-items at all. The tool isn't "understood"; it *is*. It can be understood only *because* it is, and such understanding can never adequately mirror its being.

Strangely enough, Zimmerman even goes so far as to cite Heidegger's remark that natural things ("steel, iron, metal, mineral") are also ready-to-hand,[153] without recognizing that such a list can soon be expanded well beyond the bounds of anything understandable to the laborer. The cobbler most likely has never heard of quarks, and has perhaps rarely if ever thought about being itself; nonetheless, both of these help to sustain his business and support his life as a whole. Even if it were true that entities could not *mean* anything without Dasein (and this is untrue, as will be shown in chapter 3), it would not follow that they cannot *be* anything. The meaninglessness of the word "quarks" to the cobbler does not annul their sustaining force over the matter that composes his body no less than his shoes. In the end, the example of the workshop tells us nothing much at all about cobblers and the type of knowledge they require. The analysis is far too general for that.

I have already mentioned that Zimmerman's overly specific reading of tool-being leads him down the familiar path of openly raising language to the pinnacle of philosophy. In doing so, he appeals to the views of Gerold Prauss of Freiburg, who has written a fine commentary of his own on precisely these themes.[154] In spite of the excellence of Prauss' book, I find it necessary to disagree with him even more than with Zimmerman. The basic mistake made by Prauss is not an uncommon one. Reading the difference between tool and presence-at-hand as a taxonomy of human deeds, he points to a developmental process through which Heidegger eventually overcomes the supposed naiveté of the tool-analysis. Zimmerman glosses this nicely: "Science is not merely theoretical but practical, at least insofar as it employs experimental devices. Likewise, practical behavior always involves an element of understanding, even if it is not explicitly theoretical in character."[155] In the opinion of Prauss and Zimmerman, this statement reflects only a *later* awareness by Heidegger of the interpenetration of theory and practice. I find this claim astounding, given that the whole of §69 in *Being and Time* is devoted to precisely this insight—that praxis is not blind, and that even theory has its praxis. Besides, this is not even the relevant level on which to approach the question. Readiness-to-hand *never* served to describe a particular sort of pretheoretical experiences (for example, building treehouses) as opposed to an utterly distinct type of theoretical behavior (for example, solving Fermat's Last Theorem). As argued throughout this book, the two dimensions (tool and broken tool) are *equally* present in every least scintilla of both human and nonhuman reality. Even in *Being and Time*, there exists no entity and no situation in which this dualism could possibly vanish, whatever Heidegger's feelings may be. Hence, Zimmerman and Prauss are on the wrong track when they date the intermixing of the two moments to much later in Heidegger's career.

This approach to the problem leads both authors to endorse the following lamentable claim: "Instrumental activity, then, does not *precede* language but instead is made possible by linguistic understanding."[156] Even if this were true, it would still be irrelevant, since Heidegger's tool-analysis is *not about instrumental activity*. To state that language is constitutive of the *use* of hammers does not solve the problem; such a maneuver is far from proving that language precedes the *being* of the hammer, a layer of reality that the linguistic turn must overlook altogether as long as it wishes to survive with its current prestige intact. It would still have to be demonstrated (and it cannot be) that readiness-to-hand means usefulness. In other words, even if "language" is the condition of possibility for the tool's being *accessible*, such accessibility only takes care of one side of the tool's reality. For the tool-being of the hammer is precisely what is *inaccessible* in it. Although Prauss and Zimmerman are willing to concede that

Heidegger to some extent defines things *in themselves* as ready-to-hand, they are clearly uncomfortable with this notion. As Zimmerman objects:

> But by describing tools "in themselves" as ready-to-hand, did not Heidegger tend to conceal the fact that tools become tools only when someone *uses* them? Our everyday conviction may be that the means-character belongs to the tool itself, but this conviction is misguided. The tool itself is made for a purpose that is achieved only when someone uses it. The user is informed in advance by knowledge about his or her situation, about the capacity of the tool, about the task to be accomplished. The practical activity of using the tool, then, is not productive of but instead derivative from the knowledge which leads one to pick up the tool in the first place.[157]

On one level, this is an admirable passage: Zimmerman is right to subordinate individual present-at-hand substances to the referential contexture from which they emerge. But my own view is that this is an idea once but no longer liberating. It is an idea that fights the *last* war instead of the next one, attacking a straightforward notion of independent substances that is defended today only by a handful of crusty old-guard outcasts. Surely there must be more interesting targets out there somewhere; why kick substance when it's down? By choosing as his strategic enemy the view that the tool has a function "in itself," Zimmerman backs himself into a corner in which the humanization of the tool becomes his only alternative. And tool-being is certainly nothing human. Here as before, the problem is framed too narrowly, with only explicit handy devices in mind. In cases other than that of manmade hardware, the above argument by Zimmerman is clearly not relevant at all. Does the moon become moon only when someone "uses" it as equipment for astronomy or as the backdrop for a serenade? Does the air become air only when someone breathes it? The tool-analysis is *nothing but* a refutation of this kind of deflationary realism. If our encounter with all such entities is thoroughly determined by our own projections, this is still only *half* of Heidegger's "temporality."

As Zimmerman sees it, there are very concrete reasons for Heidegger having gradually phased out his renowned hammer-example: "Later Heidegger de-emphasized pragmatic-instrumentalist activity, which he at one time made the basic feature of human behavior, because he realized that this instrumentalist account of human existence was too reminiscent of the instrumental attitude present in the technological understanding of things."[158] But this passage only works when we begin from an incorrect understanding of tool-being. It is quite impossible to regard the analysis of equipment as an example of "instrumental reason," for the simple reason that the ready-to-hand has a *universal* field of application. Even if we imagine a situation in which all instrumental reason were absent, tool-being would still be there, lurking in the shadows. In the end, technology is a *spe-*

cific phenomenon for Heidegger, present in greater or lesser degrees in every situation, but equipment is not anything narrowly specific. Tool-being has nothing more to do with instrumental devices than with angels or with flowers along the Ganges. I have argued this point from the first page of the present book.

When it comes to Rorty's nemesis, the transcendent realm of type-A objects, Zimmerman lies well within the contemporary mainstream: "To exist means to be a never-ending process of interpretation, with never a hope of arriving at an 'essential' identity."[159] But this misses the point. The fact that Dasein never *arrives* at an "essential identity" does not mean that there *is* none. In other words, we have already seen that Dasein can never encounter tool-being without somehow converting it into presence-at-hand (all efforts to claim otherwise must fail, even when they are Heidegger's *own* efforts). But this does not mean that tool-being in itself has no existence outside of language. The confusion arises from regarding equipment as a form of human interpretation. While it is true that the tool-analysis dethrones any form of traditional substance in favor of the system of reference, it is equally true that Dasein's projection is a projection *of the tool.* By reading readiness-to-hand as "practical interpretation," *Zuhandenheit* is converted into *Vorhandenheit*, an equivalence more impossible than that of black and white or night and day.

In the present case, the unnecessary continuation of the war against substance only blinds commentators to an undeniable trace of the "reality principle" in Heidegger's works. As even Zimmerman acknowledges, "understanding" is nothing subjective: "Instead, 'the understanding of being' is in effect identical with the event of being itself. . . ."[160] But even so, he fails to avoid the stale claim that this is a special discovery of the *later* Heidegger, one that allows the philosopher to redeem himself from the supposed instrumental subjectivism of his early years. In its own right this would not be so awful—after all, there is no *a priori* reason to prefer the early Heidegger to the late. But this appeal to the later phase inevitably prepares the way for a far more unfortunate song, one which Zimmerman loves every bit as much as Schürmann does. I need only quote *part* of one of Zimmerman's sentences to explain what I mean: "The shift of Heidegger's attention from the structure of human Dasein to the *play* of being itself. . . ."[161] We have now encountered this appeal to "play" often enough that it begins to seem like an inevitable final symptom of the human-centered reading of equipment. After all, if the entire tool-analysis is confined to the immanent realm of Dasein from the start, then there really isn't much choice of escape routes. With every instant of time effectively subjectivized (whatever the protests that this isn't really being done), being will inevitably have to be sought *outside* of such instants. Being turns into an "emergent process," standing above all instants even while threading them together. Although this assumption fits quite nicely with the usual reading of Heidegger's temporality, it is the *wrong* reading—as Levinas saw, and as I will argue again below.

Once again, I have argued against any connection between Heidegger's tool-analysis and his reflections on technology. It is hardly surprising that the gaping rift between these themes has been overlooked, since the description of equipment has never been pushed far enough for its utter universality to be seen. Jackhammers are ready-to-hand; bird's nests are ready-to-hand; grains of dust are ready-to-hand; black holes and pulsars are ready-to-hand. Equipment isn't "useful"; it *is*. It can prove to be useful or harmful or indifferent *only insofar as it is*. Heidegger's theory of equipment has nothing more to do with technical devices than with the most noninstrumental and useless entities that might be imagined. I have repeated this remark numerous times throughout the book because experience shows that many readers endorse it only reluctantly.

But is there really no link between the themes of tool/broken tool and technology? Unfortunately, there *is* such a link in Heidegger's eyes; I say "unfortunately" because the link he offers is not very convincing. As is well known, Heidegger develops his reflections on technology in an indirect way, and not through a reflection on various motorized devices. It is not Heidegger's style to talk about microwave ovens and heart transplants. Here as elsewhere, he claims that a wider issue is at stake than "mere" specific entities. And not surprisingly, it has much to do with the themes of concealing and revealing. As he puts it in *The Question Concerning Technology* : "But how does bringing-forth happen, be it in nature or in handwork and art? . . . Bringing-forth brings hither out of concealment forth into unconcealment."[162] When something is produced, in whatever realm of human activity, it is brought to light from the shadows of its being. Here already, Heidegger's account of "production" proceeds via appeal to the familiar tool/broken tool model that is also given the inappropriate title of "truth." Heidegger reminds us further that "production" in Greek philosophy refers not primarily to a physical making, but rather to a form of knowing: "From earliest times until Plato the word *tekhne* is linked with the word *episteme*. Both words are names for knowing in the widest sense."[163] As with every other term that appears within the compass of Heidegger's thought, it is said that knowledge must be traced back to its originary movement of emergence from hiddenness: "Knowing provides an opening up. As an opening up it is a revealing."[164] In sum: "Technology is a mode of revealing. Technology comes to presence in the realm where revealing and unconcealment take place, where *aletheia*, truth, happens."[165]

Wherever we go and whatever we do, we are always surrounded by the unconcealed, *claimed* by it: "Wherever man opens his eyes and ears . . . he finds himself everywhere already brought into the unconcealed."[166] The other side of the story is equally true. We are not only surrounded by unconcealment, but also drift about in a permanent reign of *concealment*: "All coming to presence, not only modern technology, keeps itself everywhere concealed to the last."[167] I have already argued that this tells us no more than that there is a ubiquitous relation between ready-to-hand and present-at-hand, a duality beyond which nothing and no one can step. But now as always, Heidegger wants to do more than offer a universal claim of this kind. He also holds that there are specific *brands* of concealing and revealing. That is to say, he regards modern technology as an exceedingly *special* case of the concealed/revealed dynamic, insofar as it harnesses nature and stores its force in an available reservoir of energy. "But does this not hold true of the old windmill? No."[168] For Heidegger, the hydroelectric dam must be viewed quite differently from the windmill of our grandfather's youth.

Since we are dealing with Martin Heidegger here, it is a safe bet that the difference between these two artifacts is not meant to be any sort of ontic distinction, not any squaring-off of "mere properties." He certainly must mean more than that the windmill's power is employed instantaneously while that of the dam is stored for future use. After all, this understanding of modern technology would easily fall prey to counterexamples: for example, the Medieval shepherd stockpiles wool for market days yet to come. Clearly, this is not what Heidegger wants to say. Instead, any difference between the standing-reserve and simple contraptions such as windmills must have an *ontological* character. In the present context, this can mean only one thing: the windmill and the dam must not only conceal and reveal the world in different ways (for this would already be true of the difference between an axe and a shovel). Instead, Heidegger seems to hold that the windmill and the dam have altogether different *kinds* of relations to the interplay of concealing and revealing, to the same duel that permeates every square inch of his world. Unless such a clear distinction can be demonstrated, the supposed gap between dam and windmill will remain unconvincing. Unfortunately, Heidegger's attempt to establish such a distinction fails in a familiar way. For he wants to claim that technology *annihilates* the very depth-dimension of things, reducing them to a false nearness and availability: "The coming to presence of technology threatens revealing, threatens it with the possibility that all revealing will be consumed in ordering and that everything will present itself only in the unconcealedness of standing-reserve."[169] But this is the same paradox we have encountered twice already. On the one hand, the duel of light and shadow is everywhere. On the other, Heidegger wants to say that in *specific* cases, light can predominate a bit more over shadow, or the reverse, with technology being only the limit case of sheer manipulable revealing. I have already argued that this cannot be the case, since *every* situation is haunted by an *identical* strife between darkness and light. But if this claim is untenable, then so is Heidegger's entire theory of technology, for the same reasons as were his theory of truth, his theory of space, his theory of time, and his theory of theory itself. Heidegger might still claim that even if technology doesn't *really* denude the world of all its mysteries, it is a danger insofar as it makes us *think* that it does so, makes us *believe* that the cosmos has been adequately revealed as a stockpile. This is a debating point, one that can be dealt with at some other time. But in a practical sense it strikes me as false. Despite the considerable virtues of pristine nature, despite the urgent need to address the coming ecological catastrophe, I don't see that this issue has much to do with the question of concealing and revealing. And on a personal level, I actually feel myself more chilled by the mystery of being when taking nighttime walks surrounded by flashing technological infrastructure than when taking a weekend hike amidst wildflowers. Perhaps the latter experience is superior to the former in many ways. But even if so, this has nothing to do with urban landscapes reducing being to a present-at-hand stockpile. Quite the opposite.

Some readers might be wondering when this book is going to address Heidegger's famous essay on the artwork. Unfortunately, that essay is highly disappointing for reasons that should now be clear. Heidegger's attempt to define the artwork as a strife between world and earth runs up against the difficult fact that he has already defined *all* of reality as a strife. It is not only a Greek temple that reposes in the reality of its being while unfolding itself to the gaze of mortals—the same is true of a superhighway or a tax attorney's office. The best option left to Heidegger would be to say that even if strife is present at all moments, the artwork brings forth strife *as* strife. But here as elsewhere, the as-structure is ill-equipped to attempt such distinctions. All points in the cosmos are torn asunder by Heidegger's dual forces. This is his great discovery, austere enough and global enough to be worthy of Parmenides. It also gives us the true sense of the term "fundamental ontology," as suggested once already. Even among Heideggerians, there is probably no one still alive in the world today who would proudly proclaim himself or herself a "fundamental ontologist." The reason is simple: this term is taken to refer to a phase in Heidegger's thought that the thinker himself soon overcomes. It is used as an all-embracing title for his supposed juvenilia, and defined most frequently as follows: "fundamental ontology is ontology approached through the analysis of human Dasein." I hold that this connection between fundamental ontology and Dasein is inessential, and that a more accurate definition of the term is possible.

In fact, the primary meaning of fundamental ontology is not that it analyzes human existence as the horizon for the question of being. Instead, fundamental ontology defines the philosophical collapse of all specific entities into a single *fundament*, the dissolution of every being into the repetitive play of darkness and light, tool and broken tool. If fundamental ontology is one half of philosophy according to Heidegger, the so-called "metontology" would be the other. This term itself has an extremely short lifespan in Heidegger's works (although the related term "meta-metaphysics" enjoys a brief mention in the late 1930s). Even so, the new metontological discipline is precisely what is lacking in all of Heidegger's supposed concrete analyses, which implode all too quickly into camouflaged refrains of the war between veiling and unveiling. Unless and until some sort of metontology emerges from Heidegger's own literary remains (and the chances grow increasingly slim), he will have as little to tell us about technology and artworks as he does about time. That task has been left to us in the present day, and it cannot possibly be achieved if we continue in our obsession with human access to objects rather than with objects themselves. In a sense, the object-oriented philosophy to be outlined in chapter 3 is an attempt to draw a primitive metontology out of Heidegger's works.

Heidegger brings his famous technology essay to a close by comparing the double-faced essence of technology to the relation of two stars in their courses. Having done so, he pursues the astral metaphor further: "The question concerning technology is the question concerning the *constellation* in which revealing and concealing, in which the coming to presence of truth, comes to pass."[170] He never put it better than this. This problem of specific constellations of revealing and concealing is precisely what Heidegger needed to solve, and *never managed* to solve. Instead of drawing up a detailed map of every constellation in the sky, Heidegger's astronomy contains only a static pair of binary stars, forever circling each other in profound but unchanging orbit, bathing every planet in the same pulsating light. Still, even if he fails to work out the geometry of stellar constellations, Heidegger at least goes so far as to *name* his highest hope. This occurs in the formidable Bremen lecture of 1949, "Einblick in das, was ist." Here, the messianic tone is not lacking: in some future *Kehre* that may come to pass, with or without our own efforts, entities would no longer be the stockpiled present-at-hand hulks that oppress us today. Heidegger suggests the possibility "that with this turn, the truth of the essence of being expressly enters into beings."[171] This is reminiscent of a memorable passage from early in the *Beiträge*: "The time of the construction of the essential configuration of beings from out of the truth of being has not yet come."[172] But this remark applies to Heidegger every bit as much as to his contemporaries.

§18. The Fourfold

> The experience of sleep does not mean a mere recollection that I fell asleep. It does not aim at sleep as a mere occurrence. (Heidegger, 1966/67)[173]

Among most readers of Heidegger, no major concept has left as unfavorable an impression as *das Geviert*: the fourfold. Among those readers who were never fans of Heidegger to begin with, the effect is of course far worse, and the fourfold is simply dismissed as an example of pious gibberish. As a result, most favorably disposed commentators leave it out of consideration altogether, with Heidegger's friends trying to prevent him from embarrassing himself among his enemies. But this lack of respect for the quadrate (a perfectly reasonable alternate translation despite Schürmann's objections) rests on a simple and avoidable misunderstanding. In fact, there is a sense in which the fourfold is *more* intelligible than the more popular conceptions of time, truth, and theoretical comportment. For unlike these other concepts, *das Geviert* actually has a truly original character, and cannot simply be identified with the familiar axis of tool/broken tool. By doing no more than pursuing the recurrent theme of tool-being in all its guises, we are led to an improved understanding of a concept that has been an impossible nut to crack for more than fifty years. But before unfolding the theme of the four in a new way, it will be useful to give a brief overview of the usual attempts to understand this notion. The more recent generation, split between analytic and Derrida-inspired Heideggerians, tends to avoid this concept altogether. For this reason, it is necessary to return to the work of one of those older commentators whose early disseminating mission required that even Heidegger's most inscrutable themes not be omitted from mention. Given the need to move as quickly as possible to the final chapter, I confine myself to a discussion of the venerable William Richardson,[174] although Otto Pöggeler[175] and Vincent Vycinas[176] would have been equally suitable choices.

Richardson's 1967 book *Heidegger: Through Phenomenology to Thought*, was the first extensive treatment of Heidegger in English; in some respects, it remains the most thorough and scrupulous commentary we have. But of the 641 pages in this encyclopedic commentary, a scant *six* are explicitly devoted to the problem of the fourfold. Richardson himself is not to blame for this starvation diet. When he tells us that he "[does] not feel obliged to solve the problem [of the fourfold] (*if it can be solved*),"[177] he speaks for almost every horse in the field. The lack of an obvious developmental bridge between *Being and Time* and the mirror-play of the four, the notorious preciousness of Heidegger's own descriptions of earth and sky, even his failure to insist with his usual vehemence that *das Geviert* be taken seriously—all of these factors have resulted in a concept so baffling that recent commentators have rarely felt obliged even to *mention* it, let alone solve it.

Even so, there are no grounds for Richardson's Schürmannesque assumption that Heidegger's "four" is only poetic slang for "many." Richardson feels that the key to this topic is Heidegger's insight into the "richness" of Being,[178] its "polyvalent plenitude."[179] But for anyone familiar with the 1949 Bremen lecture, that seedbed of all of Heidegger's later work, the crucial role of the number four cannot be so easily denied. In Heidegger's own eyes, at least, the world is not just "polyvalent," but specifically *tetravalent*. We make it too easy on ourselves if whatever we cannot understand is dismissed as unimportant.

The link between Richardson and Schürmann goes well beyond this particular point of agreement. Also striking is the fact that both of these prominent interpreters want to divorce the fourfold from any relevance to *specific* things, even though this is precisely the context in which Heidegger introduces his notorious tetrad. While Heidegger explicitly serves up declarations about actual jugs and bridges, Richardson studiously downplays this aspect of the theme: "What, then, is a thing? Heidegger resorts once more to the phenomenological method, which, *as far as it goes*, is masterful."[180] In this passage there can be found one alarming red flag, and one subtle but dangerous mistake. The red flag is italicized here for the reader's convenience. While Richardson offers no specific complaints about Heidegger's jug-analysis, he seems to believe that no concrete analysis of a thing can *ever* go deeply enough. Any account of a specific thing would have to be qualified with the caveat: "this is good... as far as it goes." Presumably, Richardson holds that the real action lies in the deeper "possibility" of any individual thing, or in the "play" which alone enables the thing to be a thing and which marks the passage from "Heidegger I" to "Heidegger II." I have already criticized this standpoint in another context. But the widely-read Richardson and Schürmann are two pillars of the view that specific entities in Heidegger must amount to philosophical poison.

But this leads us to a subtler and even more familiar error connected to Richardson's very use of the term "phenomenology." In Richardson's view, phenomenology is fine, "as far as it goes." This attitude takes on tangible form even in the very subtitle of his book: "Through Phenomenology to Thought," which is obviously supposed to refer to *progress* on Heidegger's part. While I am wary of the fashionable disrespect for Husserl today (which views him only as a poster boy for the discredited "philosophy of consciousness"), it is important that the real difference between the Husserlian analyses and Heidegger's own not be effaced. In the passage cited above, Richardson seemingly reads the term "phenomenological" to mean no more than "pertaining to concrete examples, such as mailboxes or jugs."

But as already stated in connection with Bernet, there is an essential difference between Husserl's "phenomenon" and Heidegger's "thing." The difference is *not* to be found in the usual claim that Dasein is historically situated while the phenomenological subject is a lucid and rootless observer; Husserl leaves plenty of room, at least in principle, for a layered *historical* structure of reality. Instead, the real difference lies between the *intentional* and *equipmental* view of objects. In the case of Husserl's now proverbial mailbox, the object is gradually displayed in a series of intentional views, each of them passing from tacit horizon into explicit awareness. With Heidegger it is otherwise: for him, the jug is not primarily the object of an intention, not even that of a suppressed intention or one not yet born. Instead, the object is already silently unleashed in the zone of its jug-being or bridge-being; quite apart from any presentation of itself, an entity is the sheer execution of receiving its wine, of holding vigil over the river it straddles. The tool-analysis, often explained away as a meditation on human action, yields nothing less than the *autonomy* of the things themselves from all such action. It is this insight alone which places Heidegger on higher ground than his greatest teacher. As I have argued already, the "hermeneutic circle" is not enough, since with this term it is still a question of an ambiguous *human* predicament, with no insight given into the inner vitality of the jug in and of itself.

It is only in *this* way that Heidegger can and does overcome phenomenology. Richardson thinks otherwise, and for this reason engages in the same misuse of the word "phenomenology" that is made more frequently by others in connection with the term "ontic." I have mentioned that while "ontic" is often taken to mean "pertaining to *objects* as opposed to the *conditions* of such objects," what it actually means is "pertaining to presence-at-hand as opposed to *readiness-to-hand*." The real movement of Heidegger's thought is not from beings toward a disembodied play or opening, but rather from mere presence into the most inexhaustible secret contours of objects themselves. If anything, Heidegger's writings on the fourfold serve to *magnify* the attention that was paid to specific beings in the context of the tool-analysis, as if he were finally cashing in on a brilliant initial investment in equipment. Only Richardson's prejudices allow him to slight this process, as if it were a kind of half-serious relapse into "phenomenology" in the old sense. In fact, such concreteness is precisely what needs to be *retained* from Husserlian phenomenology, and what is most lacking in the vast majority of present-day continental philosophy.

Having discussed this topic earlier, I revisit it here only by way of consolidation and review. More pertinent at the moment is Richardson's attempt to define the four terms of *Geviert*. Here, we find the unfortunate tendency to read the four parts of the quadrate as ontic zones, a tendency widespread even among those commentators who usually *denounce* such ontic methods. Recalling the fourfold terms of earth and sky, gods and mortals, Richardson explains these puzzling names as best he can:

> earth, for water comes from the springs in the earth, wine from grapes on the vine; sky, for the springs are fed by rain from the sky, wine-grapes nourished by the sun; mortals, for what is poured out may quench man's thirst or warm his heart; gods, for the liquid may be used as a libation to the gods.[181]

In offering this interpretation of the problem, Richardson is faithful enough to Heidegger's own literal statements on the matter. But the quadrate obviously cannot be taken in this sense of four *types* of entities, an ontic catalogue thoroughly alien to Heidegger's style of philosophizing. Such a reading could only lead us to an entertaining but implausible taxonomy of the following kind:

- Earth = mineral springs, vines, cornfields, maple groves, caverns, iron ore, dirt, etc.

- Sky = the sun, the moon, galaxies, clouds, snowstorms, the four seasons, air, etc.

- Mortals = Heidegger, Charlie Chaplin, Bismarck, Sappho, Edith Piaf, etc.

- Gods = Jehovah, Baal, Wotan, Indra, Zeus, etc.

For obvious reasons, this interpretation of the fourfold would be unacceptable. Nowhere else does Heidegger "stoop to the level" of trying to categorize different kinds of objects, and he is certainly not doing it here. And while few commentators would openly sanction a list of this kind, they would either offer nothing better in its place, or fall back into it along hidden paths.

But it is imperative that we *avoid* claiming that the jug is related to earth "insofar as water comes from the springs in the earth," or to sky "insofar as springs are fed by rain from the sky." If this were how Heidegger had meant to proceed, it is clear that his own choice of four terms would be nothing better than arbitrary. After all, instead of saying that rain comes from the *sky*, why not cite the more obvious reflection that rain is *water*—we would then have a new fourfold of earth and water, gods and mortals. Nor is wine only a libation for the gods; more often, I simply share it with visitors. Then why not a fourfold of earth and sky, *visitors* and mortals? There is simply no method consistent with Heideggerian philosophy for selecting four exemplary *entities* that would deserve promotion into the ranks of *das Geviert*. To do this would be to escape onto-theology only to endorse onto-polytheism—a grotesque maneuver under any circumstances, but particularly in Heidegger's case.

Nor am I taking unjustified pokes at an exaggerated version of Richardson's paraphrase. This talented scholar knows perfectly well what he is doing, as is clear from some of his further pronouncements: "The 'sky' here suggests nothing supra-sensible but is conceived in what another language would call a purely 'physical' way."[182] The quotation marks around "sky" and "physical" are not enough to get Richardson off the hook, since he has already included in his own explanation of *Himmel* the fact that the sun is responsible for ripening grapes. The so-called "scare quotes" are equally ineffective in the following passage:

> Earth and sky, taken together, then, would suggest the entire "world" or "physical" nature. If we take them thus and think them together with "gods" (clearly designating the entire realm of the divine) and "mortals", we are reminded of the trilogy that characterized classical metaphysics: God, man, "world."[183]

There are two significant problems with this claim. The first is that it would have made little sense for Heidegger, even if he had *meant* to retrieve the classical trilogy of God, man, and world, simply to jazz up the triad by splitting "world" into the new terms of earth and sky. If the fourfold were meant to allude to classical metaphysics, Heidegger could easily have stuck with the readily available number three, which already saturates so much of his philosophy. And furthermore, why should "world" be split in two rather than "God" or "man"? Why not dream up instead a fourfold of gods/angels/mortals/world (following Rilke rather than Hölderlin), or gods/demi-gods/commoners/world? Or, hitting even closer to home, gods/men/women/world? Until this question is answered (and it cannot be), Richardson's own parallel between the fourfold and classical metaphysics remains unconvincing.

The second and more serious problem with the analogy is that the metaphysical concepts of God, man, and the world referred to *types* of entities. Richardson himself acknowledges this: "[The classical trilogy] is a hierarchy of beings, of course, and we are dealing here clearly with Being."[184] But even this disclaimer does not save Richardson, since both his historical reference and his paraphrase of Heidegger's own difficult explanations show him to be secretly convinced that Heidegger *is* offering some new classification of entities. Nothing could be further from Heidegger's way of thinking.

Then what *does* Heidegger really mean by this inscrutable notion of the quadrate? The best place to look for an answer is certainly "Einblick in das, was ist." While *too much* noise was made about the 1989 centennial-year release of Heidegger's *Beiträge zur Philosophie* (an intriguing but rather disorganized folio) then *far too little* celebration accompanied the bombshell 1994 publication of the "Einblick" essay. It is surely the latter work, and not the *Beiträge*, which has the best claim to the title of Heidegger's second *magnum opus*. While this may be an unconventional view, it would instantly become the majority opinion if the theme of the fourfold were held in high esteem (which currently it is not). There can be no doubt that something new and exciting is underway in the "Einblick" lecture, even if it some of it turns out to be a simple reformulation of insights available in earlier works with a bit of digging.

The central theme of "Einblick" is *the thing*, which in Heidegger's view has *never* been grasped in its reality. In the history of philosophy, he claims, the thing has always been understood from an external standpoint, as something produced or represented or defined: "For this reason, Plato, who represents the presence of what comes to presence from the standpoint of its appearance, has thought the essence of the thing as little as Aristotle *and all later thinkers*."[185] And when it comes to the question of the thing, the challenge offered by Heidegger to Plato, Aristotle, "and all later thinkers," is nothing other than the ignored and ridiculed fourfold. Whatever may be thought of my own upcoming efforts to shed some initial light on *das Geviert*, we should not fail to register what is already obvious. With his opening complaint that everyone from Plato and Aristotle onward have reduced the thing to presence and appearance, Heidegger is allowing the fourfold object to spearhead his fresh efforts to overcome the history of metaphysics.

In the remainder of this section, my purpose is to show that the fourfold does have an easily intelligible structure, even if it is still a vague and frustrating one. By the end of this discussion, there should no longer be a question as to whether the fourfold is *meaningful* or not. The proper question will only be: "where does it get us?" In the end, *das Geviert* might be one of two things. If the majority is correct, it might be the ludicrous dead end of a pragmatist turned blood-and-soil mystic. But if I am correct, it might be a time bomb bequeathed by Heidegger to twenty-first-century philosophy, a weapon with which his name will forever be associated. My own view is that Heidegger's fourfold marks the elusive summit of the philosophy of the past one hundred years. Naturally, a claim of this kind cannot gather its evidence from a philological examination of various Heideggerian texts. What is required is that we at least give the concept some sort of minimal "test flight," a demonstration of its possible new uses as well as its remaining weaknesses.

The moment has come to turn directly to Heidegger's own exposition of the quadrate, beginning with earth and sky. As concerns the former: "earth is the serving bearer, blossoming and fructifying, spreading out in rock and water, rising up into plant and animal." Sky is introduced with equal flourish: "The sky is the vaulting path of the sun, the course of the changing moon, the wandering glitter of the stars, the year's seasons and their changes, the light and dusk of day, the gloom and glow of night, the clemency and inclemency of the weather, the drifting clouds and blue depth of the ether."[186] I have already insisted that these definitions cannot be treated as lists of manifold *examples* of earth and sky. The guiding factor here is not that all of the terms listed under "sky" are to be found up in the air rather than down on the ground—an ontic distinction alien to Heidegger, and too easily refuted by "transgressive" cases such as meteorites, (which have fallen from the sky to become embedded in earth) or volcanic gases (which move in the opposite direction). Rather, the key to "sky" is that all of the listed cases are specifically discernible objects or processes, tangible forces to be reckoned with in our lives—stars, seasons, day, night, weather.

It will immediately be noted that the description of "earth" has an entirely different structure. If Heidegger had meant to distinguish certain *kinds* of entities as earthly rather than heavenly (such as potatoes or moss), he could easily have done so. At the very least, he could have echoed his description of sky, saying something like: "Earth is the blossoming and perishing of the flower, the fertility of the soil, the scent of the quivering pines, the sadness and silence of the swamp, the ripeness of corn and cane." That he does *not* do this is so jarring for any attentive reader of his lecture that the vastly different conceptual overtones of earth and sky are clear. Instead of giving us tangible, specific metaphors for earth, Heidegger describes it only as "the serving bearer, blossoming and fructifying." But despite the earthly connotations of "blossom" and "fruit," this description is no more applicable to walnut trees than it is to starlight.

In an important sense, the same universal applicability also belongs to "sky." The difference between *Erde* and *Himmel* is no childlike rift between down on the ground and up in the air. As I have argued in connection with Richardson, anyone who wants to suggest otherwise will have a tough row to hoe, since nowhere else does Heidegger split up entities according to ontic categories drawn from common sense. And even if he did so in this one case for some reason, it would have to be explained: why just *these* four? And this is why I would like to suggest that the real difference between earth and sky can be found in the vastly different verbal structure of Heidegger's account of the two. All of the examples given of "sky" are specific entities—star, day, cloud, season. All of the examples given of "earth" are vague circulating forces that only burst into view through some *specific* entity. As a reminder, here is what he says about earth: "earth is the serving bearer, blossoming and fructifying, spreading out in rock and water, rising up into plant and animal." Earth is not the plant and animal, not the rock and water, and not a blossoming fruit, but is the "serving bearer" that spreads and rises into these. My point here is that the common-sense, "ontic" difference between earth and sky should be abandoned by commentators here.

Contrary examples, even bizarre ones, should be cited to establish this point. If we imagine some of the most down-to-earth entities of all time, we will find that they still must belong to sky rather than to earth. For example, it is likely that no large oak tree has ever been taken very high above the ground, not even as cargo in an aircraft. Nonetheless, an oak tree has far more in common with the terms under Heidegger's "sky" than those under "earth." It is a specific entity, and not merely a concealed "serving bearer." And we can get even earthier than an oak tree. What about mushrooms or a salt-mine, entities buried even more deeply in the earth? Here too, we find objects that are not merely suppressed murky forces that blossom and spread into others, but actual discrete objects, whether they belong to rhizomal networks or not. By the same token, the "serving bearer" that "spreads" does this not just for natural entities rooted in the soil. It must do the same for clouds, comets, and distant rings of ice. This will perhaps be less surprising than what I said about sky, given Heidegger's well-known tendency to use the word "earth" as a code word for the dark potencies and withdrawn being of things—which I have already argued should be identified with the equipmental contexture.

If we read the terms in this way, earth and sky lose their incomprehensible character. Earth is the concealed, the bearing and supporting system on which all else forever rests but which itself forever recedes from view. Sky is the sphere of revealed entities, the stars and comets but also potatoes and lakes that seduce us with their blatant energies. In the first instance, following the terminology developed throughout this book, we can identify earth with tool, sky with broken tool. But this is only half the battle, since earth and sky are much easier to grasp then the other terms of the quadrate. Still, I would like to make sure that the reader firmly grasps this first principle for interpreting Heidegger's fourfold: earth and sky are not types of beings, but names for the concealed and revealed. Like tool and broken tool, "earth" and "sky" both belong in equal measure to *all objects*. This first half of the fourfold is none other than the single repetitive dualism into which all other terms in Heidegger's philosophy collapsed during the course of chapter 1. Let your thoughts rest here for a moment: Aristotle notes that it is more pleasurable to review familiar truths than to learn unfamiliar ones, and we are about to move to unfamiliar terrain.

If earth and sky merely repeat a dualism already known to us, gods and mortals seem to present a trickier pair. The first of these terms is introduced as follows: "The gods are the hinting messengers of the godhead.

From out of the concealed sway of the latter the god appears in his essence, *which withdraws him from all comparison with what comes to presence.*"[187] As for the other quadrant of reality: "The mortals are the humans. They are called the mortals because they can die. To die means: to be capable of death *as* death."[188] Here as before, it cannot be a question of distinguishing between humans and gods in the everyday sense of these words: just like earth and sky, gods and mortals are mirrored for Heidegger even in the simplest jug.

"The gods" does not refer to a distinct class of divine beings, but to the "concealed sway" that is mirrored in *every* entity. It is true that the gods are referred to as "hinting messengers" whereas only the *godhead* is described as a concealed sway. It is also true that the passage cited above says that the god "appears in his essence," which seems to run counter to the usual impossibility in Heidegger of any entity being *truly* revealed in its essence. But these inconsistencies are trumped by the final line of the passage, in which the appearance of the god "withdraws him from all comparison with what comes to presence." If the god *appears*, it appears only as that which withdraws. The basic mode of the god is concealment; like earth, the gods belong to the concealed segment of reality, the secluded underground of reality that never comes to presence.

At the same time, the term "the mortals" cannot refer to a limited set of six billion human entities, nor to any privileged group of them. The crucial factor here is not the connotation that mortals are "people." The important part of Heidegger's description is that mortals are capable of death *as* death. The mortals, then, belong to the kingdom of the as-structure, to the zone of reality as "revealed." And to repeat, "the mortals" cannot refer to one type of entity (people) as opposed to others, since Heidegger is quite explicit about the fact that the mirror-play of the fourfold plays itself out *in objects*. Heidegger would probably never go as far as I do in de-emphasizing the privilege of human Dasein, but he still is arguing nothing like a separation of entities under four different sub-headings. All four terms must somehow mirror each other in the heart of clouds, trees, people, *and* gods, and are not separated from one another and distributed in isolation among these entities.

The reader should now let this point sink in as well. Contrary to expectation, gods and mortals begin by seeming rather similar to earth and sky, to such an extent that they might even appear indistinguishable. The mortals are those who are capable of death "as" death. They are not merely buffeted by death as by a concealed underground force but, thrown out into the nothing, openly comport themselves toward it. Still, this is not primarily a statement about human beings, but about the being of *all* that they encounter. To say that the mortals are capable of death as death does not imply any special relation of this topic to illness or funerals. Being-toward-death means being thrown out into the nothing, means grasping the finitude of all that exists, means asking "why is there something rather than nothing at all?" Prior to any specific traits it might have, every jug, bridge, and temple is something rather than nothing. This is the sense in which the moment of "the mortals" sparkles forth even from nonhuman entities. The important thing is that, like the moment of sky, "the mortals" belongs to the realm of explicit presence, to the dominion of the as-structure. The same analogy holds good for the other pair. Unlike mortals, the god belongs to the sphere of concealment. This allies the gods with earth, which also nourishes and fructifies only in utter withdrawal from our explicit concern.

This undercuts the understandable tendency by many interpreters to pair gods with sky and mortals with earth: "After all, much of world mythology places the gods somewhere high up in the air, while everyone knows that people live on the ground." But the dynamics of the fourfold run at cross-purposes to this general trend, which would work only if Heidegger were actually talking about four different *kinds* of objects. Instead, the cryptic concealment of earth and gods places them in the zone we know as "tool"; the explicit openness of mortals and sky roots them in the domain of "broken tool." Here is another point at which to pause briefly so as to let the interpretation sink in. Gods and earth belong together, in concealment; the mortals and sky belong together, in the as-structure.

The remaining question is whether there is any difference between earth and gods, and by the same token any difference between sky and mortals. If each pair consists *solely* in concealment or unconcealment, we can safely abandon Heidegger's quadrate, and return to the simple dualism of the initial tool-analysis. In attempting to answer this question, the issues grow a bit subtler, although they remain every bit as intelligible as before. For it is here that our earlier discussion of the 1919 lecture course begins to pay improbable dividends. In §8 and §9 above, the simple tool/broken tool opposition was complicated for the first time: there appeared an easily graspable contrast within the realm of appearance itself. In 1919, Heidegger made clear that the realm of explicit awareness was already polarized into dimensions that might be roughly termed "quality" and "sheer existence." We were introduced to the object as "specific something" and the same object as "something at all." I suggested that this was not a minor bit of pedantry on the young Heidegger's part, but that it marked a new dualism in his thought that had both clear ancestors and clear heirs. The most recent ancestor is the two reductions in Husserl, the obvious inspiration for this aspect of Heidegger's 1919 course. In addition to the eidetic reduction that takes a mere obvious phenomenon and gradually unveils its suppressed essential features, there is the phenomenological reduction that brackets experience as a whole. On the one hand, then, the phenomenon is a specific something, on the other it is "something at all." Going back beyond Husserl, the remote historical source for this distinction would seem to be the classical split between essence and existence.

If these concepts are the ancestors of 1919, then the heir is to be found within Heidegger's own career—the fourfold. For it is this crucial but completely overlooked second axis that renders Heidegger's fourfold intelligible for the first time. As we proceed, the reader is advised not to mix the following analysis of the fourfold with the question of whether this concept will turn out to be *useful*. My purpose for now is simply to show that *das Geviert* does have meaning: that it is not just pious hand-wringing nonsense pasted together out of arbitrary poetic slang, but presents us with Heidegger's most diligent attempt to develop a philosophy of objects. At the end of my account of the fourfold, I have included a visual diagram of my interpretation for the reader's convenience (see figure 1 below). It may be useful to refer to it now and consult it whenever necessary.

In any event, we are now reminded of Heidegger's account of a realm of unconcealment in which entities are torn between their specific character and their sheer reality-in-general. This topic is openly addressed in 1919, and I have argued further that the sister texts "What is Metaphysics?" and "Vom Wesen des Grundes" also reflect this puzzling new dualism. And this strange rift within the visible realm *is the distinction between mortals and sky.* Never forget that the Heideggerian sky has nothing to do with the sun and moon *as opposed* to cornfields. The sky comprises all recognizable entities, embraces all possible explicit qualities—blue objects, sour or bitter objects, smoky objects, stellar entities up in the sky, ruins buried in the soil. The kingdom of the as-structure, we know, is always shattered into a mob of alluring fragments. "Sky" is saturated with quality, and it is plural—there are many, many entities lying before us. Heidegger's analysis of broken tools already served to emphasize this. But at the same time, entities such as pencils, keys, ice-balls, and coral snakes are not only characterized by having certain specific features. Rather, each of them is also "something at all," rather than nothing; each of them simply *is*. But there is a difference between Heidegger's treatment of this theme in 1919 and in 1929. In his earlier reflections, it is *specific* entities that are something at all rather than nothing. The 1919 course allows for trillions of cases of "something in general"—any object at all will do quite nicely. But in 1929, with the treatment of Angst in "What is Metaphysics?," there is only a single "something at all," one that negates the whole of beings at a single stroke. Angst pays no attention to pencil or ice-ball, but cares only that beings as a whole are something at all rather than nothing. This discrepancy is an issue best left to another occasion, except to say that Heidegger is closer to the truth in 1929—the moment of "something at all" is best applied to the world as a whole, as implied by the sense of Heidegger's Angst *and* Husserl's second reduction. But what is relevant to us here is another aspect of Angst.

The one most crucial feature of Angst or being-toward-death is that such attunements are not concerned in the least with "something specific." If our theoretical comportments at a given moment are fascinated by a specific type of chemical, we are concerned with what typifies that chemical, what makes it unique. But we can also consider the chemical ontologically, and say that "whatever it is, it is something rather than nothing." In Heidegger's universe, this can also happen to us against our will, when Angst steals upon us and undermines the particularity of every entity now spread before us. When this happens, it can be said that we are confronted with being *as* being, nothing *as* nothing, death *as* death. As I have already argued, the term "mortals" refers not to people as distinct sorts of entities, but to this very moment of being *as* being. I conclude that sky is a new incarnation of Heidegger's "specific something," and the mortals a fresh term for "something at all." The distinction in Heidegger's early Freiburg years between the "formal-logical objective something" (a.k.a. something at all) and the "object-type something" (a.k.a. something as "slippery" or "burning" or "cone-shaped") is the unsuspected source for the ongoing and ubiquitous duel of mortals and sky. In more technical terms, it could be said that the difference between sky and mortals is none other than that between "generalization" and "formalization," the very forms of theoretical disclosure that so fascinated Heidegger during his student years. Given this surprising link to the vocabulary of phenomenology, this half of the fourfold has less to do with the raptures of Hölderlin than with the driest schemata of Husserl's seminars.[189] In a sense, if we consider an entity as split up into sky and mortals, we are merely repeating Husserl's insight about the two kinds of reduction.

But an analogous relationship immediately suggests itself between earth and gods, the two terms that refer to the suppressed netherworld of being. As described several paragraphs ago, earth withdraws into a hidden infernal unity, as the sustaining and nourishing system from which all else derives. Earth *is* the all-embracing and withdrawn "referential contexture," so familiar from Heidegger's tool-analysis, where it is introduced less musically but with precisely the same features. As an alias for the equipmental contexture itself, earth is not only invisible, but utterly *total*. In this respect, earth is analogous to Angst ("mortals"). That is to say, rather than having any *particular* reality, the earth is the sheltering totality: it is not something specific, but something which *is*. The difference between earth and mortals, of course, is that earth withdraws and "the mortals" belongs to the kingdom of the as-structure. Earth is a sheer concealed execution of "something at all," and not some *explicit* form of "something at all" as revealed in Angst. We now have *three* Heideggerian zones rather than the simple two of tool and broken tool. Within the scope of the latter, we now have two distinct realms: the myriad particularities of sky, and the sheer "somethingness" of Angst (mortals). And within the scope of concealment, we have our third term "earth," which takes over the familiar characteristics of tool-being in the broad sense I have advocated: concealment and totality. Heidegger remarks famously that in a strict sense there is no such thing as "an" equipment. By the same token, in the strict sense there is no such thing as "an" earth, but only a single concealed supporting totality—being itself. Earth is a name for being.

But just as there is a civil war underway above ground between sky and mortals, a similar conflict is underway in Hades. For it is not only the as-structure that is complicated by the emergence of a further dualism. The term "gods" becomes a second member of the concealed tool-empire itself. In a strict sense, there *is* such a thing as "a" god. The gods are plural, the hinting messengers who withdraw from all presence. Although both earth and gods share the basic polarity of *concealed*, there remains an obvious difference between them. Earth is the concealed double to the unveiled as-structure of the mortals: it is reality *at all*, regardless of what that reality may consist in. The rumble of the sustaining earth simultaneously underlies every flower and every skull and every ocean; it is not different "earths" in each of these cases. On the other hand, gods are the concealed double to the specificity of the unveiled sky. In the world of the as-structure, we never just confront something in general, but clouds, bread, or bicycles. So too with the empire of tool-being, which is pluralized in the form of "gods"—giving us not just a solitary sustaining earth, but specific withdrawn entities that repose in a concealed depth, irreducible to any network into which they might enter.

The result is that tool-being has a quadruple structure for Heidegger (see figure 1). The diagram in figure 1 is meant only as a summary of the foregoing discussions, and is invested with no special significance other than that of a handy reference.

I would like to conclude this discussion of Heidegger's fourfold with a final set of negative remarks, and then a prospectus of how his quadruple object might be studied in the future. To begin with the negative, we can imagine that a fountain pen sits directly before us. We have already seen how the mainstream commentators would try to relate this pen to *das Geviert*. It would probably be said that the fountain pen is used by *mortals*, perhaps to write down a prayer to the *gods*; it is made of metals buried in the *earth*, and reflects sunlight that comes from the *sky*. Something similar could be said with respect to a plate of spaghetti. After all, it is eaten by *mortals* on Sunday after church where *God* was worshipped; the

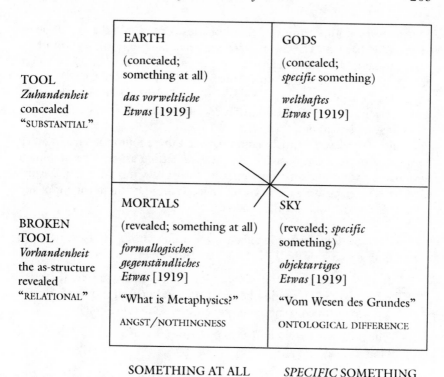

Figure 1 Heidegger's Fourfold *das Geviert*

spaghetti is made from grain that flourishes in the *earth*, ripened thanks to rain that falls from the *sky*. Endless examples of this kind are possible. By now, I hope that every reader is convinced that any separation of reality into four different *kinds* of objects is the least Heideggerian strategy that can be conceived. The only alternative, as stated by the philosopher himself, is that the mirror-play of the four is at work in *every* entity.

The *real* clarification of the four terms proved to be quite a bit more dry than the parodies above, to such an extent that it might still seem useless to some readers. To these readers, I would once more advise patience. The goal for now is simply to *state* the structure of the four. To incite the reader to *appreciate* it, to *dream* about it, to be lost in *fever* over it—these are the ambitions of a book yet to come.

As I have argued, the "sky" in a wine-filled goblet does not mean that wine-grapes were ripened under a sunny sky. Instead, it means that this is a silver goblet of a specific shape filled with wine of a specific vintage. Sky is an *ontological* notion. "Mortals" does not refer to the obvious fact that human beings drink from the cup, but means only that the cup *is* or its cylindrical shape *is*. The mortals are an *ontological* notion. On top of all this, the same dualism is repeated on the subterranean level. Quite apart from my own meaning-projections, in which the goblet is forever enmeshed, the goblet really is a sustaining reality withdrawn from my every grasp (earth), and is something of a specific character (gods). Earth and gods are *ontological* notions.

Heidegger describes the relation between these four moments in every entity as a mirror-play, though without ever getting as far as developing a systematic account of what mirroring means or how it plays out in specific objects. The stage has now been set for a solution of the meaning of the fourfold. So far, we know the following about it:

- The fourfold does not refer to four different kinds of entities, but points to a global play of four forces in all entities

- It is formed from the intersection of two distinct Heideggerian dualisms: the opposition between tool and broken tool, and the difference between something specific and something at all

- The relation between the four terms in any object is that of a "mirror-play"

In an upcoming book on "quadruple philosophy" I will attempt a full solution of this structure—linking it to two important currents in the history of philosophy, and trying to exploit it for the purposes of contemporary issues. The final chapter of the present book raises some questions that must be addressed before any such solution is possible. The question asked in chapter 3 is: what *sorts* of problems arise from the concept of tool-being developed so far in this book? What will emerge from this question is a new and offbeat variant of the old substance theory, so unfashionable today.

For the remainder of this book, there will be no further exposition of Heidegger's own writings. Instead of engaging in additional commentary, we ought to see if there are any additional ways to push beyond the punishing tool/broken tool dualism toward some more concrete vision of ontology.

But before beginning chapter 3, I would like to add one final section to the present chapter, as a kind of appendix. Since the rest of this book will defend a highly unusual brand of realism, it may be useful to begin by confronting one of today's most dynamic opponents of any philosophy of things themselves. I am referring to Slavoj Žižek, whose recent book *The Ticklish Subject* offers a highly original vision of where Heidegger's shortcomings might lie.

§19. The Specter of Realism

Any reader who has never attended a public lecture by Slavoj Žižek is urged to do so at the earliest possible opportunity. With rare personal charisma, best described as a cross between Lech Walesa and John Belushi, Žižek brings added electricity to an already challenging corpus of printed works. To read these works is as invigorating as waking from a good nap or taking an intravenous dose of sugar. If this is the future style of philosophy, then God be praised: irreverent jokes turn out to be pivotal arguments; surprising ideas erupt from every page. Among the most central of these ideas is Žižek's concept of retroactive causation—a theme in one respect very close to the present book, and in another respect diametrically opposed. While making a strong case for the unique position of Jacques Lacan in recent French philosophy, Žižek formulates what may be the most original critique of realism that can be found in the present day. The current section contains an account of his version of retroactive causes, intermixed with my own response on behalf of the tools themselves. I have chosen passages from two of Žižek's books that are especially relevant to the concept of tool-being. The first is his reading of Heidegger as presented in chapter 1 of *The Ticklish Subject* (1999). The second, taken from *The Sublime Object of Ideology* (1989), is a revealing assessment of the Kripkean theory of reference that displays Žižek's anti-realism in all its glory and all its bias.

The reading of Heidegger in *The Ticklish Subject* begins with a point already endorsed in the present book—the impossibility of a true intersection between ontic and ontological. Žižek follows this difficulty in its effects on Heidegger's politics: "On the one hand, [Heidegger] rejects every concern for democracy and human rights as a purely ontic affair unworthy of proper philosophical ontological questioning . . . on the other hand, his insistence that he is not convinced that democracy is the political form which best suits the essence of technology none the less suggests that there is *another* political form which suits this essence better."[190] As is well known, he locates this form in the "inner truth and greatness" of the Nazi movement, for at least a short period. But the paradox would remain even *absent* the stain of Hitlerism: as Žižek observes, certain Heideggerian Marxists view *communism* as the political form that best suits the essence of technology. We might also imagine Heideggerian monarchists, anarchists, Greens, or social democrats who could make the same claim for their own preferred systems. All such cases would be equally paradoxical: "Heideggerians are . . . eternally in search of a positive, ontic political system that would come closest to the epochal ontological truth, a strategy which inevitably leads to error. . . ."[191] Žižek notes that "the problem lies in this very expectation that a political movement that will directly refer to its historico-ontological foundation is possible."[192] This expectation is "metaphysics" in the worst sense of the term, the attempt to praise specific entities as privileged incarnations of a realm that is supposed to be withdrawn from *all* presence. In fact, the gap between external ideology and its "inner truth and greatness," between ontic and ontological, is *constitutive*.[193]

Even more usefully for our purposes, Žižek follows the paradox as it unfolds in Heidegger's tool-analysis. By treating presence-at-hand as a derivative mode of human immersion in the ready-to-hand, Heidegger establishes a familiar opposition between a primary reality and a second-hand realm distant from the primary one. As argued throughout this second chapter, there are compelling reasons to object to Žižek's interpretation of the tool-analysis as an attempt to collapse "the modern Cartesian duality of values and facts."[194] But we have already seen that in reading *Zuhandenheit* as "values" he is far from alone. More important here is Žižek's clear understanding of Heidegger's unsuccessful correlation of the differences between immersion and presence on the one hand, and authentic and inauthentic on the other. For example, "when a premodern artisan or farmer, following his traditional way of life, is immersed in his daily involvement with ready-at-hand objects that are included in his world, [for Heidegger] this immersion is definitely not the same as the *das Man* of the modern city-dweller."[195] For Heidegger, then, there are two sorts of immersion in one's surroundings, a good kind and a bad kind, one of them presumably corresponding more closely to the "inner truth and greatness" of the world. The same problem occurs on the level of explicit presence, since "there are also two opposed modes of acquiring a distance: the shattering existential experience of anxiety, which extraneates us from the traditional immersion in our way of life, and the theoretical distance of the neutral observer who, as if from outside, perceives the world in 'representations' . . ."[196] Here, too, Heidegger wants to say that one kind of presence corresponds to the very essence of Dasein, while representation is a mere inauthentic form of presence-at-hand. I have argued that the only feasible opposition in Heidegger's thought (aside from the strange second axis) is that between ready-to-hand and present-at-hand. In this sense, all modes of "absorption" must be ontologically identical, whether we speak of the poignant wisdom of soft-spoken peasants, the cynical absorption of Berlin lawyers, the unthematic living through of a great historic destiny, or the lazy use of a jackhammer. So too must all modes of the as-structure be ontologically identical: Angst, vandalized taxis, shattered windows, theoretical comportment, vision, hearing, and smell. Žižek is perfectly right to point to the impossibility of correlating ontic choices to the ontological gap between presence and absence.

It should also be clear that human existence never occupies the point of either pure immersion or pure awareness: "the 'specifically human' dimension is thus neither that of engaged agent caught in the finite life-world context, nor that of universal Reason exempted from the life-world, but the very discord, the 'vanishing mediator' between the two."[197] This ambivalent discord goes by many names in Heidegger, among them *geworfener Entwurf*, thrown projection. I have argued in this book that projection is no more primary than the thrownness, and hence, that the future has no real priority over the past. This is at odds with the usual reading of *Being and Time*, a reading encouraged by many of Heidegger's own statements. It is at odds with Žižek's reading as well: "The point is that the future has a primacy: to be able to discern the possibilities opened up by the tradition into which an agent is thrown, one must already acknowledge one's engagement in a project—that is to say, the movement of repetition, as it were, retroactively reveals (and thus fully actualizes) that which it repeats."[198] Obviously, Žižek has nothing to gain from following the orthodox commentaries on Heidegger, and does not defend the priority of the future in a spirit of keeping with tradition. Rather, there is a clear motive for championing futuricity that arises from his own deepest theoretical concerns. By cementing the priority of the future at this early stage, Žižek is setting the table for his doctrine of retroactive causation, in which the Real is not a "real world" outside of the human sphere, but the very *gap* between appearance and the non-appearing that is first *posited* by the fantasy of the human subject. As he puts it: "Daily habitat and excess are not simply opposed: the habitat itself is 'chosen' in an 'excessive' gesture of groundless decision."[199] Or in even clearer terms: "one can never reach a 'pure' context prior to a decision; every context is 'always-already' retroactively constituted by a decision."[200] Not only do my perspectives and projections affect how the context is *seen*, but the context is *created* by the very act of decision.

Nonetheless, Žižek will say later in his chapter that "we are not idealists"[201]—the "we" here is spoken in the first person. But clearly, any theory (like Žižek's) that grants priority to a subject retroactively positing its environment over any notion of a world in itself would also have to make the contrary claim: "we are not realists." This strange tension haunts Žižek's entire theoretical position. On the one hand, there is no real world of things themselves located in sheer isolation from the symbolic realm; these things themselves are nothing more and nothing less than the retroactive positings of a subject that never encounters them. Yet Žižek wants to avoid any extreme form of idealism. And more than this, he even responds with traces of irritation to any attempt to identify his position with idealism, as seen in his (currently uncontroversial) defense of Fichte against any charge of solipsism—the Fichtean *Abstoss* does not come from outside like things in themselves, but it still constitutes "reality," or rather is still the Real in a Lacanian sense.[202] The present book roughly accepts

Žižek's concept of retroactive causation, though without accepting the attitude of "deflationary realism" with which Žižek frames this concept. In the end, his problem will turn out to be that he restricts retroactive causation to a narrowly human realm, and orbits around the same unique gap between human and world that dominates most contemporary philosophy. But humans are not the only entities that encounter phantoms rather than things in themselves. I have argued that the as-structure also characterizes the strife between bananas and fruit flies, and even the collision of mindless rocks. In these cases too, objects do not encounter each other in direct presence, but only as a kind of caricature or objectification—the rock did exist beforehand, but never quite in the way in which the other rock objectifies it, which requires the *perspective* of this other rock.

Whereas Žižek apparently wants to restrict retroactive causation to the fantasy life of human subjects, I have insisted that even inanimate objects display this sort of fantasy. The murky depths of rock-being gain specific, tangible form not only through the retroactive positing of a human who encounters the rock, but even through inanimate entities that are forced to encounter it "as" such-and-such, "as" a specific obstacle or blessing. This has two consequences that Žižek would probably not wish to accept: (1) Retroactive causation is a global ontological structure, and not a narrowly psychoanalytic one. Whatever distinguishes human beings from animals and rocks cannot be found in this structure alone. (2) Given that retroactive cause occurs on every layer of reality, there is nothing ontologically special about human retroaction, meaning that Žižek's noncommittal distance from the question of realism is untenable. By the time human fantasy comes on the scene, the "real world" really *is* out there, and it is far more bizarre than today's realists suspect. It is in fact layer after layer of reciprocal projection and retroactive causality, with objects always "fantasizing" one another into a specific configuration of accessible properties rather than caressing one another to their very depths—an impossible desire.

Moreover, given the ontological dimension that Lacan and Žižek have provided for so many psychoanalytic concepts, perhaps "fantasy" and "desire" are more than metaphors. As Ken Burak whimsically puts it: "could there be hysterical rocks as opposed to obsessive ones? Could there be psychotic trees?"[203] Whatever Žižek might think of these almost farcical possibilities (which I myself take quite seriously, as long as they are "reduced to their bare-bones ontological foundations," as Burak adds), they certainly put his strategy in a new light. The fact that he sees retroactive causation as a death-blow to realism shows that he is repulsed by something that truly is quite repellent: the vision of the real world as a set of independent present-at-hand blocks that somehow get filtered down into a distorted human perception. But this is no longer the only version of realism on the market. *The Ticklish Subject* is already famous for its opening rhetorical flourish, an echo of Marx and Engels: "A specter is haunting

Western Academia . . . the specter of the Cartesian subject."[204] But a different specter haunts Žižek's work . . . the specter of Billiard Ball Realism. And when faced with such a bland theory as this one, the proper response is not Žižek's limited claim that the whole of nonhuman reality is a retroactive fantasy projection (a claim that is also, somehow, supposed to escape idealism). The best strategy is simply to dig a few inches into the world of objects and see that billiard balls are already in the same predicament as humans are—they too never have *access* to the tool-beings themselves. Even *they* cannot encounter reality itself, but only projections that never quite measure up to the object of their "desire." There *is* a surplus of the world beyond our projection of it; the world is *not* just a pure signifier representing a void, but is that which always withdraws from signification. The same fate awaits all objects in the cosmos.

Žižek follows his solid remarks on Heidegger with a lengthy and exciting reading of Kant and German Idealism, which I can only summarize briefly. As might be expected, Žižek strongly downplays the role of the noumenal in Kant. For him, what is most interesting in Kant is the very *gap* between phenomenal and noumenal, a gap that can be found in the structure of transcendental imagination. The noumena are not pre-existent, unformed cookie dough to be cut into shapes by the categories, but serve as "phantasmatic support"[205] for the imagination. Or in even blunter terms: "The pre-synthetic Real, its pure, not-yet-fashioned 'multitude' not yet synthesized by a minimum of transcendental imagination, is, *stricto sensu*, impossible: a level that must be retroactively presupposed, but can never actually be *encountered*."[206] But this does not address the issue of realism at all—the crucial opposition is not between presupposing and *encountering*, but between presupposing and *being*. It is obvious enough that the world cannot be directly *encountered*, and of course any access we have to it involves a retroactive constitution that cuts its being down to size and displays it by way of the as-structure. But if objects themselves must be projected in order to be determinate, this does not mean that they have no being of their own prior to such projection. Heidegger's tool-analysis teaches us precisely the opposite lesson, but Žižek follows the usual readings of this analysis as an opposition between fact and value, rather than as a more fruitful opposition between actuality and relation. Consider Žižek's appeal to quantum physics, "according to which an event 'becomes itself,' is fully actualized, only through its registration in its surroundings—that is, the moment its surroundings begin to take note of it."[207] Whatever the views of present-day quantum physicists may be, Žižek does not actually mean that an event fully becomes real only when *its surroundings* begin to take note of it. What he really means is that it only becomes fully real when a *human observer* begins to take note of it, retroactively projects it as something encountered. But I have argued that projection is a universal ontological structure that has no *special* connection with the gap between symbolic and Real in the human sense. The same fissure is everywhere, whether in vegetables, monkeys, or translucent crystal.

For Žižek, the special place of Kant in the history of philosophy comes from his radical vision of a *phantasmatic* gap between phenomenal and noumenal. As he sees it, Heidegger grasped the importance of this gap at the outset of his career, but lost his feel for it after the *Kehre* and therefore stripped Kant of his previous special historical role. On this point, we find significant agreement between yet another strange pair of commentators, with Richard Rorty's voice faintly audible beneath Žižek's: "what Heidegger actually encountered in his pursuit of *Being and Time* was the abyss of radical subjectivity announced in Kantian transcendental imagination, and he recoiled from this abyss into his thought of the historicity of being."[208] As Žižek observes, Heidegger holds that Kant's ethical theory, with its apparently strong *noumenal* component, regresses into an opposition between two worlds (eternal/temporal) rather than maintaining the standpoint of the finite temporality of Dasein.[209] According to Žižek, the crucial point missed by Heidegger is that there was never actually any cosmos in Kant at all. Or rather, there *should* not have been a cosmos in Kant, if not for his lingering wish for some kind of unity—for Žižek, it is actually Hegel who in a "breathtaking achievement"[210] makes the decisive break with all naive realisms, all possible materialist residues of the supposed thing in itself. In this way, there emerges the Lacanian model of the subject that Heidegger missed, a subject not "immersed in its life-world," but one able to create a fissure in being and retroactively posit its own context. Further support for this notion, says Žižek, is found in Schelling's "uncanny X"[211] of God qua ground in the uncompleted drafts of the *Weltalter* essay, the insane God which withdraws beyond all existence and all determination, and which must finally posit itself within the symbolic realm to escape its own blind rotary drives.[212] But the same objection would have to be made to Schelling that has already been made to Žižek. In Schelling's works, the uncanny power of withdrawal from surroundings seems to belong primarily to the blind rotary God, and secondarily to human freedom. Despite Schelling's magnificent sensitivity to nature, I am aware of no passage where he grants the uncanny X of withdrawal to *specific* entities such as donkeys, thistles, coniferous trees, or spoons. Yet this is precisely what must be done.

Concluding his chapter, Žižek aims some good-natured irony at mainstream Heidegger commentators, accurately stating that

> one of the clichés of today's American appropriation of Heidegger is to emphasize how he, along with Wittgenstein, Merleau-Ponty, and others, elaborated the conceptual framework that enables us to get rid of the rationalist notion of

subject as an autonomous agent who, excluded from the world, processes data provided by the senses in a computer-like way. Heidegger's notion of "being-in-the-world" indicates our irreducible and unsurpassable "embeddedness" in a concrete and ultimately contingent life-world: we are always already *in* the world, engaged in an existential project against a background that forever eludes our grasp and forever remains the opaque horizon into which we are "thrown" as finite beings.[213]

I quote this passage in full because, although composed in the spirit of mimicry, it provides an excellent overview of the orthodox readings of Heidegger. (Žižek, the great philosophical mockingbird of our time, is both witty enough and a good enough listener to provide similar wry summaries of virtually all of his opponents' positions.) In a positive sense, what he thinks is missed by this interpretation of Heidegger, and ultimately even by Heidegger himself, is Lacan's insight into the radically contingent, "mad" subject who is partially torn away from the fabric of reality. This jeopardizes the usual common sense conception of the world as a preexistent reality lying around prior to human awareness. But in Žižek's view, it also jeopardizes *Heidegger's* concept of world. He asks if

the Kantian destruction of the notion of the world via antinomies of pure reason does not affect world as the finite horizon of the disclosure of entities to an engaged agent? Our wager is that it does: the dimension designated by Freud as that of the Unconscious, of the death drive, and so on, is precisely the pre-ontological dimension that introduces a gap into one's engaged immersion in the world.[214]

It is Žižek's claim that Heidegger forever misses this "pre-ontological dimension that introduces a gap." For Heidegger, it is always a question of immersion, and of a corresponding passage from implicit to explicit awareness of a world in which we are already immersed. In an interesting passage, Žižek accuses Heidegger of *missing* Husserl's second reduction, saying that Heidegger's Angst is *not* enough to free us from the contexture of the world.[215] For Žižek, the problem with Angst seems to be that it points toward a concealed "real world" of being instead of the preontological gap of fantasy that surmounts all noumenal realisms:

The key question, therefore, is: how does this shattering experience of anxiety, which extraneates *Dasein* to its immersion in its contingent way of life, relate to the experience of the "night of the world," of the point of madness, of radical contraction, of self-withdrawal, as the founding gesture of subjectivity? How does the Heideggerian being-towards-death relate to the Freudian death drive? In contrast to some attempts to identify them (found in Lacan's work of the early 1950's), *one should insist on their radical incompatibility.* "death

drive" designates . . . the "immortal" insistence of drive that precedes the ontological disclosure of Being, whose finitude confronts a human being in the
experience of "being-towards-death."[216]

In defense of Heidegger, it should be said that Žižek is right to distinguish the two positions, and wrong only in which of the two he chooses to
defend. The idea that the human subject has a *special* capacity for self-withdrawal and retroactive phantasmatic positing of the world comes from an
artificially limited sense of the as-structure (in this respect, Žižek falls into
the same boat as the orthodox Heideggerians he so delightfully teases).
Mistaking the gap between reality and appearance for the narrower gap
between world and human, he exaggerates the status of human retroaction. Instead of being just one sort of projection among others, human
fantasy is held to undercut any truly independent existence of the Real; as
a result, Heidegger looks naive for thinking that Angst discloses being *in
its reality.*

But simply remove the human-centered model that Žižek is working
with, and you will find that the same structure holds equally good for all
levels of reality. Both plankton and bingo chips encounter other objects
and project them, encountering them only "as" such-and-such and not
entering into direct intimate contact with their being. All objects constitute their surroundings retroactively—objects are *retroviruses,* injecting
their own DNA back into the nucleus of everything they encounter. It is
not just humans who do this. Moreover, as a second objection, this process
does not occur in isolation from a reality that exists independently of all
such projections. There are plenty of problems with Heidegger's account
of Angst, but the fact that it tries (unsuccessfully) to reveal the independent reality of being is *not* one of them. It is crucial that retroactivity be
seen in realist terms, however strange such a realism may seem. By contrast,
Žižek is an idealist indeed. But this idealism, which Dreyfus termed "deflationary realism," has become the dominant philosophical horizon of our
time. By defining the human subject as a retrovirus, Žižek shatters the spell
of typical hermeneutic and deconstructive theories of the tedious play of
presence and absence. But by placing the outer world in the suspension of
epokhe, or of Lacanian fantasy, he reduces the many trillions of other retroviruses to a state of phantasmatic nullity. Thus, from the standpoint of the
present book, Žižek is both a great hero and a great opponent.

To clarify these points of disagreement, I will quote briefly from Žižek's
fascinating interpretation of Kripke, which can be found in his breakthrough book *The Sublime Object of Ideology.* I have already referred to
Kripke in my account of Dreyfus' reading of Heidegger. As is well known,
what Kripke opposes is the descriptivist theory of meaning, the view of
Russell and many others that the name of a thing is merely a shorthand

substitute for a series of descriptions of it, of known properties of that thing that can be tabulated and used to define it. In opposition to this tendency, Kripke regards the name as a "rigid designator," one that points to some inaccessible "X" lying behind any descriptions that might be given of it. Even if all of our current descriptions of a thing turn out to be false, if gold actually turns out to be green in pure light or to have fewer neutrons than we once believed, or even turns out not to be an element at all, the name "gold" still refers to that same inaccessible *stuff* that it has referred to all along.

And it is here that Žižek is at his very best. As if it were not refreshing enough that this gun-slinging Slovenian postmodernist actually gives a detailed examination of Kripke and Donnellan's disagreement with Searle (a dispute completely unknown to most continental philosophers), he also relates Kripke's rigid designator to issues in psychoanalysis and popular culture. By denying that a thing can ever be adequately defined by descriptive properties, Kripke seems to be establishing the rigid designator as a kind of unfulfilled/unfulfillable desire. Or as Žižek hilariously puts it, citing Kripke's own examples of gold and unicorns:

> How could we overlook the libidinal contents of these propositions of Kripke? [*laughing*-g.h.] What is at stake here is precisely the problem of the "fulfillment of desire": when we encounter in reality an object which has all the properties of the fantasized object of desire, we are nevertheless necessarily somewhat disappointed; we experience a certain "this is not it"; it becomes evident that the finally found real object is not the reference of desire even though it possesses all the required properties. It is perhaps no accident that Kripke selects as examples objects with an extreme libidinal connotation, objects which already embody desire in common mythology: gold, unicorn. . . .[217]

Much like Heidegger's politics and (according to my reading) Heidegger's ready-to-hand, the rigid designator refers to "an impossible-real kernel"[218] that can never be made present. Interestingly and disturbingly, Žižek points to a similar structure in anti-Semitism, which he says is not yet active when it is merely said that Jews conspire and swindle, but only comes into effect when we hear the reverse formulation: that they conspire and swindle *because they are Jews*.[219] In this way, Jewishness becomes a rigid designator for an inaccessible real substratum that is held to somehow, in mysterious ways, *cause* the nefarious behavior in question.

And here we again approach the heart of Žižek's entire philosophical position. We read that Pétain, capitalizing on the overwhelming incomprehension that followed the French military debacle of 1940, gained his early political success by providing a *retroactive* reading of the situation in terms of certain specific causes: "In this way, what had been experienced a moment ago as traumatic, incomprehensible loss became readable, obtained meaning."[220] As one would expect, Žižek does not take Pétain's explanation at face value: "But the point is that this symbolization was not inscribed in the Real itself: never do we reach the point at which 'the circumstances themselves begin to speak,' the point at which language starts to function immediately as 'language of the Real'. . . ."[221] To use terms drawn from the case of Heidegger's politics, Pétain chose a particular ontic explanation to suit the hidden, ontological cause of the downfall of France. The problem, as Žižek fully realizes, is that this incommensurability of the two spheres holds good for *all* experience, not just for major political decisions. And when reality comes to be seen as nothing more than phantasmatic support for the symbolic realm, one obvious question is whether this deflation of the Real offers adequate resistance to arbitrary attempts at manipulation. Žižek says that "the predominance of Pétain's symbolization was a result of a struggle for ideological hegemony."[222] Few readers will want to go to bat for Pétain, but it is hard to see how Žižek could escape saying the same thing about *any* political act, or indeed about any experience at all—that it is a "struggle for ideological hegemony," even though this objection presumably bores Žižek to tears at this stage of his career.

The root of the difficulty can be found in Žižek's slide from the claim that the impossible-real kernel can never be *encountered* to the claim that it only *exists* in human retroactive positing in the first place. The same slide can be found in his account of essentialism, which he strikingly views as a form of the very descriptivist theory of meaning that Kripke attacks (an ironic reversal, since it is usually *Kripke* who is attacked as an essentialist). As Žižek says, summarizing the position of Ernesto Laclau:

> Let us take, for example, notions like "democracy," "socialism," "Marxism,": the essentialist illusion consists in the belief that it is possible to determine a definite cluster of features, of positive properties, however minimal, which defines the permanent essence of "democracy" and similar terms—every phenomenon which pretends to be classified as "democratic" should fulfill the condition of possessing this cluster of features. In contrast to this "essentialist illusion," Laclau's anti-essentialism compels us to conclude that it is impossible to define any such essence, any cluster of positive properties which would remain the same in "all possible worlds"—in all counterfactual situations.[223]

But one can also imagine a realist response to this situation. It could be said with equal justice that all of these political terms are rigid designators referring to an underlying reality that manifests itself only imperfectly in various cases, and even manifests imperfectly in any of the *definitions* that might be given of democracy, Marxism, and the like. While denying that essences can ever become perfectly *present* in the world, such a theory would still claim that they *exist*. In fact, this is the standpoint of the present book, and it is much closer to the position of Kripke than Laclau's theory will ever be.

But Žižek wants nothing to do with such a possibility, and makes an inference that is now quite widespread—because the thing itself can never appear, it is therefore meaningless to talk about its actually existing. This is a far cry from Kripke's own conclusions, and one wishes for a more thorough justification of this slide from criticizing the ability of deeply hidden essence to appear in incarnated form to criticizing their very existence as anything other than phantasmatic projections. With this insufficiently grounded step, the safety of the linguistic turn in philosophy seems to be assured. The rigid designator is the *point de capiton*, the Lacanian "quilting point" that retroactively forms the Real in its own image. But Žižek makes a far stronger claim than this, asserting that "the rigid designator . . . is not a point of supreme density of Meaning, a kind of Guarantee which, by being itself excepted from the differential interplay of elements, would serve as a stable and fixed point of reference."[224] Which leads him to a disappointing conclusion:

> On the contrary, it is the element which represents the agency of the signifier within the field of the signified. In itself it is nothing but a "pure difference": its role is purely structural, its nature is purely performative; in short, it is a "signifier without the signified." The crucial step in the analysis of an ideological edifice is thus to detect, behind the dazzling splendour of the element which holds it together ("God," "country," "party," "class" . . .) this self-referential, tautological, performative operation.[225]

No passage could stand in greater opposition to the spirit of the present book, which champions the underground execution of objects in opposition to the "performativity" that deploys them in contexts and networks, and which deeply regrets the notion that signification could be "self-referential."

On the bright side, Žižek masterfully links the rigid designator to the very heart of psychoanalysis by identifying it with *transference*. For Žižek, transference is what ascribes significance retroactively to the Real: "We are 'in transference' when we believe that real freedom is 'in its very nature' opposed to bourgeois formal freedom, that the state is 'in its very nature' only a tool of class domination, and so on."[226] Certainly, he admits that this process is "necessary": "The paradox lies, of course, in the fact that this transferential illusion is necessary, it is the very measure of success of the operation of 'quilting': the *capitonnage* is successful only in so far as it effaces its own traces."[227] But even so, Žižek's model is that

of poking holes in ideological edifices, of trying to unmask any preten-
tious claims of the rigid designator to refer to an independent reality.

But what if transference were not only the condition for a successful
psychoanalysis or the victory of an ideology? What if it were also the condition for physical causation itself? What if, along with hysterical rocks and
psychotic trees, there were bricks and raindrops entering into transference
and either "traversing the fantasy" or prematurely withdrawing from this
process? In one of his references to the preontological realm present in
thinkers from Kant to Lacan, Žižek also says that "in Derridean terms, we
could designate it as spectrality."[228] *But the object is a retrovirus, not a
specter.* No mere phantasm haunting the gap between the subject and its
unfulfillable desire, the object fills the world with force, color, music, and
electrical charges; it summons and cajoles its neighbors, or crushes them
into splinters. Instead of continuing to embrace the hip "specter" of realism, contemporary philosophy should begin funneling arms and humani-
tarian aid toward some sort of guerilla realism—a fresh insurgency on
behalf of objects themselves.

Chapter Three

Elements of an Object-Oriented Philosophy

For since every body contains in itself many forms of natures united together in a concrete state, the result is that they severally crush, depress, break, and enthrall one another, and thus the individual forms are obscured.

—FRANCIS BACON,
Novum Organum, Book 2, 24

§20. Prehension

The book began with a simple account of Heidegger's analysis of tool-being, a ubiquitous reversal between tool and broken tool. In one respect, human beings inhabit a sphere of explicit perception, seduced by pleasant odors and colorful spectacles, our attention absorbed by the numerous people and animals and solid objects we encounter. The objects that surround us are specific phenomena, accessible in some way. This is the realm that Heidegger describes as that of the as-structure. Soon, I will show that the as-structure is actually of far broader scope than this, but for now we can remain with this usual way of conceiving it.

It should also be acknowledged that there are times when Heidegger wants to say that the "as" is not reducible to sheer presence-at-hand. The term *Vorhandenheit* has a strong negative charge attached to it in all of Heidegger's works, and some of the entities that he describes are less laden with it than others. Furthermore, those who admire his theory of unconcealment like to observe that the as-structure partly overcomes what is *vorhanden* insofar as it to some extent reveals the *being* of the thing. This is true enough. But equally true, as we have already seen, is the fact that the being of the thing is never revealed *directly*. It is mistaken to say that in the passage from hammer to failed hammer, the previously concealed hammer-being becomes visible in the second case, or even "more" visible than before. For whatever it is that we see or know or learn about the hammer when it fails, this is never enough to replace the sheer *execution* of its hammer-effect. Tool-being is never convertible into any form of the as-structure, not even partially. The best model for the conversion of tool-being into the as-structure is not that of partial progress toward an unattainable goal; in this sense, Heidegger's account of the modification of theoretical comportment must be abandoned completely, and a new alternative developed. What this alternative might be remains unclear for the moment. In any case, there is an absolute difference between the modes of tool and broken tool, and the latter can simply be identified with *all* forms of the as-structure. One layer of reality, then, can be described as that of the broken tool.

But this is only half of reality, since the analysis of equipment entails that entities are much more than luminous facades. Even before breaking into view as an explicit object, a metal fence serves to generate a reality in which the junkyard dog cannot threaten me. Before being recognized by name as a particular spice, an ounce of tarragon infuses a refreshing sub-flavor into the soup a friend has prepared for us. Anything, prior to erupting in its explicit form, is real simply by exerting its efforts in the cosmos, by breathing its life into a world that would not have been the same without it. In other words, before any object is present-at-hand, it is ready-to-hand: sincerely engaged in executing itself, inaugurating a reality in which its characteristic style is unleashed. The tool-being of the object lives as if *beneath* the manifest presence of that object.

Throughout this book, I have spoken of the as-structure as being "derivative" of the kingdom of tool-being. But I have used this expression loosely, since it hardly matters which of the two dimensions we regard as "primary." Alphonso Lingis has observed that Heidegger's claim that functional form precedes independent substance is countered by Levinas' attempt to reverse this argument and grant primacy to a revised version of substance.[1] The claim of the present book is that neither decision can be preferred over the other: they are equiprimordial. Heidegger's world is nothing but a ceaseless metabolism between these two layers of the universe. This final chapter of the book is an attempt to clarify the ontological status of these layers, and to catch them in the act of their basic sorts of interaction. It is time to pass beyond the bounds of Heidegger's explicit concerns and examine for ourselves the obscure private dynamics of tool and broken tool.

Quite apart from the bridge as something perceived, there is the subterranean bridge-being. The bridge is set loose on the earth as a distinct and independent power, giving birth to a universe in which canyon-effect and river-effect are more or less neutralized, partially surpassed in their former role as obstacles. At any point in reality, the world of the as-structure is only a belated echo of a deeper realm of brute efficacy. Any specific incarnation of the tool turns out to be only a kind of ghostly energy, siphoned from that tool in its hidden reality amidst all other beings. I have argued further that this bare opposition between "as" and "non-as" contains nothing that would allow us to distinguish between human and animal reality. Given the surprisingly rudimentary character of the as/non-as duality, *any* sentient organism must be said to inhabit the sphere of the broken tool. Whether we speak of humans, amphibians, insects, or birds, this is the space in which life unfolds. No genuine *ontological* distinctions between the species have emerged so far, whatever our preconceptions on this question may be. But at the same time, all such creatures are embedded in an environment that at least partly withdraws from them. We all stand at the mercy of the invisible kingdom of equipment, stationed unwittingly in a cryptic empire of force-against-force.

From these considerations, it might seem that we can redefine the opposition between tool and broken tool as equivalent to that between causation and perception. For on the one hand, there is the brute actuality that invisibly performs its labor; on the other, there is the free and clear space of transcendence, which partly rises above the dark empire of meaning. The awareness of organisms would lie in their ability to create a distance between themselves and the things. It seems this way at first, and so far I have tended to present the issue in just this way. But the time has come to admit to the reader that I have been guilty of a deliberate over-simplification, motivated by the need to prevent chapter 1 from growing absurdly complicated. It is time to dispense with this oversimplification and replace it with one of the central conceptions of this book, already hinted at in several passages above. In fact, it is impermissible to replace the tool/broken tool distinction with the difference between causality and vis-ibility. For it turns out that *even brute causation already belongs to the realm of presence-at-hand*. Instead of human awareness on one side and colliding billiard balls on the other, we find that both of these realities belong on the same side of the fence. Even the mindless interaction of the eight ball and the nine ball will have to count as an instance of the *broken* tool. Given this vast expansion of the as-structure beyond its previous domain, it will need to be asked what is left of subterranean tool-being at all.

The earlier discussions of *Vorhandenheit* as equivalent to sentient per-ception was meant as nothing more than a loose initial hint, and was always inadequate for pinning down the most decisive features of presence-at-hand, though not for reasons that any commentator has ever seen before. As stated repeatedly, the contrast is between: (a) our external encounter with broken or visible equipment, and (b) that same equipment in the real-ity of its execution. However hard we exert ourselves in uncovering the depths of things, whatever is revealed in the as-structure still only drifts along the surface of reality. Apart from the bridge that we openly encounter, bridge-reality is hard at work, silently exalting or diluting the status of every object it confronts. We have already seen that *any* percep-tion of the bridge fixes the withdrawn bridge-being into the biased con-tours of a specific profile. The sniper always encounters the present-at-hand bridge rather than the bridge itself. The despondent sleepwalker also encounters it as present-at-hand, as do each of the seagulls and wasps cur-rently in the vicinity. None of these observers can encounter the tool-being of the bridge "in person." All of this should be clear enough by now. But I propose to push these claims a step further. Bridge-being is forever with-drawn, not only from sentient eyes and ears and brains, but even from the merest forms of physical mass. As already signaled above, *causality is just another form of the as-structure*.

It is not sense-perception that first generates the duality between tool and broken tool. Note that this can already be guessed from Heidegger's own ambiguous references to the "as." In most cases, he identifies the as-structure exclusively with explicit awareness; for simplicity's sake, I have restricted myself so far to *this* usage of the as-structure. But Heidegger also knew that there was a kind of as-structure at work even in the unthematic encounter with equipment, on that plane of reality that lies beneath all explicit awareness. In §2, I briefly extended the as-structure even further, to cover the case of inanimate objects bouncing against a paper screen. I now ask the reader to consider the situation of two massive geological plates pressing against one another near a vulnerable point in the earth's crust. To say that each of these giant rocks does not encounter the other "as" rock is to be guilty of embezzling a common-sense definition of the as-structure and illegally importing it into ontology. Clearly, the first rock *does* encounter the second rock *as* rock, in spite of not being openly conscious of it in the specific animal sense. The evidence for this is simple: one rock encounters the other as a highly specific reality, responding to the properties of its neighbor in whatever way it can. A geological plate encounters its competitor *as* a barrier, and does not simply push it aside as if it were negligible soil or plywood. It does not encounter the second rock as a tree, nor does it melt when it touches it. Instead, it confronts it only as a stony antagonist of roughly equivalent power. By the same token, a weaker object (clay, for example) would not resist these massive plates with the same degree of tenacity they display in confronting one another; obviously, if these mighty objects should ever begin to move in the wake of seismic activity, they are well-equipped to obliterate most of what they touch.

From early on, I argued for this mutual determinacy of tools in connection with Heidegger's "for-the-sake-of," contending that a fully determinate encounter with other entities does not belong to human beings alone. Even if it were granted that Dasein alone is fully *conscious* of beings as beings (and this is far from clear, as shown by the apparent intellectual and emotional complexity of wolves, parrots, ravens, and dolphins), it would not follow that only humans can encounter discrete objects. Far from it! Screen thwarts gravel, and gravel collides with dust; dust is blocked by paper; paper is gouged with knife, but not with musical sounds. This existence of determinate relations at the subsensory level was raised as a theme quite early in the book. What is new here is the claim that such relations are *already a species of the as-structure*. It was only for purposes of clear exposition that I first defined this structure, in the usual way, as "awareness." Against such a definition, it can be seen that in any raw physical interaction, even that between two contemptible pebbles in some remote galaxy, the as-structure is already fully at play. In short, tool-being is not at all what we have thought it was up till now. It must lie at a still deeper level than that of force or relation. It is no longer an effect as opposed to an appearance, but rather an executant *being* that is neither of these. We are now a long, long way from the usual attempts to read *Zu-* and *Vorhandenheit* as praxis and theory. The book has entered upon a new and unexpected course.

Another unusual example might help clarify the issue at stake. Let's imagine that, for whatever reason, some sort of bulky metallic appliance is abandoned on a frozen lake. For now, I see no reason to accept the animistic claim that such a stove or washing machine "perceives" the lake in the usual sense. Even so, some sort of determinate encounter clearly does occur between them. This soulless piece of metal certainly does not enjoy immediate and intimate contact with the tool-being of the lake, as if sheer causal proximity were sufficient for capturing that lake in its withdrawn execution. (The fact that we are discussing an artificial object is irrelevant; the present analysis would also hold good if we replaced the appliance with a naturally occurring chunk of ore.) Even in this case, the appliance reacts to some features of the lake rather than others—cutting its rich actuality down to size, reducing it to that relatively minimal scope of lake-reality that is of significance to it. Note that the tool-being of the lake comprises an indefinitely large array of features, most of them irrelevant to the object lying on its surface. Simplifying somewhat, we can say that the stove reduces the lake to the single aspect of a frozen surface, to sheer "equipment for remaining stationary." This sort of analysis is familiar enough to readers of Heidegger, at least in a human context. When the lake supports the appliance, this act of supporting unfolds entirely within the as-structure, not within the kingdom of tool-being. This raises the following question: if the fact that the frozen lake supports an object is *not* its tool-being, then *what is?*

To explore this question, imagine that the ice now cracks or melts, so that the appliance smashes through the surface and sinks into the frigid depths of the lake. I hold that the resulting interaction between stove and ice is philosophically *identical* with the more familiar case of Dasein and the broken hammer. For what is decisive in the famous account of the "broken tool" is not that implicit reality comes into conscious view, as if *human surprise* were the key to the reversal within being. Rather, the important factor is that the heavy object, while resting on the ice as a reliable support, did not exhaust the reality of that ice. The appliance could have been resting either on thin ice or on an eternal pillar of granite, and the supportive effect (prior to the disaster) would have been precisely the same, ignoring for now the specifically *icy* experiences that the appliance may also have undergone. The same would hold true for any object in such a predicament: none of the entities near the lake are in position to sound out every last fugitive echo of its being. Just like explicit perception, causal reaction is always only a response to a *limited* range of factors in the causative entity; other features are passed over, concealed from the object that runs up against it.

When one billiard ball strikes another, it treats its victim as a simple mobile mass, and remains unattuned to its other concealed treasures—the richness of its imperfect plastic texture, its suddenly irrelevant color or its vague synthetic fragrance. No object ever unlocks the *entirety* of a second object, ever translates it completely literally into its own native tongue.

After all, we can always imagine the appearance of some *new* entity on the scene, one that would respond to a previously undisclosed reality in even the most uninteresting plastic ball. Modifying our previous example, let's say that the icy lake is not composed simply of water, but of *contaminated* water. Obviously, this contamination is unimportant for our metallic appliance (assuming that this poison does not also affect the freezing temperature or other factors that might be pertinent to it). But for the fish and ducks who also inhabit the lake, the water has now become instantly lethal. Given the absence of marine animals, however, this property would never be brought to the stage in any way at all. In this sense, Žižek is right to hold that the reality of the lake is constituted *retroactively* by the entities encountering it. Until some vile sadist releases trout into the toxic lake, there is a sense in which it is not yet really lethal. Poisonousness is not a static feature sitting around in the lake just waiting to be discovered, but a relational property that requires the trout no less than the lake. All of the properties by which we can *define* the lake are going to be relational in this way, meaning that there is no good way to *specify* its tool-being. But the fact that we cannot specify it is no reason to grant privilege either to the *network of negotiations* between things (Latour) or the *fantasizing subject* who posits the gap between the fish-killing lake and its hidden being (Žižek). Both of these approaches view as superfluous any talk of the withdrawn objects themselves. But the fact that we *know* these objects only through their appearances precisely *does not* mean that they only *are* through their appearances. This is the whole point of Heidegger's tool-analysis.

Put differently, no entity is reducible to the *hic et nunc* of its specific unleashed energies. The tool-being of the ice must exceed its current relation to all other objects in the vicinity. Heidegger has already shown us the way in which human Dasein inevitably converts the richness of bridge-being into a narrowed silhouette by means of some specific projection. In just this way, even the most stupefied physical mass reduces to sheer caricatures each of the obstacles and barriers it runs up against. Thus, some sort of objectification occurs even at the level of sheer matter; the realm of presence-at-hand is not the product of human sensation, but of *the perspectival stance of any entity whatever*. Prior to existing as any specific causative force, an object is the concealed actuality of its tool-being. It is the enactment of a reality that other objects may hope to test or measure, but which they can never aspire to *replace*, however intimately they may stroke its contours. No description of the bridge by a human being, and no touching of the bridge by the sea or hill that it adjoins, can adequately mimic the work of this bridge in its being. No perception of the bridge-thing, however direct a perception it may be, can accomplish the very actuality that the bridge brings about. The bridge is irreplaceable in an *absolute* sense.

To repeat, the tool-being of an object is the reality of that object quite apart from any of its specific causal relations, and unexchangeable for any grand total of such relations. Even if we were to catalog exhaustively the exact status of every object in the cosmos vis-à-vis this bridge, it would still be possible to conceive of other entities that might occupy a different stance or relation to it, if only they had entered the fray of the world. In this way, bridge-being is sheer reality, devoid of all relation. Tool-being withdraws not just behind any perception, but behind any form of causal activity as well.

Among other consequences of this shifting position of causality, the ontological status of sentient awareness has been radically altered: it no longer has the entire as-structure to itself, and therefore has lost its previous ontological distinction. It is true that Heidegger seems to interpret the difference between tool and broken tool as one between sheer equipmental effect and the vision that transcends or "clears" that effect. Whereas tool-being is permanently trapped inside itself, locked in the performance of its reality, the as-structure is supposed to step beyond this underground of tools. As a result, Dasein is to be defined by way of its "freedom." The human being is the site of *Lichtung*; freed in part from the concealment of being, we humans should be the negating animals.

But it is important that we oppose this view of reality. *Ontologically* speaking, there is no difference between the activity of a trained human eye and the crash of two colliding boulders. In other words, conscious awareness can no longer serve as one of the basic orienting poles of reality. Explicit awareness is not a special negating instrument, not one that *perceives* where less fortunate beings only *interact* in their blind physical way. The idea that perception or freedom work by *negating* is a myth: we never manage to free ourselves from the plenum of tool-being, not even partially. Instead, the as-structure of human Dasein turns out to be just a special case of relationality in general. We ourselves are no more and no less perspectival than are rocks, paper, and scissors. Instead of defining tool and broken tool by the common pair of causation and perception, I will refer to them instead as actuality and relation. I ask only that the reader not jump to conclusions based on the various senses carried by these terms in the history of philosophy. They are used here only as rough placeholders, and must gain their full sense only from the weight of the analyses that follow.

The results of this section should be summarized once more for the reader's convenience. It looked at first as though the world were divided between dark functional action on the one side and luminous perceptible forms on the other. Now, it has turned out that *both* of these realms belong on the side of the as-structure. The "as" applies not just to humans, dogs, and insects, but even to the miserable interaction between clots of tar and mud in a remote swamp. From this strange revision of the tool/broken tool axis, two new philosophical questions emerge. First, if both human consciousness and raw physical collision now belong to the same ontological realm, how can we account for their obvious differences? Second, if tool-being now lies even *further* from us than bare causality does, can anything useful be said about it, or is it only pushed away to an infinite noumenal distance?

Concerning the first question, all that is clear so far is what needs to abandoned. The human being can no longer be viewed as a "creature of distance," one who transcends mere effects in order to see those effects "as" effects. Instead of rising above the infernal world of equipment into a sunlit ethereal space, Dasein's movement actually occurs in the *opposite* direction. With respect to sheer brute causality, Dasein does not move upward into the ether (an impossible movement), but *downward* into the bowels of the earth. Instead of creating an open space in which entities come to light, we actually burrow beneath them, toward the tool-beings that remain untouched by any relationality whatsoever. To become aware of these tool-beings is not to rise above them, but to make oneself ever more vulnerable to them, increasing the surface area of our being that can come into contact with them. In this way, consciousness is not an epiphenomenon, but an *infraphenomenon*. Theory has little in common with a forest clearing, but resembles an ever-extending network of subway or freight tunnels. I cite this image only to suggest an alternative possibility. But one further conclusion is immediately suggested by all of this. The model of knowledge as transcendence is a model of irony and critique. By rising above the things, it seems that we no longer take them for granted, and that in this way we have unmasked their pretensions. To this day, intellectuals remain in heated competition to see who can debunk the pretensions of the others the most thoroughly, thereby attaining an even more neutral, "cleared" standpoint. An analogous attitude can be found in the ethical realm, in which "transgression" takes the place of critique for those who believe they have risen beyond all the nullities by which uncritical minds are duped (for example, religion, virtue, mainstream sexual mores). But maybe this critical stock character, who has dominated intellectual life in the West for several centuries, begins to look less prestigious as soon as the model of knowledge-as-distance falls apart. If acquiring knowledge of things means to enter into even closer contact with the things rather than to stand beyond them, then maybe critique reverses into sincerity—and maybe Deleuze is right that transgression gives way to treason (at least the traitor seeks new citizenship *somewhere*), and irony to humor (at least the comic implicates *himself* in his buffoonery).[2] Perhaps instead of rising *beyond* good and evil, the more radical step is to move *beneath* them.

The second question was as follows: if tool-being can no longer be described in terms of practical action or brute causality, then what can be said about it at all? That is the central question of this final chapter, and an answer emerges only slowly.

In the example of the stove and the ice, we saw that the importance of cracked ice as failed equipment by no means lies in a contrast between what that ice *tacitly does* to certain beings and what those beings *perceive* of this action. The two halves of the tool are not "acting" and "seen"; the implicit/explicit distinction of hermeneutics does not do justice to the double life of tool-being. Instead, what we have is the difference between the tool itself and any particular *relation* of this tool to neighboring objects. Tool-beings are hard at work just being themselves; no relation can possibly exhaust this reality. If numerous entities encounter any given object, each runs across it as a vastly different causal power to reckon with. Each of them frames it from a specific perspective, opens itself up to it as a distinct and limited kind of impact. My claim is that the sum total of all such impacts never adds up to the reality of the tool-being—there is always more where that came from. Every entity forever holds new surprises in store. In every inch of reality, equipment belongs to an utterly different order from relationality. This idea is to serve as the building-block for the remainder of chapter 3.

It is likely that Heidegger would find this idea puzzling. For him, the concealed system of the world is what is primary. Already in chapter 1, I argued that the primacy he grants to world over entities is not just a primacy *for human life*. This mistaken notion comes from the idea that world is a human structure, that the natural world really is a set of isolated present-at-hand material blocks, and that only human praxis constitutes them as a total system of meaning. But in fact, objects themselves are already delivered over to the world, their forces mutually determining one another, their identities partly dissolving into a single all-embracing system. As a result, the contexture of holistic relation does not just precede our *awareness* of beings, but must even precede these beings themselves. (This is not my own view, but rather the logical outcome of Heidegger's views.)

This holistic theory of reality is one of the common features in virtually every major twentieth-century philosopher. But it is especially strong in two of them: Heidegger and Whitehead. Both of them regard the traditional theory of substance as a mortal enemy. And both try to undermine substance by granting preeminence to a massive system of relations in which all objects are stationed. For these reasons, it is surprising that Heidegger and Whitehead are so rarely linked. Surely, part of the reason must be that the fans of these two thinkers tend to be so *temperamentally* incompatible—in one case Protestants or ex-Protestants who read Emerson and Peirce, in the other case, darker-minded types who pass their nights in the company of Hölderlin and Trakl. But while no one would invite these two groups to the same dinner party, their philosophical heroes have a surprising amount in common.

For Heidegger, any distinct entity that might be encountered is already a fragment somehow chipped away from the world as a whole. This leaves little room for any nonrelational concept of objects, except in the naive sense of *Vorhandenheit* that he condemns. The relationality of function or meaning saturates every square inch of Heidegger's "world." But Whitehead formulates the same thesis even more clearly. In this section I have argued for a revised concept of tool-being, for a reality of the thing that recedes from all relation. If Whitehead were reading this book, he would instantly condemn this notion as a clear case of what he calls "vacuous actuality," the mistaken concept of an entity that could exist in a vacuum apart from any contact with other entities. Those who remain skeptical of the Heidegger-Whitehead link ought to note the parallel between this concept and Heidegger's "presence-at-hand." Both "vacuous actuality" and *Vorhandenheit* are used to refer to the concept of isolated, inert matter in physical science. Heidegger and Whitehead each try to supplant this vacuous material with a global network in which everything affects everything else.

Since I am now arguing for a concept of objects that withdraws not just from perception, but from any relation at all, both Heidegger and Whitehead become direct opponents of my theory. *Tool-Being* is a theory of vacuous actuality. But it is important that we not understand "vacuous" according to the terms in a thesaurus, where we might read: "ignorant, nonexistent, stupid, thoughtless, trivial, vacant." Instead, I take "vacuous" *literally*, as referring to the reality of tool-beings *in vacuo*, apart from any accidental collision with other objects. This is not as strange as it may sound; indeed, it is not even unprecedented.

Instead of entering into preliminary disputes about this concept, we should begin by setting out its features as fully as possible: my critics are requested not to kick the ponies until the whole circus has arrived. But there is one foreseeable complaint that ought to be warded off from the start. Namely, it might be said that by divorcing tool-being from any actual causal relation, I am defining it only as a center of *potentiality* for other relations that might someday exist but do not yet exist. As sensible as this might sound, the example of the icy lake establishes just the opposite: tool-being is not potentiality at all, but sheer *actuality*. To illuminate this claim, it be should noted that there are two distinct ways in which the tool might be regarded as a potential:

(1) In one sense, if we view equipment as a "potential" for relation with other things, this is to slip back into the cardinal error of viewing tool-being *from the outside*, measuring it by the kinds of effects it might have on other objects. But this means to view it as something encountered by some

other entity—that is, as something-present-at-hand. Tool-beings are potentials only insofar as other objects might be brought into the vicinity and hooked up to them in some way, brought into some determinate relation with them. But I have already insisted that no such link, and no *total summary* of such links, can do anything more than unveil the tool-being in some distinct, inherently exaggerated profile. Although I agree that every tool-being is a font of abundant possibilities, such possibilities belong only to the sphere of the tool's *relations* with its sister-entities, not to the tool-being itself. Relations can only hope to take the pulse of equipment, unlocking some tiny part of it.

Heidegger sees this question very differently, and often trumpets potentiality as more important than actuality. This privileging of the potential is valid only if we follow Heidegger in taking "actual" to mean "present-at-hand." It is already an admirable step when Heidegger says that the being of a thing is irreducible to any of the "actual" features we might spy on its luminous or petrified surface. But Heidegger should have taken an additional step. Even if possibility is "richer" than presence-at-hand, there is something richer than all possibility.

This can be explained in several steps. Beneath the plateau of visible hammers and bridges, there is the raw causal energy of these objects, each bumping up against the others with varying degrees of violence or softness. On this level, the invisible forces of hammer and bridge are locked in an utterly distinct set of arrangements with the other beings in the world; it is deployed in a total set of relations with them. This is the contexture of meaning: it is the tool-system; it is "world." Admittedly, this contexture of tools does sound richer than any presence-at-hand, just as Heidegger claims. But even richer than this contexture is tool-being—richer than relation is actuality. For this reason, we should reverse Heidegger's terminology, and say that *actuality is richer than potentiality.* After all, the sort of potentiality he has in mind is always nothing better than potentiality *for further relations.* My greatest complaint about Heidegger here is that he only does tacitly what Whitehead does openly, reducing the being of objects to their total relational situation in the system of equipment. In attempting to overcome substance, both thinkers overreact, and reduce beings *only* to their relational status, *only* to their exhaustive position in the gigantic cosmic system known as world. Neither Heidegger nor Whitehead realizes that even direct physical relations are only second-degree silhouettes of a deeper reality *in vacuo*: tool-being.

(2) But there is an additional sense in which tool-being might be regarded as "potentiality": namely, its potential for alteration, growth, or movement. And this is a kind of potential that Heidegger, like Whitehead, is ill-equipped to make sense of. My complaint can be expressed very simply—if an object can truly be reduced to its current total set of relations,

then it holds nothing in reserve, and there would be no reason for any change to occur. If the icy lake is supposed to be truly reducible to its relation to stove, fish, and mountain, then what happens when I point a butane torch at the surface of the lake? Something new will happen that never happened before—a hole will be melted in the ice. But what I am melting is *the ice*, not the ice as previously *encountered by* stove and fish and mountain (obviously not, since I am doing something to it with the torch that they were unable to do). Change only happens because the lake is a reality irreducible to the presence-at-hand of all its relations. Intellectuals have gotten very much into the habit of poking holes in all remaining versions of the old substance-concept, and measuring their own critical liberation by the extent to which they are able to do so. For this reason, it may seem a bit counterintuitive to ask the reader to *restore* a necessary concept of substance, even one of a new kind. It may seem at first like I am trying to get away with murder. But I have tried to make my case in a very straightforward way. If an entity always holds something in reserve beyond any of its relations, and if this reserve also cannot be *located* in any of these relations, then it must exist somewhere else. And since this surplus or reserve is what it is, quite apart from whatever might stumble into it, it is actual rather than potential. But it is not present-at-hand, because I have shown that presence-at-hand turns out to be *relational*, against what is usually believed.

Although these speculative questions are of compelling interest, Heidegger would surely dismiss them altogether. For him, tool-beings can never be anything like underlying substrata, not even in the de-physicalized form that I am advocating. Instead, Heidegger views entities as determinate forces always stationed at a definitive site with respect to all other entities. They always belong to the entire system of equipment, and in a strict sense it is a unified system with no room for individual beings. This raises an issue that is pivotal in Whitehead's *Process and Reality*, but which lurks in the midst of *Being and Time* as well. For the plain-spoken Whitehead, the hammer at midnight and the "same" hammer at 12:01 A.M. cannot be regarded as two successive states of one unitary thing. They must be understood as *two different entities altogether*. He likes to tell us that they belong to the same "society," but this term is introduced only after the fact, only as a way to explain why they *seem to me* to be the same hammer. To speak of a unified hammer-object that undergoes changes, that endures through all its "adventures in space and time," is to fall back into the traditional substance-philosophy. In Whitehead's terms, what is real is the hammer as an "actual entity."[3]

These actual entities are supposed to contain the full run of their relations to every least speck of dust in the cosmos. If I the author had been born left-handed rather than right-handed, the moon would not be the very moon that it is, since the network of its relations would thereby have altered in some faint way. While Heidegger rarely deigns to pose cosmological questions of this kind, his tool-analysis begins by yielding precisely the same result. For him no less than for Whitehead, there cannot be a single moon-substance that would survive the fluctuations in the entities that surround it. The moon, along with all comets, satellites, restaurants, Marxist revolutions, and my own left hand all belong to a global system of relations far more profound than any of these objects taken as individuals. To change one is really to change them all, since every last one of the parts is derivative of the environmental whole. This is the inevitable result if we say that every actual entity is to be defined as the sum total of its perceptions (Whitehead). It is equally inevitable if we say that every object exists fundamentally in the network of functions and purposes (Heidegger).

In passing, this provides additional grounds for referring to Heidegger's philosophy as a kind of covert Occasionalism. For even if Heidegger *were* capable of discussing the real passage of time (and I openly assert that he is not), his tendency to ignore individual tool-being in favor of the swirling relations of the tool-system means that no entity is capable of enduring from moment to moment. The Bay Bridge under blazing sun and the Bay Bridge in the rain must be completely different entities, since the total system of meaning has been permanently altered from one state to the next. Under these circumstances, the world *might as well* be annihilated and recreated in every instant. Malebranche may or may not be right; Heidegger's reflections on "time" say nothing either for or against such a hypothesis.

Whitehead expresses things more directly than Heidegger, telling us that an actual entity (that is, a tool-being) is not a durable unit that "undergoes adventures" in space and time.[4] The reality of a being is confined to the thorough particularity of a transient moment. To give especial emphasis to this point, he often calls actual entities "actual *occasions,*" so as to erode any lingering connotations of a long-lasting substance. For Whitehead, what endures through time is not Socrates, but a community of closely related Socrates-events strung along throughout the span of what *appears* to be a coherent individual life. It is in the same vein that Whitehead offers his famously outlandish solution to the problem of personal immortality, which has not been without influence in theological circles. As he sees it, I cannot even endure as the same entity from one moment to the next, let alone into eternity.

Again, it is hard to imagine Heidegger taking any of these claims seriously ("Ontic, all of them!"). Even so, he does not escape the same ramifications that Whitehead has the courage to state more bluntly. Heidegger too would have a difficult time saying that the "same" Dasein endures from moment to moment, since Dasein seems utterly defined by a specific set of projects at each moment, and there is little room in this philosophy for a Dasein-substance that would remain the same through a shifting series of projects. If there were something in Dasein "deeper" than the totality of its relations at every moment, what could it be? A physical body? A soul? Hardly, since any such answer would require a durable present-at-hand substratum that would contradict the rest of Heidegger's philosophy. My claim is that Heidegger and Whitehead both paint themselves into this corner through their shared fear of the traditional concept of substance, which both of them coldly condemn as often as possible. But a traditional theory is by no means the only alternative. Fear of this classical demon does not justify the equally untenable claim that tool-beings are exhausted by the circumstances in which they currently happen to be embedded. Fear of water should not cause us to jump into fire, even if fire and water are all that can be seen. Sometimes, all that is required is a bit of patience. Before jumping in either direction, we ought to consider the possibility that the Heidegger/Whitehead critique of substance is an idea once but no longer liberating. In some respects, this critique remains the pinnacle of twentieth-century philosophy. But the century has recently changed. Given the difficulties of the supposed all-embracing context, we are obliged to recover the integrity of objects without relapsing into theories that these two thinkers have helped us overcome.

This section has raised the question of the precise ontological status of tool and broken tool. Having initially described this difference as one between conscious perception and dark causal reality, I now state that *both* of these domains belong on the side of the as-structure, and have nothing to do with tool-being. Whether it be Dasein listening to music, or the mere collision of two silver atoms, both cases unfold within the as-structure. To draw attention to this all-pervasive character of the as-structure, I have entitled the current section by referring to one of Whitehead's own most intriguing terms: "prehension." This word designates the mutual objectification with which *all* actual entities confront one another, and thereby stakes a philosophical claim outside the limited realm of Dasein. Whether implicitly or openly, the as-structure spreads over the field of the world. Everywhere, entities prehend one another: child prehends toy, rock prehends paper, tar prehends oil. But tool-being lies somewhere else altogether.

The great virtue of Whitehead, lacking in Heidegger, is precisely this recognition that the as-structure has a cosmic dimension. Of all the great philosophers of the past century, it is Whitehead who has done the most to free us from the constraints of the philosophy of human *access* to the world. Perhaps this is why his philosophy has had a narrower range of influence than those of his worthiest rivals, Heidegger among them. Nothing of this kind can be found in Heidegger's own works. Even in texts where it is said that Heidegger has made a fateful shift from Dasein to being, what is at stake is still only being as revealed *to Dasein*, and not being as it impacts upon fruit, dust, and horses. By contrast, Whitehead does grasp this cosmic dimension of philosophy, and in this way begins to recover the breathing room that philosophy deserves.

But I still prefer Heidegger, and still consider *him* the indispensable philosopher of the past century. The reason is as follows: what is lacking in Whitehead are the resources to restore objects to their full status in the world, whereas Heidegger unearths such resources in spite of himself. This may seem paradoxical at first glance. After all, Whitehead simply plows through the obstacles that often seem to confine Heidegger within a Dasein-centered model of reality. In this way, he seems to install an ontological democracy in which humans are no more central than grasshoppers or ice. But the real beneficiary of Whitehead's *coup d'état* against transcendental philosophy is not the objects—it is the *empire* of objects, the network that binds them together as mutually prehending actual entities. Defenders of Whitehead like to claim that he alone has managed to reconcile the two aspects of entities as atomic individuals and as components in a larger process. But their claims are unconvincing. For Whitehead, an actual entity can always be resolved into its prehensions; to claim any excess for it beyond these prehensions is to posit a vacuous actuality. All of an actual entity's relations are *internal* relations, and for this reason it is difficult to see how there can be specific entities in Whitehead's system at all.[5] What we find instead is an empire of prehensions. Ultimately, this is the same thing as a total system of tools. The great paradox is that Whitehead begins with the integrity of individual objects but ends up devouring them all in a total system of relations.

But the opposite paradox holds for Heidegger, who begins by devouring individual objects in a total network of significance, only to restore their integrity. Although Heidegger's tool-beings seem to withdraw from perception into the system of effects, they actually withdraw from this system as fully as they do from perception, and attain a strange reality that lies outside of all contexts. This inevitable withdrawal of beings from all relation, which splinters up Heidegger's own talk of the concealment of *being*, is what places Heidegger a full step closer to the future of philosophy than Whitehead. Pushed to the limit, the tool-analysis reverses its own inherent dogma. Meanwhile, Whitehead believes he has *already* accounted for individual beings, and remains content with the radical implosion of entities into the network that Heidegger both celebrates and inadvertently overturns.

We can now return to the central task of deciphering the *relation* between the moments of tool and broken tool. Chapter 1 called for a renewed theory of specific entities, a thematic investigation into the secret contours of objects. Now that the concept of prehension has helped clarify the status of the subterranean realm, we are in better position to probe the concrete interplay between tool and broken tool, with all the difficulties it generates. It will also be helpful if, in passing, we can discuss *both* of Heidegger's two key axes of division, as seen in both the 1919 lecture course and the concept of the fourfold. To this end, we are blessed with a stroke of good fortune. For it turns out that two important philosophers of the postwar era, each a student of Heidegger during the same key period of his career, launched their own philosophical efforts with a detailed analysis of *one* of the two Heideggerian dualisms. Oddly enough, each of them seems to have done this in total ignorance of the other's work, the greatest possible confirmation that the fault lines I have identified in Heidegger's system are no arbitrary concoction.

Emmanuel Levinas (1906–1995) continues to enjoy increasing fame, in large part due to his ethical works, which will be left out of consideration here. My primary interest is in his earliest original writings, those of the late 1940s. The central topic of these works is a Heideggerian theme: the relation between an existent and its existence, between the single anonymous rumbling of being and the assorted fragments that somehow shatter away from it. For Levinas no less than for Heidegger, tool-being emits shadows and contours: being *resembles* itself. We know this as the simple opposition between tool and broken tool, which Levinas still reads as the difference between unitary being and the myriad specific beings liberated by the work of consciousness.

Xavier Zubiri (1898–1983) is largely forgotten today, except by certain enthusiasts of contemporary Catholic thought, and by fans of his distinguished teacher, Ortega y Gasset. Although Zubiri's highly technical work has little resonance with today's most fashionable trends, he developed an ontology of rare innovation and rigor, one whose best days may be ahead of it. This is most visible in his major book: *Sobre la esencia* (*On Essence*). In this weighty volume, we read about the "functional identity" of two distinct orders in every tool-being. Zubiri says that entities do have a specific quality, but that they are also real in the sense that *anything whatever* is real. And this is none other than Heidegger's *second* axis, the "something at all" revealed in Angst, and in Husserl's second reduction.

What is especially strange about this coincidence is that it arises directly from the subject matter rather than from any mutual influence between the two thinkers. Although both authors followed Heidegger's courses as students at Freiburg during roughly the same period (c. 1930), they are so drastically incompatible in vocabulary and tone that it is unlikely either could even have *read* the other, let alone profited from the exercise. Even today, I find it extremely difficult to read both Levinas and Zubiri during the same *week*, so different are the moods and styles of reading that each requires of us. The reason that this odd couple of ontology has never been linked before is quite simple. Only a line of reflection already guided by Heidegger's neglected *Geviert* makes it possible to grasp the inner unity of this impossible pair: the eloquent Parisian essayist and the dry but systematic Basque, the theorist of the Talmud and the defender of the Eucharist.

Whatever their obvious differences, both have followed Heidegger in exploring the new continent at the heart of objects, much as Verrazzano and Ponce de Leon followed Columbus. Now as then, plenty of dark forest still remains—and in this case, we disturb no one by traveling through it.

§21. Contributions of Levinas

Levinas is more widely known for his major works of ethical philosophy (*Totality and Infinity, Otherwise Than Being*) than for the early treatises that concern us here. He himself would be pleased by this widespread preference for his later writings, quick as he is to tell us that his works of the 1940s have only a preparatory character.[6] Most discussions of Levinasian philosophy quickly zero in on the notion of "the Other"; it is here that both his friends and enemies reach a final verdict as to his legacy. But for the moment, I ask the reader to forget all of the ongoing disputes over "alterity." More important for the moment is Levinas' pioneering interpretation of Heidegger, which receives inexcusably little attention from Heideggerians. Even the fans of Levinas are guilty of downplaying these "preparatory" studies, composed under dramatic circumstances during the war. But if there is a sense in which the later ethical works were born from the Talmud and the Torah, their true intellectual background is Heidegger's theory of time. Even a proper account of alterity must begin with the very writings of Levinas that I will now discuss. Reference will be made to *De l'existence à l'existant*, and more briefly to *Time and the Other*. Taken together, these works are a neglected shining moment in postwar philosophy.

Levinas sees Heidegger's central discovery as that of the relation between a being and its being. This ontological bond forms the subject matter for his own *Existence and Existents*, the slight shift in terms from Heidegger's own occurring only "for reasons of euphony." As the author puts it: "Heidegger distinguishes subjects and objects—the beings that are, existents—from their very work of being. . . . The most profound thing about *Being and Time* for me is this Heideggerian distinction. . . ."[7] Readers of Heidegger will easily recall the powerful role of the ontological difference in his thought. In chapter 1, I made an even stronger claim, attempting to show that this difference quickly takes on *overwhelming* scope. All of Heidegger's numerous attempts to discuss specific regions of reality (space, time, animal organisms . . .) invariably collapse into an omnipresent fissure between the sparkling perceptibility of the object and its hidden seismic reality. The single goal of the ensuing discussion of tool-being has been to develop a more concrete account of this relation between the two currents in the entity, an aspiration for which Levinas is the most direct forerunner. As he tells us, "a thing is always a volume whose exterior surfaces hold back a depth and make it appear."[8] Tool-being is this very reversal between the entity and its being, the bridge that spans *de l'existence à l'existant*.

With a familiar Heideggerian ring in his voice, Levinas claims that this relation between existence and existents is obscured by nothing other than the traditional concept of time. This concept regards temporality only as a process transpiring "through time," a story that always unfolds only *between* any given instants. As a result, the mind tends naturally to slip into the notion of some highest being or remote principle, a *theon* that would remain aloof from any of the distinct moments of time even while working its effects upon them. Levinas accepts Heidegger's criticisms of this view of being as a supreme entity, and tries instead to capture being in its very labor. For Levinas, a moment is not something merely inert and present-at-hand, such that temporality would have to lie *outside* of any moment, an external superhero redeeming us from the horrors of stasis. Rather, the relation between an existent and its existence is a contract sealed *in the space of a single instant*: "Is [the relation of being and beings] not rather accomplished by the very *stance* of an instant? . . . Is not an instant a 'polarization' of being in general? . . . An instant is not one lump; it is articulated."[9] The entire philosophy of Levinas revolves around this articulation.

Like Heidegger, Levinas points to the ambivalent polarization that must occur even in a single instant. But unlike Heidegger, Levinas ventures beyond this total determinacy of the instant so as to offer a *genuine* theory of time, whether successfully or not. And it is only *here* that the celebrated "alterity of the Other" emerges in his thought. His claim, probably inspired by Bergson, is that time in the *real* sense can never be found in the insularity of the moment; Heidegger's version of "time" condemns every entity to utter solitude. To arrive at the genuine notion of time, we need to move beyond the concept of future as a "projection" (which can easily be stuffed into a single instant, as happens with Heidegger), toward time as a *disruption*—as novelty, surprise, imperative. In this way, the ponderous strife within every instant is challenged *from the outside*, whereas for Heidegger the drama that threatens any moment occurs *within* that moment. The theory of time becomes a theory of the Other. Clearly, the famous ethical work of Levinas arises directly from the very crisis that the current essay has described: the collapse of all songs into the mantra of tool and broken tool. There is a sense in which Heidegger's avoidance of ethics goes hand in hand with his surprising avoidance of the question of time.

The relation of a being and its being, which always occurs in a single instant for Levinas, can be described in greater detail. The being of a thing consists in its *work* of being. But obviously, this "work" does not occur in pristine isolation, as the doubling of existence with "existents" already indicates: "An act is not pure activity; *its being is doubled up with a having* which both is possessed and possesses."[10] Even so, the act remains utterly concealed from view: "light is doubled up with a night."[11] Individual entities surge into view from amidst the anonymous labor of being. By way of introducing a new technical term, Levinas speaks of "the upsurge of an existent into existence, a *hypostasis*. This entire essay intends only to draw out the implications of this fundamental situation."[12] There is little in all of this that would bother Heidegger. But there is also a subtle but decisive shift of emphasis, which Levinas himself does not formulate in an explicit way. What it amounts to is an improved status for concrete things.

For both Heidegger and Levinas, reality is a strife between unified being and manifold specific beings. But there is an important difference: while Heidegger situates this duel *between* beings and being itself, Levinas says that beings *are* the between. The philosophical implications of this delicate shift are enormous. Above all, it means that the homeland of ontology is no longer regarded as located *outside* of specific entities, a realization that comes to Heidegger only occasionally ("The Thing," "Building Dwelling Thinking," "The Origin of the Work of Art"). This subtle ontological alchemy undertaken by Levinas means that the concrete strife between objects such as rocks, drills, fossils, tomatoes, walnuts, and icicles can no longer be seen as mere superficial distractions that lure us away from the deep. The famous ontological *Zwischen* now occurs *within* the things rather than above or beneath them; the difference between almonds and rivers is no longer simply "ontic." Levinas brings us to a point where it is no longer a mark of urbane sophistication to take a smirking ironic distance from the most colorful details of the earth. Discussions of paper, silk, or rubber are no longer "reactionary" simply because they point to tangible objects.

To repeat an earlier claim, we should worry about concrete objects of this kind *only if they are taken as present-at-hand.* But we have seen that this possibility was dead as soon as Heidegger's most rudimentary analysis of tools appeared. This is not to say that Heidegger's ontological difference should be replaced with a return to discussions of atoms or sense data— quite the contrary. It is not I, but only mainstream Heidegger commentators, who wrongly consign the dazzling carnal zone of shapes and colors to the exclusive reign of positive science. It is these same interpreters who back themselves into a corner, assuming that we can never have a philosophical discussion of spearmint, but only of the "emergent process" by which all spearmint is possible, a clearing or granting or even "thanking" that would be irreducible to any particular spearmint leaf. In this way, mainstream Heideggerians continue to fight the last war instead of preparing for the next one. They remain so fixated on the step beyond present-at-hand entities (accomplished by Heidegger many decades ago), that they assume that entities can be interpreted *in no other way* than onti-cally. This sort of endless deferral misses the sincere relation to objects that characterizes the life of every good sensualist who savors a night of amaretto and pearls, or every child who relishes the combat of plastic dinosaurs in a sandbox.

Allow me one additional formulation of this theme, to ensure that the point is truly driven home. Against the belief that cleverness arises only from abandoning all specific beings and rising "critically" beyond them, we should turn the tables on this approach. Instead of structural aloofness and quasi-transcendental doubt, what philosophy now needs above all else is an injection of sheer naiveté—not the pathetic innocence of a burglary victim, but the innate candor with which circus clowns handle everything from cowbells to puppies to dynamite.

For those who do not care for poetic formulations of this kind, the point can be repeated in respectable technical terms. The usual tendency is to place Heidegger's *fundamental* difference on one side of reality, *specific* differences on the other. The turn to philosophy would consist in washing one's hands of any specific differences whatsoever. But such a turn leads only to voluntary paralysis, a self-imposed intellectual coma. The reality of objects does not unfold in some sort of ontic junkyard, as if ontology were confined to some sanitized palace in the sky. As stated repeatedly above, there is no such thing as an ontic object that would exist in isolation from ontological horizons: "ontic" refers not to objects, but to a certain kind of human *comportment* toward objects, the kind that takes them as merely *vorhanden*. Paper and silk are not unworthy of our philosophical efforts— they are tool-beings erupting from the system of the world and seducing us with their enticing surfaces. The specific contours of objects are noth-ing less than specific contours of the ontological difference itself. *Being itself reverses into beings.*

This book has focused repeatedly on Heidegger's basic distinction between the universal, invisible system of equipment and the deluge of fragmented objects that coast along its surface. The early work of Levinas describes a very similar sort of fundamental difference. But whereas Heidegger describes the work of being as a comprehensive system of ref-erences, Levinas gains access to it as the impersonal *il y a*, a simple "there is" that lies at the basis of all particularity. Whereas Angst places the entire world at a distance from us, the *il y a* shows us that no such distance is possible, closes off any escape hatch from the world. In his own words: "Let us imagine all beings, things and persons, reverting to nothingness. . . . Something would [still] happen, if only night and the silence of nothingness."[13] By imagining the banishment of all quality or personality from the universe, Levinas wants to arrive at the sheer labor of existence—the fact that every object simply is what it is, does what it does: "This impersonal, anonymous, yet inextinguishable consummation of being, which murmurs in the depths of nothingness itself we shall designate the '*il y a*'... [or] 'being in general'."[14]

For Levinas as for Heidegger, it is not only a thought experiment that brings us to this limit case. There are special scenarios in human life that give compelling vividness to the *il y a*. The most notable is insomnia: "The impossibility of rending the . . . anonymous rustling of existence manifests itself particularly in certain times when sleep evades our appeal."[15] On such occasions, specific existents disintegrate into an impersonal, inextinguishable night: "One is detached from any object, any content, yet there is presence."[16] With this inescapable *il y a*, which returns in the heart of any negation, Levinas wants to guide us to a point *prior* to the "hypostasis" of beings amidst being. Insomnia should allow us to achieve direct reconnaissance on being itself, prior to any sealing of a contract between being and beings.

Despite Levinas' wonderful discussion of insomnia, this is impossible for the same reason that Heidegger's pure *Angst* was impossible. The anonymous work of existence occurs in the sheer labor of things at being what they are, and not in any supposed *access* we might have to this labor, not even a noncognitive sort of access. The *il y a* that emerges in insomnia, however devoid it may be of specific features, already stands at an infinite remove from the infernal work of objects. It is not being itself that is experienced by the insomniac, but only being *as* being. No two realities could be more different. The impersonal realm of "being in general" remains fully withdrawn even in the endless night vigils described by Levinas, just as they do in Heidegger's various fundamental moods. In this way, the *il y a* is only a kind of front man or ambassador for anonymous being itself, which is too busy enacting a world to be able to meet the insomniac directly. There remains an unbridgeable gap between being in general and this being in general *as experienced*. We should not forget that it is not Angst and insomnia that sustain the reality of the cosmos: only *being* does this.

This means that the *il y a* does not allow us to retreat behind hypostasis at all, but only points to a special *kind* of hypostasis. Along with the eruption of green, heavy, or slippery things from the anonymity of the world, there is also an upsurge of impersonal featureless being. This flareup of impersonal being as opposed to specific beings cannot be confined to occasional sleepless nights, just as Heidegger's "something at all" did not occur only during episodes of anxiety. To say "*il y a*" or "something at all" is to refer not to a special event, but to a permanent and universal feature of reality as a whole.

But this points to another decisive factor. Like Heidegger's Angst, the *il y a* of Levinas is meant to be divorced from any specific being, to point to the single underground rumbling of the world as a whole. By way of contrast, the world of hypostasis is supposed to be made up of specific beings, scattered in their diversity across my field of consciousness. But our explicit encounter with "something at all" in insomnia shows that the kingdom of the as-structure is already split in half. I have treated Levinas as the leading explorer of Heidegger's *first* axis of division: the polarization of reality between tool and broken tool. But with his introduction of the *il y a*, Levinas runs across the *second* Heideggerian axis as well—hardly a surprise, given the close analogy between his insomnia and Heidegger's Angst. For the moment, I mention this point only to draw the parallel between these two authors, and not to make the premature claim that Levinas helps unlock the secret of Heidegger's quadruple object.

But there is a key difference between them that may endow Levinas with a greater capacity to appreciate the problem he has on his hands. Both Heidegger and Levinas try to bring being as a whole to presence through situations of privileged access. In both cases, they are wrong that being as a whole has actually become accessible, since being in its labor cannot be captured even in a fundamental mood. Hence, both of them are forced to fracture the as-structure in half, a move with a significance that is still unclear. But whereas Heidegger tends to regard Angst as the sheer *nihilation* of particular beings, Levinas sees each being as making a specific *contract* with the work of being, setting up a specific hypostasis in the cosmos. Once again, Levinas takes an extra step toward grasping the positive reality of entities rather than dismissing them as derivative. In focusing our attention once more upon the integrity of specific objects, Levinas goes a long way toward his stated goal of "leaving the climate of Heideggerian philosophy."[17]

To repeat, "being in general" for Heidegger sweeps all entities aside, standing them up against a void. But since Levinas is fascinated by the *relation* between the entity and its being, the rift in question must occur in the midst of *all* specific things: perhaps we can speak both of paper as paper, and paper as something at all. The key to the structure of reality would lie not *between* being and beings, but in beings themselves. This is also suggested from certain remarks that Levinas aims at Heidegger's tool-analysis, a topic that does not usually play a central role in his reading of his forerunner.

What Levinas tells us about equipment is that Heidegger tends to emphasize the way in which objects are suppressed and swallowed up by some ulterior purpose (tools), but that he himself prefers to describe them in their explicit finality (broken tools). Air is not just equipment for breathing: "We breathe for the sake of breathing, eat and drink for the sake of eating and drinking, we take shelter for the sake of taking shelter, we study to satisfy our curiosity, we take a walk for the walk. All that is not for the sake of living; *it is living*. Life is a *sincerity*."[18] It is unlikely that this passage was meant as a blistering criticism of Heidegger, who obviously realized that the invisible system of references only tells half the story. But it does herald the shift of emphasis described several pages ago, tacitly redefining the "ontic" realm as the zone where ontology stakes its genuine claim. In the words of Levinas: "What seems to have escaped Heidegger—if it is true that in these matters something might have escaped Heidegger—is that prior to being a system of tools, the world is an ensemble of nourishments."[19] Consciousness does not penetrate back behind the objects that surround it; it does not outflank the countless elements that bombard it like snowflakes or hailstones. Instead, consciousness is *sincere*. Life is fundamentally an enjoyment. It is nothing but an absorption or involvement, even in those darkest moments of life when we maintain a cynical distance from the pleasures of well-cooked food.

But enjoyment is pluralistic. If world war or a beloved person can thoroughly absorb our attention, so too can relatively minor entities: violins, olives, ink, the pointless chant of hooligans in the street. What all such entities have in common is that all of them take a stance within the world and command our attention, lure us into taking them seriously even if only to ridicule them. Thus, it is not only insomnia that displays an absorbing hold of reality over us. The same inescapable being is present in the allure of fresh pomegranate, or in the anguish of a brutal migraine. "There is" an exotic fruit here before me. "There is" a crushing pain in my head. In this way, *the* il y a *is atomized*. Although Levinas seems to grasp this point instinctively rather than openly, it is one of his two great philosophical discoveries (along with the connection between time and the Other, which lies beyond the scope of this book). Being is no longer the all-embracing term, visible only in exceptional cases, that both Heidegger and Levinas tend to imagine. Instead, it is scattered across the full multitude of entities that inhabit the world, defining each thing as being just what it is, *whatever that may be*. It defines the primordial unity by which *each* thing encounters us. The world is already congealed into units, and does not confront us as a disconnected set of points woven together after the fact. But if the *il y a* is transformed in this way into the unity of countless specific objects, then being is always the being of beings in an even more fundamental sense than the one that Heidegger sometimes admits. The provisional lesson should be clear: an entity is not only hard at work in being what it is, but is equally effective at drawing me into its orbit *as an individual thing*. The object is fundamentally a *coquette*, as the maltreated Baudrillard so beautifully describes.[20]

Levinas is a student of Heidegger, not of Whitehead. This means that the wider sense of the term "prehension" is completely missing from his works. For Levinas, hypostasis is always the work of *consciousness*, and seemingly only the human kind. It is consciousness that generates hypostasis, liberating the ceaseless drone of insomniac being into specific objects. In this way, his description of the strife between anonymous being and singular entities remains trapped in the very interpretation of tool/broken tool that was just criticized: namely, "explicit perception" vs. "concealed relational system." As a result, his discussion of sincerity is really only a meditation on the *human* enjoyment of bread or shelter or sexual nakedness. But since I am now arguing that the as-structure holds good for *any* encounter between any entities at all, the Levinasian theme of sincerity has to be broadened as well. Even a rock and a pane of glass encounter one another in their sincerity. The unitary rock is not simply an abstraction based on a collection of stony *matter* contiguous in space: rather, it is a genuine *form*. Split the rock up into independent particles, and it would not be the same thing for the window. The same goes for the human encounter with bread or wine. It is not particles that I encounter, but forms. For the first time, the theme of "formal causation" enters the discussion of objects. Let me point out in passing that the classic examples of formal cause, in Aristotle and elsewhere, have always come from examples of *tools*. And here is the real reason for my retaining the term "tool-being," which is not meant only as a marker for its point of origin in Heidegger's analysis of equipment.

But I will drop this new theme for the moment. What is important here is to note that Levinas' insights soon expand far beyond the framework he intended. We have already seen the importance of not skewing the entire analysis of being and beings in the direction of sentient consciousness: human awareness is already far too complicated a phenomenon to shed any light on the general ontology of the as-structure. The drama described by Heidegger and Levinas is already perfectly evident on the brutal level of soil, minerals, and salts. But with certain limited exceptions (Schelling, Schopenhauer, Whitehead, and parts of Nietzsche, Peirce, and Dewey), post-Kantian philosophy has shown little confidence in its ability to describe the action of soulless matter itself. Like Heidegger, Levinas shares this bias in full, and almost always appeals to the sphere of human being when posing philosophical problems.

But there are moments when Levinas seems vaguely uneasy with this prejudice. One such moment is his exciting dismissal of the notion of equipment as an instrument of human praxis. More important than the use-value of a tool, he says, is the fact that it suppresses work and swallows up distance.[21] To use a term from cybernetics, the tool is a "black box," a simple integral unit that conceals an inferno of numerous interior powers and relations—forces utterly indifferent to any human "use" of them. But this insight is developed only hesitantly, and Levinas continues to show little concern for the strife between inanimate objects. His theory of the Other is a theory of the infinite challenge posed by the *human* Other, and tells us nothing about the imperative force unleashed upon me by a beautiful sunny day, let alone about the forces exchanged between two boulders in my absence. While there is no denying the special ethical status of human reality, it hardly exhausts the field of *ontological* alterity.[22]

§22. Contributions of Zubiri

In most parts of the world, Xavier Zubiri remains a far more obscure figure than Levinas. In the United States, he is best known as the final guide word on volume 7/8 of the standard Collier-MacMillan *Encyclopedia of Philosophy*.[23] For this reason, his name is easily visible at virtually every house party on the American philosophical circuit. His obscurity is undeserved, and is due mostly to the unfashionable status of "first philosophy" in our time. Zubiri's major work, *Sobre la esencia*, first appeared in Madrid in 1962; largely unread in our country, it is arguably one of the most original works of philosophy published since World War II. An English translation, *On Essence*, has been available for nearly two decades, and can often be found in the remainder bins of used book stores for less than a good carton of juice.[24]

But even if it were read more widely, its success would not be guaranteed, since many of its innovations are likely to remain hidden from a first reading. And it must be admitted that some of the book's misfortunes are self-inflicted: hampered by dense exposition and a sometimes arid vocabulary, Zubiri's work can have the initial flavor of rear-guard Thomism. Even so, Zubiri is not arguing for a "return" to *anything*, as becomes clear in his book through numerous moments of unexpected drollery and the massive presence of camouflaged Heideggerian armaments. The present book cannot provide the sort of systematic treatment that his work deserves. I will try to identify quickly the linchpin of Zubiri's system and relate it to the concept of tool-being. This is not such a difficult task, given Zubiri's agreement with Heidegger on several pivotal issues:

1. The reality of a thing cannot be identified with its presence, its unconcealment, or (against the pragmatist reading) its usefulness for any particular human agent.

2. The reality of the thing is composed of *both* the fact that it is something specific, and the fact that it is something at all. Zubiri himself refers to the poles of this second Heideggerian axis as the "talitative" and "transcendental" dimensions. I will take the liberty of renaming these terms in the pages that follow. The talitative dimension refers to what everyday language loosely calls the *essence* of a thing. But since Zubiri reserves a stricter meaning for that word, we can call the talitative pole the *consistency* of a thing, as when we speak of the consistency of a liquid or a dessert. The transcendental pole can be renamed the "singularity" of the thing, as it refers to the thing as a unity that encloses all of its qualities.

3. The reality of a thing cannot be regarded as a substance endowed with properties. Instead, the thing is always a *system*, a system that unifies all of its numerous "notes."

The title of Zubiri's book could hardly be more traditional: *On Essence*. But he begins his discussion of essence with a negative remark, insisting that he does not use the term in the sense of the traditional existence/essence opposition. In the first of several jarring parallels with Levinas, Zubiri takes a subtle critical slap at all attempts to locate the drama of existence *outside* of any given moment. The existence/essence distinction, he says, arises historically only with the doctrine of creation *ex nihilo*.[25] This theological approach is able to understand essence only in causal terms; it demands our recognition of the fact that a thing can be described as having a certain "whatness," and also described simply in terms of the fact *that* it exists. For Zubiri, such a distinction is harmless in its own right. The problem comes when this dualism is interpreted as the result of *createdness*. On the one hand there is a disembodied essence, and on the other a remote causal agent who either brings the essence into existence or does not do so. To put it in Heideggerian terms, the problem with the existence/essence split is that it reads the "existence" side of the equation as a simple presence-at-hand, as an obvious factual state of occurring rather than *not* occurring.

Levinas and Zubiri are united with their teacher Heidegger in condemning this interpretation of "existence." Things do not simply occur or fail to occur. Rather, an entity such as a piece of wood embodies a genuine tension between two moments of reality, neither of them reducible to sheer occurrence. On the one hand, there is what I have termed the "consistency" of the wood, the fact that it displays a set of diverse features: smoothness, hardness, perhaps hollowness. On the other, there is the "singularity" of the wood, its individual reality as anything at all. But this refers not just to the sheer factual presence of the wood, as if in contrast to the possibility of its *not* existing. There is not a binary decision here between occurrence and nonoccurrence. The question of the thing's existence is not to be answered with a "yes" or "no," but must be described as a thing's real enactment of itself amidst the system of the world. The upshot: this dual friction between the consistency and singularity of a thing is one that unfolds only *within* the thing, and does not arise at the *external* point where it is brought into occurrence by a carpenter or deity. Nothing in this part of Zubiri's argument will surprise readers of Heidegger's *Basic Problems of Phenomenology*.

Whatever one might think of Zubiri's reading of Medieval philosophy, it is interesting that he independently raises the same problem as the otherwise flashier Levinas: the ambivalence at play in the heart of *specific beings*. Both authors are on the hunt for the specific facets of the *metabole* embodied in every object, and are thereby one step closer to the metontology that in Heidegger never escapes the drawing board. Having already discussed the Levinasian version of the contract between existence and existents, I now briefly describe Zubiri's approach to the problem, which takes a somewhat more challenging turn. Zubiri is fully aware of the Heideggerian difference between the essence "in and of itself" (tool) and the essence as "respective to us" (broken tool). Indeed, it is a cornerstone of his philosophy. But rather than simply dwelling on this more manageable theme, Zubiri also confronts the duel that erupts both *within* the as-structure and *within* tool-being. He often does this only implicitly, and for the most part fails to credit Heidegger's own anticipations of the theme. Nonetheless, Zubiri's uncanny flashes of insight begin to reveal possibilities for ontology that are barely sensed by Heidegger himself—and sensed even less by those of his successors who remain fixated on a human-centered model of reality, whatever their attacks on "humanism."

The first of Zubiri's lightning-flashes appears with his resurrection of the term "physical," which he uses interchangeably with the word "real." The physical is neither the bodily nor the material. Instead, it refers to that dimension of a thing's reality that is *unrelated* to the fact of its being thought or perceived—namely, it refers to what I have argued must follow from Heidegger's tool-being. As an example, Zubiri describes the weight and color of an apple tree as physically distinct moments of this tree. Independently of any observer, there are the realities of "tree-weight" and "tree-color," unleashed like wild dogs amidst the rest of reality. The weight and color of the tree are really there, executing their being amidst all that is. They are also *truly distinct*, since each moment inflicts itself upon its sur-roundings in distinctly different ways. The tree-weight specializes in com-pressing the soil and grass beneath it, or in crushing a nearby house as it falls during a storm. By contrast, the tree-color has its own limited role: bombarding the universe with distinct wavelengths of reflected light. In this way, these two moments are *physically* distinct in the total reality of the apple tree. But the case is quite different if we try to distinguish between the "life" of the tree and its "vegetation," since these amount to precisely the same quality. Only a human observer would draw a distinction between them—in a scientific context, it might be useful to insist on a difference between the life and vegetation of the tree. But no such difference really exists *in the tree*, which is a *physical* whole, not a conceptual one. In this sense the essence of the tree, its basic *physical* reality, is also *the metaphysi-cal par excellence*. I warmly endorse this Zubirian use of the term "meta-physical," ignoring the contemporary tendency to reserve it as a pejorative tag for philosophies of presence.

By introducing the term "physical" in this sense, Zubiri positions him-self to rephrase the old existence/essence question in a fresh way. We have already seen that the weight and color of a tree are supposed to be physi-cally distinct. Asking further about this distinction, Zubiri asks: "Is the essence something *physically* distinct or different from the existence?"[26] With respect to the traditional use of these terms, Zubiri's answer will be that there is no such physical distinction. The thing exists only physically, only in the deployment of its essence amidst the cosmos. But we might pose a related question, and ask whether there are *any* structural physical distinctions in the heart of the essence. In terms of the present book, we might ask about Heidegger's second distinction between something spe-cific and something at all: namely, Zubiri's distinction between the consis-tency and singularity of the thing. Are these physically distinct moments in an object, or only a conceptual difference introduced by ontologists?

For the moment this question can be left in the background, so as to develop in more detail Zubiri's concept of physical reality. A reality is defined as that which acts on other things by virtue of its notes.[27] This term "note" is meant as a replacement for the word "property," which Zubiri regards as biased toward reality viewed *conceptively*, that is, from the external standpoint of a relation rather than from the thing in and of itself. To speak of a *property*, he says, is to speak of the idiosyncrasies that distin-guish one thing from another; in this way, the property is an extraneous feature grafted onto some underlying substrate, and always viewed from outside rather than from within. As opposed to properties, the notes of a thing make up even the most intimate *parts* of that thing: "matter, its structure, its chemical composition, its psychic 'faculties', etc."[28] Instead of qualities *belonging* to a substance, Zubiri's notes *are* the reality of the thing itself (which he calls a "substantivity" rather than a "substantiality," for reasons to be clarified below).

Here as everywhere, Zubiri insists on a distinction between the *real* notes of a thing and its *conceptive* notes. The former make up the basic reality that supports all the other kinds of notes. This becomes especially relevant in the case of items of equipment. Zubiri holds that tables, farms, or knives are not *realities* in the strict sense of the term. The physical reality of each of these objects is a certain irreducible *factum*, a set of notes that include a shape, a weight, a color, a determinate tensile strength. The fact that the knife is used for cutting is only *derivative* of its physical essence, the essence that supports every possible "use" of the knife, every relation or respectivity in which it might happen to become ensconced. This is obviously a complete reversal of Heidegger and Whitehead, who both hold that the full *system* of relations is always prior to any individual essence. As Zubiri crisply puts it, the essence of a thing is essence *of*, not essence *for*. Granted, the "essence of" is inevitably bound up with countless "fors," simply by existing in the world and having a determinate effect on all that it encounters. But this does not eliminate the fact that the "of" and the "for" are utterly distinct moments of the thing. This physical essence *of* the thing is precisely what the present book has called its *tool-being*: not its "usefulness," but its brute actuality apart from any manifestation of this reality to human thought or to any *other* entity.

To speak of essence in Zubiri's sense is, roughly, to speak of tool-being in the sense in which I have used it. The theme covered by both terms is the reality of the real *in vacuo*, as opposed to the theory of the thing as always stationed amidst a network of references. For Heidegger and Whitehead, this stance within a network is ontologically exhaustive—nothing remains of the thing outside it. But for Zubiri, as for the present book, the network into which any object is thrust can only scratch the surface of its *actuality*. Essence, he says, is "the physical structural moment of the thing taken in itself."[29] For this reason, the essence is always individual: each dog has its own private essence. Any shared dog-quiddity is purely derivative, the second-hand product of an observer trying to abstract some sort of "dogness" after the fact.[30] To approach the essence as a quiddity amounts to converting it into a form of presence-at-hand, into what Zubiri terms the merely *conceptive* essence. The true physical reality of a thing, also described as its reality *simpliciter*, admittedly does not define the *whole* of that thing's reality. After all, it is also a part of the apple tree's reality that it can be cut down and used as firewood. But "cuttability" and "burnability" are not part of the ultimate radical reality of the tree, which recedes from every human view. And although this is only implicit in Zubiri, the radical reality of the tree also recedes from any *causal* interaction, as argued in the case of the icy lake in §19. The essence *of* the apple tree is not the same as its essence *for* humans or *for* lightning bolts.

To use Zubiri's own example, air as "travellable" is not part of the physical/essential reality of air. Until quite recently, this travellability was an untapped potential, and "in every case, possibility and real note are two completely different dimensions of the thing."[31] Consider another, nontechnological example. Silver has the capacities of reflecting light and floating in water. But according to Zubiri, *neither* of these abilities belong to the absolute reality of the silver. They are a kind of *secundum quid*, and do not belong to silver *simpliciter*. Put differently, the essence of silver or anything else does not refer to properties that emerge "under a given set of conditions." For Zubiri, essence is *entitative*, not operational. In other words, the essence is the very act of a thing's being, and not its ability to act on other things.

For this reason, the essence must remain withdrawn from any attempt to apprehend it: "the radical structure of reality is not necessarily definable in a *logos*."[32] The resulting distinction has a Heideggerian ring: *proper* reality (tool) vs. *actualized* reality (broken tool).[33] In this way, Zubiri says, reality resides in the thing *two* times.[34] We have the thing and its shadow, tool and broken tool. Essence is simply itself (the "ultimate" moment) but also and equally a relation to other (the "grounding" moment).[35] For Zubiri, "the essential notes are those notes . . . which are not due to the connection of the reality in question with other realities. . . ."[36] Adding an equivalent pair of terms, he distinguishes between the *constitutive* and *quidditive* kinds of essence, of which the latter are only representations, simulacra of a prior and proper reality.[37]

Throughout this book, I have spoken of the action or activity or actuality of things, but in a sense diametrically opposed to Heidegger's own use of these terms. I have not been speaking of the "ergic" character of things as able to accomplish distinct ends in the world, as able to produce an *ergon* in the sense so often lambasted by Heidegger. Activity of *this* kind is always something quite different from the primordial physical essence, the tool-being of the thing. As an example of this, Zubiri points to the case of a chair.[38] The chair is something we can sit in, or something to stack books upon. But again, these traits are not *physically* real: "the chair . . . *qua* chair, is not real, because 'chair' is not a character which belongs to it 'of itself' [*de suyo*]".[39]

The reader's first thought might be that this is because of the overtly *artificial* character of the chair. But the traditional *physis/tekhne* opposition is not an issue here; Zubiri's point would hold good even if chairs blossomed naturally from the earth. We can see this when he discusses the numerous inherent possibilities of a *cave*. The fact that a cave can be used as a habitation pertains only to the cave as "meaning-thing," as essence *for* human life, and not as sheer essence *of* the cave itself. By the same token, in modern times it is possible even to create certain artificial products which, once created, behave with an independent "naturalness." As examples of this, Zubiri cites the cases of insulin and nuclear acids, which "once produced, act formally in virtue of the properties which they possess,"[40] bearing no trace at all of their artificial origin in the laboratory. Perhaps future developments will prove Zubiri's point all the more, as we become increasingly enmeshed with strange entities of this kind: species of fertile artificial vegetables, sexually reproducing androids, and so on. To conclude, the term "nature" should refer not to the *origin* of a thing, but to its manner of reality.[41]

To nail the point home, the normally solemn Zubiri provides a series of refreshingly whimsical examples of the kind that also permeate Aristotle's works, unnoticed. For instance, we can consider the case of a specific dog, which may be either gaunt or obese. With uncharacteristic sass, Zubiri insists that the size of the dog's meals or its family history of weight disorders is not what is philosophically interesting: what ought to concern us is the gauntness or obesity itself, irrespective of what may have caused it.[42] In an equally irreverent example, he asks the reader to imagine that a house is falling to pieces before our eyes. Here too, the *cause* of this process is irrelevant to the question of its physical essence: "Even when we see the house falling to pieces because someone is destroying it, what is decisive is seeing that the house *is actually* falling to pieces and not seeing that it is falling to pieces because someone is destroying it."[43] He sums up this point with the flair of a single aphorism: "In the final analysis . . . when all is said and done, things, whether caused or not, are already here."[44]

But there is more to this claim than meets the eye, since it not only focuses our attention on the tool-being of the things prior to any causation. More than this, it also tends to grant to tool-being a central role *within* the sphere of causation. As Zubiri puts it: "the truly surprising thing in experience is that what is already real ceases to be real *by reason of an intrinsic condition*."[45] Does this passage not suggest a kind of Leibnizian windowless causation? After all, if the house collapses primarily "by reason of an intrinsic condition," even if we see it being bulldozed by a gang of aggressive vandals, then clearly Zubiri has minimized the power of things to act externally upon one another.

Unfortunately, Zubiri never addresses this metaphysical problem directly. Instead, he adopts the unsatisfying placeholder solution of a "double causality" that includes both of these elements: (a) efficient cause, and (b) the sort of cause that pertains to a thing's *predisposition* to be vulnerable to particular sorts of forces.[46] This solution is inadequate, since it merely repeats the dualism between subterranean physical essence and external relationality that Zubiri has already demonstrated, without clarifying the issue of how the essence "of itself" can ever be affected by anything external to itself. If someone pours vigorous acid onto a flower and burns it away into nothingness, does this destroy the physical essence of the flower in and of itself, or only the "conceptive" essence of the flower as something encountered by the malignant chemist himself? Or in terms of the present book: given the claim that tool-being recedes even behind the *causal* realm, do tool-beings remain unscathed by their inevitable causal duels with other entities? How can the vandals affect the essence of the house or the acid affect the essence of the flower? Do such duels occur only on the level of the as-structure? On these questions, Zubiri has no help to offer, since he is satisfied with drawing a distinction, when what is needed is a clear *depiction*.

We have now heard a great deal about what Zubiri thinks essence *is not*, but relatively little of what he thinks it *is*. Whatever essence may be, we know that it cannot be regarded as as an ultimate substance, as some sort of framework that would later support accidental or peripheral attributes. By means of a perilously subtle terminological distinction, Zubiri proposes that the essence of a thing is not a substantiality, but a "substantivity." Often, hair-splitting shifts of this kind conceal an intellectual sleight of hand that secretly preserves what really ought to be rejected. But in the present case, the difference is reasonably clear, even if it cannot ultimately be maintained. For Zubiri, substantivity turns out to be a synonym for "system." His rejection of substance in favor of substantivity is a turn away from the present-at-hand givenness of ultimate building-blocks, and toward the encompassing unity of an ontological *machine*, whose totality must always precede any of its parts. This will lead to puzzling consequences, as described in §24 below.

All along, Zubiri has been turning our attention away from the systematic relations between entities back toward these same entities *in vacuo*, the essences or tool-beings "of themselves." Ironically, he now wants to define these essences *as systems* rather than as distinct pregiven units. But there are two senses in which the physical essence can be regarded as a system. First, it is the performance of some total reality amidst the cosmos, and therefore part of a network of effects. This is a sense of "system" that Zubiri rejects, since the Heidegger/Whitehead theory of networks reduces essence to its effect on other things rather than to its own inherent reality. But second, in a way that Zubiri accepts, the essence *is itself* a system, insofar as it integrates numerous notes. In this way, the essence or tool-being is itself a network that unifies various parts or components. While irreducible to relations, the tool-being exists only *as* a sum of relations.

This is where some paradoxes begin to emerge from Zubiri's account of essence. On the one hand, he wants to distinguish between physical reality "of itself" and the derivative relational reality that turns things into mere "meaning-things." There is first the real knife, and second the non-real *cutting* knife; first the real chair, and second the nonreal chair that one *sits* in; first the farm as a real plot of earth, and second the same farm as derivative *cropland*. These use-values arise only when the sheer physical essence has gotten caught up in a system of meanings and functions, when it has gained a secondary reality *in respect to* some other reality. Hence, there is a marked tendency for Zubiri's opposition between "physically real" and "respective" to become an opposition between simples and composites, an opposition I will criticize in §24 below.

I have said that Zubiri both denies that the essence is part of a system *and* defines it *as* a system of various notes. We can recall the earlier example of a piece of silver. Zubiri speaks of silver as having a real essence "of itself"; in contrast, the silver's shininess and buoyancy are derivative, since they require an exterior relation between the silver itself and light or water. The composite effects of "floating silver," or "beautiful shining silver," are regarded as external couplings of several discrete essences. But the question that needs to be asked is why *silver itself* is considered exempt from the zone of relationality. How can we really speak of it as having ultimate integrity? Also, what is the essence of the "silver itself" in the first place? Zubiri sometimes refers to it as the "atomic-cortical structure" of the silver, which is less materialist than it sounds but more vague than it sounds—he simply never clarifies the phrase. What if I were to tell Zubiri that only the protons and electrons *in* the silver have real physical essence "of themselves," and that the silver as a whole is merely a derivative effect, a "respectivity" of these particles? It is fine to say that floating silver is only a relational compound of silver and water, but we have no way of knowing whether the silver and water have a real essence, or are only the compound effect of "smaller" essences.

Indeed, the entire analysis can be pushed as far as contemporary physics is willing to take us. Why not say that even a lonely proton in the chunk of silver *is itself* a composite machine built out of quarks and even more minuscule fragments? So far, no smallest unit has been identified, and it seems unlikely that any will ever be demonstrated. Unless Zubiri wants to be a strange sort of atomist who grants essence only to tiny, tiny unverifiable particles while treating all larger units as merely relational, he is going to have to drop the absolute distinction between essential and respective. The obvious solution, the one advocated by this book, is to recognize that the difference between essence (the substantial) and respectivity (the relational) is not a difference that splits between two *locations* in reality. That is to say, Zubiri ought to stop pointing to various entities when he describes this term, stop saying that a farm or chair is "merely respective," merely "essence *for*." Since Zubiri already defines the essence as a unifying system, he also ought to be willing to say that every unifying system is an essence. If the physical essence of silver is not threatened by its swarming inner nation of "notes," then why not grant a real tool-being to my act of smoking a water-pipe, despite the fact that this act combines cafe furniture and various metal parts of the sheesha with all of the tobacco and molasses and water that fill it? I will revisit this issue in §24, in the course of a discussion of Aristotle and Leibniz.

Zubiri's distinction between the physical essence and the conceptive essence is the same as Heidegger's rift between tool and broken tool. But Zubiri is in agreement with the present book when he holds, against Heidegger, that the essence or tool-being is prior to the relational machinery of the world: in a sense, the part comes before the whole. The tricky consequence of this is that Zubiri wants to be able to commend certain essences (silver, apple tree, physical knife) as having natural integrity and others (floating silver, burning apple tree, rusting knife) as being contaminated from the start by a relation to other essences. The perplexities of this claim have not yet been addressed. Nor have we heard much so far about the famous second axis of Heidegger's ontology, which I suggested could be found in Zubiri's *magnum opus*. In the coming section, then, I will give Zubiri a bit more time on stage.

§23. Refining the Problem

As we have seen, Zubiri's basic philosophical strategy is to draw attention to the reality of the essence *de suyo*, "of itself," apart from any human contact with it. In comparison with most contemporary philosophy, this is enough to qualify him as an unusually hard-headed realist. For this reason, it might seem that Zubiri has less interest in the specifically human real than in purely "objective" reality. But in fact, his strategy is motivated by precisely the *opposite* wish. By drawing an absolute line between essential realities and merely respective ones, Zubiri is actually trying to *guarantee* a special status for human reality in the world. If he distinguishes between physical reality and perspectival reality, his use of the term "perspectival" is confined only to *human* perspective, and perhaps in some limited sense to sentient animals. Never does he *openly* consider that the physical reality of a knife manifests itself differently to a brick wall than it does to a melon. Like Heidegger before him, Zubiri tends to interpret inorganic beings as pregiven slabs of matter that bear a fixed and uniform consistency, even if he does so in an unorthodox way. For both authors, the perspectival drama of the as-structure is strictly quarantined within the human realm. In this sense, they lag behind the speculative verve of intellectual gamblers such as Leibniz and Whitehead.

This lack of fascination with the inorganic realm leads Zubiri into two additional difficulties. The first difficulty arises from the fact that he only grants genuine "substantivity," and thus real essence, to two sorts of entities: (1) Beings whose *substantive* unity also enjoys a *substantial* unity. The best example of this would be a chemical compound. Hydrogen and chlorine can be combined to form hydrochloric acid, thereby generating a new substantiality with unforeseen properties not foreshadowed in either of the individual components. Another example would be the way that a group of molecules compose the joint *physical* reality of a knife (ignoring for the moment its "derivative" cutting ability). (2) Beings composed of a "functional combination." This happens when the parts of an entity do not fuse into a single substance despite having one *substantive* functional unity. Such beings are generally known as *organisms*,[47] although there are also moments when Zubiri seems to grant this status only to *human* organisms.[48]

What is most disconcerting here is the first case. If we forget the question of organisms for the moment, and focus on the inorganic physical essence, the criterion of whether or not a thing is physically real turns out to be a traditional concept of *substance,* which in practice always has a largely empirical value. Two molecules in a piece of metal are generally held to be part of the same substance insofar as that piece of metal can be moved around in a stable state, without the molecules easily losing their configuration within the rigid structure. Zubiri holds that the same thing *cannot* be said of the relation between a single person's heartbeat and thumbprint, or between the small and large intestines. Although all of these entities belong to the same organism, thereby contributing to a single *substantive* unity, they should not also be regarded as *substantially* one. For they remain independent domains correlated in an organic whole; they do not dissolve into a new and higher substance.

But it is difficult to see any way (other than the ontic, common-sense way) of establishing this thesis. Zubiri still hasn't really established a closer bond between the hydrogen and chlorine in a drop of HCl than between a woman's left eye and her right middle toe. And this is not yet the worst of it. Like many others working in the Aristotelian tradition, Zubiri holds that if there is no real fusion in the organism, there is even less in the case of machines, which Zubiri describes as sheer "mixtures" rather than combinations. A bridge has no essence; its properties are "merely additive."[49] Whereas the functional union of kidneys and lungs and blood cells in an organism at least gives rise to something genuinely new, this is supposedly never the case for tools or machines. If a new bridge lacks only the center trestle to be completed, and I go to the trouble of laying that single trestle, Zubiri would still say that I have still created nothing new—at least nothing that could be said to have an essence. Rather, I have only managed to create something respective or relational, something that has meaning only for the human entities who will use it.

This sort of assumption is a key weakness of most forms of realism, one that Whitehead should be praised for avoiding. Instead of proceeding slowly with the analysis, and not making any distinctions that cannot withstand the strictest ontological scrutiny, realists tend to jump the gun. Not satisfied with demonstrating that the thing in and of itself is irreducible to any of its manifestations, Zubiri wants to import numerous, apparently reasonable distinctions from everyday life for use at a much higher level. As obvious a difference as there seems to be between pieces of metal, organisms, and machines, it is impermissible to give lengthy orations on this difference without first demonstrating that this common-sense distinction is also a distinction on the level of their *being*. To turn Zubiri's own terminology against him, the fact that there is a *conceptive* difference between these entities does not prove that there is a *physical* difference as well.

For this reason, I reject the substance/organism/machine distinction as an ontic solution to an ontological problem. It is irrelevant here that certain combinations of substances seem to behave as a single substance (protons in a silver atom), while others apparently retain a greater independence (a car's tires and its windows). In fact, the unity of a chemical compound is every bit as problematic as the couplings between a physical knife and the relational human *use* of it. There is little reason to call the former an essence and the latter only an accidental mixture. For even the sleek integral unity of the physical knife is already made up of a swarming microcosm of metallic pixels, and even smaller confederations of dwarfish components. The fact that all of these metal-points tend to move together in a certain uniform proportion is ontologically unconvincing: on a deeper level, there is no reason to regard the connection of these molecules as any more natural ("physical") than an absolutely random combination of objects.

To cite an example from history, if a horde of independent molecules can combine into a larger physical knife-essence, there is no reason why this knife-essence cannot combine with an entity called Brutus to become a weapon-essence. In Zubiri's world, this assassin's tool cannot have a real essence, since it is a merely conceptive or relational sort of reality. But I hold that *any* entity becomes relational as soon as it is viewed from below. Zubiri regards the essence as a unity of *real notes*—nowhere does he claim that the thing is inherently one and that only from the outside does it look like many (this is what separates Zubiri from Leibniz). No, Zubiri's essence is alaready a union of inherently plural notes. In this sense, *every* essence is a kind of machine: a swarming composite when viewed from below, but a sleek nonrelational unity when viewed from above. Viewed from one side, it is an assembly of diverse components; viewed from the other, it is a simple "black box" whose internal seismic turmoil need not concern us in the least.[50] Consequently, either *every* being has an essence, or *no* being does. But to choose the latter option would be to reduce a thing to its perspectival reality, its existence here and now in the total network of meaning. Since this entire book has worked to establish a being of things that withdraws from any of their relations, we are left with only the first option. Everything must have an "essence" of the Zubirian kind, even those he dismisses as merely respective, such as farms and sitting-events and cutting-events.

Some light can be shed on this point if we make use of an especially absurd example. It would be possible to construct an utterly pointless machine by combining an irrelevant series of materials into a flamboyant final product (children often do this for entertainment's sake). For example, we might attach a plastic tube to a piece of camel-hair fabric, then tie this fabric to a light fixture so as to suspend the tube in mid-air, and finally pour water through the tube into an empty bowl on the floor. The resulting invention could be called a "water-pouring machine." In ontological terms, such an apparatus would provoke Zubiri's utter contempt. After all, where is the genuine combination here? It is nothing but a ridiculous set of diverse pieces performing no important practical function; such a machine will certainly have no essence. But I disagree with this assessment: in fact, the machine in question has as specific an essence as any object under the sun. To see this, note first that each piece of the machine plays an utterly distinct role in the total system. If not for the empty bowl on the floor, we would have a completely different system: one that would *spill* all of its water, damaging linoleum and perhaps arousing the anger of the person living in the apartment below. If not for the tubular shape of the plastic, the water would not attain the speed and force achieved by a lengthy concentrated stream, thereby altering the final temperature and air-content of the water immediately after pouring. If the entire apparatus had not been hanging near the ceiling, the amount of air cooled by the water during its fall would be considerably decreased, and the air-currents in the room would have altered decisively as a result. The fact that the tube is suspended by means of a camel-hair fabric rather than cotton or gauze does not seem especially relevant to the pouring, although it might lend an offbeat aesthetic charm to the scene for any human observers, and also helps fireproof the machine and thereby augment its general durability. To say that none of these features would alter the water-pourer *qua* water-pourer is of no help. This simply begs the question, since it may well be that to consider this specific entity *qua* some aspect or other is to view it only conceptively. In and of itself, it may well be that there is no such thing as a water-pourer, but only an individual machine with highly determinate notes that later gets *objectified* as a "useful water-pourer." This question has not yet been decided.

Moreover, as I argued in §19, the reality of this ridiculous machine cannot be reduced to its system of relations in the here and now. Alternative scenarios could easily be imagined that would place this apparently ludicrous machine in a far more sinister light. For example, any number of hazardous materials might have been siting in the bowl, ready to explode when combined with water. If the machine had been constructed by the sadist imagined earlier, ants might have been exploring the bowl, in position to be exterminated once the water began to flow. Each modified set of conditions exposes a new face of this very real and very distinct machine. The machine itself is not reducible to any of these scenarios, and retains a reality independently of all of them. Then the water-pouring machine *does* have an essence, one that remains withdrawn from any of its total relational environments. This fact becomes far more compelling if we change our tone, and speak not of futile childhood contraptions, but of diesel engines or nerve gas.

I conclude that essence is a moment of *every* entity, and cannot be restricted to a certain limited class of entities (the "physically real" in Zubiri's sense). This claim raises numerous metaphysical issues. For example, as I write this sentence, the following assembly of objects now lies on my bedroom table: a stapler, two computers, five pens, three pencils, a wallet, sunglasses, eleven dimes, and six nickels. Does this chaotic grouping of entities have its own unique essence? But one of the computers has recently been advertised for sale [already sold by the time of this printing—g.h.]. If someone purchases the computer and removes it, was there a group essence of these objects that has now been transformed by this event? Nor does the question arise only in the drastic case when one of the items is actually sold. If I simply turn one of the pencils forty-five degrees to the northwest, does this change the essence of the group as a whole, assuming that there is such a thing? Is it possible that it changes "in some respects and not in others"?

We should also ask about the impact of *external* events on this group of objects. Let's say that the economy enters a grievous inflationary spiral tomorrow morning, ruining the value of the nickels and dimes; or let's say that Chicago is darkened for months by an unprecedented fog, rendering the sunglasses useless. Does the essence of this system of objects retain its integrity no matter what happens in the outside world? Or, since we have seen that every essence also has a composite internal reality in spite of itself, is the essence of the system of objects on my desk irretrievably shaken by every minor event in the cosmos? We have seen that the latter answer is the one given by Whitehead (explicitly) and Heidegger (implicitly).[51] In their zeal to rid philosophy of substances, they have created a landscape on which every entity throbs in sympathy with every other, shaken to the core by every tiniest occurrence in the total system of meaning. Against this severe form of holism, we need to reestablish the firewalls that protect every entity from its neighbors. To do this without relapsing into a conservative version of substances may prove to be one of the great challenges for philosophy over the next several decades.

The reader will recall what Zubiri tells us about knives: a knife is a genuine reality, but the knife insofar as it cuts is not physically real. My own contention is that the knife is in a far more problematic position than Zubiri realizes. For there are actually *three* things that happen simultaneously in this case: (a) The knife is a composite made up of innumerable parts, each a dazzling universe in its own right, and each with its own physical reality whether the knife as a whole continues to exist or not. Rust the knife away into nothingness, and its component quarks will probably never know the difference; (b) In another sense, the knife is a mere component swallowed up into larger unities, whether these be assassination scenes, cooking scenarios, or mere hardware store vignettes; (c) The knife is also a simple "black box," a unitary object which has an obvious integrity apart from any use to which it is put, *and* whose own ambivalent internal parts can safely be ignored as irrelevant. My claim is that every entity has all three of these aspects at all times. In an obvious way, they are nothing more than the three moments of Heidegger's supposed "temporality": the thing as harboring a concealed universe in its breast ("past"), the thing as significant only in the light of the projections we make upon it ("future"), and the thing as a union of these two moments ("present").

Here, I have the same objection to both Zubiri and Heidegger: both of them make this threefold structure revolve around *human awareness,* with fatal consequences. Since they fail to see the perspectival structure already at work in inanimate matter, they wrongly apportion these three moments among different *types* of entities, rather than seeing that all of them permeate *every* entity to an equal degree. For both thinkers, the physical knife is sheer *Vergangenheit,* an unproblematic unity forever fixed by Nature herself. It is only the human being who sweeps this knife-thing away into a further drama of meaning: it takes Brutus to convert the knife-essence into a killing-essence. In this way, Zubiri gives his "essence" the literal Aristotelian character of *to ti en einai,* or "what being was." He also follows Heidegger in granting to human beings the unique ontological privilege of dealing with the "unreal," with the essence as encountered only through some projection. For both of them, it seems that colliding boulders affect each other as real physical essences, while only humans view entities *conceptively.* To work out the way in which the three dimensions of the thing interpenetrate is a difficult task. Do they bleed into one another completely, or are there ontological firewalls between them, protecting their status as distinct domains? How are these dimensions disjoined and recombined through normal physical causes, and how is it that we humans employ our unique intellectual powers to probe their depths? In any case, Zubiri avoids these crucial problems by turning essence into the special privilege of a limited class of "real" objects.

In other words, Zubiri tries to handle the problem by claiming that there are *natural* termini within the interlocking system of wholes and parts. Supposedly, the physical knife is a substantial/substantive whole, and is in no important way a "part" of any larger scenario: it becomes carving-knife or cooking-knife only relatively or conceptively. To repeat an earlier complaint, I regard this as an ontic solution to an ontological problem. Zubiri allows common sense to pull off a bloodless *coup d'état* at the precise moment when he had begun to open our eyes to a zone of incomparable strangeness— that of the essence withdrawn from all relation, even from brute *causal* relation (as overlooked by Heidegger, Levinas, and Whitehead alike).

Zubiri's mistake was to try to locate essences at *discrete* points in the world, confining them to particular natural places in the hierarchy of beings. He did not want to believe that essences are ubiquitous, because this seemed to threaten his understandable wish to wall off the essential from the "respective." But we cannot say that only the physical knife or only the silver have an essence. Along with these, protons have an essence, as do superstrings, magnetars, assassinations, and banquets. Another well-known question that will have to be raised is whether even *possible* objects have an essence that makes them real.[52] On the other hand, both silver and knife seem to be mere *respectivities* as soon as we decide to focus on their interior component mechanisms, since it makes little difference to most electrons whether they exist in a molecule of silver or sulphur. To sum all of this up in a single phrase: the ontology of tool and broken tool cannot be pieced together by claiming that some objects are *always tools* and others *always broken tools*. This is just another variant of the error with which Heidegger was charged in chapter 1, the fallacy of identifying ontological structures with distinct *kinds* of entities.

To say that every entity is both tool and broken tool is to say that every entity is half physically real, and half merely relational. No entity can be assigned unequivocally to one side of the equation or the other. But this implies something more than we have seen so far. It is not only the case that every entity has a deeper essence—rather, every *essence* has a deeper essence as well. This will be simpler if we revert to our own earlier terminology: not only does an object have tool-being, but this tool-being *in turn* has its own tool-being. For example, I have often spoken of the visible or tangible bridge as opposed to the subterranean bridge-being. But the tale does not end with this distinction. The tool-being of the bridge is indeed a unitary force distinct from any of the successive sensual or causal profiles it might present to other entities. However, this underground bridge-effect is not as pure as it claims to be. For we have seen that *it too* is merely respective or relational, that *it too* fails to exhaustively express the essence of the trestle-being and cable-being and bolt-being that comprise it. Will this lead to an "infinite regress" of tool-beings? For now, we can simply call it an indefinite regress, and move on to other problems that arise from the emerging concept of substance.

The preceding paragraph has a rather strange implication. The initial argument of this book was that *Vorhandenheit* and *Zuhandenheit* are not two distinct classes of entities, but two *modes* of being that belong to *every* entity. But we have now pushed Heidegger's insight far enough that the situation has reversed into its opposite. In a sense, it has now turned out that the hammer in use and the hammer in its tool-being are not simply two sides of the same coin, but two different coins altogether. In an unexpected sense, presence-at-hand and readiness-to-hand turn out to be *two distinct beings*.

The bridge now lying before me is encountered from a specific angle, in a specific mood, in the glare of a specific amount of sunlight. Let's say that a friend is also with me, one who does not enjoy my own exuberant state but is oppressed by fear or sadness, and who is perhaps a full foot shorter or fifty years older than I am. For all of these peripheral reasons, my friend will "project" the bridge differently. Furthermore, let's say that a number of cardinals, seagulls, and minnows have massed near the bridge. For all of the living creatures gathered among me, the bridge is confronted only as part of a total situation, a colossal environmental whole composed of numerous different entities. I have argued that the bridge "of itself" (Zubiri) is something quite different from this system: namely, a sheer integral bridge-being that makes its mark on reality, while forever withdrawn from the swirl of exterior factors into which it is embedded.

The withdrawn bridge-being is not affected at all by whether it is now noon or evening, January or February, national holiday or wartime. This book has defended a difference between the bridge as "prehended" by other entities, and the same bridge in its underground execution apart from all perspectival inflection. In short, we have the bridge and its prehender as distinct realities, and then the relation in which these entities encounter each other. While wishing to maintain Heidegger's absolute gulf between thing (tool) and relation (broken tool), I have now opposed the notion that certain sorts of events are always things, and other sorts always relations. In other words, the bridge is not simply an innocent entity that is later hijacked by the as-structure so as to manifest itself in such and such a way. Rather, the tool-being of the bridge has already committed a hijacking in its own right, appropriating bolt, cable, trestle, and asphalt, devouring them into its own being. The bridge, like any tool-being, is already a system, a machine in which numerous components are arranged in some form or another. The object is a kind of *formal cause.*

Another way of putting it is as follows. Behind the reality of the bridge *as* bridge, there is a bridge-being. But this bridge-being cannot simply be placed on one side or another of Heidegger's "temporality." In comparison with the bridge as encountered by me, the bridge-effect is indeed something withdrawn (i.e., "past"). But with respect to bolt-being and nail-being and trestle-being, the bridge-effect is the joint effort of subsystems that interact with each other *as* each other (i.e., "future"). As a result, what looks at first to be pure *Zuhandenheit* turns out to be already infected with the as-structure. It turns out that there is no point in the ontological realm that can claim a naive executional purity.

To put it differently, the seagull's relation to the bridge "as" bridge is composed of bridge-entity and seagull-entity; neither of them is ever completely "used up" by this relation. Likewise, the tool-being known as "bridge" is only a functional relation among numerous subsystems arranged in a certain effective way; it is more substantial than any context it enters, and more contextual than any substance that inhabits it. The way in which bolt and nail and trestle are mutually arranged, contacting one another *as* something specific, is *ontologically* no different from the way in which I myself confront the bridge. Instead of the notion of an entity as a hard durable unit, but also instead of a theory telling us that only contexts are real and not objects, we arrive at a concept of the entity as a certain *respectivity* of parts, a machine or formal cause.

But if every entity is already made up of a set of relations, the converse is also true: *every set of relations is also an entity.* The physical knife combined with Brutus gives rise to a new sort of assassin-entity. There is still no *ontological* reason to assume that the knife and Brutus are separate substances at all. We cannot use familiar everyday units or "natural kinds" (knife, person) as default termination-points for the interwoven contextures of meaning that make up the world. "Assassin" is no more and no less a composite of person and knife than "silver" is a composite of protons. For as I have argued, the human as-structure is not really different in kind from the inanimate, *causal* version of this structure.

The predicament now becomes somewhat difficult. On the one hand, the reality of a thing lies behind any of its relations, irreducible to them. On the other hand, any relation (such as Brutus plus knife) must be regarded as a new entity, since "durability" is irrelevant here—Brutus the Assassin seems every bit as real as a silver-atom. But if every relation automatically generates a new entity, if any special status is denied to durable substance over transient accident, there descends upon us a host of unpleasant problems. Is any arbitrary pairing of entities enough to create a brand new entity? Can I genuinely claim that a special subsystem is formed by, say, the Washington Monument, a fruit stand in Munich, the moon, and the set of all current U.S. Marines? If so, then ontology would begin to resemble a form of paranoia. Like Judge Schreber[53] piecing together outrageous machines from pointless sets of elements (gods, sunbeams, birds) the ontologist would be able to declare an infinite number of new entities by the merest fiat. Is there no difference between *real* systems of entities and those that are posited by means of a paranoid metaphysical collage like Schreber's? These references to paranoia are only half in jest: what better name for a philosophy which claims that *everything affects everything else*? As I have said, Whitehead contends that the tiniest shift of a pebble in the asteroid belt changes all of us into completely different entities. Likewise for Heidegger, for whom the slightest fluctuation in my mood changes the entire contexture of equipment into something different. What is this extreme holism if not a sort of ontological paranoia? Leibniz advocates this view with unmatched clarity: "As a result, every body is affected by everything that happens in the universe . . . 'All things conspire,' said Hippocrates."[54]

But this sentence could have been uttered by Schreber as easily as by Hippocrates or Leibniz. "All things conspire": it is the madman's axiom even more than the scientist's. And with it, we simply relapse into the philosophy of networks that I have criticized repeatedly. Contemporary philosophy excels in its critique of traditional substance, but in so doing has turned everything into an infinite system of conspiratorial relations. Individual things have lost their privacy completely, as though their phones were tapped and their essences bugged by the system as a whole. In order to counter the excesses of this tendency, a number of further questions should be asked. Which relations are *real* relations and therefore constitute real entities? What are the porous firewalls that protect one object from being affected by another, even while admitting the seductive or ruinous influence of others? I have also described entities as machines, insofar as a machine both performs an isolated discrete task *and* is swallowed up into larger systems. To prevent this claim from settling into a dull truism, it would be necessary to diagram the *specific features* of this process. How do tool-beings or machine-beings interlock, and how can they affect one another in the first place if they are supposed to be withdrawn from all relation? How are the components of a given machine liberated, and what energies are liberated along with it? And finally, is it possible to offer a good criterion by which to distinguish between different types of machines: organic, inanimate, rational, aesthetic? In short, it is necessary to flout Heidegger's own tastes by defining philosophy roughly as a form of machine-analysis or even machine-*building*.[55]

To repeat, we would seem to be trapped in a shaky compromise position. On the one hand, there is the Leibniz/Zubiri belief in a *real* distinction between simples and compounds. In Zubiri's case this is perfectly clear: an event such as *farming* has no essence, but is only a relation between the essences of farmer and land. The difference with Leibniz, of course, is that the farming is held to be part of the essence of this man from all eternity, and thus enters into the substance through a back door (and not through a window). But such predestination does not change the terms of the problem. The event of farming is merely imploded into the simple substance of this man; there is still no direct contact between separate monads so as to form a new system. The exact contrary to this is found in the Heidegger/Whitehead theory. For them, there are no real "simples," since what is primary is a universal compound from which all simples are only derivative.

What we are forced to defend, then, is a combination of these two views. In one respect, Zubiri is correct that there is a reality to the thing quite apart from its alliances and adventures at any given moment. In another respect, Heidegger and Whitehead are right to say that an entity is determined by the systematic attachments into which it enters. In other words, there is no absolute line in the sand between monad and global machine.[56] Every entity displays both aspects. But more than this: the tool-being of the hammer and the hammer *as* hammer are not simply two faces of the same entity, as I have said up till now. They must be two separate entities. For by hypothesis, the hammer as hammer has been *prehended*, and therefore has already come into relation with me as a different entity. Merely by prehending the hammer, I have created a new entity, a monstrous fusion of my own tool-being and the hammer's.

All of these consequences are interesting. But the present section ought to close with a look at the second Heideggerian axis, a topic which Zubiri is better prepared to address than Levinas. We have now repeatedly discussed an ongoing tension between tool and broken tool, a duality which in its previous form now lies in rubble: the moment known as "tool" is "broken tool" when viewed from the other side, and vice versa. I leave this difficulty in peace for the moment, so as to turn to the second tension in the heart of things. It was already clear that Zubiri tends to allow real essences only to certain privileged units—for instance, to knife or silver as physically real apart from any of their relations. But insofar as these ultimate essences can also be viewed as *systems* made up of notes, "the system . . . is that 'of' which all and each one of the notes 'are'."[57] This unitary system of the essence or monad is of course not just a unity, but a unity unlike all others, something completely individual. Leibniz sees this quite clearly: "However, monads must have some qualities, otherwise they would not even be beings. And if simple substances did not differ at all in their qualities, there would be no way of perceiving any change in things, since what there is in a composite can come only from simple ingredients . . . ."[58] Leibniz again: "This diversity must involve a multitude in the unity or in the simple. For, since all natural change is produced by degrees, something changes and something remains. As a result, there must be a plurality of properties and relations in the simple substance, although it has no parts."[59]

Thus, it is not surprising to hear Zubiri say that this plurality of properties is supposed to belong not to a substance, but to a system: essence should be regarded not as a *quid*, but as a "constructivity," something constructed from out of notes.[60] The essence is not a root-substance onto which the various notes of the thing are then grafted; instead, it *is* the system in which all of these notes are jointly deployed. In the essence seen as constructivity, the thing "of itself" goes to work: "Operatively, the 'entire' thing is involved in the action, with all its notes, precisely because this thing possesses a primary 'integrity' which is what is involved in the action."[61] In a sense, the *systematic* character of the thing thoroughly overpowers the *specific* character of its notes: "The stricter and stronger the constitutional unity, the greater is the character of a 'whole' possessed by the reality constituted in this way, and the more it acts as a whole." He concludes this reflection with an intriguing metaphysical remark: "In the limit case we would have absolutely simple action."[62] Zubiri seems to imply that, in this sense, any specific quality or note of a thing is already a degenerate form of its basic systematic integrity.

To pose the problem from a different and more intelligible angle: why speak of "notes" in the plural at all? Suppose that somewhere, a ripe lemon reposes in the utter systematic unity of its lemon-being. Just as in the earlier example of the apple tree, Zubiri would want to speak of the shape and color of the lemon as physically distinct notes. But this seems impossible if the lemon is to be considered "of itself" rather than in relation to some ulterior term. Strictly speaking, the lemon does not possess *notes* but *a note*, a single bulk package of quality. It is the lemon as a whole that sets up shop in reality, bombarding the cosmos with its unique lemon-effects. Its various notes seem to become separated only insofar as the outer world swarms with additional entities, each of them open to it in rather different ways. In reality, the color and weight of the lemon cannot possibly be physically distinct. What happens is that the bowl in which the lemon sits is vulnerable to its weight, absorbing the downward thrust of the lemon-mass resting within it; meanwhile, it turns a blind eye to the brilliant color of that lemon, which is of relevance to few of the entities scattered around it.

There are other subtle aspects to this lemon-being that are not now detected, but could be if only certain absent entities would arrive. For example, perhaps the lemon gradually emits a faint acid into the air. This acid may have no effect on the sturdy wooden and metallic objects currently assembled in the room—but it will severely damage a rare piece of antique parchment that will soon be delivered into the vicinity. All of this suggests that the notes or qualities of the lemon belong to the domain of respectivity or relation, rather than to the lemon "of itself." I will once again cite Leibniz, the all-time master of the themes now under discussion: "The passing state which involves and represents a multitude in the unity or in the simple substance is nothing other than what one calls *perception* . . . ."[63] Here, Leibniz seems to affirm what Zubiri denies: that individual qualities of an entity have reality only through the eyes of *another* entity. It is only the parchment which can prehend acid-emission as a distinct feature of lemon-being; indeed, only the parchment *makes* it a separate feature in the first place.

If this were true, it would mean that there are not two distinct axes in reality at all, but only one. The difference between the unity of a thing and its features would be identical with that of tool and broken tool—with that of absolute withdrawn action and specific qualities, or tool as real and tool as perceived. The very least that can be said here is that Zubiri *reverses* Leibniz's model. It is not that perception comes upon a unified substance and splits it up, but rather that a substance unifies all the specific notes. For Leibniz the unity is on the bottom, for Zubiri it is on top. In this sense, Zubiri holds that the parts precede the whole, and the perception of a substance would not artificially create many properties in it (as Leibniz has it) but *would* simply free up a plurality of notes that were already there. This leads to a more general point. I have already found it necessary to say that substance is not always substance and relation not always relation: there is a regress at work. Zubiri would not agree with this, but he would agree with something else. The essence prior to its being encountered, the essence "of itself," is not a simple unity for him as it is for Leibniz. Zubiri's essence is composed of a tension between specific notes and unifying system.

Allow me to cite a number of passages that testify to Zubiri's preoccupation with this theme. Early on in my summary of Zubiri, I mentioned his question as to whether the existence and essence of a thing are *physically* distinct. On the one hand, this question is answered in the negative. Zubiri argues, in Heideggerian fashion, that this traditional difference has its roots in a causal theory of creation, one which interprets the term "existence" in an uninteresting binary way: the thing either is or is not present-at-hand. But for Zubiri, higher than existence or being is "reality," a term that also contains all of a thing's essential *notes*. Hence: "Only as grounded on this formality, that is, in the reality *qua* reality, will we be able to discover its two moments of essence and existence."[64] But even as Zubiri downplays this traditional pair of terms, it gives way to a strikingly similar pair, which turns out to be precisely the same as the second dualism found in Heidegger (and even in Levinas). Zubiri makes no attempt to hide the classical roots of his new theme: "Now, every reality is, from antiquity, capable of being considered from a double point of view."[65] On the one hand, there is that aspect of the thing that distinguishes it from all other entities; on the other hand, there is the aspect according to which the thing is simply *real*: "The first constitutes the order of 'suchness'; the second is the 'transcendental' order."[66] Before commenting further, I might repeat Zubiri's own modest warning: "It is hoped that the reader will indulge, not only the re-appearance of concepts which have already been explicated, but also the wearisome repetition of the explications themselves."[67]

We can begin with the "transcendental" character of essence, which is absolutely identical with the young Heidegger's "something at all." Zubiri describes the transcendental unity of the essence as follows: "This unity, in a word, is, before all else, the terminus of the generating physical subsystem."[68] In layman's terms, the unity is the systematic *form* in which all of the component notes of a thing are arranged: "For example, it is not enough for me to produce wheels and springs, but wheels and springs such that they constitute 'one' watch."[69] But this unity has a purely formal character, and is held by Zubiri to be nothing qualitative at all: "This peculiar way of being *above any suchness whatsoever* in the sense of being related to all without being one further suchness, is what Scholasticism called 'to transcend'."[70] That is why he gives it the name "transcendental."

With this, Zubiri is openly declaring that there must be a dualism *within* the essence (which is precisely what Leibniz denies), since the transcendental unity of the thing rises above all suchness. Returning to his earlier discussion of reality *simpliciter*, as in the reality of the silver *simpliciter* apart from any of its floating or light-reflecting activities, Zubiri again speaks with a vaguely familiar tone: "[*Simpliciter*] can mean either the conjunction according to which something is reality, for example, silver or iron, or it may mean that with it, we have a reality without qualification: *it is the ambiguity between suchness and the transcendental.*"[71] Alter the terminology slightly, and this could easily be Martin Heidegger in 1919 (Heidegger says *formaliter* instead of *simpliciter*). For if there are two kinds of theoretical comportment, this is because there are at bottom two kinds of essence: tool and broken tool alike are both defined by this "ambiguity between suchness and the transcendental." The object is both a unified system and a system *of* such-and-such qualities. The visible world both *is at all* (Angst) and is composed of numerous beings that have broken free from the system of being (ontological difference).

Expressing this in yet another pair of terms, Zubiri says that the thing is defined by both "richness" and "solidity."[72] The thing is rich in notes, but the notes must be unified under the aegis of one constructive system in order to make up a single thing. To say it once again: "Actuality . . . does not mean only that the act is in the state of being actually executed, but also that what is executed has intrinsic *determined* actuality. . . ."[73] This duality between union and specific notes, says Zubiri, already occurs in the essence "of itself," and is not first generated by an external perceiver as in Leibniz. Naturally, the same dualism is repeated on the level of the essence as "respective" or encountered by other things: here too, the thing is encountered as a unified thing, but as a thing of many notes. Still, much like Heidegger, Zubiri provides few details as to how these two moments interact.[74]

The foregoing exposition has had to be somewhat dry. But I hope its *results* will be anything but dry for the reader's tastes. Zubiri, even more clearly than Heidegger, is concerned with a fourfold object—an "essence" packed with tensions and ready to explode. Whereas for Heidegger this structure remains so vague that lots of digging is required to unearth it, Zubiri places it at the exact center of reality, at the core of every object. The old Heideggerian opposition between tool and broken tool is rewritten as the difference between the nonrelational essence "of itself," and the "respective" essence that is seen or used by other essences. But we also find in Zubiri the second, more elusive Heideggerian opposition between the thing as specific and the thing as something at all. In Heidegger this was shadowy enough that some readers may even have found my earlier exposition of it to have been a bit of a stretch. But in the present case, all appearance of stretching is gone: Zubiri explains the second axis as a difference between the various aspects of the essence and the formal unity that combines them. The object lives torn by a dual tension in its breast. On the one hand it fluctuates between the vacuum of its tool-being and the power of its impact on neighboring beings. On the other hand it is itself a systematic empire swarming with interior parts. The object is a seismic object. It is an atom—not the billiard ball atom of the materialists, but that of Enrico Fermi, waiting to be split apart so as to release its energies into the sky.

My hope is that at this point, the reader will agree with me on four important points: (1) Zubiri's quadruple structure and Heidegger's have precisely the same significance. They are identical. (2) The fourfold structure clearly belongs to the innermost life of objects. There is nothing arbitrary about it. (3) The fourfold is not a conceptual abstraction, but plays itself out *in* the life of objects, as they "severally crush, depress, break, and enthrall one another" (Francis Bacon). It is an ambivalence of objects themselves, and not of human *access* to them. (4) Unfortunately, neither Heidegger nor Zubiri do much to clarify the dynamics between the four parts of the essence. Just as Heidegger's as-structure was inadequate to explain the relationship between tool and broken tool, Zubiri's distinction between "transcendence" and "suchness" is far from vivid enough to explain the relation between these two moments. Heidegger and Zubiri have barely scratched the surface of objects. But they have given us a first primitive "atomic theory" on which further models and thought experiments can be based. To accompany the earlier diagram of Heidegger's fourfold, I have constructed an analogous chart of Zubiri's model of essence, which the reader may find useful to consult at this point (see figure 2 below).

I will close this section with a brisk itemized review of its contents:

- The familiar tool/broken tool dualism is exhibited in a strange new light. Not only does tool-being withdraw from all relation: it itself turns out to be a relational system. Hammer and broken hammer are no longer two faces of the same entity, but *two different entities altogether.* For while hammer-being reposes in utter isolation from me, hammer *as* hammer is linked with me in a perspectival relation; the hammer and I form a new kind of "machine," and are not simply ourselves. Since we cannot use mere durability as an *ontological*

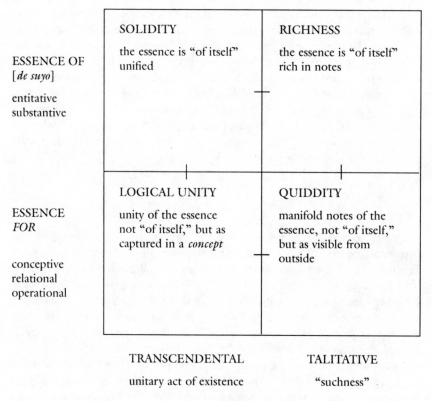

Figure 2   Zubiri's Model of Essence

criterion of what counts as substance, an atom of silver is no more a unity than is Brutus-and-his-knife. Every relation is *ipso facto* an entity. Therefore, the hammer in its sequestered reality is a different object from the hammer in its "machinic" link with me.

- As a result, we are forced to navigate *between* the extremities defined by Leibniz/Zubiri on the one hand and Heidegger/Whitehead on the other. It is necessary to see that the reality of the thing is something distinct from any relations into which it might fall. But it is equally necessary to be just a touch paranoid, and to acknowledge a sense in which everything in the cosmos is co-determined by everything else.[75] In their strictest forms, these views are mutually exclusive.

- Zubiri defends a distinction that is identical to Heidegger's second axis. The difference in question is that between the thing as *one* thing, and the thing as possessing *specific* notes. This is a difference that occurs both in the essence of itself *and* the essence as something respective to us. Although Zubiri is clear that the notes cannot exist on their own apart from the unity of the thing,[76] they are still distinct from that thing. Since this dualism repeats itself both at the level of the essence in itself and that of the essence as encountered from outside, Zubiri is dealing with a quadruple object, one that is the same as Heidegger's own. But the relations between these four terms in any object remain largely unclear. Before seeing whether they can be clarified at all, it will be useful to engage in another brief historical discussion.

§24. Classical Milestones

Contrary to widespread practice, there is an important sense in which the historical approach to a philosophical problem must always come *second*. For no sort of neutral access to the history of philosophy is ever possible. The decision as to which classic texts we look to for assistance will always be determined by how the problem at hand is conceived in our own minds, as could be seen clearly in §10 above. It is sometimes claimed that the Heidegger-Aristotle relation is the best point of entry into Heidegger's thought. But no mere reading of Aristotle, however painstaking it may be, can guarantee that we have found the *proper* point of comparison between these thinkers. For those who read the tool-analysis as an account of human productive activity, then of course the *Nicomachean Ethics* will seem to be the ideal point of comparison. But for the present book, which reads the tool-analysis as a global account of the dual reality of every concrete entity, the *Metaphysics* provides a far more useful parallel. This was the reason for my claim that a thorough phenomenology of equipment must precede any attempt to trace this notion to its possible classical roots.

But it should also be noted that the coined phrase "tool-being" does not necessarily make any claim to originality. Indeed, there are at least two senses in which it may be derivative. In the first place, this term restricts itself solely to elaborating Heidegger's own central discovery. However unorthodox this elaboration may be, it still owes its life to the things that Heidegger has seen. In the second place, to whatever degree this book *does* depart from Heidegger's own intentions, it might still be nothing more than an unwitting historical parasite, at least in part. It is possible, however unlikely, that the foregoing interpretation of Heidegger somehow yields nothing more than an exact replica of some past philosophy. Perhaps it turns out that the progressive analysis of tool-being succeeds only in repeating a familiar insight found in Kant or Locke, Leibniz or Aristotle. If this turned out to be the case, there should be no hesitation in jumping on the bandwagon of whichever past philosopher turns out to have beaten the tool-analysis to the punch. There is no good reason to have anything at stake in Heidegger's being a more *advanced* figure than his forerunners.

The proper balance in any philosophical work between historical presentation and direct argument cannot be dictated *a priori*, but must be hashed out through the development of the concepts themselves. One must try to choose the method that yields *real results*, in strict accordance with the mission of whatever is being written. The primary mission of the current book is not to discover historical auguries of the tool-analysis, but only to show that this analysis, if placed under sufficient scrutiny, undergoes a strange metamorphosis into a speculative metaphysics of objects. But it will be helpful to offer another brief comparison of Heidegger's tool-being with certain milestone figures in the history of philosophy. As suggested above, the most relevant of these figures is probably Aristotle. (This is especially the case insofar as we have just finished a lengthy discussion of Zubiri, and will soon refer to Leibniz yet again.) And the best place in Aristotle to help refine the concept of tool-being is obviously the *Metaphysics*. Although this monumental work is far richer than any brief treatment that can possibly be given of it, a brief treatment will be enough to lend additional flavor to Heidegger's theory of the tool and its reversal.

The first question, of course, is what aspect of the *Metaphysics* has the most to teach us about Heidegger's inadvertent theory of objects. The result of the preceding sections clearly suggests that the Aristotelian theory of *substance* is the proper analogue for tool-being, in both a supportive and a critical sense. Important similarities quickly emerge. The tool-being of a thing is what that thing simply *is*, quite aside from any of the faces that it manifests to view. And as Aristotle tells us in Book Beta: "he knows most fully who knows what a thing is, not he who knows its quantity or quality or usefulness."[77] As I have argued throughout this book, equipment in Heidegger cannot possibly mean "usefulness." The fact that this has been overlooked is the reason that so many parallels have already been drawn between *Zuhandenheit* and *poiesis*, while to my knowledge *none* have been drawn between the more closely related *Zuhandenheit* and *ousia*. However suggestive the name "tool-being" may be of the shoemaker's workshop, the ready-to-hand has less to do with production than with substance.[78]

The tool-being of a thing, as we have seen, is never some sort of general serviceable trait that might also belong to other things as well. I cannot say that the being of an umbrella is "equipment for remaining dry," and then argue that the same tool-being also belongs to an unfolded newspaper, a veranda, a railway platform, the hood of a rubber coat, and all other umbrellas. As Zubiri would say, such a procedure can only transform tool-being into something second-hand, abstracted after the fact from the singularity of a raw concrete event. The tool-being is not a handy functioning "universal," but always an *individual*, always the discrete execution of some localized and unexchangeable reality. It is fundamentally *prote ousia*, not *deutere ousia*. As we read in some of the canonical passages of Book Zeta: "For firstly the substance of each thing is that which is peculiar to it, which does not belong to anything else; but the universal is common, since that is called universal which is such as to belong to more than one thing."[79] And furthermore, "substance means that which is not predicable of a subject, but the universal is predicable of some subject always."[80] Like tool-being, Aristotle's substance is not a sheer predicable quality, but always a specific "this": "it is plain that no universal attribute is a substance, and this is plain also from the fact that no common predicate indicates a 'this' [*tode ti*], but rather a 'such' [*toionde*]."[81] Against Plato's doctrine of the *chorismos* or separation between the world of Ideas and the sensible realm, Aristotle famously contends that the substance of a genus or species is *not* separate from that of its individual.

Instead of the quality, which is the "such" considered as something common to many particulars, we can speak of the "form" as always the form of some *concrete* thing. Even so, Aristotle regards it as pointless to evict all matter from philosophy in favor of forms, for "indeed there is some matter in everything which is not an essence and a bare form but a 'this.'"[82] Everywhere, we find an interpenetration of "this" and "such," "matter" and "form." This is not only the case for physical objects, as can be seen from the following passage: "The semicircles, then, will not be part of the universal circle, *but will be parts of the individual circle... for while one kind of matter is perceptible, there is another which is intelligible."[83]

The "this" and the "such" are united in the concrete thing, which alone is the primary substance (naturally, I am aware that other views of the Aristotelian primary substance are often defended). But in the first instance, this Aristotelian distinction is *not* the same as Heidegger's tool/broken tool. For there is nothing in Aristotle's "quality" or "form" that immediately suggests a perspectival structure. Aristotle's distinction between the thing as a set of universal predicates and the thing "as it really is" is not the same as that between the as-structure and the equipmental stratum that rumbles beneath it.

With their shared objection to the primacy of quality or quantity or usefulness, these two philosophers to a large extent achieve *opposite* results. Aristotle attacks the primacy of these notions in order to subvert the claims of any realm other than that of the thing in its concreteness. Heidegger launches the same attack, but with the motive of pointing to another realm *within* the thing in its concreteness. As I have argued in this book, Heidegger aims to pay tribute to the concealed second world of tool-being, while Aristotle wants to implode Plato's second world into the first. For Heidegger, the strife between tool and broken tool *by definition* extends far beneath the layer of human perception. For Aristotle, form and matter are fundamentally neutral with respect to this theme. His distinction has much more to do with the concreteness described by Zubiri: that which is composed of the thing in its talitative "suchness" and the same thing in its transcendental unity. After all, the "this" is nothing if not a specific unity, a "this" in opposition to all that is *not* this.

Another way of describing the difference is as follows. For Aristotle, the thing is always a single distinct concrete thing, a single intersection of form and matter. But for Heidegger, the thing is doubled. Aristotle's purpose is to denounce an old *chorismos*; Heidegger's purpose is to create a new one. Whatever criticisms Heidegger might make of the matter/form relation in its historical development, all that concerns us here is that this relation is not the same as that of tool/broken tool. Aristotle's matter and form belong to *both* the present-at-hand and ready-to-hand realms, which are not openly distinguished by Aristotle, who lacks the twentieth-century obsession with the way in which context alters reality. But the fact that Aristotle draws no such distinction is in many ways an advantage, for Heidegger's attempt to double individual things with a deeper referential contexture tends to weaken any sense of the concrete individual. As we have seen, if we take "being" or "the system of meaning" quite literally, all specific things would be dissolved into a single all-encompassing network. For Heidegger, the unity of being is a kind of substrate for the many particular things. Aristotle, however, wonders in advance whether this can really be the case:

But if there is to be a being-itself and a unity-itself, there is much difficulty in seeing how there will be anything else besides these—I mean, how things will be more than one in number. For what is different from being does not exist, so that it necessarily follows, according to the argument of Parmenides, that all things that are are one and this is being. . . . For whence is there to be another one besides unity-itself? It must be not-one; but all things are either one or many, and of the many each is one.[84]

It might seem for a moment as if the alternative is equally untenable, for:

if we do *not* suppose unity and being to be substances [emphasis added], it follows that none of the other universals is a substance; for these are most universal of all, and if there is no unity-itself or being-itself, there will scarcely be in any *other* case anything apart from what are called the individuals.[85]

But of course, this is the side of the dispute that Aristotle means to discard. He is obviously not the least bit rattled in Book Beta by the idea that none of the universals can be substance, since in what follows he will cite precisely this inability when he defends the central status of concrete things. It is not unity that is the root of substance, but substance that is root of unity: "the things that are primarily called one are those whose substance is one."[86]

Later he states this in even more straightforward fashion: "'being' and 'unity' are more substantial than 'principle' or 'element' or 'cause,' *but not even the former are substance*, since in general nothing that is common is substance; for substance does not belong to anything but to itself and to that which has it, of which it is the substance."[87] While being and unity are *common*, the substance is *one*. This unity applies to the substance in all categories, of no matter what character, and is therefore not a genus. Rather, it is what the Scholastics, and following them Zubiri, will call a "transcendental." Whether a given thing be cold or smooth or rancid, it is inevitably *one* thing: inevitably *this*. But although *every* concrete substance is one, all are of course distinct by virtue of that which distinguishes them: "It is clear, then, from these facts that, since its substance is the cause of each thing's being, we must seek in these differentiae what is the cause of the being of each of these things."[88] For *everything* with a true unity has a *cause* for why it is one: "In the case of all things which have several parts and in which the totality is not, as it were, a mere heap, but the whole is something besides the parts, there is a cause. . . ."[89] The sort of "cause" referred to here has all manner of varieties. Things may be unified by means of simple physical union—or even by virtue of "viscosity"! They may be unified in a definition as belonging to one and the same substance; they may also be unified by a specific configuration, as when the various parts of a shoe have to be stitched together effectively or else be reduced to a random pile of isolated pieces of leather or canvas. But however the qualities may be unified in a specific thing, they are not grafted onto the substantial unity as if *after the fact.* This can be seen even from one of Aristotle's frequent facetious examples: "it is not by accident that the nose has the attribute either of concavity or of snubness, but in virtue of its nature."[90]

Nonetheless, the quality of being a snub nose rather than an aquiline nose, or of being a snub nose rather than a snapping turtle, are not *equivalent* to the substance. No amassing of qualities, however detailed the process may become, can ever replicate the living unitary substance: "Now none of these differentiae is substance, even when coupled with matter, yet it is what is analogous to substance in each case. . . ."[91] To define ice as "water frozen in such and such a way" or a cancer cell as "DNA coded in such and such a way and embodied in such and such a way" is an analogy only; it is only "what most resembles full actuality," and not the full actuality of the thing itself. Hence, to speak of any of the specific qualities of a thing is inevitably to work from a derivative standpoint, and not one that can ever grasp the substance directly. After all, the matter of the thing is inevitably too opaque and obscure for our powers of reasoning. In the previous section, we encountered Zubiri's difficulty in trying to infuse quality into a realm divorced from all relation. This is precisely the same problem faced by his ancestor Aristotle in trying to say that universals (which are necessarily *common* and therefore not substantial) must also belong to substance, so as to prevent all substances from becoming identical featureless clods. It is also the same problem faced by Leibniz, who tries to solve it by saying that the individual qualities of the unified monad emerge only thanks to a perceiver, as we saw in the previous section. Aristotle expresses this with supreme eloquence in Book Zeta:

> But our result involves a difficulty. If no substance can consist of universals because a universal indicates a 'such,' not a 'this,' and if no substance can be composed of substances existing in complete reality [more on this later—g.h.], every substance would be incomposite, so that there would not even be a formula of any substance. But it is *thought* by all and was stated long ago that it is either only, or primarily, substance that can be defined; yet now it seems that not even substance can. There cannot, then, be a definition of anything; or in a sense there can be, and in a sense there cannot.[92]

Whatever the solution to this aporia may be (if indeed there is a solution), all qualities and accidents require a subject *of which* they are qualities and accidents. This is the *ontological* meaning of the principle of noncontradiction, as opposed to its merely logical meaning: "There must, then, even so be something which denotes substance. And if this is so, it has been shown that contradictories cannot be predicated at the same time."[93] With his underrated droll wit, Aristotle draws the consequences of denying this fact, consequences actually *embraced* by Anaxagoras, Bruno, and others: "Again, if all contradictory statements are true of the same subject at the same time, evidently all things will be one. *For the same thing will be a trireme, a wall, and a man,* if of everything it is possible either to affirm or deny anything. . . ."[94] Given that the same thing does *not* seem to be a trireme, a wall, and a man, Aristotle's argument carries the day:

> For if anyone thinks that the man is not a trireme, evidently he is not a trireme; so that he also *is* a trireme, if, as they say, contradictory statements are both true. And we thus get the doctrine of Anaxagoras, that all things are mixed together; so that nothing really exists. They seem, then, to be speaking of the indeterminate, and, while fancying themselves to be speaking of being, they are speaking about non-being; for it is that which exists *potentially* and not in complete reality that is indeterminate.[95]

In the realm of actual substance, then, there is no contradiction. But what counts as an individual substance, and what *fails* to measure up to this criterion? Aristotle's examples of substance are every bit as broad as one would expect: animals, plants, the *parts* of animals and plants, fire, water, earth, stars, moon, sun.[96] It is no coincidence that all of the entities on his list, whether animate or utterly insensate, occur *naturally* in the universe. Anticipating the refusal of Leibniz and Zubiri to grant substantiality to composites, Aristotle invokes the distinction that Heidegger and Whitehead must implicitly reject: "the continuous by nature [is] more *one* than the continuous by art. A thing is called continuous which has by its own nature one movement and cannot have any other. . . ."[97] Aristotle, like Leibniz after him, shows a deep suspicion toward any *ad hoc* attempts to slap together a substance by artificial means: "Those things are continuous by their own nature which are not one merely by contact; for if you put pieces of wood touching one another, you will not say these are one piece of wood or one body or one *continuum* of any other sort."[98] There follows a list of criteria for substancehood that any consistent Heideggerian would have to dismiss as "ontic," but which still have the virtue of Aristotle's ever-surprising sense of humor: "Things, then, that are continuous in any way are called one, *even if they admit of being bent*; e.g. the shin or the thigh is more one than the leg, because the movement of the leg need not be one."[99]

The italicized phrase, in conjunction with the attempted gradation between legs and shins, sets a precedent of the sort that Heidegger *must* refuse for as long he wants to remain true to his own philosophy.

Obviously, it is inconceivable that Heidegger could ever endorse "physical flexibility" as a criterion for oneness. It would be no great shock if Aristotle were to tell us that a rock is more of a unit than is a stretchy piece of plastic, or that a two-piece hammer is less unified than a simple butter-knife but more so than a complicated nuclear submarine. But if Heidegger or Whitehead were to say such things, it would be a scandalous piece of hypocrisy. The fact that a rock is more durable than a fragile pane of glass cannot, in the Heideggerian philosophy, serve as evidence that the rock has more of a unitary tool-being than the glass does. The reason for this is simple: Heidegger and Whitehead do not aim at a substantial theory of entities, but a rigorously *functional* one. For them, the hammer is not primarily a substantial unity-of-differentiae, but primarily a relational effect upon all other entities. And in the realm of ontological function, there *are* no gradations: either there is a particular tool-being having such-and-such an effect, or there is not. In each case, the relational system is completely determinate. All of the hammers and aqueducts and supernovae in the cosmos currently stand in utterly specific relation to one another. There is no "wiggle room" for any of these things to be more or less themselves than they already are. As we have seen, this is because both Heidegger and Whitehead take their cue from the world as a whole, and tend to disdain the notion of objects as discrete walled-off zones, as cryptic batteries where energy and personality are held in reserve from whatever is currently going on.

Now, the Heideggerian phrase "ontic" can easily be abused to the point of self-parody, as often happens when Heidegger and his followers heap arrogant and preposterous scorn upon everything from space exploration to psychoanalysis to Central American revolutions to boxing matches. But this term "ontic" does have its legitimate uses, and the present case is one of them. What I object to in the Aristotle/Leibniz/Zubiri model is the employment of the word "substance" to refer to certain special entities at the expense of others, and even to rank some substances (the less bendable ones) as *more* substantial than their rivals. There is an *ontic* prejudice at work here: the tendency to determine the substantiality of an entity by looking at its causal *source* rather than its formal structure. In all of these thinkers, with occasional exceptions on Zubiri's part, it is the natural body that tends to be viewed as a substance, while the human-fabricated machine is dismissed as an unnatural mixture or collage.

The present book has argued that the functional holism of Heidegger and Whitehead liberates us from any *naturalistic* theory of substance. Indeed, I believe that this is the primary achievement of both Heidegger's critique of presence-at-hand and Whitehead's slams against "vacuous actuality." But it is also my view that both thinkers push their "whole-before-the-part" doctrine to the point that individual entities tend to vaporize altogether. What is necessary is to retrieve the integrity and isolation of discrete substances without positing them as a limited set of privileged durable units. As mentioned throughout this book, the philosophical world has just spent an entire century nurturing everything that pertains to contexts and wholes. It is individual rocks and flowers that are now crying for our attention; *this* is now the more fertile cropland for twenty-first-century philosophy. And it is my view that Heideggerian tool-being, interpreted properly, is the swiftest vehicle to propel us toward a new theory of objects.

By adamantly refusing to grant more tool-being to a shin than to a leg (after all, both a solid hammer and a bendable rubber hammer would have to be *equally* ready-to-hand for the tool-analysis, even if in different ways), Heidegger frees us from the ontic and ultimately *physical* criterion of substantiality. Zubiri senses this, and replaces the durable overtones of "substance" with the equipmental echoes of "substantivity." Nonetheless, he follows through on the old mistake. At the same time, Heidegger at least offers us the proper *resource* for overcoming his own excessive brand of equipmental holism. This resource is the inevitable fact that the individual tool-being must be even *more* free of the as-structure than Heidegger himself believes, free even of "world." For this reason, it must lie partly outside of any relation to other tool-beings. To reconcile these two separate insights is a necessary task, but one for which Heidegger and Aristotle are both able to provide only limited assistance.

One of the ways they *can* help is by tacitly disagreeing with one another on the question of wholes and parts. For Aristotle, the substance has no parts. That which we normally refer to as the "parts" of a substance are material parts without being actual parts: "For even if the line when divided passes away into its halves, or the man into bones and muscles and flesh, it does not follow that they are composed of these as parts of their essence, but rather as matter; and these are parts of the concrete thing, but not also of the form. . . ."[100] These parts are material *elements* of the substance, and in their own right are neither genuine parts of the substance nor new additional substances. For Aristotle, there is obviously no way in which any substance can be a composite formed of others. We have already seen that no substance can be pieced together out of qualities or universals (just as no tool-being can ever be built out of "broken tools"). Thus, if the substance *were* to consist of parts, it would *have* to consist of substances and the "this," and not only of the "such." But even this option is regarded as impossible: "A substance cannot consist of substances present in it in complete reality; for things that are thus in complete reality two are never in complete reality one. . . ."[101] In any unity, the parts must exist only *potentially.* The actuality must be completely devoid of real internal components.

From the perspective of Heideggerian tool-being, the problem with the theory of substance is that it wants to define substantiality not as a structural moment of *all* entities (as Zubiri in his best moments does), but as a prize conceded only to *certain* entities that are not merely "artificial" unities. It wants to celebrate the oneness of the parts of a leg-bone while denigrating the connection between the engine and tires of a Volkswagen. To repeat, the notion of natural substance makes illicit use of our ontic biases to draw a supposed ontological distinction between substances and *non*-substances ("a leg-bone is one solid piece even in newborn babies, but a Volkswagen must be assembled carefully by skilled technicians . . . ").

If ever there were a moment when Heidegger had a good case against the Aristotelian tradition, this is that moment. The notion of substance is in some ways the one concept that Heidegger was born to undermine, even if this procedure is destined to be only partially successful. Although Aristotle's method of undercutting the pretensions of "quality" or "suchness" may be the original forerunner of Heidegger's subversion of presence-at-hand, Aristotle *ceases* this process at a specific point in his analysis. Once he has gone back beyond the noisy assertions of quality, he arrives at the irreducible substance–at that which is no longer a derivative surface-effect of anything else, that which is utterly innocent of any *composite* status. This remains the case despite Aristotle's (and Leibniz's) disclaimer that it is difficult or impossible ever to know the substance in any way other than analogically, since he at least regards it as possible *in principle*: after all, the ultimate simple substances are *really there*, whether we can fully arrive at them or not. But to say that the substance is simply and purely *there*, free of any *further* reality that would withdraw beyond its apparent simple unity, is equivalent to saying that the substance is straightforwardly *vorhanden*, however secluded from human vision it might be.

Put differently, the mistake lies in holding that the substance has to be a natural ultimate point, one that would be ruined by any sort of composition. It will be useful to draw an example from a particular type of substance; I select Aristotle's "moon" as an especially beautiful case. As he would tell us, the various rocks that make up the moon are a part of the concrete individual "moon," but not of its form [*morphe*] or formula [*logos*]. The first of these can be destroyed, while the second is indestructible (Leibniz derives the immortality of his monads from this distinction). Insofar as the various moon-rocks are still part of the moon, they are substances only *potentially*, their individuality revoked by the higher actuality of the vast lunar oneness.

But again, it seems arbitrary to claim that the moon is the substance in this case, rather than its component rocks or the solar system as a whole. There is no good way to decide which of these is the real substance and which is the aggregate without flimsy appeal to so-called common sense ("the moon is obviously *one* object, while the solar system is made up of *many* objects."). Besides, if the formal unity of a thing can survive even its destruction as a concrete individual, then what is so painful about conceding that the solar system or two pieces of wood glued together might be further large-scale substances? And if it is true, as this book contends, that any such assortment of substances will always generate a new formal unity, it makes little sense to say that its component parts lose their status as individuals except potentially. After all, if we push things far enough, the ultimate formal unity or ultimate assemblage of entities is none other than Heidegger's "world." And it is impossible that world should be the only actuality, since this would mean that all specific entities would be nothing other than suppressed potentials. There would be no specific entities at all, which is precisely my complaint about both Heidegger and Whitehead.

If this were the case, the cosmos would be dissolved into a single all-encompassing empire, with all of its regions and districts and internal organs dissolved like sugar in a bottle of rum. But just as Heidegger's "world" fails to cancel the singularity of its inner provinces, so too must Aristotle's substance fail to nullify the distinct actuality of each of its elements. In short, the distinction between form and concrete individual is useful only if it is meant to give *unity* to the form beyond any mere aggregation of constituent parts. But if this distinction is wrongly employed to mean that the form actually swallows up the elements of the concrete individual, it becomes a philosophical albatross. In that case, the only thing saving Aristotle from the predicament of a single all-encompassing world-system is his tendency to posit preexistent termini, natural kinds that never enter into any wider systems. Since Heidegger's general philosophical position does not allow him this luxury, it is he rather than Aristotle who forces us to the decisive point here. That is to say, it is Heidegger who is forced to confront the real *coexistence* of total system and fragmented composition in the same entity (though Zubiri confronts it even more directly). In other words, while Aristotle's distinction between unities and composites is apportioned among different entities, Heidegger's version of this distinction rips apart the inner life of *every* entity. Aristotle's strict distinction between natural units and artificial composites means that this is one problem he never has to face.

For Aristotle, then, there are natural unities ("substances") which maintain their dignity no matter what sort of artificial unity they may fall into, and which also temporarily neutralize the actuality of their internal elements. For Heidegger, no such thing is possible. The hammer is always siphoned away into countless systematic unions. And although he never sees this, the hammer is also made up of trillions of minuscule tool-beings which are by no means utterly dissolved in it. While a substance is supposed to be independent of any of its internal or external conglomerates, a tool-being always shares in both of these, is always part *and* whole.

Now as earlier, it might be objected that this will lead to an "infinite regress," since any tool-being we identify will always be decomposable into further tool-beings *ad infinitum*. Without attempting to solve this difficulty at the moment, I would simply point out that Heidegger's criticism of presence-at-hand requires *nothing less* than a ceaseless regression behind or beyond any supposed natural terminus. The tool-analysis demands a furious regress of tools within tools within tools. This does not become clear from Heidegger's own analyses, since he would never admit that the concealed being of a hammer is *itself* a relational compound (that is my own twist to the scenario). But for the moment, the only obvious alternative to the infinite regress is to adopt a *finite* regress, and hence to posit some natural stopping point in reality, which is what I have just criticized in the Aristotelian substance.

Earlier, I suggested that Aristotle's distinction between the thing as "such" and as "this" has more to do with Heidegger's *second* dualism than with his first. That is to say, the interpretation of the thing as "such" and as "this" is the remote ancestor of Heidegger's 1919 difference between "something at all" and "specific something," or Zubiri's schism between the "transcendental" and "talitative" dimensions of the thing. By contrast, the strife between tool and broken tool does not seem to be found in Aristotle at all. Given the tool-being's reversal between concealed night and visible daylight, the more obvious historical parallel would be with Kant's distinction between noumenal and phenomenal. To compare Heidegger and Kant on this point would be a fascinating but controversial exercise, one that in any case lies beyond the scope of this book. However, I will make one remark on this theme to show how I would be inclined to approach the question of the crucial relationship between Heidegger and Kant.

It must not be forgotten that Kant's rift between thing in itself and thing as appearance revolves entirely around the question of *human* reality. Nowhere does he suggest that two colliding bricks encounter one another as phenomena rather than as noumena; indeed, he is never clear as to whether they encounter one another at all. Heidegger's own hopeless crush on human Dasein faithfully mirrors this aspect of the Kantian standpoint, as has been observed by those critics who refer to the *Daseinsanalytik* as a "transcendental argument." But I have tried to show that the tool-analysis actually has more in common with Leibniz than with Kant, despite Heidegger's own reluctance to ascribe any sort of perceptual structure to inanimate matter. Tool/broken tool is less a distinction of noumena and phenomena than of substance and relation, since it inevitably descends into the midst of birds, rocks, viruses, and atoms.

Whitehead, more of a philosophical outsider and hence more of a risk-taker than Heidegger, sees this more clearly than his contemporary.

§25. Two Paradoxes

This book claims that the two central dogmas of contemporary continental philosophy are: (1) anti-realism, and (2) holism. The concept of "prehension" is aimed at the first of these, since it points to a real zone of tool-beings located at a distance from all human contact—indeed, at a distance from all causal interference whatsoever. When I refer to the tool-being as a kind of independent substance, as a black box unpenetrated by the contexts in which it is immersed, my target is the second, holistic dogma: "Everything is linked; all things conspire." In comparison with traditional materialism and all other theories of substance that downplay the relational character of the thing, the holistic ideal is a marvelous breakthrough. But for the purposes of contemporary philosophy, this battle has largely already been won. And it has *certainly* already been won among Heideggerians, for whom the meaning-contexture always remains prior to any specific entity.

In this sense, holism has become an idea once but no longer liberating. To say that all things mirror each other, to say that every part necessarily bears traces of the whole that embraces it, is no better than a half-truth. There is indeed a sense in which all things conspire, but it should not be forgotten that a tomato and a shoelace are two very different conspiracies. Aristotle was right to say that if holism were strictly true, if Anaxagoras were correct that everything mirrors everything else, then the same thing would be a trireme, a wall, and a man. But this is not the case. Instead of a central master agency dictating the course of cosmic events, there are an infinite number of local conspiracies. In one sense, there is indeed vast ontological collusion between the CIA, the Illuminati, the Israelis, the Masons, the Russian Mafia, Oliver North, big oil companies, the sun and moon, bricks, snakes, icicles, and sugar cane. But in another sense they fail to listen to one another at all, too exhausted with their own internal conspiracies to engage in foreign operations.

Whatever the holistic boasts of Heidegger and Whitehead, being is not *only* an empire: it has local governments as well. A watermelon is not a mere ontic phantom, enslaved in some wider system of differential meaning or projected against the very possibility of its possibility for human Dasein. The melon is also the defender of its own private terrain, master of its castle. Within this castle it conceals most of its personality until the moment when circumstances cause further of its energies to be unleashed. Eventually, the black box shatters; eventually, the atom is split. In this way, the object is a kind of minefield or time bomb, concealing its explosive reality until it is somehow brought into play. The remainder of this book seeks to review what has already been determined about the structure of objects, and to shed further light on this structure with a handful of piercing questions capable of lingering in the reader's minds as worthy of our labor and our dreams.

By way of review: two *separate* dualisms were identified in Heidegger, both of them also found in the chief work of his realist descendant Xavier Zubiri. For both conceptual and biographical reasons, I argued that the intersection of these axes is the source of Heidegger's notoriously elusive "fourfold." My claim was that his quadrate results from a crossing "X" of tool and broken tool with a second opposition between a thing's qualities and its sheer systematic unity. The seemingly abstract quadruple object that results from this crossing *really is* the same as Heidegger's earth and sky, gods and mortals, all allowances made for his more romantic terminology. Scratch the surface of the fourfold, listen *behind* its poetic overtones, and you will find nothing other than the double paradox of actuality and relation that the present chapter has tried to describe. Given this, the problem with Heidegger's fourfold is not that it is "meaningless"—its meaning is all too clear. The more dangerous question is whether it is *irrelevant*.

It is easy enough to speak in Heideggerese and say that a pouring jug gathers the four and cradles their mirror-play in a onefold. The problem is that the same thing can also be said of *any* entity, whether it be a pencil or a red caboose. In other words, the fourfold is still only a complication of the *earlier* duality, and does not yet allow us to say much about the specific stock characters that inhabit the world. *Das Geviert* is still only the name for a kind of potent sauce that is poured over the whole of reality, causing everything to taste exactly the same. Expressed in more technical terms, the fourfold still belongs to fundamental ontology, and not yet to the metontology that Heidegger never attained. It is still a radical and austere foundation into which all beings implode, and not yet a principle of variation that would shed light on the interaction between forests, radio towers, coffee beans, and icebergs. To speak in more traditional language, what Heidegger needed was something like a new theory of categories, or at least a set of laws governing the interaction between systems of objects and their resistant, withdrawn fragments. Having never done so, he has left us high and dry amidst the monotonous drumbeat of tool and broken tool, or at best the slightly more intricate song of earth and sky, gods and mortals.

The additional framework within which all further problems of toolbeing should be formulated is that of the "machine" theory of entities, invoked at the close of §21. The word "machine," of course, is employed in a metaphorical way that has no more to do with factories than with wildflowers; objects *qua* objects can be described as ontological machines, even if they are the least mechanical entities on the globe. The reasoning behind this statement will easily be recalled. Zubiri (like Leibniz, among others) draws a distinction between simple essences and the relational composites in which they become entangled. At first, this might seem analogous to the distinction between tool and broken tool. But they are not quite the same, for I have already argued that no real end point can ever be discovered to the chain of tool-beings wrapped inside of tool-beings. Just because Zubiri's "respective" entities floating silver and shining silver require water or light to come into being does not mean that we should exalt "silver *de suyo*" above them. After all, this silver "plain and simple" can also be regarded as a mere relational whole of protons and electrons that also exist *de suyo*; in turn, each of these particles might be viewed as a composite system in its own right.

When Leibniz (like Aristotle) admits the difficulty of verifying where the true substance lies, and recommends that we refer to certain substances as substances only "by convention,"[102] he posits a hypothetical solution in some ultimate unit. Against the supposition of such an ultimate unit, this book has defended the notion that composites *do* have a real essence or tool-being, as shown quite clearly by the case of Zubiri's silver. Although the silver would vanish if its interior proton-system were to dissolve, it also has a formal reality which outranks any mere assemblage of protons. If these protons were scattered at random across the universe instead of being effectively arranged, the silver-reality would also be hopelessly lost. In this sense, a piece of silver is a machine, a *formal* reality by which subsidiary entities are arranged in an efficacious pattern. It is a real unit, and not just an aggregate surface effect at the ontological mercy of its parts. Contra Leibniz and Zubiri, a steam engine is also a *genuine* unit, a rather different force to reckon with than all of its parts would be if disassembled in a chop shop and strewn across America.

But both of these authors are brilliant men, not fools. Both are fully aware of the truism that in the case of the machine, the whole is somehow greater than the sum of its parts. The problem is that they *still* want to distinguish between the merely relational or "aggregate" status of the steam engine and the *genuine* reality of some of its components. But in fact, the silver *de suyo* is also a machine; this is not true only of floating or reflecting silver. Just as the steam engine is made up of dozens of elements, silver *simpliciter* is not just a black box, but also the formal union of trillions of minuscule internal organs.

At the same time, it would be wrong to conclude that every entity is only a relational effect, only a network that is fully deployed in its current state. This is not the case. Despite their status as machine-like integrations of countless distinct components, the silver and the engine both have an inherent unitary reality, one not exhausted by the fact that the silver is "currently floating" or that the engine is "currently powering a Chinese warship." As argued in §19 above, no entity ever exhausts the reality of another, never makes contact with the darkest residues of its heart. Far beneath any prehension *of* the silver or *by* the silver, there is the silver in its real execution, silently resting in its vacuum-sealed actuality (a.k.a. "vacuous actuality"), waiting to inflict injuries or blessings on entities yet to arrive—injuries and blessings that will be something altogether different from the preexisiting entities that give rise to them. In other words, we cannot try to say that there are certain "real" substances that have a tool-being as opposed to others that do not. Even the most bizarre combinations of entities are a reality never exhausted by any perception or use of this combination. This led in turn to the surprising additional realization that tool and broken tool are not two faces of the same entity, but two separate entities altogether.

This concept of the entity as both withdrawn from all relation and itself *composed* of relations marks the chief point of contention between the present book and the authors just mentioned. I have argued that both Leibniz and Zubiri *underestimate* the machine, viewing it as an inessential composite that exists only by the grace of the genuine purebred substances comprising it. For these authors, machines are always composites and never simples. Displaying the inverse prejudice, Heidegger and Whitehead *overestimate* the machinery of relation (whatever Heidegger's negative views on "machines" in the everyday sense). For them, there are no simple terms that are not already ensconced in a composite system of entities. But against *both* prejudices, I have said that there is nothing inherently simple in the world and nothing inherently composite. On the one hand, even a raw piece of silver is already an integrated network of assorted tool-beings. On the other hand, even the most pointlessly eclectic machine possesses a formal unitary tool-being distinct from that of its components and withdrawn from every attempt to sound its depths.

Whatever may become of this unusual concept of tool-beings, it already achieves two purposes. First, Heidegger's criticism of presence-at-hand is retained: an object is neither an obvious physical mass nor a sheer presence to other objects, but always something more. Second, this concept of tool-being breaks down every distinction between simple ultimate essences and the ulterior relations in which they become involved. Or rather, it *preserves* this distinction, and denies only that *specific* entities can be assigned to one side of the fence or the other. Zubiri's "silver *de suyo*" has no more special status than does useful silverware. It is not possible to say that the former has a real essence or tool-being and the latter only a secondary or "mixed" character. The same holds for Leibniz's monad, which in addition to its freedom from external relations, is also wrongly granted the parallel *ontic* reward of durability, ungenerability, indestructibility. Another way of putting this is to say that the concept of tool-being repels any conception of a root matter that later takes on form, of a substance to be modified by accidents, or of a monad whose invulnerability to relationships is immediately conflated with immortality. There are now two distinct results that remain in need of closer integration: (1) the "machine" theory of the entity, and (2) Heidegger's dual axes, resulting in a quadrant-model of reality.

I have argued that no simple distinction can be made between relational and nonrelational entities, since every entity is both of these. For this reason, I have also said that every relation is in turn a new entity. But a problem immediately results from this claim. For the moment, this has nothing to do with the well-known controversy over whether "possibilities" really exist, but is concerned with the infinite permutations in which the *actual* things can be considered. The reluctant but committed claim of this book is that every relation is also *ipso facto* a new entity. But Leibniz, in his famous correspondence with Arnauld, makes an interesting preemptive strike against such a claim: "the composite made up of the diamonds of the Grand Duke and the Great Mogul can be called a pair of diamonds, but this is only a being of reason."[103] As Leibniz sees it, to grant any sort of reality to such a composite of diamonds also invites a disastrous uprising of every bizarre pseudo-substance: "If a machine is one substance, a circle of men holding hands will also be one substance, and so will an army, and finally, so will every multitude of substances."[104] The end of this sentence ("and finally, so will every multitude of substances") is meant as a *reductio ad absurdum*, a deadly blow to the opposing position. But in fact, the result is absurd only if one accepts the very connotation of substance that must be rejected: namely, immunity to alteration and decay. For otherwise, why would an army or a circle of men holding hands be considered any less worthy of unity than a human soul?[105] After all, no one is claiming that "every multitude of substances" is immune to decay; many such multitudes degenerate or rust away by the minute. The point of calling an army a "substance" (a tool-being, in my terms) is not to say that it lasts as eternally as a human soul, but to say that it has a genuine reality that is never sufficiently measured by the various probes and tendrils that are extended toward it by other entities. The hammer has a tool-being quite apart from its manifest visibility, and even quite apart from its brute causal interactions. The same holds true for a human being, a cat, a grand piano, a laser, and a modem, whatever Leibniz may think.

The question is whether it is also true of a pair of diamonds, a circle of men holding hands, and of the set of living and dead humans containing Leibniz, Martina Hingis, and Hammurabi. Does this incongruous assortment of people have a genuine tool-being of its own? Against what seem to be the fears of Leibniz, the danger of this whimsical association of names is not the multiplication of substances *per se*. For since there is only a rather minimal range of traits attached to the term "tool-being," I am making no claim as to the immortality of this strange trio. Nor am I claiming that every "being of reason" is on the same footing as every *real* unity: for I am not just referring here to the *ideas* that we have of these three people, but to their subterranean reality as forces to reckon with in the cosmos. The difficulty is clear. On the one hand, we can say that *any* possible permutation of objects forms a new tool-being. But this has the disadvantage of multiplying entities to the point of near absurdity. The other solution would be to say that Leibniz/Hingis/Hammurabi has a real tool-being only if this combination has some real *effect* on the world. But this amounts to saying that tool-being becomes real only by way of an *external relation*, which has been anathema to this book since §19.

In his reflection on the unreality of a "pair" of diamonds, Leibniz makes use of an entertaining thought experiment. He tells us that if we imagine the diamonds being brought closer and closer together, this still does not make them a substance. Even if we bring them closer until they touch one another directly, they are still not one substance. Finally, even if we fuse them together with some sort of glue, they are still not a single substance. Aristotle would be pleased to hear it. While this argument against equating substantiality with physical proximity is convincing, there is another unspoken possibility that would perhaps be more threatening to Leibniz. What if instead of a physical combination, we ask about the possible *functional* union of two distinct substances?

We can imagine that Leibniz's employer, the Duke of Braunschweig, has been kidnapped by a shadowy international gang. A ransom note threatens him with death unless a single, nonnegotiable price is delivered to the criminals: the Duke will be spared only in exchange for the diamonds of the Grand Duke *and* the Great Mogul. The next morning, the learned librarian and ducal emissary Leibniz is placed in charge of negotiations to secure these diamonds. We can imagine that the notoriously generous Great Mogul is willing to help: a deal is struck, and Leibniz delivers the first part of the ransom to the kidnapping syndicate. But the Grand Duke refuses to part with his own prize diamond, owing few political favors to Duke Johann Friedrich, the unlucky captive. There is now an obvious sense in which the two diamonds *do* form a single unit (ransom-machine). This is proven increasingly each day as Leibniz's follow-up negotiations with the Grand Duke continue to flounder; it is proven definitively a month later, when in the aftermath of Leibniz's final diplomatic failure, the Duke of Braunschweig is murdered by his captors.

The scenario can easily be expanded to cover a far more ludicrous situation. After all, large diamonds are a vulgar prize, coveted only by the most insipid criminals. As a more interesting alternative, we might imagine that the Duke of Braunschweig's tormentors are motivated not by financial gain, but by an avant-garde sense of black humor. Rather than asking Leibniz to provide the world's most famous diamonds as ransom, they decide to send him on a humiliating scavenger hunt for pointless miscellaneous items. To be specific, the kidnappers might demand a particular late landscape by Poussin, a genuine arrowhead from North America, a lock of hair from the late Elisabeth of Bohemia, and a specific rare Korean manuscript by an anonymous Zen master. Moreover, the kidnappers are coldly insistent upon receiving precisely *these* objects in exchange for the liberation of Johann Friedrich, and will accept no substitutes. Obviously, the scenario is flexible enough to fit *any* combination of objects. The kidnappers might even add a touch of paradox and cruelty by including an item on the list that they know to be nonexistent: say, "a copy of St. Anselm's epic poem on the Battle of Hastings." In this sense, any permutation of real and unreal objects seems able to acquire a ready-made tool-being on the spot. Nor is it only human life which is able to produce such an effect: certain far-fetched scenarios are possible in which, even in the absence of any human beings, the two large diamonds might act in such a way to attain an end that *they alone* can attain. Not wishing to strain the reader's credulity any further, I leave these cases to the imagination.

In any event, there should be no objection to our merely using the word "substance" to refer to any of the kidnappers' odd systems of entities. It costs us no more to call them substances than to call them relations, since we have already rejected most of the traditional features of substance. Having abandoned their physical durability and endless lifespans, we have no pressing motive to limit their number. The *real* problem is the unwanted infusion of relationality into the tool-being that was supposed to be free of it. After all, it seems to be only the whim of the kidnappers that unifies the Poussin painting, the arrowhead, the lock of Elisabeth's hair, and the Korean manuscript. Let's call this unity a "thing," for lack of a better term. Now, just as with any other thing, its tool-being must be something that exceeds its particular effects on other entities, withdrawing behind any perception of it or causal access to it. But paradoxically, it is the kidnappers alone who *constitute* the assorted objects as one thing by forming a relation to it. Since the scenario now under discussion is far-fetched, no one will care. But the problem is not so trivial once it bleeds over into every other functional unity in the cosmos.

Earlier, it was necessary to reject the Aristotle/Leibniz/Zubiri distinction between natural simples and natural composites. As a result, the absurd set of ransom-objects listed above has no more and no less unity than that of a silver atom or a sugar refinery. All of these are formal systems that exceed any set of parts. And as shown in §19 in the case of the stove on the frozen lake, the tool-being of *any* entity withdraws from whatever relational complex it finds itself in. But from the example of the kidnappers, it seems that it is only by being *for* another entity (i.e., Leibniz or the kidnapping gang) that the absurd mixture of ransom-objects attains any unified tool-being at all. But if that is the case, then *every* entity will exist only because it has an effect on other entities—even a durable atom of silver will have a real tool-being only because of the effects it is able to have on the other entities surrounding it. If a ridiculous collection of ransom-objects only comes into being thanks to the kidnappers, it might also be said that the atom comes into being only because there are other atoms capable of colliding with it. To treat these two cases differently is only to betray a common-sense prejudice in favor of solid physical things over immaterial functional couplings. This may be a good strategy in day-to-day life, but as an ontological principle it is too haphazard to be acceptable. In short, in trying to strike a compromise between substance theories and relational theories, the concept of tool-being seems to be saddled with the difficulties of *both*. From this, two basic paradoxes result:

PARADOX NUMBER 1: "The object is both free of all relations and seemingly *created* by relations." In a certain sense, the tool-being of a thing exists in vacuum-sealed isolation, exceeding any of the relations that might touch it. But now it also seems true that some sort of relationality is needed to create at least *some* tool-beings. Until the Duke of Braunschweig is abducted, the pair of diamonds remains nothing but a "being of reason," which seems to give the kidnappers the appalling godlike power of creating substances. However, neither of the philosophical positions that I have critcized is any better equipped to clarify the situation. The substance theorists simply draw an arbitrary distinction, based in everyday prejudice, between natural simples and natural composites, when in fact every entity *vacillates* with respect to this distinction. This allows them to dismiss the proposed ransom package as no more than a "being of reason." Meanwhile, the relational theorists arbitrarily state that every tiniest change in the system of the world shakes every object to its core. For them, the case of the kidnappers is no paradox at all, because there are no objects anyway, only *events*. But this position has no basis besides the contemporary mania to avoid any doctrine of independent substances. For the moment, the solution to the kidnapping paradox remains unclear. But the important thing is that it is posed at all—a genuine metaphysical problem rising like suppressed vapor from the marshes of Heidegger's philosophy.

PARADOX NUMBER 2: "Where *is* presence?" Now that we have ascribed the status of entities even to relations, the accessible zone of presence-at-hand seems to have withered away altogether. That is to say, even my perception of the hammer is no longer just a derivative relation unfolding in the derivative sphere of the as-structure. The systematic encounter between me and the hammer is now defined as a unique *entity* in its own right, a kind of machine-like connection between two objects. We already know that the hammer has a withdrawn tool-being that is not exhausted by any perception or use of it. But the same holds true for my *perception* of it, for that combination of myself and the hammer that defines a brand new entity. After all, human perceptions no less than objects contain innumerable tacit strata and muffled overtones that can always be explored much further.

But this means that there is no longer a single corner of reality that is devoted *heart and soul* to the as-structure. There is no free transcendent clearing, in human Dasein or elsewhere, in which the opacity of tool-being would be effectively countered by the aloof observation of the as-structure. Everywhere, the world is a plenum crowded by tool-beings, by formal units that retreat behind any external contact with them. But if this is the case, then how does perception occur at all? Or more generally: how does *relation* occur at all? The solution to this second paradox is equally unclear. But just as with the first one, the interesting thing is the fact that it can be posed at all on the basis of Heidegger's writings. It is these sorts of metaphysical questions, and not the endless play of presence and absence for a thrown human being, that will soon make up the new face of Heideggerian philosophy.

§26. Tools in a Vacuum

Gradually, a number of unexpected features have emerged from the tool-analysis. While Heidegger shows little taste for speculative problems of any sort, such problems become uncircumventible as soon as the tool-analysis is pushed beyond the pragmatic/productive fetters in which it is often imprisoned. What Heidegger's discoveries *imply* is a fresh ontology of objects of a kind that may seem by turns wild or anachronistic. But I have tried to show that they issue directly from the vital heart of contemporary philosophy.

The question now is as follows: what model of the world begins to emerge once we push Heidegger's tool-analysis to its most extreme form? It should be noted that the truly *pivotal* claims of this book are now behind us. I have offered the model of reality as a reversal between tool and broken tool, with the tool-being receding not just behind human awareness, but behind all relation whatsoever. This duality has been crossed by another opposition of equal power: the difference between the specific quality of a thing and its systematic union. Furthermore, the world is not split up evenly with a nation of pure tool-being on one side and a land of sheer relations on the other—every point in the cosmos is *both* a concealed reality and one that enters into explicit contact with others. Finally, in the strict sense, there is no such thing as a sheer "relation"; every relation turns out to be an entity in its own right. As a result, there is no cleared transcendent space that gains a distance from entities to reveal them "as" what they are. There is no exit from the density of being, no way to stand outside the brutal play of forces and vacuum-packed entities that crowd the world. We ourselves are only one such entity among innumerable others— perhaps this is the real meaning of Socrates' strange speculations in the *Phaedo* about other beings inhabiting hollow spaces both above and below us. All of these themes make up the core of what has been said in this book, which *lives or dies* with the question of whether they are true or not. The same cannot be said for the discussions that follow, which are intended only as initial probings beyond these basic principles.

The result of the previous section was the point about tool and broken tool being utterly *separate* entities rather than two faces of one and the same entity. This resulted from an inability to distinguish any longer between relational reality on the one hand and a tool-being *free* of all relation on the other. It becomes unworkable to try to point one's finger somewhere in reality and say "*right there* is real substance," while treating other features of reality as mere compounds made up of pure discrete simples. Tool-beings can no longer be viewed as a special set of genuine foundational realities in comparison with which all else would be derivative.

The brokenness of the broken tool turned out to be a matter of relationality. My encounter with the hammer (no matter whether I perceive it or only use it) objectifies the silently withdrawn hammer-effect, reduces it to some limited profile of itself. No perception of the hammer can ever step into the hammer's place and execute its hammer-force. But the same thing turned out to be true of inanimate causal reality. One rock does not exhaust the reality of another by smashing into it: here too, the as-structure is present. In order to avoid the brash technique of referring to the collision of rocks as a "perception," I introduced Whitehead's term "prehension" in §19 above. Whether the rock is prehended by as I look at it, by a rattlesnake slowly winding across it, or by another rock slamming into it as it falls—all of this is *ontologically* the same. Any attempt to develop an explanation of human awareness from out of the primitive material of the as-structure is doomed to failure. A more complicated approach to consciousness is needed, as the usual cavalier explanations of human superiority by ontologists are as tedious as they are baseless.

The contrast between tool-being and its relations permeates all of reality, both animate and inanimate. In addition to objects in their prehensive relations with one another, there is something withdrawn behind any of these relations, irreducible to them. In addition to the tools immersed in Heidegger's "world," there are also *tools in a vacuum*: this latter region is where tool-beings are located. Although Whitehead employs the term "vacuous actuality" as an insult, it can be salvaged as a neutral description for the true reality of objects. The actuality of the object belongs always and only to a vacuum.

So much by way of review. The new problem that arose most recently was that the distinction between tool and broken tool actually began to implode. The supposed snow-white innocence of withdrawn equipment ended as soon as it became apparent that tool-being is also *inherently relational*. Zubiri argues against Leibniz that the plurality of a substance is not merely generated by an external observer. The substance known as hammer-being is a union of numerous internal notes (though Zubiri, following Aristotle, does not want to grant these notes the status of substances). The search for some sort of ultimate integral substantial stratum appears for now to be fruitless: *every* tool-being is a relational compound harboring vast interior galaxies and being siphoned upward into larger ones. But if a piece of silver exists through the mutual prehension of its atoms and other minuscule parts, then there is no reason to say that my perceptual relation with the hammer is not an entity in its own right. Once we abandon the prejudices stemming from the fact that physical matter is hard and enduring while perceptions are frail and fleeting, neither the silver nor my acts of perception are more or less composite than the other. There is no ontological reason to say that one of them is *only* an entity, and the other *only* a set of relations *between* entities.

All of this led to a radical transformation in the viewpoint defended by this book. Until now, the question has been that of the relation between the tool-beings themselves and the surface apparitions that they generate. But now that these apparitions have acquired the status of real entities in their own right, the term "broken tool" becomes merely relative. In the end, *the world is completely devoid of perceptions, and utterly jam-packed with entities.* The transition from hammer to broken hammer no longer occurs between two separate planes of reality, but between two separate *objects.* Put differently, there are no *images*—only *things.* Or perhaps even more provocatively, the being of beings is *always* itself a being; it is simply not a *present-at-hand* being, which is Heidegger's truly important point. The relation between a tool-being and its various objectifications (in perceptions, collisions, etc.) must be reinterpreted as a relation between numerous distinct entities. How these are able to interact or interpenetrate at all is a question well worth asking.

But first, it may be useful to say a word about the relation of whole and part. The way in which I opposed a strict distinction between the dimensions of tool and broken tool was to claim that every tool-being is already a composite reality. The hammer in its subterranean reality is not only a chaste and inviolable unity, but already the end result of a conspiracy of inner components. The same goes for silver and gold, as well as for Leibniz's prize diamonds. Who knows—perhaps it even holds true of animal and human souls. From the time of Aristotle, little respect has been granted to the constitutive *elements* of any substance. On those occasions when it is conceded that these elements have any genuine individuality at all, they are still only allowed the status of a *potential* individuality. Here we find another connection between Aristotle and Heidegger, far more interesting than those that are more frequently asserted: Aristotle's insistence that the components of a unity have merely *potential* singularity heralds one of the key difficulties that plagues Heidegger's notion of a functional system, as I will now discuss.

Being and Time asks us to regard all of the items in a room as mutually referential: desk, ink, walls, sink, aquarium, trash can. None of these things exists in the first instance as a present-at-hand entity. There is first and foremost the embracing unity of a room-effect. Any notion of the objects in the room as independent solid units that accidentally enter into combination is instantly rejected as superficial. What comes first is the referential system as a whole. But the problem becomes—what *is* the status of these specific objects within the room? In answering this, it should first be noted that Heidegger employs the terms "actuality" and "potentiality" in precisely the opposite sense from how I have been using them in this book. Higher than the actual is the potential, Heidegger tells us; potentiality is always *richer* than actuality. *Wirklichkeit* is usually a pejorative term for Heidegger, just another slang phrase for the stockpile of represented or present-at-hand entities as opposed to the being that exceeds them all. It is for the surpassing depth of being beneath all presence that Heidegger reserves the name "potential." Richer than any specific objectification of beings, he believes, is their bottomless surplus, their potentiality for coming to light in any number of possible ways beyond their current forms of presence. For Heidegger, the realm of the potential is that of the suppressed, submerged, underground reality lying beneath all specific entities. By contrast, he holds that the unified individual thing—a single house, a single pair of pliers—belongs to the kingdom of the *actual*.

In one respect this is similar to Aristotle's approach, in another quite different. Let's begin with the most obvious similarity. For Aristotle, too, the realm of potentiality is submerged, and in some respects even *opaque* to the human observer; it is a nearly inscrutable "matter" that can never truly be grasped outside of the tangible form that configures it. But one clear difference between the philosophers is that "actuality" is obviously not a pejorative term for Aristotle. In the *Metaphysics* (just as later in Zubiri), it is the actual which stands higher than the potential. Despite this disagreement, there is a sense in which both Aristotle and Heidegger accomplish the same result with their different choices: in both cases, the full system of the thing triumphs over its constituent elements. For Aristotle, the unified whole of an actual substance is what is primary; its interior elements are compressed within it, existing as individuals only *potentially*. For Heidegger, who has little interest in the fate of individual substances to begin with, the primary unity is that of "world," with individual things regarded as no better than secondary eruptions from the all-embracing system of reference. In short, their apparent disagreement on the question of actuality and potentiality hides a fundamental *agreement* concerning the unreality of parts in comparison with wholes.

It was also argued in chapter 1 that if we take Heidegger's conception of world *literally*, there would be no such thing as specific objects at all. The worldhood of the world is the very principle of speed, with all entities coupling infinitely in an overarching world-effect. The obvious problem that results is the necessity of explaining why anything ever moves or changes at all. Here as elsewhere, Heidegger returns us to the position of Parmenides or, at best, of Anaxagoras. If the cosmos is truly one, devoid of any *genuine* specific regions, then nothing would conflict with anything else, and the universe would resemble an infinite placid lake. But this is untrue: being is *not* a body without organs, but a kingdom in which localized districts have already been carved out. The world is not just Heidegger's "world," but always a world populated with distinct forests, atoms, and omens. For this reason, it is misleading to claim that only the world as a whole has primary reality, that its constituents are only *potentially* there. On the contrary, the parts of the world are *really* there, defending their private integrity even while besieged by the worldhood of the world.

But the same problem that holds for Heidegger's "world" also holds for the supposed aloofness of Aristotle's substances from their "potential" elements. If the material components of a substance were truly devoured by that substance, even if only temporarily, it is inconceivable that they should ever be able to break free and regain their independence. Yet this happens all the time. The elements can never possibly reemerge unless they are already susceptible to being jarred loose from the system they inhabit. But these characteristics belong *to the parts*, and not to the whole in which they are supposedly absorbed as mere suppressed potentials. In general, the concept of potentiality is too often an easy way out for those who do not wish to take the trouble to show how the various elements of a whole are actually *inscribed* in it. This allows such people to treat wholes as simple homogeneous totalities, then reintroduce their parts into the discussion as if by magic whenever circumstances should require it.

I conclude that it is justified to reinterpret the relation between tool and broken tool as that between part and whole—as long as we avoid the assumption that some things are by nature simple parts, and others by

nature second-hand composites. Consider it this way. The hammer as manifested in the as-structure is by definition linked to me and indeed to every
other entity in its orbit. If we look beneath this sum of relations toward the
withdrawn tool-being of the hammer and all other entities in the vicinity
(including I myself) we retreat into a set of parts that the system had previously devoured. It is the same as if we were to disassemble an object such
as a ferris wheel and identify numerous bolts, beams, and gears in its mechanism, each of them formerly suppressed by the ferris wheel as a whole.
The first and most obvious objection will be that this is a naively *materialist* reading of the tool-analysis. Far from it! Above all else, the "parts" in
question here are *form*, not matter. When taking apart the ferris wheel in
my mind, I do not immediately posit a set of inert iron granules from
which all pieces of the wheel are molded. I begin more proximately with
bolt-machine and engine-machine. In turn, each of these pieces is composed of formal parts: bolts and screws are never terminal points of reality,
but always composite relational systems. Yes, I will eventually reach the
atoms of iron from which the ferris wheel is ultimately built. But even these
tiny parts are not inert specks of present-at-hand matter—they too are
machines, grand totalities concocted out of sub-mechanisms perhaps still
unknown. What separates this model from all materialism is that I am not
pampering one level of reality (that of infinitesimal particles) at the expense
of all others. What is real in the cosmos are forms wrapped inside of forms,
not durable specks of material that reduce everything else to derivative status. If this is "materialism," *then it is the first materialism in history to deny
the existence of matter.*

To summarize: if I perceive hammer *as* hammer, this is a system made
up of hammer and me. The encounter between us is something quite different from both of us. The tool-being of the hammer is a system made up
of whatever formal parts it requires to function as a hammer. Still further,
each of these parts relies on numerous internal mechanisms, each of them
with a tool-being that is never fully exhausted by the hammer. Instead of
materialism, this is perhaps a new sort of "formalism," with Francis Bacon
one of its unlikely predecessors. I refer not to the vulgarized Bacon of the
textbooks ("Do as many experiments as possible, and use the results to try
to dominate nature . . ."), but to the forgotten Bacon of *Novum Organum*
Book II, who lampoons efficient causation as *ridiculous*. This is not a side
of Bacon that hard-core empiricists care to remember.[106]

There are two immediate implications of all of this for Heidegger.
First, there is a sense in which his critique of presence-at-hand *does* imply
an infinite regression of tool-beings into further component tool-beings.
But to avoid the infinite regress is either to say that there is only a *finite*
regress (substance theories), or that there is no regress in the first place
(relational theories, which deny any depth beneath the network of the

world into which one could retreat). To call a halt to this movement by positing some final substantive atomic entity, exempt from all internal composition, would amount to defining that entity as a sheer present-at-hand building block. Taking the tool-analysis to its logical extreme, we discover that *no* entity is irreducible, since each is a formal union of its elemental components, which have an independent reality and are *not* held in a kind of limbo as "potentials." If the choice is between defending the infinite regress and defending presence-at-hand, the reader is advised to choose infinite regress. And for the moment, it is only an *indefinite* regress anyway.

The second implication is as follows. I have traced the movement from the tool-being of a thing down toward its ever-tinier elements. But the same movement yields interesting results if pursued in the *opposite* direction. Not only is each thing a galaxy of parts—each thing is also a part of the larger system known as "world." Despite Heidegger's vehement objections, perhaps "world" and "being" really are just the union of all beings— but it must be their union as a churning, electrified whole rather than as just a pile of durable present-at-hand cinder blocks. The world may indeed be a colossal referential machine, just as Heidegger says. But against what he further assumes, the elements of the world do retain *individual* integrity despite their absorption into the entire system. The tools withdraw into a vacuum, an "extraworldly" refuge. But where might this refuge be? On the one hand, tool-being commits us to the existence of tools in a vacuum. On the other hand I have argued that there are no gaps in the cosmos, that the world is stuffed absolutely full with entities. But this seems to suggest that although the tool-being of a hammer withdraws into a vacuum apart from any relations, this vacuum can only be the body of *another* entity, since there are no other kinds of places.

On this note, recall the troubling disappearance of relationality from this rough model of the world. Once physical durability was discarded as a purely arbitrary criterion for substance, it followed that a causal relation between two rocks is also a system that forms an entity, and that "hammer plus me" is also a system forming an entity ("hammer-encounter," we might call it). Is something now missing from the world? Yes: any sense of a wide-open "clearing" has been abolished. We no longer have any opposition between a brute realm of effects and a starry, windy space of transcendent vision. For even a perception becomes a new kind of entity, so that our face is always pressed up against subterranean reality as against a wall or a plate-glass window; there is no longer any breathing room in being. We never manage to rise *above* the massive clamor of entities, but can only burrow around *within* it. For the moment, the mechanisms of this process remain obscure. But at least we know what is missing: the sanctuary of the human as-structure, with its free transcendence and partly liberated vision, has been jettisoned in favor of a dense and viscous universe stuffed absolutely full with entities.

The central distinction throughout this chapter has been between tools in a system and tools in a vacuum. It has been clear since §19 that genuine tool-being withdraws even behind *causal* contact with other entities. An additional claim, now under discussion, is that there is no system which is not also an entity, so that even my *perception* of the hammer must count as an entity or object. And as such, it displays the same trait of withdrawal that marks all other entities. No amount of introspective digging in my memory will ever adequately reproduce the fresh impact of the perception itself; no form of reminiscence ever recaptures it completely. My perception of the hammer is something quite distinct from anything that I ever feel or know or recall about it. The perception is itself a tool-being, and as such it resides in a vacuum uncontaminated by all relation, irreducible to all external contact. We have seen that this vacuum of the thing's existence is threatened on two sides. On the inside, its unity is threatened by the swarming combination of interior tool-beings that enable it to exist, and which it unifies with its living action. On the outside, its integrity is threatened by the innumerable networks that draw it into themselves, dissolving it into the ether of a sleek, unified reality. Despite this dual threat, the entity somehow manages to be itself, undisturbed by the storms of relation that rage to the north and south of it.

I have already mentioned that a challenging difficulty results from all of this. The world has been said to contain no relations—nothing other than entities. But entities are always primarily withdrawn tool-beings, and as such, they are sealed away in a vacuum devoid of all relation. If this is true, then the world is packed with noncommunicating vacuous zones, onto-logical bubbles, none of them able to transmit energy or influence to the others. There are neither windows nor doors to be found. Any contact between distinct entities would seem to be impossible; for the same reason, any sort of alteration in the universe would also seem impossible. Is there any way to avoid these consequences by pointing to a medium through which tool-beings might genuinely interact? How can one vacuum impart its secrets to another? And what happens, ontologically speaking, when one entity perceives another, or lightly grazes it, or outright *crushes* it?

Given that direct ontological contact between substances now seems impossible, the time has come to revive some form of *occasional cause*. The traditional invocation of God as the source of such causes is both super-fluous and unconvincing—after all, it would still have to be explained how *God* can touch the substances directly, and it is far from clear that even a deity could do so. The occasional causality I have in mind would have to occur on a more local level, and not away on high in the sphere of the divine. If a faulty electrical cord sets fire to a rug, even though the withdrawn tool-being of these objects never really comes into contact, then we must ask through what medium they affect one another at all. And in a strange sense yet to be determined, that medium will have to be *another object*, because according to the results of this book there is nothing in the universe *but* objects. To clarify this point would require a broader onto-logical theory not set forth at the present time—my purpose here is only to show the way in which Heidegger accidentally brings us to the border-lands of such a theory.

A few paragraphs ago, it was mentioned that my perception of a ham-mer forms a new systematic entity, one in which the tool-being of the ham-mer and the tool-being of I myself mutually encounter one another, each failing to exhaust the treasures of the other. It is interesting to note that this perception has as its object the hammer, and not *itself*. The perception is a unified reality that nonetheless undergoes an interior disintegration. What all of this means, if the terminology is stripped down to the bone, is that the perceptive entity (the system made up of me and the thing) per-ceives not *itself*, but rather the elements of which it is composed. In other words, *relation is already a descent into its own particles*. The system that includes me and the hammer burrows down into itself, decomposing itself before our eyes in spite of its necessary status as a *single* entity.

In any case, we are left with the following scenario—the world as a duel of tightly interlaced objects that both aggrandize and undermine one another. The movement of philosophy is less an unveiling (which relies on an illegitimate use of the as-structure) than a kind of *reverse engineering*. Teams of industrial pirates often lock themselves in motel rooms, working backward from a competitor's finished product in an effort to unlock and replicate the code that generates it. In the case of the philosopher, the fin-ished product that must be reverse-engineered is the world as we know it; the motel room is perhaps replaced by a lecture hall or a desert. Behind every apparently simple object is an infinite legion of further objects that "crush, depress, break, and enthrall one another." It is these violent under-ground currents that one should attempt to reverse-engineer, so as to unlock the infrastructure of objects. Whatever the details of its functioning may turn out to be, this infrastructure must be made up of *tools in a vac-uum*—a concept for which Martin Heidegger serves as the unwitting fore-runner.

Notes

INTRODUCTION

1. Heidegger generally uses the term "object" in a specific pejorative sense that differs from his more positive use of the term "thing." For him, the object is the thing reduced to the correlate of a representation. I choose not to follow this usage, as the term "object" is old enough and flexible enough that it does not deserve to be sacrificed to his prejudices.

2. This viewpoint is visible throughout Kisiel's encyclopedic *The Genesis of Heidegger's* Being and Time, but is made especially clear in his refreshing glossary entry for the term "Ereignis" on page 494.

Chapter One
THE TOOL AND ITS REVERSAL

1. See §10 and §11 below.

2. The term "tool-being" was first suggested in April of 1992 by Raven Zachary of Dallas, Texas.

3. It is not enough to say that what is at stake is "transcendence" rather than a primacy of practical reason. For even this view follows Heidegger's words too closely, and repeats the central mistake by interpreting this transcendence as a property of *human Dasein* rather than of objects themselves.

4. See §14 below.

5. "Readiness-to-hand is the way in which entities as they are 'in themselves' are defined ontologico-categorially" (*Being and Time*, p. 101). The quotation marks surrounding the phrase "in themselves" by no means serve to mock the idea that there could be things independent of Dasein. Rather, they are employed to distance Heidegger's use of the phrase from the traditional sense of the *an sich*: a noumenal realm that still has the mode of presence-at-hand, even if in the privative mode of "absence."

6. *Being and Time*, p. 99.

7. On this point, the reader is urged to consult a brilliant work by the unjustly forgotten José Ortega y Gasset: "An Essay in Esthetics by Way of a Preface," in

Phenomenology and Art. This essay's lucid critique of all representation in 1914 [sic], at a moment when the young Heidegger was still barely mastering the phenomenological method, has to qualify it as a neglected landmark of twentieth-century philosophy.

8. *Being and Time*, pp.95–96.

9. Ibid., p. 97.

10. I will "complicate" this opposition between visible and invisible soon enough; as a first step, it is perfectly capable of setting us on the right road.

11. *Being and Time*, p. 105.

12. Ibid., p. 120. From this passage it is clear that there are no grounds for regarding "world" as something distinct from the actual system of equipment, whether as a horizon of possibility lying beyond that system, or as an empty, featureless site in which it is inscribed. For "that wherein Dasein as such already is" is neither of these abstractions, but rather an utterly *determinate* totality of things. Heidegger's occasional warnings about identifying world with "the sum of equipment" are plainly aimed only at the belief that a concept of world can be obtained by tabulating an inventory of the set of all present-at-hand hammers and chisels and other entities currently lying around in the cosmos. The tool-system as I define it here (as invisible, total, non-substantial, and so on) has been cleansed in advance of all of the ontic features to which Heidegger objects.

13. Although Heidegger uses the terms *Sinn* and *Bedeutung* separately, there is no genuine distinction in his works between what they signify, despite his tendency to use the former term for more serious matters (for example, being itself) and the latter for specific entities (for example, hammers). Both terms point ambiguously to an explicit end-point *and* to a concealed reality lying hidden from view. The "reference" of the hammer can be either the act of hammer-being that lies behind its visible wooden hulk *or* the larger construction project into which it is dissolved. Likewise, the "meaning" of being can be either its nonrepresentable reality *or* its meaning as projected in any of the epochs of the history of being.

14. One excellent reason can be found in a remark by Edgar A. Poe, who states bluntly of a newly deceased author that "during the larger portion of his life, he seemed to breathe only for the purpose of perpetrating puns—things of so despicable a platitude that the man who is capable of habitually committing them, is seldom found capable of anything else" (*Poe: Essays and Reviews*, p. 1471).

15. My account of the question of being can be found in §12 below.

16. For this reference I am indebted to Irene Schaudies of Antwerp, Belgium.

17. In his lucid book *Heidegger and Aquinas*, John Caputo gives a fierce critique of those Thomists who want to exempt terms such as *actus* and *esse* from the sphere of the forgetting of being. On page 120, he does so by insisting that such conceptions are inevitably forms of *Vorhandenheit*. Without offering here an opinion about St. Thomas or the traditional concepts of action, it can be definitively stated that what I have called the "action" of the tool is *anything but* present-at-hand. Caputo's understandable fear of allowing being to degenerate into "efficiency and productivity" leads him to overlook the immeasurable difference between withdrawn tool-being and any form of *Vorhandensein*. His related claim is that the meaning of being has to be regarded as an "emergent process" of *aletheia*

or *physis* rather than as an act. While argued clearly enough, this sort of retreat is precisely what needs to be avoided. See my related criticism of Reiner Schürmann in §15 below.

18. "to think the 'difference' only as being itself . . . [and] no longer as the being of beings." (*Wegmarken*, p. 134, footnote c), but also "that being never comes to presence without beings..." (ibid., p. 306). Any claim to solve the problem chronologically by saying that the *later* Heidegger's tendency is simply to turn from entities toward *Sein* is faced with major difficulties in connection with the theme of the fourfold, which enacts its mirror-play only in *the thing* (cf. "Das Ding"), as well as in connection with language as the one-fold differentiation of world *and thing* (cf. "Die Sprache").

19. This is evident at every point of Heidegger's career, even to the point of monotony: "For [Greek ontology], the world is the *aei on*, the always already present-at-hand..." (*Basic Problems of Phenomenology*, p.115); "Plotinus: *noeta* over against *aistheta*, but even in the sphere of *aistheta* again only present-at-hand things, indifferent being-present-at-hand . . ." (*Gesamtausgabe*, hereafter GA, 22, p. 156); "World [in Kant]—i.e., present-at-hand nature in its totality . . ." (GA 31, p. 204); "But is [Dilthey's] definition drawn from experiences which aim at a primary experience of the being of man? Or does it not come from the experience of man as a present-at-hand thing of the world. . . ?" (*History of the Concept of Time*, p. 125). Countless further examples are available, as any veteran reader of Heidegger will easily recall. Indeed, in my own copies of the *Gesamtausgabe* volumes, it is probably no exaggeration to say that I have underlined several thousand formulations of this kind.

20. *Being and Time*, p. 97.

21. Ibid., p. 116.

22. Most famously, see the contemptuous footnote in "Vom Wesen des Grundes," which refers to the charge of anthropocentrism in *Being and Time* as "[an] objection that is now passed all too eagerly from hand to hand . . ." (*Wegmarken*, p. 162).

23. "A chair does not have the mode of being of being-in-the-world; instead it occurs within the intraworldly present-at-hand" (*Basic Problems of Phenomenology*, p. 166). Far from it! This is clearly false even on Heidegger's own terms, since it contradicts the most interesting result of his analysis of equipment. The being of a chair might not be an issue for the chair in the same way that human being is an issue for itself. But this doesn't mean that the chair exists only as an extant sum of wood pieces, nor would Heidegger insist on such an absurdity if we were to press him on it. Among other features, the chair has the being of supporting the sitter, a role that *cannot possibly* have the mode of presence-at-hand. Here we can see Heidegger's unfortunate tendency to conflate being-in-the-world with *awareness* of the world—in fact, these are two utterly distinct structures.

24. And to repeat an earlier remark, the word "action" is not used here in any special historical sense, but only as a placeholder term for whatever it is that the reality of tool-being may turn out to be.

25. *Being and Time*, p. 79.

26. Ibid.

27. Ibid.

28. I use this Leibnizian term loosely, with the sole aim of adding color to the present description.

29. The following statement from *History of the Concept of Time* is especially interesting, and especially neglected: "[The question of being] can be attained in any entity; it need not be intentionality" (*History of the Concept of Time*, p. 137).

30. This is shown above all in the biographical writings of Kisiel.

31. It may even be doubted whether the existential analytic has much to tell us about human being at all. *Being and Time* actually gives us surprisingly little information about specific experiences such as "the call of conscience" and the relation to "death." Such terms, lifted directly from the sphere of ontic experience, are quickly converted into distracting passwords for the simple event in which basic ontological structures such as "temporality" and "world" become present *as* what they are.

32. The impatient reader is advised that a consideration of the as-structure is only pages away.

33. This is already the explicit concern of Emmanuel Levinas in his neglected early work *De l'existence à l'existant*, which I will discuss in §20 below. In this way, Levinas is probably the most direct forerunner of the central claims of the present book, but he adopts a different approach from my own, locating the pre-thematic anonymity of being in the insomniac's *il y a* rather than in Heidegger's imperial system of implements. As will be shown below, this fascinating approach fails insofar as Levinas still regards human consciousness as the sole agent capable of breaking up the anonymity of being into numerous specific beings.

34. *History of the Concept of Time*, p. 188.

35. Ibid. Emphasis added.

36. Thanks are due to Alphonso Lingis for offering this concise formulation of the problem (in a letter to the author of September, 1995).

37. *Being and Time*, pp. 97–98.

38. *Hölderlin's Hymn "The Ister,"* p. 74.

39. In this context, it has been suggested that I ought to focus my attention on the "not" rather than on the "mere." The reason I cannot follow this advice is clear—my theme is neither the possibility and limits of a negative theology, nor the more general topic of language and negativity. In fact, I am arguing that Heidegger's "*bloß*" actually illuminates two *positive* realities: the "mere" realm of presence-at-hand, and its counterpart, the permanently concealed yet effective kingdom of *Vollzug*.

40. Strangely enough, Heidegger seems to have pirated this turn of phrase from the pseudo-Scotus of the Habilitation Thesis; see the epigraph to §10 below.

41. *Being and Time*, p. 136.

42. *Essai sur les donées immédiates de la conscience*. Translated as *Time and Free Will*.

43. See *Zur Bestimmung der Philosophie*. GA 56/57, p. 74.

44. This is the case throughout most of *Being and Time*.

45. "Thus, the human being is . . . a creature of distance," in the final paragraph of "Vom Wesen des Grundes" (*Wegmarken*, p. 175).

46. The issue resurfaces, of course, in Heidegger's later writings on technology: the radio is a shrinking-machine that destroys distance, but does not thereby give us "true" nearness. Insofar as this critique merely repeats what we have already learned about the general incommensurability between being and representation, it can hardly be recommended as a specific contribution to the theme of technology, except in the sense of a basic intellectual framework. Marshall McLuhan, among others, is a far more fruitful writer than Heidegger on the question of technology.

47. See *Zur Sache des Denkens*.

48. The failure to do this is what fuels the stifling dominance of the *Bildungsroman* approach to Heidegger, which seeks to identify as many minute changes in the thinker's trajectory between 1915 and 1976 as possible. Against this attitude, it becomes increasingly clear that Heidegger is simple enough to be taught rapidly to intelligent teenagers (and important enough that he should be). The waters are only muddied when dueling scholars quarrel excessively over shop talk.

49. In the *Beiträge zur Philosophie*, this *Zeit-Spiel-Raum* is first mentioned on p. 6.

50. *Being and Time*, p. 145.

51. Ibid., pp. 401–18.

52. Ibid., p. 403.

53. All of these historical moments are summarized quite effectively, of course, in *The Basic Problems of Phenomenology*.

54. *Being and Time*, p. 408. Emphasis added.

55. Ibid., p. 405.

56. See the opening sections of *History of the Concept of Time* for an especially clear account of this view.

57. *Being and Time*, p. 407.

58. Ibid., p. 408.

59. Ibid., p. 409.

60. Ibid., p. 358.

61. Ibid., p. 409.

62. Ibid., p. 412.

63. Ibid., pp. 411–12.

64. Ibid., p. 411.

65. Oddly, it has been objected to this thought experiment that I ask the reader to "imagine" something, and that since Heidegger argues in *Kant and the Problem of Metaphysics* that imagination is inherently temporal, my experiment fails. But this is like trying to defend materialism by saying that idealists cannot object to materialism without using their brain or blood cells: a textbook case of begging the question.

66. See especially *Creative Evolution*, throughout.

67. Among other passages, the reader is referred to footnote xxx on pp. 500–501 of *Being and Time*, where Bergson is grouped with Hegel and Aristotle as exemplars of the doctrine that time is a sequence of now-points.

68. See Levinas' *Existence and Existents*, as well as §20 below.

69. Ibid., p. 415.

70. Ibid.

71. Ibid.

72. Ibid., p. 401.

73. See the *Metaphysical Foundations of Logic*, p. 157.

74. Ibid.

75. It is for this reason that the existing accounts of metontology are of limited use for my own treatment of this theme. My claim is that metontology is not just a discrete intuition that appears in a given Heideggerian text. Rather, it is the necessary but undeveloped counter-concept that would begin to free us from Heidegger's universal implosion of all singularities into the monotonous interplay of tool and broken tool. Insofar as this implosion has not been admitted by commentators, who continue to pursue Heidegger's various topics as though they were truly distinct themes, an appropriately wide understanding of the mission of metontology has also never emerged. Some of the standard accounts of metontology can be found in chapter 2 of D. F. Krell's *Intimations of Mortality*, chapter 2 of Robert Bernasconi's *Heidegger in Question*, and William McNeill's article "Metaphysics, Fundamental Ontology, Metontology."

76. Concerning the important role of Levinas in my reading of Heidegger, see §20 below. The works of Jean Baudrillard are also relevant on the theme of simulation, but these works are so non-Heideggerian in terminology and tone that excessive space would be required to demonstrate the strange but undeniable Heidegger-Baudrillard connection.

77. Thus, the present book's reading of the 29/30 course finds itself in substantial disagreement with that of Krell's *Daimon Life*. While arguably no other commentary exhibits a better scent for potential metontological themes, Krell is far too liberal in his assessment of Heidegger's capacity (as well as his own) to provide any concrete discourse on such issues.

78. *Being and Time*, p. 149.

79. *Fundamental Concepts of Metaphysics*, pp. 220 ff.

80. "Thus it is only a further sign of the prevailing groundlessness of thought and understanding today when we are asked to regard the house as a machine for living and the chair as a machine for sitting" (ibid., pp. 215–16). Heidegger's target here is certainly not his own earlier analyses of equipment, but probably the Bauhaus movement and perhaps even American pragmatism. The same is true of his mocking statements against "knives and forks," which are sometimes strangely misinterpreted as if Heidegger were disavowing his own notion of tool-being. I will return to this issue in chapter 2 below, §10 and §11.

81. Ibid., p. 226.

82. "Das Ding." Emphasis added.

83. 1929/30, p. 312. Emphasis added.

84. Ibid.

85. Ibid.

86. Among other difficulties, the supposedly privileged relation of theory to the as-structure could not be maintained for long in any room containing Jacques Derrida (see *Speech and Phenomena*, throughout).

87. *Being and Time*, p. 111.

88. 1929/30 course, p. 308.

89. See *Erläuterungen zu Hölderlins Dichtung*, pp. 33–34. Note also Heidegger's stated preference, when discussing Rilke, for the stentorian *Sonnets to Orpheus* and *Duino Elegies* over the livelier imagination and versification of the poet's earlier *Buch der Bilder* and *Neue Gedichte* (see "Wozu Dichter?," in *Holzwege*). Heidegger shows himself fully at home in mining Rilke's obscure declarations about "das Offene" for his own philosophical use. It is unlikely that he would display equal skill in unfolding the lyric treasures of "The Buddha" or "The Panther," poems whose content hardly allows the reader to grind any axe in particular.

90. As is especially the case throughout much of the Germanien/Rhein lecture course, GA 39.

91. *Being and Time*, p. 111.

92. *Wegmarken*, p. 312.

93. *Fundamental Concept of Metaphysics*, p. 369.

94. See the opening to "Einblick in das, was ist," in GA 79, *Bremer und Freiburger Vorträge*. I will offer a more detailed criticism of Heidegger's views on technology in §17 below.

95. To give just two examples, I would recommend McLuhan's classic *Understanding Media* and Latour's engrossing *Aramis*.

96. In passing, I would like to suggest that the notion of philosophical ideas as instituting or building reality rather than unveiling it is perhaps the real meaning of Deleuze's cryptic and unorthodox view of philosophy as a "creation of concepts" (see above all the final book with Guattari, *What is Philosophy?*)

97. Published in *Zur Bestimmung der Philosophie*, GA 56/57. A fair-minded reading of this course tends to confirm Kisiel's suggestion that it contains *all* of the central Heideggerian themes, whether "early" or "late." (See *The Genesis of Heidegger's* Being and Time, p. 458.)

98. It is my view as well as Kisiel's that the frequent occurrence of this word at such an early date helps to shift the burden of proof back onto those who would advocate a developmentalist reading of Heidegger. To argue that 1919's *Ereignis* offers a "merely verbal similarity" with the later usage of the term is to assert that the mainstream view of Heidegger's mental evolution should rank higher than the voice of the texts themselves. This opinion is unacceptable for obvious reasons.

99. *Zur Bestimmung der Philosophie*, p. 73.

100. Ibid., p. 67.

101. Ibid.

102. Ibid., p. 72.

103. See already the 24-year-old Heidegger's 1913 dissertation on the theory of judgment. In connection with the "*es*" of '*es blitzt*' ("it lightens"), the young Heidegger asks: "Do I mean to express a property or a current state of the mysterious 'It', or does the judgment have a completely different sense?... The judgment says, rather, that something *happens*; the thought rests on the *taking-place*, on the sudden *befalling*" (GA 1, p. 185).

104. *Zur Bestimmung der Philosophie*, pp. 205-14, "Über das Wesen des akademischen Studiums."

105. Ibid., p. 206.

106. This reference to the *commedia dell'arte* is obviously my own, not Heidegger's.

107. Ibid., p. 74.

108. Ibid. Here I make use of MacQuarrie and Robinson's earlier rendering of *Entfernung* as "de-severance," rather than the more recently popular translation of "de-distancing." In the present passage, which does not talk about spatiality at all, "de-severance" seems to be a more effective choice.

109. Ibid., p. 75.

110. Ibid.

111. Ibid., p. 76.

112. Ibid., p. 85.

113. Ibid., p. 109.

114. Interestingly, the two show a nearly exact correspondence with Husserl's distinction between "*Generalisierung*" and "*Formalisierung*." (See *Ideen I*, p. 26 ff.) In fact, Heidegger uses precisely these terms in his 1920/21 presentation of the same theme (GA 60, *Phänomenologie des religiösen Lebens*, pp. 57-62). In some respects, this later treatment offers a superior exposition. I have chosen to discuss 1919 instead due to its lucid early analysis of equipment, as well as its unique status as Heidegger's earliest surviving lecture course. But there can be no question that the ultimate source of Heidegger's second axis is Husserl's difference between the eidetic and phenomenological reductions, with the necessary changes being made to account for Heidegger's less idealistic stance.

115. Ibid., p. 114.

116. Ibid., p. 116.

117. Ibid., p. 115.

118. *An Introduction to Metaphysics*, p. 1.

119. For this reason, it is necessary to reject Krell's otherwise interesting claim that Angst is unique among the moods in not having a temporal character (see his *Intimations of Mortality*).

120. GA 56/57, p. 117.

121. In GA 79, *Bremer und Freiburger Vorträge*.

122. *Wegmarken*, p. 123. Emphasis added.

123. Ibid.

124. See §12 below.

125. *Wegmarken*, p. 138.

126. Ibid., p. 162.

127. Ibid., p. 138.

128. Ibid., p. 167.

129. Ibid.

130. Ibid., p. 163. Emphasis added.

131. Ibid., p. 105.

132. Ibid., p. 115. Emphasis added.

133. Ibid., p. 117. Emphasis added.

134. In preparing the final version of this chapter, I have benefited greatly from the extensive comments of Daniel Selcer and Henry Staten.

Chapter Two
BETWEEN BEING AND TIME

1. From the Habilitation Thesis on Duns Scotus (which actually deals, of course, with writings of the pseudo-Scotus Thomas von Erfurt). The citation renders Heidegger's translation of the original Latin: "Numerus non solum est unus aggregatione sicut acervus lapidum." *Frühe Schriften*, GA 1, pp. 233–34.

2. "The Fate of the Distinction Between *Praxis* and *Poiesis*." In *Heidegger in Question*, pp. 2–24.

3. The reader is referred to Tamaniaux's *Heidegger and the Project of Fundamental Ontology*, and Volpi's "Being and Time: A 'Translation' of the Nicomachean Ethics?" (in Kisiel and Van Buren, *Reading Heidegger from the Start*, pp. 195–211) and "Dasein as *praxis*: the Heideggerian assimilation and the radicalization of the practical philosophy of Aristotle" (in Macann, *Critical Heidegger*, pp. 27–66.)

4. Bernasconi, *Heidegger in Question*, p. 5. (Cited from *History of the Concept of Time*, p. 194.)

5. Ibid., p. 4.

6. Bernasconi, *Heidegger in Question*, p. 4. (Cited from *Kant and the Problem of Metaphysics*, pp. 165–66.)

7. *Kant and the Problem of Metaphysics*, p. 212.

8. Bernasconi, *Heidegger in Question*, p. 8.

9. Ibid., p. 9.

10. *Delimitations*, p. 142.

11. Bernasconi, *Heidegger in Question*, p. 11.

12. Ibid., p. 22. Naturally, a full critique of this tactic would have to be directed not against Bernasconi, but against Derrida's much-admired "Geschlecht II," a task that lies beyond the limited framework of the present book.

13. Ibid., p. 15.

14. Ibid., p. 17.

15. Ibid., p. 14.

16. GA 56/7, *Zur Bestimmung der Philosophie*, p. 83 and p. 206, respectively.

17. *Heidegger's Pragmatism*, p. 17.

18. Ibid., p. 19.

19. Ibid., p. 24. Emphasis added.

20. Ibid., p. 20.

21. See *Kant and the Problem of Metaphysics*, throughout.

22. Okrent, *Heidegger's Pragmatism*, p. 31.

23. Ibid., p. 39.

24. Ibid.

25. Ibid., p. 41.

26. Ibid., p. 261.

27. Ibid.

28. Ibid., p. 281.

29. I will discuss Rorty in more detail in §16 below.

30. Ibid., pp. 280–81.

31. Since I am using a version of this article taken from a web site, there is no way to provide page numbers for my citations.

32. See Lafont's interesting book *Heidegger, Language, and World-Disclosure.*
33. Concerning Žižek, see §19 below.
34. See Kripke's *Naming and Necessity.* Naturally, this work is already a well-known classic among analytic philosophers; as it was first published in 1972, it can even be considered old news, as brought out most amusingly in its several references to Richard Nixon. But given the continued sectarian dispute in American academic philosophy, it is likely that many of my colleagues in continental circles have not even looked at Kripke's book. If they do so, I can promise them a pleasurable reading experience.
35. GA 60, *Phänomenologie des religiösen Lebens,* p. 113.
36. As mentioned in §3 above, Heidegger does already claim in this 1925 course that the question of being can be raised with respect to *any* entity, not just the being of intentionality. To this extent, he seems to endorse the claims I make in this section. Even so, he does not seem especially *interested* in developing this theme of the being of inanimate objects.
37. See Hopkins' maverick argument in his *Intentionality in Husserl and Heidegger.*
38. *Metaphysical Foundations of Logic,* p. 134.
39. Ibid.
40. *Being and Time,* p. 215.
41. GA 28, *Der deutsche Idealismus,* p. 340. Emphasis added.
42. *History of the Concept of Time,* p. 110.
43. Ibid., p. 111.
44. Ibid., p. 110.
45. Ibid., p. 114,
46. *History of the Concept of Time,* p. 200.
47. Ibid., p. 136.
48. *Being and Time,* p. 68.
49. Ibid., p. 174.
50. "Phenomenological Reduction and the Double Life." In Kisiel and Van Buren, eds., *Reading Heidegger from the Start.*
51. Ibid., p.256.
52. Ibid.
53. Ibid., p. 257.
54. Ibid., p. 258.
55. Note that Bernet's Husserl, having discovered both the tool-analysis and the question of being well before Heidegger, is a rather imposing historical giant. In this respect, I am puzzled by Hopkins' dissatisfaction with Bernet's credentials as a defender of Husserl.
56. Ibid.
57. Ibid., p. 263.
58. Ibid., p. 264.
59. Ibid., p. 266. Emphasis added.
60. Ibid., p. 267.
61. Ibid.
62. See his autobiographical "Preface for Germans" in *Phenomenology and Art.* The exact dating of Ortega's reaction against Husserl can be found on page 61.

63. *History of the Concept of Time*, p. 172.
64. *Philosophy and the Mirror of Nature*, p. 12.
65. *Intimations of Mortality*, pp. 47–48.
66. Ibid., p. 48.
67. Ibid., p. 29.
68. GA 49, *Die Metaphysik des deutschen Idealismus*, p. 50.
69. *Being and Time*, p. 376.
70. Ibid., p. 377.
71. Ibid.
72. See §2 above.
73. *Metaphysical Foundations of Logic*, p. 211.
74. *Basic Problems of Phenomenology*, p. 306.
75. Ibid., p. 307.
76. *The Metaphysical Foundations of Logic*, pp. 145 and 149, respectively.
77. GA 21.
78. *Double Truth*, p. 57.
79. Ibid., p. 59.
80. Ibid., p. 61.
81. Ibid., p. 63.
82. Ibid., p. 66.
83. Ibid.
84. Ibid., pp. 63–64. And see section §12 in the present book.
85. See §11 above.
86. Ibid., pp. 67–68.
87. Ibid., p. 68.
88. Ibid.
89. Ibid., p. 79.
90. Ibid., p. 71.
91. GA 66, *Besinnung*, p. 340.
92. See his two-in-one cult classic, *Computer Lib/Dream Machines*.
93. *Heidegger on Being and Acting*, p. 9.
94. Ibid., p. 204.
95. Ibid., p. 205.
96. Ibid., p. 206.
97. Ibid., p. 210.
98. Ibid., p. 207.
99. Ibid.
100. Ibid., pp. 208–9.
101. Ibid., p. 210.
102. Ibid., p. 211.
103. Ibid.
104. Ibid., p. 217.
105. Ibid., p. 211.
106. Ibid., p. 348. Footnote 158.
107. Ibid., p. 223.
108. Ibid.
109. Ibid.

110. Ibid., p. 348. Footnote 158.

111. In GA 79, *Bremer und Freiburger Vorträge*.

112. Ibid., p. 52.

113. Badiou, *Deleuze: The Clamor of Being*, p. 19.

114. Rorty, "Wittgenstein, Heidegger, and the Reification of Language," in *The Cambridge Companion to Heidegger*.

115. Ibid., p. 337.

116. Ibid., p. 339.

117. Ibid., p. 340. See Dummett's *The Seas of Language*.

118. Ibid., p. 337. See Davidson's *Inquiries Into Truth and Interpretation*.

119. Ibid., pp. 341–42.

120. Ibid., p. 342.

121. Ibid.

122. Ibid., p. 344.

123. Ibid., p. 345.

124. Ibid., pp.346–47.

125. Ibid., p. 337.

126. In using the term "fantasy" here I am borrowing from Žižek's description of the retroactive constitution of reality by a human subject, although I am extending it well beyond the human realm *and* rejecting Žižek's anti-realist sense of "fantasy." For a full discussion of this topic see §19 below.

127. Throughout the present book I have tried to reverse the usual assumption that presence-at-hand means "independence from perception" and readiness-to-hand means "participation in a total network of meanings and purposes," by arguing that presence-at-hand is precisely what is *generated* by perception and readiness-to-hand precisely what *escapes* all relation.

128. Rorty, "Wittgenstein, Heidegger, and the Reification of Language," p. 348.

129. Ibid., p. 349.

130. *Unterwegs zur Sprache*, pp. 11–33.

131. Ibid., pp. 20–21.

132. Ibid., p. 21.

133. Ibid.

134. Ibid., pp. 29–30.

135. Ibid., p. 19.

136. Ibid., p. 22.

137. Ibid.

138. Ibid., p. 24.

139. Ibid., pp. 24–25.

140. Ibid., p. 32.

141. Ibid., p. 26.

142. Ibid., p.28.

143. Ibid.

144. Ibid., p.29.

145. Ibid.

146. Ibid., p.32.

147. Ibid.

148. From the published English translation of *On the Way to Language*, p. 11.

149. *Heidegger's Confrontation with Modernity*, p. 137.
150. Ibid., p. 138.
151. Ibid.
152. Ibid.
153. Ibid., p. 140.
154. *Erkennen und Handeln in Heideggers "Sein und Zeit."*
155. *Heidegger's Confrontation with Modernity*, p. 142.
156. Ibid.
157. Ibid.
158. Ibid., p. 143.
159. Ibid., p. 147.
160. Ibid., p. 148.
161. Ibid. Emphasis added.
162. *The Question Concerning Technology*, p. 11.
163. Ibid., p. 13.
164. Ibid.
165. Ibid.
166. Ibid., pp. 18–19.
167. Ibid., p. 22.
168. Ibid., p. 14.
169. Ibid., p. 33.
170. Ibid., p. 33. Emphasis added.
171. GA 79, *Bremer und Freiburger Vorträge*, p. 71.
172. GA 65, *Beiträge zur Philosophie*, p. 5.
173. GA 15, *Seminare*, p. 239.
174. Richardson, *Heidegger:Through Phenomenology to Thought*.
175. Pöggeler, *Martin Heidegger's Path of Thinking*.
176. Vycinas, *Earth and Gods*.
177. Richardson, *Heidegger*, p. 570. Emphasis added.
178. Ibid., p. 571.
179. Ibid., p. 572.
180. Ibid., p. 567. Emphasis added.
181. Ibid., p. 571.
182. Ibid., p. 572.
183. Ibid.
184. Ibid.
185. Ibid., p. 7; emphasis added.
186. In this case I simply refer the reader to the English translations of these passages, as contained in *Poetry, Language, Thought*, p. 149.
187. GA 79, *Bremer und Freiburger Vorträge*, p. 17. Emphasis added.
188. Ibid. Emphasis added.
189. See *Ideas I*, §13. In the secondary literature on Heidegger, an eye-popping hint at the appearance of the fourfold in the early Heidegger can be found in a diagram of the 1919 course printed in Kisiel, *The Genesis of Heidegger's* Being and Time, p. 22. As far as I am aware, Kisiel himself has never suggested that this diagram, found not in the published GA 56/57 but only in the student transcripts deposited in Marbach, actually presages *das Geviert*.

190. *The Ticklish Subject*, p. 12.
191. Ibid., p. 13.
192. Ibid., pp. 14–15.
193. Ibid., p. 15.
194. Ibid.
195. Ibid.
196. Ibid., p. 16.
197. Ibid.
198. Ibid., p. 18.
199. Ibid., p. 16.
200. Ibid., p. 19.
201. Ibid., p. 36.
202. Ibid., p. 45.
203. Burak, e-mail to the author of November 20, 2000.
204. *The Ticklish Subject*, p. 1.
205. Ibid., p. 60.
206. Ibid., p. 33.
207. Ibid., p. 57.
208. Ibid., p. 23.
209. Ibid., p. 46.
210. Ibid., p. 60.
211. Ibid., p. 55.
212. See also Žižek's *The Abyss of Freedom*.
213. *The Ticklish Subject*, p. 62.
214. Ibid., p. 65.
215. Ibid., pp. 63–64 on Husserl and pp. 65–66 on Angst.
216. Ibid., pp. 65–66. Emphasis added.
217. *The Sublime Object of Ideology*, pp. 91–92.
218. Ibid., p. 97.
219. Ibid., p. 96.
220. Ibid., p. 97.
221. Ibid.
222. Ibid.
223. Ibid., p. 98.
224. Ibid., p. 99.
225. Ibid.
226. Ibid., p. 102.
227. Ibid.
228. *The Ticklish Subject*, p. 51.

Chapter Three
ELEMENTS OF AN OBJECT-ORIENTED PHILOSOPHY

1. See Lingis, "A Phenomenology of Substance," throughout.
2. See Deleuze and Parnet, *Dialogues.*
3. To view the hammer as an actual entity is already to cut against the grain of at least some orthodox readings of *Process and Reality*, which claim that actual entities belong only to the "microscopic" level, and that the "macroscopic" level of recognizable everyday objects can only be referred to as a "nexus" or "society." But this reading is at odds with Whitehead's own claim that "actual entity" refers to everything from God to the merest puff of existence in empty space—neither of which strike me as inherently "microscopic." Perhaps even more importantly, there is nothing in Whitehead's own analyses to indicate that the difference between actual entity, nexus, and society refer to different *kinds* of beings; accordingly, I regard the difference between these three levels as merely relative. For a contrary view, see Donald Sherburne's useful book *A Key to Whitehead's* Process and Reality.
4. *Process and Reality*, p. 75.
5. Bertrand Russell makes a similar criticism of monadology in his *The Philosophy of Leibniz.*
6. cf. *Existence and Existents*, p. 15, and *Time and the Other*, p. 33.
7. *Time and the Other*, pp. 44–45.
8. *Existence and Existents*, p. 47.
9. Ibid., pp. 17–18.
10. Ibid., p. 27. Emphasis added.
11. Ibid., p. 22.
12. Ibid., p. 36. Emphasis added.
13. Ibid., p. 57.
14. Ibid.
15. Ibid., p. 65.
16. Ibid.
17. Ibid., p. 19.
18. Ibid., p. 44. Emphasis added.
19. *Time and the Other*, p. 63.
20. See his *Seduction*, throughout.
21. *Time and the Other*, p. 68.
22. This issue is explored in depth in the recent writings of Lingis (especially *Foreign Bodies, The Community of Those Who Have Nothing in Common*, and *The Imperative*). While Lingis ingeniously extends the imperative from interpersonal ethics to the entire field of reality, it remains for him a question of the force these objects work upon *us*. I have suggested that it is possible to go further than this, to examine imperative objects in the summons they work on the level of animals, and even on the level of raw physical causation. By expanding the insights of Levinas well beyond their usual boundaries, Lingis invites a cosmological turn that he himself appears reluctant to take.
23. *The Encyclopedia of Philosophy [7 and 8: Psychology to Zubiri].*

24. The interested reader is referred to the Chicago or Portland incarnations of Powell's Used Books.

25. *On Essence*, p. 47.

26. Ibid., p. 46. Emphasis added.

27. Ibid., p. 128.

28. Ibid.

29. Ibid., p. 123.

30. To link Zubiri with a more colorful contemporary figure, this also seems to be Deleuze's point in opposing the singularity of *repetition* to any second-hand abstracted *identity* (see *Difference and Repetition*, throughout). Deleuze's "generalized anti-Hegelianism" shares many common features with Zubiri's own opposition to Hegel.

31. Ibid.

32. Ibid., p. 139.

33. It seems to me that the notion of a "proper reality" is criticized in two very different ways that are often conflated, one of them valid and the other less so. For it is one thing to assail the notion that no entity in the world is ever truly commensurate with a "proper" reality in and of itself, but quite another to draw the unfounded conclusion that there *is* no proper reality. The present book insists that Heidegger's analysis *does* establish the existence of a realm of the "proper": tool-being, which stands at a distance from all present-at-hand entities, all broken tools, all configurations of presence.

34. Ibid., p. 140.

35. Ibid., p. 202.

36. Ibid., p. 197.

37. Ibid., p. 324. Zubiri himself does not use the term "simulacrum."

38. Ibid., p. 365.

39. Ibid.

40. Ibid., p. 130.

41. Ibid., p. 129.

42. Ibid., p. 155.

43. Ibid., p. 419.

44. Ibid.

45. Ibid.

46. Ibid.

47. Ibid., p. 171.

48. Ibid., p. 173.

49. Ibid., p. 166.

50. This point is made quite forcefully in Bruno Latour's marvelous 1999 book *Pandora's Hope*. But like Whitehead, Latour is reluctant to believe that anything substantial could exist outside of all networks.

51. Obviously, Heidegger tends to regard such questions with contempt, and his admirers have tended to follow suit. It is partly for this reason that metaphysics is a field now dominated by analytic philosophers.

52. Most famously, see Quine's "On What There Is," in *From a Logical Point of View*.

53. Daniel Paul Schreber, *Denkwürdigkeiten eines Nervenkranken*.

54. *Monadology*, §62.

55. I deliberately forego any discussions of ontological machinery in Deleuze and Guattari, although to some readers the theme of objects may seem to have more in common with these authors than with Heidegger.

56. We have already seen Zubiri's attempt to treat artificial machines differently from organic ones. For Leibniz's own enthusiastic defense of this distinction, see *Monadology* §64.

57. *On Essence*, p. 278.

58. *Monadology*, §8.

59. Ibid., §13.

60. *On Essence*, p. 428.

61. Ibid, p. 168.

62. Ibid, p. 167.

63. *Monadology* §14.

64. *On Essence*, p. 365.

65. Ibid., p. 319.

66. Ibid.

67. Ibid.

68. Ibid., p. 296.

69. Ibid., p. 302.

70. Ibid., p. 341. Emphasis added.

71. Ibid., p. 410. Emphasis added.

72. Ibid., p. 440.

73. Ibid., p. 399. Emphasis added.

74. Ibid., p. 424.

75. Although Leibniz also endorses the doctrine that everything affects everything else, his monads do not affect one another *directly*. For this reason, I have chosen to emphasize his differences with Heidegger and Whitehead on this issue, and his agreement with Zubiri that there must be ultimate simples prior to any composites.

76. Ibid., p. 424.

77. *Metaphysics*, 996b16–996b18; p. 718. (All page references are to the easily accessible English version in McKeon's anthology, *The Basic Works of Aristotle*.)

78. This remains the case in spite of Heidegger's otherwise vehement anti-substantialist doctrine, as will be argued shortly.

79. *Metaphysics*, 1038b10–1038b12; p. 805.

80. Ibid., 1038b15–1038b16; p. 805.

81. Ibid., 1038b34–1039a2; p. 805.

82. Ibid., 1036b35–1037a2; p. 801.

83. Ibid., 1037a2–1037a5; p. 801. Emphasis added.

84. Ibid., 1001a29–1001b1, 1001b4-1001b6; p. 728.

85. Ibid., 1001a19–1001a24; pp. 727-28.

86. Ibid., 1016b8–1016b9; p. 759.

87. Ibid., 1040b21–1040b24; p.809. Emphasis added.

88. Ibid., 1043a2–1043a4; p. 814.

89. Ibid., 1045a8–1045a10; p. 818.

90. Ibid., 1030b16–1030b20; p. 788.

91. Ibid. ,1043a4–1043a5; p. 814.
92. Ibid., 1039a14–1039a23; p. 806.
93. Ibid., 1007b16–1007b18; p. 740.
94. Ibid., 1007b18–1007b22; pp. 740–41. Emphasis added.
95. Ibid., 1007b25–1007b29; p. 741. Emphasis added.
96. Ibid., 1028b8–1028b13; p. 784. Emphasis added.
97. Ibid., 1016a3–1016a6; p. 758.
98. Ibid., 1016a7–1016a9; p. 758.
99. Ibid., 1016a9–1016a12; p. 758. Emphasis added.
100. Ibid., 1035a17–1035a22; p. 798.
101. Ibid., 1039a3–1039a5; pp. 805-6.
102. From the correspondence with Arnauld. See the Hackett volume of Leibniz's writings entitled *Philosophical Essays*, p. 89.
103. Ibid., pp. 85–86.
104. Ibid., p. 86.
105. Latour argues this point brilliantly in the second chapter of *Pandora's Hope*. See especially page 74. A related point is already made by Locker, who observes that an army is no more complicated than any individual soldier.
106. I am indebted to Eric McLuhan for drawing my attention to this aspect of Bacon.

Bibliography

For the reader's convenience, the bibliography is divided into three parts:

(1) Those writings of Heidegger that are of especial relevance for the argument of *Tool-Being*.
(2) A list of additional sources that decisively influenced the background ideas developed in this book.
(3) A list of those secondary sources that are cited in the book or which otherwise proved useful in refining my argument.

Relevant Works by Heidegger

All works are listed here by their current or impending volume number in the *Gesamtausgabe* published by Vittorio Klostermann, Frankfurt. The year or years listed in parentheses following the volume number refers to the original publication date, or to the date of composition for those works not published by Heidegger himself. In cases where I have quoted from existing English translations, these are cited as well.

Volume 1 (1912–1916): *Frühe Schriften*, 1978.

Volume 2 (1927): *Sein und Zeit.* 1977. [*Being and Time.* Translated by J. Macquarrie and E. Robinson. New York: Harper & Row, 1962.]

Volume 3 (1929): *Kant und das Problem der Metaphysik.* 1991.

Volume 4 (1936–1938): *Erläuterungen zu Hölderlins Dichtung.* 1991.

Volume 5 (1935–1946): *Holzwege.* 1977. ("Der Ursprung des Kunstwerkes," "Wozu Dichter?").

Volume 6.1 (1936–1939): *Nietzsche I.* 1996.

Volume 6.2 (1939–1946): *Nietzsche II*. 1997.

Volume 7 (1936–1953): *Vorträge und Aufsätze*. ("Die Frage nach der Technik"; "Bauen Wohnen Denken"; "Das Ding"). Individual edition published by Günther Neske, Pfullingen. 1990.

Volume 9 (1919–1961): *Wegmarken*. 1976. ("Was ist Metaphysik?"; "Vom Wesen des Grundes"; "Vom Wesen der Wahrheit"; "Brief Über den Humanismus"; "Vom Wesen und Begriff der *Physis*. Aristoteles, *Physik* B, 1"; "Zur Seinsfrage"). [*Pathmarks*. Translated by W. McNeill. Cambridge, UK: Cambridge University Press, 1998.]

Volume 10 (1955–1956): *Der Satz vom Grund*. Individual edition published by Verlag Günther Neske, Pfullingen. 1986.

Volume 12 (1950–1959): *Unterwegs zur Sprache*. Individual edition published by Verlag Günther Neske, Pfullingen 1985. ("Die Sprache"; "Das Wesen der Sprache").

Volume 13 (1910–1976): *Aus der Erfahrung des Denkens*. 1983. ("Hebel—der Hausfreund").

Volume 14 (1962–1964): *Zur Sache des Denkens*. Individual edition published by Max Niemeyer, Tübingen. 1988.

Volume 15 (1951–1973): *Seminare*. 1986.

Volume 17 (1923/34): *Einführung in die phänomenologische Forschung*. 1994.

Volume 19 (1924/25): *Platon: Sophistes*. 1992.

Volume 20 (1925): *Prolegomena zur Geschichte des Zeitbegriffs*. 1988. [*History of the Concept of Time*. Translated by T. Kisiel. Bloomington, IN: Indiana University Press, 1992.]

Volume 21 (1925/26): *Logik: Die Frage nach der Wahrheit*. 1976.

Volume 22 (1926): *Grundbegriffe der antiken Philosophie*. 1993.

Volume 24 (1927): *Die Grundprobleme der Phänomenologie*. 1989. [*Basic Problems of Phenomenology*. Translated by A. Hofstadter. Bloomington, IN: Indiana University Press, 1988.]

Volume 26 (1928): *Metaphysische Anfangsgründe der Logik im Ausgang von Leibniz*. 1990. [*Metaphysical Foundations of Logic*. Translated by M. Heim. Bloomington, IN: Indiana University Press, 1984.]

Volume 29/30 (1929/30): *Die Grundbegriffe der Metaphysik: Welt-Endlichkeit-Einsamkeit.* 1983. [*Fundamental Concepts of Metaphysics: World, Finitude, Solitude.* Translated by W. McNeill and N. Walker. Bloomington, IN: Indiana University Press, 1995.]

Volume 31 (1930): *Vom Wesen der menschlichen Freiheit. Einleitung in die Philosophie.* 1994.

Volume 33 (1931): *Aristoteles, Metaphysik Q 1-3. Von Wesen und Wirklichkeit der Kraft.* 1990.

Volume 34 (1931/32): *Vom Wesen der Wahrheit. Zu Platons Höhlengleichnis und Theätet.* 1997.

Volume 38 (1934): *Logik als die Frage nach dem Wesen der Sprache.* 1998.

Volume 39 (1934/35): *Hölderlins Hymnen "Germanien" und "Der Rhein."* 1989.

Volume 40 (1935): *Einführung in die Metaphysik. 1983.* [*An Introduction to Metaphysics.* Translated by R. Manheim. New Haven, CO: Yale University Press, 1987.]

Volume 50 (1941/42, 1944/45): *Nietzsches Metaphysik.* 1990.

Volume 54 (1942/43): *Parmenides.* 1992.

Volume 56/7 (1919): *Zur Bestimmung der Philosophie.* 1987.

Volume 58 (1919/20): *Grundprobleme der Phänomenologie.* 1992.

Volume 59 (1920): *Phänomenologie der Anschauung und des Ausdrucks: Theorie der philosophischen Begriffsbildung.* 1993.

Volume 60 (1918/19, 1920/21): *Phänomenologie des religiösen Lebens.* 1995.

Volume 61 (1921/22): *Phänomenologische Interpretationen zu Aristoteles.* 1994.

Volume 63 (1923): *Ontologie: Hermeneutik der Faktizität.* 1988.

Volume 65 (1936-38): *Beiträge zur Philosophie: Vom Ereignis.* 1989.

Volume 66 (1938/39): *Besinnung.* 1997.

Volume 68 (1938/39, 1942): *Hegel.* 1993.

Volume 79 (1949/1957): *Bremer und Freiburger Vorträge.* 1994. ("Einblick in das was ist," 1949).

Works that Helped Inspire the Argument of this Book

Aristotle. *Metaphysics, Physics, Nicomachean Ethics.* In *The Basic Works of Aristotle.* Edited by R. McKeon. New York: Random House, 1941. (However, the line numbers of the Metaphysics cited in my footnotes refer to the original Greek of the Oxford text cited below.)

―――. *Metaphysica.* Oxford: Oxford University Press, 1957.

Bacon, Francis. *The New Organon.* Edited by F. H. Anderson. Indianapolis: The Library of Liberal Arts, 1960.

Badiou, Alain. *Deleuze: The Clamor of Being.* Translated by L. Burchill. Minneapolis: University of Minnesota Press, 2000.

Baudrillard, Jean. *Fatal Strategies.* Edited by J. Fleming, translated by P. Beitchmann. New York: Autonomedia, 1990.

Bergson, Henri. *Time and Free Will: An Essay on the Immediate Data of Consciousness.* Kessinger, 1987.

―――. *Laughter.* Translated by F. Rothwell and C. Brereton. Green Integer, 1999.

Bhaskar, Roy. *A Realist Theory of Science.* London: Verso, 1997.

Brentano, Franz. *On the Several Senses of Being in Aristotle.* Berkeley, CA: University of California Press, 1981.

Bruno, Giordano. *Cause, Principle, and Unity.* Translated by R. de Lucca. Cambridge, UK: Cambridge University Press, 1998.

Deleuze, Gilles. *Cinema I: The Movement-Image.* Translated by H. Tomlinson and B. Habberjam. Minneapolis: University of Minnesota Press, 1986.

―――. *The Logic of Sense.* Translated by M. Lester and C. Stivale. New York, Columbia University Press, 1993.

―――. *Difference and Repetition.* Translated by P. Patton. New York: Columbia University Press, 1993.

Deleuze, Gilles, and Guattari, Félix. *Anti-Oedipus: Capitalism and Schizophrenia, Part One.* Minneapolis: University of Minnesota Press, 1985.

Deleuze, Gilles, and Parnet, Claire. *Dialogues.* Translated by H. Tomlinson and B. Habberjam. New York: Columbia University Press, 1977.

Derrida, Jacques. *Speech and Phenomena.* Translated by D. Allison. Evanston, IL: Northwestern University Press, 1973.

―――. "Restitutions." In *The Truth in Painting.* Translated by G. Bennington and I. McLeod. Chicago: University of Chicago Press, 1987.

―――. "Geschlecht 2: Heidegger's Hand." In J. Sallis, ed., *Deconstruction and Philosophy.*

Hartshorne, Charles. *Whitehead's Philosophy.* Lincoln, NE: University of Nebraska Press, 1972.

―――. *Insights and Oversights of the Great Thinkers.* Albany, NY: SUNY Press, 1983.

Husserl, Edmund. *Logische Untersuchungen.* 3 vols. Tübingen: Max Niemeyer, 1993.

Kant, Immanuel. *Critique of Pure Reason.* Translated by N. K. Smith. New York: St. Martin's Press, 1965.

Kripke, Saul. *Naming and Necessity.* Cambridge, MA: Harvard University Press, 1996.

Lask, Emil. *Die Logik der Philosophie und die Kategorienlehre.* Tübingen: J.C.B. Mohr (Paul Siebeck), 1911/1993.

Latour, Bruno. *Science in Action.* Cambridge, MA: Harvard University Press, 1987.

———. *The Pasteurization of France.* Cambridge, MA: Harvard University Press, 1988.

———. *We Have Never Been Modern.* Cambridge, MA: Harvard University Press, 1993.

———. *Aramis, or The Love of Technology.* Cambridge, MA: Harvard University Press, 1996.

———. *Pandora's Hope.* Cambridge, MA: Harvard University Press, 1999.

———. *Politiques de la nature.* Paris: Éditions la découverte, 1999.

Leibniz, G.W. von. *Philosphical Essays.* Indianapolis: Hackett, 1989. ("Discourse on Metaphysics," "A Specimen of Dynamics," "New System of Nature," "Principles of Nature and Grace, Based Reason," "The Principles of Philosophy, or, the Monadology.")

Levinas, Emmanuel. *Totality and Infinity.* Translated by A. Lingis. Pittsburgh: Duquesne University Press, 1969.

———. *Ethics and Infinity: Conversations with Philippe Nemo.* Translated by R. Cohen. Pittsburgh: Duquesne University Press, 1985.

———. "Reality and its Shadow," "Meaning and Sense." In *Collected Philosophical Papers.* Translated by A. Lingis. The Hague: Martinus Nijhoff, 1987.

———. *Existence and Existents.* Translated by A. Lingis. The Hague: Martinus Nijhoff, 1988.

———. *En Découvrant l'existence avec Husserl et Heidegger.* Paris: Vrin, 1988.

———. *Time and the Other.* Translated by R. Cohen. Pittsburgh: Duquesne University Press, 1990.

Lingis, Alphonso. *The Community of Those Who Have Nothing in Common.* Bloomington, IN: Indiana University Press, 1994. (Especially "Faces, Idols, Fetishes.")

———. *The Imperative.* Bloomington, IN: Indiana University Press, 1998.

———. "A Phenomenology of Substances." In *American Catholic Philosophical Quarterly* 71, no. 4 (1998).

McLuhan, Marshall. *Understanding Media.* Cambridge, MA: MIT Press, 1994.

McLuhan, Marshall, and McLuhan, Eric. *Laws of Media: The New Science.* Toronto: University of Toronto Press, 1988.

Nelson, Theodor. *Computer Lib/Dream Machines.* Microsoft, 1987.

Ortega y Gasset, José. *Some Lessons in Metaphysics.* Translated by M. Adams. New York: Norton, 1969.

———. *Phenomenology and Art.* Translated by P. Silver. New York: Norton, 1975. ("An Essay in Esthetics by Way of a Preface.")

———. *Historical Reason.* New York: Norton, 1986.

Peirce, Charles Sanders. *Philosophical Writings of Peirce.* Edited by J. Buchler. New York: Dover, 1955.

p.m. *bolo'bolo.* New York: Semiotext(e), 1985.

Scheler, Max. *Selected Philosophical Essays.* Translated by D. Lachterman. Evanston, IL: Northwestern University Press, 1973.

Schreber, Daniel Paul. *Denkwürdigkeiten eines Nervenkranken.* Berlin: Kadmos, 1995.

Serres, Michel, and Latour, Bruno. *Conversations on Science, Culture, and Time.* Ann Arbor: University of Michigan Press, 1995.

Virilio, Paul. *Speed and Politics.* Translated by M. Polizzotti. New York: Semiotext(e), 1986.

———. *The Aesthetics of Disappearance.* Translated by P. Beitchmann. New York: Semiotext(e), 1991.

Whitehead, Alfred North. *Process and Reality.* New York: The Free Press, 1978.

Žižek, Slavoj. *The Sublime Object of Ideology.* London: Verso, 1989.

———. *The Abyss of Freedom.* In Žižek and Schelling, *The Abyss of Freedom/Ages of the World.* Ann Arbor, MI: University of Michigan Press, 1997.

———. *The Ticklish Subject.* London: Verso, 1999.

Zubiri, Xavier. *On Essence.* Translated by A. R. Caponigri. Washington, DC: Catholic University Press, 1980.

Secondary Works Cited in the Book and Other Works of Especial Relevance

Benjamin, Walter. *Illuminations.* New York: Schocken, 1969.

Bernasconi, Robert. *Heidegger in Question.* Atlantic Highlands, NJ: Humanities Press International, 1993.

Bernet, Rudolf. "Phenomenological Reduction and the Double Life." In Kisiel and Van Buren, eds., *Reading Heidegger from the Start: Essays in His Earliest Thought.*

Blattner, William D. "Existential Temporality in Being and Time (Why Heidegger is not a Pragmatist)." In *Heidegger: A Critical Reader.* Edited by H. Dreyfus and H. Hall. Oxford, UK: Blackwell, 1992.

Boeder, Heribert. "Der frühgriechische Wortgebrauch von Logos und Aletheia." In *Archiv für Begriffsgeschichte* 4 (1959).

Caputo, John. *Heidegger and Aquinas.* New York: Fordham University Press, 1982.

———. *Demythologizing Heidegger.* Bloomington, IN: Indiana University Press, 1993.

Dastur, Françoise. "The Ekstatico-Horizonal Constitution of Temporality." In *Critical Heidegger.* Edited by C. Macann. London: Routledge, 1996.

Dreyfus, Hubert. *Being-in-the-World: A Commentary on Heidegger's Being and Time, Division I.* Cambridge, MA: MIT Press, 1991.

———. "Heidegger's History of the Being of Equipment." In *Heidegger: A Critical Reader.* Edited by H. Dreyfus and H. Hall. Oxford, UK: Blackwell, 1992.

———. "Coping with Things in Themselves: Heidegger's Robust Realism." Available on the internet at http://socrates.berkeley.edu/~frege/dreyfus/ Short_Realism_Bielefeld.html.

Encylopedia of Philosophy. Vols. 7 and 8: *Psychology to Zubiri, Index.* New York: MacMillan, 1967.

Frings, Manfred. "The Background of Max Scheler's 1927 Reading of Being and Time." In *Philosophy Today* (Summer 1992).

Gadamer, Hans-Georg. *Truth and Method.* New York: Seabury Press, 1975.

Gethmann, Carl Friedrich. *Dasein: Erkennen und Handeln.* Berlin: de Gruyter, 1993.

Haar, Michel. *The Song of the Earth: Heidegger and the Grounds of the History of Being.* Translated by R. Lilly. Bloomington, IN: Indiana University Press, 1993.

———. *Heidegger and the Essence of Man.* Translated by W. McNeill. Albany, NY: SUNY Press, 1993.

Haugeland, John. "Dasein's Disclosedness." In *Heidegger: A Critical Reader.* Edited by H. Dreyfus and H. Hall. Oxford, UK: Blackwell, 1992.

Hopkins, Burt. *Intentionality in Husserl and Heidegger: The Problem of the Original Method and Phenomenon of Phenomenology.* Norwell, MA: Kluwer, 1993.

Irigaray, Luce. *L'oubli de l'air- chez Martin Heidegger.* Paris: Minuit, 1983.

Janicaud, Dominique, and Mattei, Jean-François. *Heidegger: From Metaphysics to Thought.* Translated by M. Gendre. Albany, NY: SUNY Press, 1995.

Kisiel, Theodore. *The Genesis of Heidegger's Being and Time.* Berkeley, CA: University of California Press, 1993.

Kisiel, Theodore, and Van Buren, John, eds. *Reading Heidegger From the Start: Essays in His Earliest Thought.* Albany, NY: SUNY Press, 1994.

Krell, David Farrell. *Intimations of Mortality.* University Park, PA: Penn State University Press, 1986.

———. *Daimon Life.* Bloomington, IN: Indiana University Press, 1992.

Lafont, Cristina. *Heidegger, Language and World-Disclosure.* Translated by G. Harman. Cambridge, UK: Cambridge University Press, 2000.

Meinong, Alexius. *Über Gegenstandstheorie / Selbstdarstellung.* Frankfurt: Felix Meiner Verlag, 1998.

Okrent, Mark. *Heidegger and Pragmatism: Understanding, Being, and the Critique of Metaphysics.* Ithaca, NY: Cornell University Press, 1988.

Pöggeler, Otto. *Martin Heidegger's Path of Thinking.* Translated by D. Magurshak and S. Barber. Atlantic Highlands, NJ: Humanities Press International, 1987.

Prauss, Gerold. *Erkennen und Handeln in Heideggers 'Sein und Zeit'.* Freiburg/Munich: Karl Alber, 1977.

Richardson, William. *Heidegger: Through Phenomenology to Thought.* The Hague: Martinus Nijhoff, 1967.

Rorty, Richard. "Wittgenstein, Heidegger, and the Reification of Language." In *The Cambridge Companion to Heidegger.* Edited by C. Guignon. Cambridge, UK: Cambridge University Press, 1993.

Sallis, John. *Delimitations: Phenomenology and the End of Metaphysics.* Bloomington, IN: Indiana University Press, 1995.

———. *Double Truth.* Albany, NY: SUNY Press, 1995.

Schürmann, Reiner. *Heidegger on Being and Acting: From Principles to Anarchy.*

Translated by C.-M. Gros. Bloomington, IN: Indiana University Press, 1987.

Sheehan, Thomas J. "'Time and Being,' 1925-27." In *Thinking about Being: Aspects of Heidegger's Thought.* Edited by R. Shahan and J. Mohanty. Norman, OK: University of Oklahoma Press, 1984.

Taminiaux, Jacques. *Martin Heidegger and the Project of Fundamental Ontology.* Translated and edited by M. Gendre. Albany, NY: SUNY Press, 1991.

———. *Dialectic and Difference.* Atlantic Highlands, NJ: Humanities Press International, 1985.

———. "Poesis and Praxis in Fundamental Ontology." *Research in Phenomenology* 17 1987).

Tugendhat, Ernst. *Der Wahrheitsbegriff bei Husserl und Heidegger.* Berlin: de Gruyter, 1967.

———. "Heidegger's Idea of Truth." In *Critical Heidegger.* Edited by C. Macann. London: Routledge, 1996.

Van Buren, John. *The Young Heidegger: Rumor of the Hidden King.* Bloomington, IN: Indiana University Press, 1994.

Volpi, Franco. "Dasein as Praxis: the Heideggerian Assimilation and Radicalization of the Practical Philosophy of Aristotle." In *Critical Heidegger.* Edited by C. Macann. London: Routledge, 1996.

Vycinas, Vincent. *Earth and Gods: An Introduction to the Philosophy of Martin Heidegger.* The Hague: Martinus Nijhoff, 1961.

Zimmerman, Michael. *Heidegger's Confrontation with Modernity: Technology, Politics & Art.* Bloomington, IN: Indiana University Press, 1990.

Index

action
  as historical concept, 298n17,
    299n24
  as reality of tool-beings, 18, 20,
    22, 26, 27, 35, 37, 39, 45,
    59, 94, 237, 239
actus. See action
aletheia (truth), 67, 98, 186
analytic philosophy, 1, 9, 104, 114,
    115, 122, 157, 168, 177–78,
    312n51
Anaxagoras, 274, 280, 292
animals, 33, 71, 73, 172, 220, 222,
    259, 260
  and humans, ontologically
    indistinguishable, 8, 60, 70
  as tool-being, 36, 42
Aristotle, 106, 108, 109, 113, 114,
    197, 249, 252, 253, 268–79,
    280, 282, 286, 290, 291,
    292, 301n67
  fails to think the essence of the
    thing, 195
  formal cause, 242
  influence on Heidegger, 105, 268
  life, discussion of in *De Anima*,
    69
  ousia, relation to tool-analysis, 270
  phronesis irrelevant to tool-analysis,
    111, 112
  poiesis irrelevant to tool-analysis, 4,
    104, 109–14, 122, 270

  praxis irrelevant to tool-analysis,
    15, 104, 109–14
  primary substance (*prote ousia*),
    172, 270–79, 292
Arnauld, Antoine, 284
artworks, 8, 188
as-structure, 2, 8–9, 32, 36, 40, 42,
    45, 46, 53, 55, 60, 61, 69, 74,
    81, 85–86, 127, 160, 219,
    220, 221, 222, 225, 232, 240,
    287–89, 294, 300n32
  for animals and inanimate things,
    50, 69–70, 208, 225
  fails as normative standard, 49–50,
    76–78, 80

Bacon, Francis, 266, 293, 296,
    314n105
Badiou, Alain, 164
Baudrillard, Jean, 242, 302n76
Bauhaus movement, 302n80
being-in-the-world
  not restricted to Dasein, 37–39, 92,
    118, 299n23
Bergmann, Gustav, 168
Bergson, Henri, 52, 63, 65, 71, 236,
    301n67
Bernasconi, Robert, 104, 106–14,
    115, 134
Bernet, Rudolf, 135–42, 150, 192,
    306n55

black box, 243, 255, 257, 280,
    282
Blattner, William, 115
Brandom, Robert, 104, 115
broken tools, 18, 45, 112, 125, 199,
    290
    as covering all beings, 46, 47, 49,
        55, 197, 241
    as reversal into visible terminus,
        (*metabole, Umschlag*) 4, 6, 10,
        24, 25–26, 31–35, 43–44,
        45–47, 49, 50, 55, 56, 60, 66,
        67, 68, 79, 81, 90, 106, 108,
        110, 128, 149, 158, 167, 176,
        220, 238, 245, 269, 288
    as separated absolutely from tool-
        being, 21, 22, 97, 120, 121,
        160, 206, 282, 283
Bruno, Giordano, 274
Burak, Ken, 208

Caputo, John, 157, 298n17
Carnap, Rudolf, 165
causality (*see also* Occasionalism), 2,
    11, 34, 120, 121, 146, 170,
    216, 221, 247, 249–50, 258,
    264, 289, 293, 311n22
    as form of the as-structure,
        221–30, 295
    retroactive causation (*see also* Žižek,
        Slavoj), 207, 208, 209, 212,
        214, 216, 224, 308n126
commedia dell'arte, 83, 303n106
constructivism, 173
continental philosophy, 1, 9, 55, 104,
    105, 114, 115, 121–22, 131,
    135, 156, 157, 168, 178, 213,
    280
    Perugia (Collegium
        Phaenomenologicum), 122
    SPEP (Society for Phenomenology
        and Existential Philosophy),
        122
Copleston, Frederick, 8
correspondence theory of truth, 98
critique/irony, 226, 237, 238

Dasein, human being, 155
    as present-at-hand, 37, 38–39
    as tool-being, 36–37, 41, 42
    as transcending world, 42, 56, 57,
        71, 74, 90–91, 103, 220, 224
    excessive role for Heidegger of, 1,
        16, 18–19, 29, 33–34, 40, 63,
        68, 103–4, 117–18, 127–28,
        132, 147, 152, 176, 185, 279
    two distinct senses of, 41–42, 127
Davidson, Donald, 122, 174
deconstruction, 123, 212
Deleuze, Gilles, 8, 88, 164, 226,
    303n96, 312n30, 313n55
Democritus, 142
Derrida, Jacques, 2, 9, 164, 190,
    216, 302n86, 305n12
Descartes, René, 60, 65, 71, 105,
    120, 122, 123, 131, 206
Dewey, John, 120, 121, 142, 172,
    242
direct reference (*see also* Kripke, Saul),
    122, 205
Donnellan, Keith, 213
Dreyfus, Hubert, 104, 115, 122–26,
    152, 157, 168, 169, 171, 182,
    212
Dummett, Michael, 165, 168
Duns Scotus. *See* pseudo-Scotus

earth, in artworks (*see also* fourfold),
    8
equipment. *See* tool-being
essence (*see also* Zubiri, Xavier), 123,
    141, 185, 248, 282
    deeply hidden essence, 172, 173
    essentialism, 173, 214–15
fantasy projection. *See* causality,
    retroactive cause
Fichte, J.G., 118, 207
Fink, Eugen, 77, 136
firewalls, preventing absurd
    substances, 257
first philosophy, 165
formal cause, 171, 242, 260, 282,
    293

enjoyment, 241
ethical theory, alterity, 236–37
existence and existents, strife
  between, 11, 69
  hypostasis, 237, 239–40, 242
  il y a, 238–41, 300n33
  insomnia, 239–40, 242, 300n33
  philosophy of objects, as forerunner
    of, 237
  sincere relation toward objects, 43,
    238, 241
  substance precedes function, 220
  world, criticizes Heidegger's
    concept of, 241
Lingis, Alphonso, 220, 300n36,
  311n22
Locke, John, 314n105
logocentrism, 173

machines, ontological, 250, 268,
  281–84, 288, 293, 294,
  313n55, 313n56
Malebranche, Nicolas, 65, 231
materialism, 172, 210, 280, 293
McLuhan, Marshall, 78, 301n46,
  303n95
meaning/reference
  as equivalent to being, 25–26
  as irreducible to human purposes,
    30–31, 34-37, 61
  as subsuming all objects, 53, 61,
    81–82, 133
Medieval philosophy, 107, 245, 265
mere (*bloß*)
  as Heideggerian technical term, 16,
    48–49, 103, 114, 127, 175,
    180, 190, 300n39
metaphysics
  contemporary analytic, 312n51
  new sense of, 5, 16, 32, 79, 80,
    127, 246, 269, 287, 288
  traditional sense of, 2, 5, 9, 16, 72,
    79, 80, 107, 112, 128, 194
metontology
  as insufficiently developed, 6, 158,
    281, 302n77

as overcoming of fundamental
  ontology, 6, 67–68, 189,
  302n75
monadic theories, 35, 273, 313n75

Nazism. *See* Heidegger, Martin,
  politics of
Nelson, Theodor, 154, 163
Nietzsche, Friedrich, 242
non-mentalism, 122
nothingness
  as Angst, 89–98, 141, 239
  as ontological difference, 89–98,
    237
  as useless for ontology, 11, 225–26

object-oriented philosophy (*see also*
  guerilla metaphysics), 1, 2, 10,
  24, 47, 49, 104, 126, 156,
  164
objects
  as accidentally rejuvenated by
    Heidegger, 5, 15, 49, 191
  as ambiguous prior to encounter
    with humans, 19
  as being-in-the-world, 35
  encountering each other
    independently of us, 30–35,
    71
  encountered determinately by us,
    47
  as false danger for Heidegger's
    thought, 6, 28
  new sense of, 16
  as ready-to-hand, 20, 21, 27
  as transcendent in themselves,
    92–94,
  twofold duel within, 32, 35–38,
    45–46, 55, 56, 58, 59, 65, 67,
    69, 86, 91–92, 96, 97, 106,
    134, 146, 155, 176, 183, 187,
    188, 189, 190, 204, 227, 236,
    240, 245, 288–89
occasional cause, 11, 65–66, 231,
  295–96

causation, 249–50
conceptivity, 257
constructivity, 263
creation *ex nihilo*, 244, 245, 264
essence *de suyo*, 248, 252, 267,
  282, 283
essence irreducible to relations, 11
essence *of* (opp. to essence *for*),
  244, 245, 247, 248–49, 250,
  251, 255, 266
on existence, 244–45
as important philosopher,
  unrecognized, 243
notes of the thing (opp. to
  properties), 246, 248, 254,
  263, 264, 290

on organisms, 253
physical as metaphysical, 245, 246,
  248, 250–51, 252–53, 254,
  256, 258
reality *simpliciter*, 247, 248, 265
respectivity, 251, 253–54, 255,
  258, 266
richness and solidity of the essence,
  265
substantivity (essence as *system*),
  250, 251–52, 253, 254,
  257, 258, 261–62, 263, 264,
  274
transcendental and talitative
  moments of essence, 244, 265,
  266, 268, 271, 279

LaVergne, TN USA
14 December 2010
208704LV00003B/6/P